MW01253917

Muslim communities in the United Kingdom have important contributions to make to the local communities and broader societies in which they live. Yet these communities, and Islam more broadly, are often the subject of misunderstanding and vilification.

Whereas Islamic legal and political traditions have, at key points, inspired and informed Western political and intellectual traditions and British Muslims have historically made, and continue to make, important contributions at every level of British life, portrayals of their religion and identity still often seem to focus on terrorism, intolerance and issues such as female genital mutilation and forced marriages.

A Fresh Look at Islam in a Multi-Faith World makes a comprehensive case for a contemporary educational philosophy in our schools, with a view to playing a key role in creating mindsets that are resistant to radicalisation and encouraging of productive intercultural relations. Dr Wilkinson's analysis of the history curriculum's potential role in creating a forum for discussion to address the ignorance that leads to the misunderstanding of our communities adds real value to this important discussion, and to the wider debate around how we educate our children.

Rt. Hon. Sadiq Khan MP, *Shadow Secretary of State for Justice, Shadow Lord Chancellor and Shadow Minister for London*

In this ground-breaking, potentially game-changing book, Matthew Wilkinson shows how critical realism can be used to inform the Islamic tradition, so as to generate a fresh and vital take on Islam. In doing so, it begins to return to that tradition the kind of intellectual fertility it had in the early middle ages, which went on to spark the European Renaissance and modern science, and restores it to an intellectual relevance, depth and rigour that it has often in recent times lacked. In particular, it will be of enormous value to teachers who wish to show their students how Islam can be a productive member of the family of faiths in contemporary times.

Professor Roy Bhaskar, *World Scholar, Institute of Education, University of London*

This remarkable integration of Islamic wisdom with critical realist theory energetically tackles some of modern Britain's most pressing issues in curriculum design and community integration.

Tim Winter, *Shaykh Zayed Lecturer in Islamic Studies, University of Cambridge Dean, Cambridge Muslim College*

Using detailed research into the experience of Muslim boys, Matthew Wilkinson examines the intellectual, social and spiritual blocks to young Muslims engaging in British democracy and to owning the open-minded intellectual tradition once characteristic of Islam. One important remedy is a rigorous history education. Young Muslims need historical knowledge if they are to connect 'being authentically British to being seriously Muslim' and to participate fully in the civic life of Britain. Far from suggesting that British history is not important, Wilkinson argues that it is centrally important, and that its completeness requires a rigour in identifying interconnections across British, European and world history. History teachers wishing to reflect on the past, present and future relationship of Islam with Britain will find much food for thought in this book.

Christine Counsell, *Senior Lecturer in History Education, Faculty of Education, University of Cambridge*

Matthew Wilkinson combines broad and deep scholarship with practical experience and penetrating philosophical analysis in this survey of Islam in a multi-faith world. He presents a persuasive case for a new theoretical approach to education regarding Islam and Muslims in Britain today and illustrates its application in some humanities subjects.

His telling remarks on religious education and citizenship, in particular, are very topical and relevant. If fully adopted, his approach could transform education in our schools and the relationship between Muslims and non-Muslims in our society.

John Keast OBE, *Chair, Religious Education Council of England and Wales*

Matthew Wilkinson is an expert in the education of young Muslims as well as in the teaching of Islam in UK schools. His book delivers exceptional insights into our secondary education system and is of value to anyone interested in reflecting on the challenges raised by living in contemporary multi-faith Britain.

Dr Wilkinson's book makes an important contribution to today's debate about how we educate our children and I have no doubt that it will become a standard work in the fields of education, Islamic and interfaith studies.

Dr Edward Kessler MBE, *Executive Director, Woolf Institute, Cambridge*

In our rapidly changing world, all of us, Christians and Muslims alike, need as much help as we can get in relating what we believe to the often confusing problems of daily living. The traditions in which we stand, properly understood, give us stability and enrichment to approach these, but they still require wisdom in application. I warmly commend this book for the thoughtful contribution it offers to the gaining of that wisdom for both teachers and learners.

Lord Richard Harries of Pentregarth, *Former Bishop of Oxford*

This book makes an important contribution to an ongoing debate both about the way subjects on the curriculum are framed and about how the diversity of contemporary British society can and does renew and refresh that debate.

Dr Wilkinson is well positioned to understand and reflect the implications of the social cohesion debate as it impinges on curriculum reform and has, here, identified many of the factors which could make a difference to how that debate is at present conceived.

As such, this book is to be very much welcomed and will start a new and engaging phase of discussion at a critical moment for fresh thinking about the way that faith in general, and Islam in particular, are addressed in our schools.

Mary Earl, *University Lecturer and Convenor, Initial Teacher Training in Religious Studies, Faculty of Education, University of Cambridge*

With his expertise and experience, Matthew Wilkinson's thoughtful narrative is valuable reading for learners, educators and policy-makers, and all others who seek to deepen mutual understanding and tolerance between believers in contemporary, multi-faith Britain. I highly commend it to all.

Rt Hon. Simon Hughes MP, *Minister for Justice and Civil Liberties*

A Fresh Look at Islam in a Multi-Faith World

A Fresh Look at Islam in a Multi-Faith World: A philosophy for success through education provides a comprehensively theorised and practical approach to thinking systematically and deeply about Islam and Muslims in a multi-faith world. It makes the case for a contemporary educational philosophy to help young Muslims surmount the challenges of post-modernity and to transcend the hiatuses and obstacles that they face in their interaction and relationships with non-Muslims, and vice versa.

It argues that the philosophy of critical realism in its original, dialectical and metaReal moments so fittingly 'underlabours' (Bhaskar's term) for the contemporary interpretation, clarification and conceptual deepening of Islamic doctrine, practice and education as to suggest a distinctive branch of critical realist philosophy, specifically suited for this purpose. This approach is called Islamic critical realism.

The book proceeds to explain how this Islamic critical realist approach can serve the interpretation of the consensual elements of Islamic doctrine, such as the six elements of Islamic belief and the Five 'Pillars' of Islamic practice, so that these essential features of the Muslim way of life can help Muslim young people to contribute positively to life in multi-faith liberal democracies in a globalising world.

Finally, the book shows how this Islamic critical realist approach can be brought to bear in humanities classrooms by history, religious education and citizenship teachers to help Muslim young people engage informatively and transformatively with themselves and others in multi-faith contexts.

Matthew L. N. Wilkinson is a Research Fellow at Cambridge Muslim College, Affiliate Lecturer at the Woolf Institute, Cambridge and Visiting Fellow at the Institute of Education, University of London.

New studies in critical realism and education

Other titles in this series:

A Critical Realist Perspective of Education
Brad Shipway

Why Knowledge Matters in Curriculum
A social realist argument
Leesa Wheelahan

Knowledge and Knowers
Towards a realist sociology of education
Karl Maton

Strong and Smart – Towards a Pedagogy for Emancipation
Education for first peoples
Chris Sarra

Imagining the University
Ronald Barnett

Critical Realist Activity Theory
Iskra Nunez

A Fresh Look at Islam in a Multi-Faith World
A philosophy for success through education
Matthew L. N. Wilkinson

A Fresh Look at Islam in a Multi-Faith World

A philosophy for success through education

Matthew L. N. Wilkinson

Routledge
Taylor & Francis Group

LONDON AND NEW YORK

First published 2015
by Routledge
2 Park Square, Milton Park, Abingdon, Oxon OX14 4RN

and by Routledge
711 Third Avenue, New York, NY 10017

Routledge is an imprint of the Taylor & Francis Group, an informa business

© 2015 Matthew L. N. Wilkinson

The right of Matthew L. N. Wilkinson to be identified as author of this
work has been asserted by him in accordance with sections 77 and 78 of
the Copyright, Designs and Patents Act 1988.

British Library Cataloguing in Publication Data
A catalogue record for this book is available from the British Library

Library of Congress Cataloging in Publication Data
Wilkinson, M. L. N. (Matthew L. N.)
A fresh look at Islam in a multi-faith world : a philosophy for success
through education / Matthew L.N. Wilkinson.
    pages cm – (New studies in critical realism and education (Routledge
    critical realism))
    Includes bibliographical references and index.
    1. Islam. 2. Critical realism. 3. Education–Philosophy.
    4. Islam–Relations. I. Title.
    BP161.3.W547 2014
    297–dc23   2014018723

ISBN: 978-0-415-81319-8 (hbk)
ISBN: 978-1-315-74565-7 (ebk)

Typeset in Times New Roman
by Wearset Ltd, Boldon, Tyne and Wear

Printed and bound in the United States of America by Publishers Graphics,
LLC on sustainably sourced paper.

For my wife, Lucy, and my son, Gabriel: without you, none of this would have been possible and none of it would have been fun.

Contents

List of figures   xiii

List of tables   xiv

Foreword   xv

Preface   xvi

Acknowledgements   xviii

PART I
Historical background and sociological context   1

**Introduction: a tale of two young Muslims, a spiritual quest,
a book to be used**   3
An enlightened student; a misguided classroom assistant 3
The issues of this book 5
The author's story 7
The book's intellectual heritage 9
Defining the key terms 11
The structure of the book 14

1 **From sacred civilisation to secular confusion: why does
   Islam need a philosophy?**   16
*The collapse of the sacred–civic balance of power that sustained
   Islamic civilisation 18*
The Protestant West shapes the conditions of modernity 19
Difficulties faced by Muslims in the embrace of modernity 20
The theological crisis and the Reformers' response 22
The 'new' Muslim diaspora: a significant 'out-group' 27
*The 'other/counter-other': the hostile reception of Islam by
   elements of non-Muslim European society 28*
*Two default positions of faith set up the Unhappy Muslim
   Consciousness 33*
The need for a philosophy for Islam in the multi-faith world 34

PART II
The philosophy of Islamic critical realism   37

2   **Shared meta-theoretical premises: 'underlabouring' and**
    'seriousness'   39
    A shared commitment to 'underlabouring' 39
    A shared commitment to 'seriousness' 42
    Philosophical seriousness: seriousness $_{(p)}$ 42
    Seriousness and Islam: seriousness $_{(r)}$ 43
    Seriousness in Islamic philosophical theology 47
    The implications of seriousness 48

3   **First Moment (1M): original Islamic critical realism**   50
    Ontological realism 51
    Epistemological relativism 56
    Judgemental rationality 59
    The Qur'an as a critical realist text 61
    Establishing the conditions for rational re-enchantment 63

4   **Second Edge (2E): dialectical Islamic critical realism: the**
    life of the Prophet Muhammad   65
    Introduction: dialectical critical realism 65
    Second Edge (2E): absence 65
    Third Level (3L): totality, partial totality and sub-totality 67
    Fourth Dimension (4D): transformative praxis 69
    Dialectical Islamic critical realism in the life of the Prophet
       Muhammad 70
    The lessons of Muhammad: the dialectics of re-enchantment 87

5   **Islamic metaReality: the Articles of Faith and Pillars of**
    Islam   88
    The philosophy of metaReality from difference to identity 89
    Islamic critical realist transcendence: a hierarchy 93
    *Demi-reality, unbelief (*kufr*) and the meanings of* Jihād 94
    The dialectics of transcendence: the exemplar of marriage 98
    The philosophy of metaReality, Islamic ethics and Shari'a 100
    The Islamic Articles of Faith 103
    The Five Pillars of Islam 108

PART III
Generating success with humanities education 115

6 **Towards an ontology of educational success: Muslim young**
 people in humanities education 117
 Introduction: from theory to research to practice 117
 1M: who are young Muslims in education? 118
 Hegemonic masculinities and femininities 122
 History, identity and Muslim young people 126
 Methodology: the fulcrum of ICR underlabours for social
 science 127
 A laminated ontology of educational success 129
 The dimensions of young British Muslims' success at history 133
 In summary: who are Muslim young people in humanities
 education? 147

7 **History education: from absence to emancipation** 151
 Introduction: ontological monovalence in education 151
 2E: the absent curriculum 152
 2E: the absent pedagogy 167
 2E: the absent parent 169
 3L: the ontology of inclusion 177
 4D: transforming communities of learners 185
 Conclusion: reimagining the nation through history education 187

8 **Religious education: learning about, from and for**
 religion-for-life 190
 Introduction: delineating the spiritual dimension of Muslim young
 people 190
 1M: who is the Muslim learner in religious education? 192
 2E: absences of 'seriousness' (e), of governmental support, of pupil
 respect and of buy-in from the Muslim community 200
 3L: the fulcrum of ICR in the classroom, the embrace of difficult
 issues and the use of transcendence 206
 4D: a transformative nexus of religious education: school, home,
 madrasa and peer group/internet 216
 Summary: religious education – a return to 'seriousness' (e) 219

9 **Citizenship education: a pathway to full critical engagement** 221
 Introduction: the complexity of civic identification for young
 Muslims 221
 1M: who is the young Muslim citizen? 223

2E: the absence of seriousness (e) in citizenship education 230
3L: a serious (e) citizenship education 236
4D: transformative praxis: taking citizenship education out of the
    classroom 245
Conclusion: a pathway to full civic engagement 246

10 Conclusion: a call for existential seriousness (r+p+e) to
     regenerate the Happy Muslim Consciousness   248
     The philosophical and political preconditions of
        seriousness (r+p+e) 248
     Removing absence to transform educational praxis 249
     The opportunity for and of Islam 251
     From the terrors of performativity to serious (r+p+e)
        transformativity 253

Appendix: Possible reasons for differences in empirical
findings about Muslim boys' identities   254

References   256
Index   270

Figures

3.1 The fulcrum of Islamic critical realism (ICR)   50
3.2 The fulcrum of ICR exemplified   54
5.1 Stratified levels of transcendence   93
7.1 The three components of the absent curriculum   153
7.2 The ontology of curriculum, including presence and absence   156
7.3 The fulcrum of ICR for history education   179
8.1 The fulcrum of ICR   207
8.2 The fulcrum of ICR transposed into religious education (RE)   210
8.3 The pedagogical modes of the fulcrum of ICR in RE   210
8.4 An example of the ICR fulcrum in use with the example of
    pilgrimage   212
8.5 Stratified levels of transcendence   215
8.6 The transformative nexus for the spiritual dimension of
    Muslim young people   218
9.1 The fulcrum of ICR transposed into citizenship education   239
9.2 The modes of the fulcrum of ICR transposed into citizenship
    education   241
9.3 Examples of the modes of the fulcrum of ICR transposed into
    citizenship education   242
10.1 The components of existential seriousness   248

Tables

6.1   Significant factors in different types of Muslim success with
the English National Curriculum for History (linear
regression)   140

8.1   The rank in popularity in different school subjects with 355
UK-based Muslim and non-Muslim boys   204

Foreword

Religious diasporas have characterised the twentieth century, and a challenge of the twenty-first century is to understand and respond to them. Matthew Wilkinson's book is a thoughtful and profound response to what the historian Tony Judt called the 'politics of social cohesions around collective purposes'.

Wilkinson successfully and excitingly draws together the philosophical insights of critical realism and an open Islamic tradition to explore the questions that underpin educational theory and practices in multi-faith societies. These issues are experienced in their most intense form in schools with high levels of religious and cultural diversity. But they go beyond such places: all of our children are growing up in a world in which diversity is commonplace – embedded, increasingly, in everything we do.

Wilkinson is a philosopher of education and turns his gaze predominantly on issues of curriculum, and particularly on the humanities and civics curriculum. But he locates his discussion of curriculum in a wider frame: the different trajectories of young British Muslims and the philosophical traditions of Islam, and draws on a rich vein of original empirical data from young Muslims in British schools.

Too many of the trajectories of contemporary life promote differences in interest, wealth and power, and provide virtual and real spaces where communities and traditions can isolate themselves, putting up barriers against the world and against exchange, as we have seen acutely in recent developments in the Middle East. Wilkinson's work is a reminder that the bases for intelligible discourse exist, that they are not only deeply rooted in long traditions but enacted in everyday encounters in schools and beyond. It is a reminder that conflict is not inevitable, that intellectual curiosity and engagement can be enriching as well as challenging and that there are intellectual traditions which have furnished us with effective tools to craft and shape that engagement in pursuit of authentic social cohesion built around the necessary collective purposes of human flourishing and social justice.

Professor Chris Husbands
Director, Institute of Education, University of London

Preface

The question of the relationship between the faith of Islam, the young Muslims who follow it and the multi-faith political and educational contexts that they increasingly inhabit is one of the most pressing issues facing the theological, political and educational worlds today. In Britain, Europe and beyond, young Muslims have become the public face of revived twenty-first-century religiosity in both its benign and, occasionally, its destructive forms. Moreover, young Muslims are negotiating complex new European Islamic identities in lands with little history of Islam or whose Islamic heritage has often been hidden or ignored.

Yet the revival of religion in general and Islam in particular is happening within prevailing political environments in which religious considerations are increasingly marginal to decision-making and in which educational policy is increasingly driven by targets, league tables and measurable indices of collective, reductive achievement, rather than indices of individual holistic success and integration. A dangerous educational gap has also developed between the importance of history, religion and citizenship in the world and the quality and status of the corresponding subjects in schools.

This book shows how the philosophy of critical realism can form an interpretative spiritual and intellectual bridgehead between Islamic praxis and contemporary multi-faith educational and social contexts. It then suggests how the philosophy that results from the engagement of critical realism with Islam, called Islamic critical realism, can be used in a practical way by history, religious education and citizenship teachers to create a serious educational provision that both is deeply informative and transformative for the lives of young Muslims and will help situate Islam and Muslims productively and authentically in a multi-faith world.

The book is born out of the author, Dr Matthew Wilkinson's, 23 years of humanities teaching of young Muslims and practice and research-based experience of Islam. Matthew embraced Islam in 1991 after reading theology at the University of Cambridge, where his Part 1 exam was recognised by a scholarship. After gaining a traditional Islamic education and British teaching qualifications, Matthew taught history, religious studies and citizenship in mainstream and Islamic faith schools in Spain and the United Kingdom for 15 years. Thereafter he gained a PhD on an ESRC studentship at King's College London on the relationship between history curriculum and British Muslim boys. More recently, Matthew has lectured in history and religious education at the University of Cambridge. He has also acted as an expert witness in Islamic theology and Muslim identity.

Matthew is currently Director of Curriculum for Cohesion, Research Fellow at the Cambridge Muslim College, Affiliate Lecturer at the Woolf Institute, Cambridge and Visiting Fellow at the Institute of Education, University of London.

Acknowledgements

After God, may He be glorified, to whom all praise and thanks are due, this book could not have been written without the belief, moral and generous financial support of the donors of Curriculum for Cohesion, who recognised the value of the ideas explained in this book. Principal among these, I would like to extend my deepest gratitude to:

The Easa Saleh Al-Gurg Charitable Foundation
The Easa Easa Saleh Al-Gurg Charitable Foundation was founded in 2010 by His Excellency Easa Saleh Al-Gurg, following a decree issued by His Highness Shaikh Mohammad bin Rashid Al-Makhtoum, Vice President and Prime Minister of UAE and ruler of Dubai. The Foundation assists in establishing and supporting charity housing projects, orphanages, homes for the elderly, day-care centres and medical facilities. It supports academic institutes, research centres and public libraries, and provides study and research grants to students and researchers. It also assists in the building of mosques and cultural centres, and supports environmental conservation projects. The Easa Easa Saleh Al-Gurg Charitable Foundation has been proud to sponsor Curriculum for Cohesion, as we believe building sustainable peace and harmony between faiths is one of the most vital tasks facing humankind.

Mr Mohammed Amin
Mr Mohammed Amin is Chairman of the Conservative Muslim Forum and was the first Muslim partner in Price Waterhouse, UK. Most recently, Mr Amin was PricewaterhouseCoopers' Head of Islamic Finance in the United Kingdom. He has made presentations on Islamic finance around the world as well as advising the UK government on this subject, and is active in a number of inter-faith and Muslim community organisations. In retirement, as well as consulting in Islamic finance, Mr Amin spends most of his time 'giving back' to the community by writing, speaking and mentoring, and active involvement in a number of charitable organisations. This activity was recognised by his selection as the Clare College Alumnus of the Year 2014. Mr Amin is a patron, lead donor and mentor for Curriculum for Cohesion.

1st Ethical Charitable Trust

The 1st Ethical Charitable Trust is a leading British-based educational charity, established in 2003. Its vision is to deepen the faith of current and future generations of British Muslims by helping Muslims look out for the rights of others. It is based on the belief that Muslims who fulfil the rights of others are best placed to lead successful lives and to leave a lasting Islamic legacy of a flourishing society. For this reason, it supports partnerships between scholars, civil society groups and educational institutions and initiatives, such as Curriculum for Cohesion.

Ahmad Tea

Ahmad Tea is a UK-based family business drawing on four generations of tea blending and tasting experience. Founded on a passion for the finest tea, Ahmad Tea is dedicated to the unique place that tea drinking commands at the heart of daily life in Britain and beyond. Its owners feel an ethical mission to help where they can. They are proud that Ahmad Tea's significant international presence allows them to become involved in good causes in many of the countries that they work with. The focus of their charity work is in the sponsorship of orphanages in Mali, Russia, Sri Lanka and Ukraine. They have been delighted to support Curriculum for Cohesion in the hope that Islam, like tea, will soon be a normal part of British life.

Muslim Aid

Muslim Aid is one of Britain's leading Muslim relief and development agencies, guided by the teachings of Islam. The charity endeavours to tackle poverty and its causes by developing innovative and sustainable solutions that enable individuals and their communities to live with dignity and by supporting initiatives that promote economic and social justice. It supports Curriculum for Cohesion because helping people increase their knowledge about a multi-faith world will enable greater social cohesion and tackle underlying causes of conflicts and poverty.

Cambridge Muslim College

The Cambridge Muslim College supports the development of training and Islamic scholarship to help meet the many challenges facing Britain today. The college is dedicated to maintaining academic excellence and pushing the boundaries of Islamic learning in the West. Drawing on resources and expertise in Cambridge and beyond, the college's mission is to help translate the many existing strengths of British Muslims into stronger, more dynamic institutions and communities. The Cambridge Muslim College has been the host institution and a sponsor of Curriculum for Cohesion.

The Martin and Judith Ainscough Charity Trust

The Martin and Judith Ainscough Charity Trust was formed following the sale of Ainscough Crane Hire Limited in 2007. Since that time, it has supported many charities, with an emphasis on helping disadvantaged people to get their lives back on track. The trust is pleased to support Curriculum for Cohesion as its organisers think that developing healthy, peaceful Muslim–non-Muslim relations is vital for the harmonious productivity of Britain.

I would also like to thank and acknowledge the role of the partner institutions of Curriculum for Cohesion in the completion of this book.

Cambridge Muslim College supports the development of training and Islamic scholarship to help meet the many challenges facing Britain today. It is dedicated to maintaining academic excellence and pushing the boundaries of Islamic learning in the West. Drawing on resources and expertise in Cambridge and beyond, Cambridge Muslim College's mission is to help translate the many existing strengths of British Muslims into stronger, more dynamic institutions and communities.

The Woolf Institute is dedicated to studying relations between Jews, Christians and Muslims throughout the ages. It consists of the Centre for the Study of Jewish–Christian Relations, the Centre for the Study of Muslim–Jewish Relations and the Centre for Public Education. The Woolf Institute is also an Associate Member of the Cambridge Theological Federation. The Cambridge Theological Federation brings together 11 institutions through which people of different churches, including Anglican, Methodist, Orthodox, Reformed and Roman Catholic, train for various forms of Christian ministry and service.

The Institute of Education, **University of London**, is the only higher education institution in the United Kingdom dedicated entirely to education and related areas of social science. It was recently recognised as the world's leading centre for studies in education and related disciplines.

I would also like to thank the **Muslim Council of Britain** and the **Department of Education and Professional Studies, King's College London**, which, in partnership, funded my PhD research from which the empirical data of this book is derived.

This book has been written in conversation with the following academic advisers of Curriculum for Cohesion, who have most kindly given of their time and expertise to ensure the highest possible academic standards have been met by this book:

Professor Roy Bhaskar is World Scholar at the Institute of Education, University of London and the founder of the philosophy of critical realism. Critical realism has had an enormous influence on the natural and social sciences over the past 25 years. Professor Bhaskar is regarded by many as one of the world's most innovative and creative philosophers. As the founder of the philosophy of critical realism and my own generous-spirited academic mentor, Roy has made an invaluable contribution to this book. Thank you, Roy.

Tim Winter (Shaykh Abdal Hakim Murad) is the Shaykh Zayed Lecturer in Islamic Studies at the Faculty of Divinity of the University of Cambridge and Dean of the Cambridge Muslim College. In 2009, Tim Winter was named one of the 500 most influential Muslims in the world by the Royal Islamic Strategic Studies Centre of Jordan. Abdal Hakim has had an important influence over Part I of the book in particular.

Christine Counsell has been a leading thinker in the development of history education, history curricula and teacher education in the United Kingdom and internationally for the past 20 years. Christine taught history in state secondary comprehensive schools for 10 years, and for three years was deputy headteacher in a comprehensive school in Bristol, UK. In 1997, Christine was appointed by the University of Cambridge to lead its secondary school PGCE history teacher training course. This teacher training programme is now considered one of the best and most rigorous in the United Kingdom. Christine kindly advised me, ably and wisely, on the history education content of the book.

Dr Julia Ipgrave is Senior Research Fellow at the Religions and Education Research Unit, University of Warwick. Her research interests include young people's religious understanding, religion in education and inter-religious encounter. She has participated in a number of UK and European projects and published widely in these fields. She is education specialist member on the Christian Muslim Forum. She has also worked for 16 years as a class teacher and school manager, for most of this time in a predominantly Muslim inner-city area. Julia's input was crucial to my thinking about religious education.

Professor Chris Husbands is Director of the Institute of Education, University of London. He was a teacher in urban comprehensive schools, where he was rapidly promoted to senior management before moving into higher education. He was a board member at the Training and Development Agency for Schools from 2006 to 2012 and is a member of the RSA Academies Commission. He has served as a board member at two examining groups, Edexcel and the Assessment and Qualifications Alliance. He has worked as a consultant or adviser to local authorities, Ofsted, the Department for Education, the Qualifications and Curriculum Agency and the National College for School Leadership. Chris made himself available for high-quality feedback about history education, one of his fields of expertise, despite the onerous duty of leading the Institute of Education, University of London, at a time of transition and change.

Dr Edward Kessler MBE is the Executive Director of the Woolf Institute in Cambridge and is also a Fellow of St Edmund's College, University of Cambridge. He has a first-class joint honours degree in Hebrew and Religious Studies from the University of Leeds and a Master of Theological Studies degree from Harvard Divinity School. He completed a PhD at the University of Cambridge. In 2006, he received the Sternberg Interfaith Award from philanthropist Sir

Sigmund Sternberg 'in recognition of outstanding services in furthering relations between faiths'. He was awarded the MBE for services to inter-faith relations in 2011. Ed's critical perspective from a Jewish and inter-faith point of view has been extremely important for nuancing and enriching the background and educational chapters of the book.

Her Royal Highness Princess Badiya bint El Hassan has a BA Hons in History from Oxford University and an LL.M. in Public International Law from the London School of Economics. She was called to the bar by Lincoln's Inn in 1998. Princess Badiya has worked with a number of initiatives to further interfaith and cross-cultural understanding, as well as projects to promote human rights in general and, more specifically, the rights of asylum seekers and refugees. She is also involved with various charities and programmes that work to support young people and women. Princess Badiya is regularly invited to give lectures on Islam, inter-faith matters, human rights and related issues. Princess Badiya, who is a patron of Curriculum for Cohesion, kindly read and commented sagely on the text from the point of view of an educated Muslim woman who has an insider's knowledge of both Europe and the Muslim-majority world.

Salah Al-Ansari is Visiting Lecturer in Islamic Studies at Heythrop College, University of London, where he is also completing his PhD on Muhammad Abu Zahra and Islamic modernism, and imam of the Margate Mosque, Kent. Salah became a *hafiz* of the Qur'an (someone who has memorised the entire text) at 13 years of age. He graduated in Classical and Modern Islamic Studies from the prestigious Al-Azhar University, Cairo, in 2000. Salah was an imam and teacher at the Central London Mosque from 2004 to 2007. He then worked in a number of mosques run by the Al-Birr Foundation in Margate, Woking and Basingstoke, where he did extensive inter-faith work in collaboration with Hampshire County Council, as well as at Palmers Green Mosque. Salah ably checked and enriched the Islamic textual content of the book.

Ms Basma El-Shayyal has taught in mainstream, supplementary and faith schools in a senior capacity for the past 20 years and was Head of Religious Education at Islamia Girls' High School until 2013. She is a long-standing member of Brent Standing Advisory Committee on Religious Education (SACRE), which advises schools on the religious education curriculum, and was made its Vice-Chair in 2013. She is also on the Editorial Board of the *International Journal of Religious Education*. Basma kindly made sure that the teaching tools for religious education outlined in this book are practicable from the point of view of a RE classroom teacher.

I should also mention the contribution of my PhD supervisors at King's College London, **Professor Louise Archer** and **Professor Peter Kutnick** (now of the University of Hong Kong), as well as **Dr Jamil Sherif**, my outside supervisor from the Muslim Council of Britain, who were most intellectually rigorous and professional in the supervision of my PhD.

I am exceedingly grateful to you all. A lot of what is good and useful in this book is the outcome of the refinement and direction offered by your advice; any mistakes or misjudgements are fully my own.

The production of this book has also been kindly and wonderfully supported by the **patrons of Curriculum for Cohesion**. Our patrons endorse of Curriculum for Cohesion as it, like them, works towards a more just, knowledgeable and harmonious society. Thank you all so much.

The Rt Hon. Sadiq Khan MP is the Member of Parliament for Tooting and Shadow Lord Chancellor and Shadow Secretary of State for Justice. He was both the first Asian and the first Muslim to attend Cabinet. From October 2008 to June 2009, Mr Khan was Parliamentary Under-Secretary of State in the Department for Communities and Local Government. He had special responsibility for community cohesion, religion and belief, race and preventing violent extremism. Apart from his parliamentary duties, Mr Khan has a keen interest in education as a governor of two primary schools, and is a patron of the Polka Theatre Company. Mr Khan's book *Fairness not Favours: How to Reconnect with British Muslims* won the prestigious Jenny Jeger Award for Best Fabian Society Publication.

Rabbi Baroness Julia Neuberger DBE was educated at Cambridge and Leo Baeck College, and has had a life of distinguished public service. Among her numerous contributions, she served the South London Liberal Synagogue from 1977 to 1989 and chaired Camden and Islington Community Health Services NHS Trust from 1993 to 1997. She was Chancellor of the University of Ulster from 1994 to 2000 and Bloomberg Professor of Divinity at Harvard University in 2006. She became a life peer in 2004 and chaired the Commission on the Future of Volunteering from 2006 to 2008. She was President of Liberal Judaism until spring 2011. She chaired the Advisory Panel on Judicial Diversity for Lord Chancellor Jack Straw, working across the political parties, during 2009 and 2010. She was appointed Senior Rabbi of West London Synagogue in March 2011.

The Rt Hon. Simon Hughes MP is the United Kingdom's Minister of State for Justice and Civil Liberties. Simon read law at Selwyn College, Cambridge, and was called to the bar by the Inner Temple in 1974. He then spent a postgraduate European Studies year at the College of Europe in Bruges. Simon joined the Liberal Party in 1971, inspired by the campaigns for international justice in places such as South Africa and Palestine. He was first elected for Southwark and Bermondsey in 1983 with a still-unbeaten record for the largest swing in any British parliamentary election (50.9%). In 2010, the constituency was renamed Bermondsey and Old Southwark, and Simon won the constituency with his highest ever number of votes. During his time as an MP, Simon has held many significant roles within the Liberals and Liberal Democrats, including Party President, Deputy Leader, Shadow Home Secretary, Shadow Attorney General, Shadow Leader of the House of Commons and Shadow Secretary of State for Energy and Climate Change.

Her Royal Highness Princess Badiya bint El Hassan of Jordan has a BA Hons in History from Oxford University and an LLM in Public International Law from the London School of Economics. She was called to the bar by Lincoln's Inn in 1998. Princess Badiya has worked with a number of initiatives to further inter-faith and cross-cultural understanding as well as projects to promote human rights in general and, more specifically, the rights of asylum seekers and refugees. She is also involved with various charities and programmes that work to support young people and women. Princess Badiya's UK commitments include her role as Founder Chairman of Mosaic and a Prince's Trust Ambassador. Princess Badiya is regularly invited to give lectures on Islam, inter-faith matters, human rights and related issues.

Sir David Calvert-Smith QC is Chair of the UK's Parole Board. He was Director of Public Prosecutions of England and Wales from 1998 to 2003. He was called to the bar at the Middle Temple in 1969 and became a Queen's Counsel in 1997. He was knighted in 2002 and sat as a High Court judge from 2005 to 2012. After beginning his career both prosecuting and defending, he specialised in prosecution work from 1986, including several cases of murder, terrorism and organised crime. In October 1998, he became Director of Public Prosecutions and head of the Crown Prosecution Service, a post he held for five years. Towards the end of his term, he piloted a new system in which CPS lawyers, instead of police officers, would make decisions about charging suspects, resulting in a 15% increase in convictions. This policy was fully implemented by his successor. In 2005, he led an inquiry for the Commission for Racial Equality into how the police forces of England and Wales deal with racism within their ranks.

Ms Sarah Teather MP is the Liberal Democrat Member of Parliament for Brent Central. Following the 2010 General Election, Sarah was appointed as Minister of State for Children and Families in the Coalition Government, a position she held until September 2012. While a Minister, Sarah was responsible for introducing the pupil premium and for publishing reforms to overhaul the special educational needs system. Sarah became an MP in 2003 when she won a landmark by-election in Brent East, becoming the youngest Member of the House of Commons at the time. Prior to her election to Parliament, Sarah read Natural Sciences at St John's College, Cambridge, before working in science policy in both the public and the private sectors.

Sir Anthony Figgis KCVO, CMG is a retired senior British diplomat who has been engaged for a lifetime in creating inter-cultural understanding. He joined

Her Majesty's Foreign (later Diplomatic) Service in 1962 and served in Yugoslavia (twice), Bahrain, Spain (twice), Germany, and as Ambassador to Austria (1996–2000). He was appointed Her Majesty's Marshal of the Diplomatic Corps in 2001 and served in that capacity until 2008. He has been Governor of Goodenough College for Overseas Graduates since 2004 and has been Chairman of the Royal Over-Seas League since 2009.

Ms Bernadette Hunter is President of the National Association of Head Teachers (NAHT) for 2013–2014. She has worked in education for over 30 years, having been a head teacher for 22 years in three different schools, and is currently head teacher of a large primary school in Staffordshire. She joined the NAHT National Executive in 2007, where her responsibilities have included chairing the NAHT Equalities Committee. Bernadette believes that in an increasingly diverse society, school leaders have an important role to play in promoting an ethos of tolerance and inclusion that helps young people explore their own faiths and cultures hand in hand with developing an understanding of the different faiths and cultures that they will encounter in life.

The Rt Rev. Richard Douglas Harries, Baron Harries of Pentregarth, was Bishop of Oxford from 1987 to 2006. He has a background of distinguished ecclesiastical and academic public service. He has been an Honorary Assistant Bishop in the Diocese of Southwark since 2006. He was the Gresham Professor of Divinity from 2008 to 2012. Lord Harries was ordained as a priest in 1964 and served as an army chaplain until 1969. He was appointed Bishop of Oxford in 1987, taking a seat as a Lord Spiritual in the House of Lords in 1993. As Bishop of Oxford, he became a founder member of the influential Oxford Abrahamic Group, bringing together leading Christian, Muslim and Jewish scholars. He is the author of many influential works of theology.

Sir Trevor Chinn CVO is Senior Adviser to CVC Capital Partners. He retired in 2003 as Chairman of RAC PLC (formerly Lex Service PLC) after 47 years' service. He served for five years from 1999 as Vice-Chair of the Commission of Integrated Transport and for 11 years as Chair of the Motorists Forum. In 2008, Boris Johnson, Mayor of London, appointed him as Chairman of the Mayor's Fund, an independent charity addressing the large scale issues of poverty of children and young people in London. He was Vice Chair of the Wishing Well Appeal for Great Ormond Street Hospital and responsible for the fundraising campaign from 1985 to 1989. He was Deputy Chair of the Royal Academy Trust and a member of the Royal Academy Management Committee from 1994 to 2004. He is on the Executive Committee Board of the Jewish Leadership Council.

Bishop Richard Cheetham read Physics and Philosophy at Oxford and was ordained in 1988 after working as a teacher and an investment analyst. He became Archdeacon of St Albans in 1999 and Bishop of Kingston in 2002.

Bishop Richard is Chair of Southwark Diocesan Board of Education and Anglican President of the Christian Muslim Forum. He has a PhD from King's College London for his thesis on collective worship in schools, and is now an Honorary Research Fellow there. He has close connections with the University of Roehampton, is President of London Southwest YMCA, and a Trustee of St George's College, Jerusalem.

Dr Muhammad Abdul Bari MBE is Chairman of the Board of Trustees at the East London Mosque and London Muslim Centre (London's first mosque). He has served east London's diverse communities in various capacities for three decades. He was Secretary-General of the Muslim Council of Britain from 2006 until 2010. He was on the Organising Committee Board for the 2012 Summer Olympics.

Mr Aaqil Ahmed currently combines being the TV Genre Lead for Religion and Ethics with commissioning the TV output as well as managing the in-house Multimedia Religion and Ethics Department in Salford and Belfast and being the BBC's overall Head of Religion. Over the past four years, Aaqil has commissioned projects as diverse as *The Life of Muhammad*, *The Preston Passion* and *Hitler's Children*. He also led the BBC in-house team's coverage of the papal visit in 2010 and the award-winning 50th anniversary *Songs of Praise* in 2011. Aaqil combines this work with a Professorship in Professional Practice: Television at the School of Media and Performing Arts, Middlesex University.

The Muslim Council of Britain (MCB) is a national representative Muslim umbrella body with over 500 affiliated national, regional and local organisations including mosques, charities and schools. Its **Research and Documentation Committee** is an academic and researcher network that supports the activities of the MCB through policy briefings, survey work and supporting research of relevance to the Muslim community.

Last, but by no means least, I would like to thank my family: my father, the late Sir William Wilkinson and my mother, Kate, who set high standards of integrity and scholarship; my beautiful wife, Mrs Lucy Wilkinson, who is also Project Director of Curriculum for Cohesion, without whose love, insightful advice and outstanding powers of organisation, this book would not have been possible: she is a blessing from God to me; and my darling son, Gabriel, who at four years old donated all his pocket money to become the first donor of Curriculum for Cohesion. He always helps me to keep life in perspective and is one of the greatest joys of my life.

Part I

Historical background and sociological context

Introduction

A tale of two young Muslims, a spiritual quest, a book to be used

An enlightened student; a misguided classroom assistant

Let us compare and contrast two experiences involving young Muslims in multi-faith educational contexts in the United Kingdom.

In February 2014, the BBC reported the story of the founder of Ieat Foods, Shazia Saleem, whose student experience at Warwick University prompted her to start up a successful ready meal company serving *halāl* (religiously permitted) versions of traditional British dishes such as shepherd's pie.

The BBC article reported:

> Ms Saleem first came up with the idea for the company when she was at Warwick University eight years ago, because she was fed up with having to buy vegetarian food to avoid non-halal meals.
>
> 'Most of my friends at university were non-Muslims, and when we did a weekly food shop together their trolleys were full of really tasty-looking ready meals, and all I could buy were things like cheese and onion pasties,' she says.
>
> 'It was really frustrating, and I used to whinge a lot that I was missing out. I thought, why wasn't anyone making halal ready meals, other than the odd curry?'
>
> 'That was when I decided I needed to do something about it. While moonlighting on other things, I then spent the next eight years putting together all the pieces of the jigsaw that needed to be in place before I launched Ieat.'
>
> (www.bbc.co.uk/news/business-26187624)

Here, then, is one out of many possible examples of a creative response of a young Muslim to student life in multi-faith Britain. It is driven by the need to be authentic to the demands of her Islamic faith and by the desire to fill a gap in the market created by a new and authentically British Muslim identity, carried out through a mixture of intelligence, persistence and hard work. It shows how Muslim young people in multi-faith contexts are beginning to find creative solutions to complex cultural challenges which arise through the healthy and normal coexistence of young Muslims with non-Muslim friends, neighbours and fellow citizens.

By contrast, at 8.50 a.m. on 7 July 2005, a British primary school classroom assistant from Leeds, Mohammed Sidique Khan, whom one of his charges had described as 'kind' and who had been regarded by teachers and parents alike as a 'role model' (BBC, 2007), blew himself up at Edgware Road Underground Station in London, killing six fellow British citizens. The place of Khan's attack was highly symbolic. The Edgware Road was and is the hub of Arab Muslim commercial life in London, where the multi-faith life of the capital of the United Kingdom takes on its most obviously Middle Eastern expression, and where Islam and other faiths, together with their cultural expressions, exist cheek by jowl. By detonating himself there, Khan was attacking the very idea of the coexistence of Islam with other faiths.

Directly after the attack, Al-Jazeera television channel aired his 'martyrdom' video.

> [O]ur words have no impact upon you, therefore I'm going to talk to you in a language that you understand.
>
> Our words are dead until we give them life with our blood.
>
> I'm sure by now the media's painted a suitable picture of me, this predictable propaganda machine will naturally try to put a spin on things to suit the government and to scare the masses into conforming to their power and wealth-obsessed agendas.
>
> I and thousands like me are forsaking everything for what we believe.
>
> Our driving motivation doesn't come from tangible commodities that this world has to offer.
>
> Our religion is Islam – obedience to the one true God, Allah, and following the footsteps of the final prophet and messenger Muhammad. . . . This is how our ethical stances are dictated.
>
> Your democratically elected governments continuously perpetuate atrocities against my people all over the world. . . .
>
> Until we feel security, you will be our targets. And until you stop the bombing, gassing, imprisonment and torture of my people we will not stop this fight.
>
> We are at war and I am a soldier. Now you too will taste the reality of this situation.
>
> (http://news.bbc.co.uk/1/hi/uk/4206800.stm)

These contrasting events and enterprises, of course, lie on the extremes of a continuum between personal, spiritual success and personal and spiritual catastrophe, on which the daily experiences of young Muslims in education might more normally be ranged somewhere near the middle. Nevertheless, on the Durkheimian principle that the normality and the pathology of a cultural group lie on a continuum, I believe that these vignettes do together illustrate some of the related issues faced by many young Muslims in education in a multi-faith world that will be addressed by this book.

The issues of this book

First, the majority of young Muslims face issues connected to their faith (or the lack of it) and their faith-based education. Both the enterprises cited above were motivated in some way by religious faith and both of them were apparently inspired by the desire to obey God. In this way, they represent heightened examples of more general identifications, which we shall explore in this book, of the centrality of Islamic faith to the identities and lives of young Muslims, which can have both benign and negative effects. Muslim young people in British schools have both been observed to mobilise around Islam both as a platform for educational achievement and engagement and as an identity through which to 'resist' formal education, which is construed as 'white' and even 'un-Islamic' (L. Archer, 2003; Shain, 2003).

It is, therefore, a premise of this book that it is not possible to do intellectual justice to the educational situation of young Muslims unless their Islamic faith is addressed non-reductively qua religious faith and not 'dumbed down' as an ethno-cultural form or an expression of gender, while recognising that both culture and gender interact as two of a multiplicity of factors that influence young Muslims' understandings of their faith.

Second, and relatedly, many Muslim young people face complex issues of ethics and morality. Both the successful young Muslim entrepreneur and the suicide bomber believe that they taking an 'ethical stance', in the former case showing a deep intuitive ethical understanding and in the latter case betraying a deep ethical confusion as to the difference between right and wrong, and correct and traditional Islamic ethical responses to fellow human beings. A more widespread ethical confusion among young British Muslims is suggested by the fact that 12% of the male population of UK prisons is Muslim even though Muslims make up a mere 4.8% of the population of the United Kingdom (UK Gov., 2012).

Third, many Muslim young people face complex issues of belonging and citizenship. Both phenomena cited here represent, in some senses, responses to being both British and Muslim. The young British Muslim entrepreneur has overcome a gap in the food market that is symbolic of the relative public absence of her faith in British life to forge a 'new' idea of being British *and* Muslim.

The British Muslim suicide bomber has categorically rejected his British nationality and the country where he was born, bred and educated, and has displaced his allegiance into a global Islamic identity. His references to 'my people' clearly refer to some 'imagined' (Anderson, 1983) connection to Muslim-majority countries and not to the British people of the land of his birth, upbringing and education, and where his rights of citizenship pertain. The words 'you' and 'Your democratically elected governments' suggest, furthermore, the perception of a Manichean division between the Muslim 'us' and the non-Muslim 'you', together with the idea that there is an essential incompatibility between democracy and Islam.

Fourth, many Muslim young people face issues of political alienation and injustice, both real and perceived, meted out in part through skewed representations of

Islam in the media. Saleem has used the media to her advantage by framing (Morey & Yaqin, 2011) her enterprise as a Muslim success story. Khan clearly feels strongly that the Muslim community as a global family (the Umma) is on the receiving end of profound miscarriages of political justice and that the media have let the Muslim community down through their 'predictable propaganda machine'. Such feelings that Muslims are always 'on the receiving end' of domestic and international power-politics are also prevalent among young Muslims of entirely peaceful persuasions (Mondal, 2008). Normal too is the sensation and perception that Muslims are cut out of the everyday discourses and institutions of majority society owing to prejudices of many different types.

Fifth, many young Muslims face issues connected with the nature and performance of gender in an Islamic way. It will not, I am sure, have been lost on the reader that while the successful young Muslim entrepreneur is a woman, the suicide bomber is a man. The experiences of negotiating gender as a British Muslim young woman and a British Muslim young man display both similarity and difference; and both experiences exhibit tensions with 'hegemonic' (Connell, 1995) masculine and feminine forms and identities that are available for young people in contemporary, multi-faith liberal democracies.

This book deals squarely with the first three of these sets of issues and touches on the last two. Its premise is that the negotiation of Muslim practice and identity is inevitably being undertaken by young Muslims in Britain and elsewhere as a default and necessary response to the contemporary multi-faith world though accommodation, renegotiation and, sometimes, rejection of contemporary, often non-Muslim, habits and cultural forms. Nevertheless, this book contends that contemporary young Muslims are missing a coherent philosophical approach, both explicitly articulated and implicitly understood, which can be accessed through education, to aid a meaningful and fulfilling life in multi-faith contemporary contexts. It works to remove this absence. Once this absence is addressed, it is a premise of this book both that the innate intelligence of young Muslims will enable them to negotiate meaningful and fulfilling lives in multi-faith contemporary contexts and that teachers, especially in the humanities subjects, history, religious education and citizenship, together with other responsible adults with whom young Muslims interact, will be well placed to guide and enhance this process. Thus, this book is intended to help the deep processes of personal and social integration that will enable young Muslims to fulfil themselves spiritually, emotionally, intellectually, civically and instrumentally in the multi-faith contexts in a sustained and systematic way.

Moreover, the broader context of the book – Britain and multi-faith societies at large – means that these issues are of concern to all of us and demand soul-searching with regards to the broader social conditions and educational environments in which young Muslim people in the West are growing up and being educated. Identities and actions are always performed and understood relationally with reference to the identities and actions of other people and other groups (L. Archer, 2003). In other words, there is an unspoken flip side to the issues documented above, which is that people of all faiths and none reflect upon implications of the 'new' Muslim presence for the creation of a harmonious society in which 'the good of all is dependent upon the good of each' (Bhaskar, 1993/2008, chapter 3). Therefore, this book is also intended to help citizens of other faiths and none, as well as Muslims, reflect upon the meanings of this 'new' Muslim faith-based presence in the heart of liberal, secularising democracies.

The author's story

You might be wondering at this juncture what a white British man called Matthew Wilkinson has to offer in this regard! What experience does he have of the issues facing Muslim young people? I am not going to indulge in a lengthy postmodernist-style apology for my life, but a little bit of personal context might help the reader understand the personal circumstances from which this book emerges.

I was born to a well-to-do, upper-middle-class Anglican Christian English family in 1969. I enjoyed an elite education at Eton College, where I was a King's Scholar and Head Boy, and at Trinity College, University of Cambridge, where I was awarded a scholarship in Theology after my Part 1 exam. Immediately after my Finals exams in June 1991, having been impressed by the spiritual depth and seriousness of the Muslim prayer, I converted to Islam in Granada, Spain, to the horror and disbelief of my family and friends. In fact, my conversion to Islam came following an intense three-year period of theological and existential soul-searching, which included a failed operation on my father in 1990 that left him blind, my first tumultuous relationship with a member of the opposite sex, and over-indulgence in the traditional pleasures of the undergraduate.

At the time, Islam and the Muslim group which I had joined gave a religious structure to my day, a way to express my belief in God and, in some ways, a surrogate family after 15 years spent in boarding school institutions of different types. It was also a rebellious reaction against the 'meaningless' professions in finance and industry which I saw my talented peers entering and that I wanted to avoid at all costs; and, indeed, against my own hedonism of the previous five years. With the benefit of hindsight, I would be rather more charitable to those professions and to the aspirations of my peers today.

My first decade (1992–2002) as a Muslim was spent with a Sufi Muslim group, during which time I studied the Book of Islam (the Qur'an), the recorded behaviour of the Prophet Muhammad (the Sunna), basic Islamic law and jurisprudence, and the Arabic language 'at the feet' of some recognised and some less-recognised teachers using traditional techniques such as memorisation from a writing board (*lawh*). It was a formative period. However, I abandoned this group when I realised, among other things, that its separatist ethos was detrimental to my own development and was hindering the progress of the pupils at the school which I had helped set up and where I taught Islamic studies, English literature and history. I realised that such separatism had no sanction in the Qur'an, which repeatedly warns against sectarianism (e.g. Qur'an, 42:13–14).

During this time, I saw some of the Muslim-majority world. In 2001, I taught English in northern Nigeria deep in the countryside near Zaria and in Zaria itself. There, astonished, I witnessed joyous street parties to celebrate the attacks on the Twin Towers in New York of 9/11, which were clearly perceived by the common man in Africa to be the 'bloodying of America's nose', in stark contrast to the scenes of disbelief and mourning that prevailed on my return to England. I went fundraising in Abu Dhabi and Dubai, studied with *shuyukh* (religious teachers) in Melilla and Morocco, and visited the mosques of Istanbul and Bursa, Turkey. Most memorably, I went on Hajj to Mecca in Saudi Arabia in 2003 and worshipped in the mosque of the Prophet Muhammad in Madina. This experience of the Muslim-majority world left me with a strong impression of peoples in whom the education and background of Islam still resonated in their personal habits of hospitality, family-mindedness and personal ethics, but whose formal practice of Islam and social and institutional fabric were fragile or even shattered.

After leaving this group, and as a married man, I qualified as a history teacher on the Graduate Teacher Partnership at Brondesbury College in Brent, London, an Islamic faith school established in 1996 by the former pop star Cat Stevens, now known as Yusuf Islam, and at the then John Kelly Boys' Technology College in the same borough, now the Crest Academy. At Brondesbury College, I taught Muslim young people history, citizenship and drama for seven years from 2003 to 2009. There, in a nurturing educational atmosphere and in the presence of usually highly articulate, intelligent and well-mannered Muslim young men, I became aware of the sensibilities, issues and dilemmas facing Muslim young people and males, myself included. During this time, attacks and planned attacks by British Muslim males on 7 July 2005 and 21 July 2005 thrust young Muslim males into the national British consciousness as never before and led to the securitisation (K. E. Brown, 2010) of the Muslim community, as the War on Terror continued to rage chaotically and with terrible loss of civilian life in Iraq and Afghanistan. During this tumultuous period (2005–2011), I also served on the education committee of the Muslim Council of Britain (MCB) and completed a PhD at King's College London in History curriculum, entitled 'History Curriculum, Citizenship and Muslim Boys: Learning to Succeed?', on an ESRC/MCB-funded studentship. Both these experiences broadened my horizons further about life as a young British Muslim.

This experience of the Muslim community with the MCB, and the PhD thesis upon which this book often draws, confirmed my prior teaching experience that there was a much-needed job of 'translation' and interpretation of the Muslim faith for multi-faith contexts and that history, religious education and citizenship in school were potentially well positioned to help with this work.

Since 2011, I have also served as an expert witness in Islamic theology in seven successful counter-terrorism trials. This means that I have had an intimate knowledge of Islam and the Muslim community in Britain over a period of 22 years in both its peaceful, intelligent and articulate and its illegal, terrorist and sinister manifestations, and a lot of what lies on a continuum between these two extremes. I am acutely aware of how gaps and absences in proper Muslim thinking and a well-conceived education are likely to be filled at best with clumsy and ill-conceived and at worst violent and extreme 'Islamic' teaching from the pulpit and, increasingly, the internet and social media.

I am, therefore, intimately aware, at an intellectual and existential level, of the issues and dilemmas that face Muslim young people, if for no other reason than the fact that many of them have also been faced by me. What does it mean to live in a Muslim minority in a Christian-majority country surrounded by people who do not believe in the truth of Islam, or even in God, and yet who are more often than not palpably good and decent human beings? What does it mean to live as an equal Muslim citizen under non-Muslim law and to abide lawfully and peacefully under the authority of people who legislate in a way that it is often not Muslim and sometimes even militates against basic Qur'anic principles? What is an authentic Muslim response to cultural forms that often encourage behaviour that may lead one away from the faith? What does it mean to obey God in a society whose members often do not believe in Him and which sometimes makes religious obedience difficult and even counter-cultural?

These types of questions and dilemmas are not easily answered; for even if one finds answers to them – which one can, within the precedents of Islamic experience and law – they still throw up powerful emotional, philosophical and educational issues for young people of faith in general and Muslim young people in particular.

The book's intellectual heritage

This book draws on three intellectual traditions in order to shed coherent, systematic light on dilemmas such as those set out above. It aims to set out a programme of systematic spiritual and educational reflection by which teachers, especially of history, religious education and citizenship, curriculum planners and others involved in the education of young Muslims can challenge young Muslims to make the most of their faith and to use it to enlighten their own lives in the service of God and the multi-faith society around them.

First, it draws upon the traditions of philosophical theology (*kalām*) and theological philosophy (*falsāfa*) that have been characteristic of Islam in its most vibrant intellectual phases, epitomised by the great Muslim religious philosopher-theologians such as Al-Farabi (872–950), Ibn Sīna (Avicenna, 980–1037), Ibn Rushd (Averroes, 1126–1198), Fakhr al-Dīn al-Rāzī (d. 1209), and, in particular, Abu Hamid Muḥammad ibn Muḥammad al-Ghazāli (1058–1111). Of course, in the Muslim classical period of the ninth to the fourteenth centuries CE the theologians (*mutakalimūn*) and rationalistic philosophers (*faylasūf*) of Islam often went to wars of words (and, at times, of the sword) to champion or refute one another's methods and positions. Famously, al-Ghazāli's *Incoherence of the Philosophers* was aimed at taming the Hellenistic trend in Islamic religious thought, which he thought was displacing the idea of a living, theistic Deity with a deistic and impersonal one and had caused theologian-philosophers to transgress the bounds of traditional Islamic doctrine as expounded in the Qur'an (Ormsby, 1984; Winter, 2008).

This was countered, equally vehemently, by Ibn Rushd's (Averroes') *The Incoherence of the Incoherence*, which aimed to unmask the faulty logic of the theologians (*mutakalimūn*) (Ziai, 2008). However, with the benefit of hindsight we can see that the integration of Hellenic rationality and the Islamic revealed traditions was to a large extent accomplished in the Middle Ages by al-Ghazāli himself, often following the logic, if not the conclusions, of *falsāfa* for the long-term enrichment of Muslim faith. However, although the successful integration of Hellenistic philosophy (*falsāfa*) with Islamic theology (*kalām*) meant that 'pure' *falsāfa* 'withered' (Winter, 2008), it would be wrong to suppose that Islamic philosophical theology died out after the al-Ghazāli–Ibn Rushd debate. It continued in the world both of Sunni and of Shi'a Islam with the 'Asharite and Māturidite schools, with such figures as al-Shahrastāni (d. 1153), Fakhr al-Dīn al-Rāzī (d. 1209), 'Adud al-al-Dīn al-Nasafī (d. 1355), al-Sharīf al-Jurjānī (d. 1413) and the Tusi school of Twelver Shi'ism (Leaman & Rizvi, 2008). These figures made use of the systematic and detailed use of the logic that had characterised *falsāfa* and was now integrated into 'mainstream' theology (*kalām*) (Leaman & Rizvi, 2008). Hereafter, therefore, this book treats the intellectual and spiritual traditions theological philosophy (*falsāfa*) and philosophical theo-logy (*kalām*) as one tradition united, post al-Ghazāli, in the mission to form a bridgehead of reason between eternal principles and truths of religion and con-temporary, contingent realities of the world, working within the broad, consen-sually accepted parameters of traditional Islamic doctrine.

Second, therefore, this book draws upon the tradition of dialectical European philosophy, epitomised by G. W. F. Hegel. Most recently, this tradition has been brought with great energy and conceptual sophistication into the contemporary academy by the founding figure of the philosophy of critical realism, Roy Bhaskar, as well as others following his lead, such as Alan Norrie, Andrew Wright and Margaret Archer. Critical realism is exceptional in its coherent articulation of a contemporary philosophy of being, of knowing and of real per-sonal, ethical and social change, and in its refusal to reduce being of all types, including spiritual being, to socially constructed epistemology or merely psycho-logical or semantic meaning. This makes the philosophy of critical realism at its original, dialectical and spiritual moments an ideal vehicle for the development of a systematic rationale to interpret Islam and Islam-in-education for a multi-faith world.

Third, it draws upon the tradition of contemporary British and American educational and curricular theory developed by the likes of Michael Young, Ivor Goodson and Michael Apple, as well as contemporary theories of gender-in-education expounded and illustrated with reference to Muslim young people by researchers in gender-in-education such as Louise Archer and Farzana Shain. These traditions and discourses have shown how educational processes, whether at classroom, school, national or international policy level, or informally at

home, can never be value-free or free of the demands and constraints of the societies and their institutions which they are designed to serve and of which they are
products. The questions is always, 'Free from and free for what?' Education is
always education *for*. In this book, education is primarily understood as *for* the
development of human success on connected and differentiated layers of spiritual,
intellectual, emotional, civic and instrumental being. This book, therefore, sets out
to be honest, clear and intellectually rigorous about the aims and purposes of
education, in terms both of what is put in *and* of what is left out of educational
architecture such as the curriculum. As an educational book, it is driven by the
desire to provide as many children and young people (and adults) as possible with
useful, content-rich, well-theorised knowledge that empowers them to fulfil themselves in a way that helps bring harmony to the world around them.

While I cite the intellectual roots and influences of this book, it is my sincere
intention that the utility and (hopefully) enjoyment of the book require no prior
knowledge of any of these traditions on the part of the reader. It is my intention
that the book should stand alone on its own terms in order to help teachers of
young Muslims, in schools and out-of-school settings, and all those seriously
interested in the place of faith in education today to think about the relationship
of Islam to the multi-faith world.

Defining the key terms

I have told the reader who I am, where this book is coming from and whom and
what it is intended for. Now let me offer a brief explanation and justification of
the way that I intend to use my terms, since almost all the key terms and core
concepts of this book come laden with pre-existing assumptions and are contested terms.

Islam, which means 'surrender to the will of God', is a complete religious
life-transaction (*deen*) between the human being and God (Arabic – *Allah*,
meaning the One worthy of worship) that is derived from two primary sources:

1   *The Revelation (lit. the Recitation) of God (the Qur'an)*. Muslims believe
    that this was sent down from God to the Prophet Muhammad through the
    mediation of the Angel Gabriel over a period of 23 years from 610 to 633 CE.
    The Qur'an conveys the message of the lordship and unity of God and the
    requirement for humans to worship and obey Him.
2   *The habitual pattern of behaviour (the Sunna) of the Prophet Muhammad*.
    This is made up of collections of sayings and recorded actions of the
    Prophet Muhammad and transmitted by his family and Companions that
    exemplify and explain the injunctions contained in the Qur'an.[1] These
    sayings were subject in the first centuries of Islamic scholarship to stringent
    processes of authentication and classification.

From the Qur'an and the Sunna, taken together, is derived Islamic law, Shari'a,
by processes of human interpretative and legal deduction. Shari'a literally means

a Path or Way: thus, Islamic law is conceived of as a religious and legal path to God.

A core part of Shari'a are the Five 'Pillars' of Islamic practice – Witnessing, Obligatory Prayer, the Social Welfare Tax, Fasting and Hajj – and the Articles of the Islamic Faith: God, His Angels, His Books, His Prophets, the Decree and the Day of Reckoning.[2] Adherence to these basic elements of practice and belief is what characterises the Muslim believer. The meanings of these obligatory Articles of Faith and Pillars of Practice and how they might be interpreted by young Muslims in a multi-faith world are explored by the philosophy of this book.

Muslims are those human beings who declare themselves (or are declared by carer adults if minors) to be followers of the religion of Islam – who believe (allowing also for lapses into unbelief and for long periods of 'dormant' belief) that there is no god except the one true God, *Allah*, and that Muhammad, may God bless him and grant him peace, is the Messenger of God. It is coterminous with no particular culture or ethnicity. 'Muslims' also refer to children born into Muslim religio-cultural families who may still be in the process of deciding about their core values and religious beliefs (Head, 1999).

Multi-faith refers to the coexistence of a wide variety of religious groups of legal parity (or near-parity in the context of established religions) in democratic, usually functionally non-religious, political jurisdictions. A multi-faith world refers to a world increasingly characterised by ethical and religious plurality, porosity and the easy mobility of ethical and intellectual ideas through human travel, trade, international publishing and the internet, which usually transcend traditional geo-religious identifiers such as Christendom or Dar al-Islam (the place of Islam). A multi-faith world is a world also characterised by the possibility of religious conversion outside of the normative religion traditionally connected with certain places, e.g. conversion to Islam in 'Christian' Europe. It is also characterised by religiously plural national citizenries who live, work and learn side by side, often in confined spaces, e.g. inner-city boroughs and districts, and in schools and universities.[3]

A *philosophy* here means a coherent body of systematic and logically inter-related theoretical ideas that are brought to bear in the service of a practical cause. In this case, I call the philosophy expounded here Islamic critical realism (ICR). By Islamic critical realism I mean a philosophical approach based on the major aims, tenets, moments and developments of critical realist philosophy that has, in this case, been brought to the service of the interpretation of the Muslim faith and Islam/Muslims-in-education. It has been brought to service in a way that makes a contribution to critical realist thinking that is distinctively its own. Hence, Islamic critical realism is both more accurate and less controversial than the other possibility, critical realist Islam. It also allows for a necessary category distinction, which is important, between the Islamic religion (*deen*) which is based on divine revelation and the prophetic example, and this philosophy of religious and educational interpretation which is put to the service of the Islamic religion, its followers and those members of societies that find its followers in significant numbers in their midst.[4]

Success is thematised in this book as the multidimensional development and self-realisation of individual human beings in productive relation to the multidimensional development and self-realisation of other human beings on four social planes (see Chapter 3). These planes are:

a   material transactions with nature;
b   inter-subjective (interpersonal) transactions between differently situated human agents;
c   social relations at the irreducible level of structures, institutions and forms; and
d   the internal stratification of the embodied personality.

(Bhaskar, 1993/2008)

The dimensions of success that characterise the internal stratification of the embodied personality at level 4 in this book are:

* the spiritual dimension;
* the intellectual dimension;
* the affective-cultural dimension
* the civic dimension;
* the instrumental dimension.

These dimensions are themselves understood as having distinct and interrelated, 'articulated' ontologies. These ideas are explained and explored in detail in Chapters 3, 5 and 6 in particular.

Education is here taken to mean the involvement of the human being individually or as part of a group in any process that engages him- or herself in systematic meaning-making in the discovery of the self (and the 'other') and of the world (and the Other, God, or equivalent). It is an activity in which teaching and learning are intrinsically (Bhaskar, 1975; Sayer, 1984), inseparably related in an oscillation of necessary knowledge–power relations between the teacher and the taught and in a process of unfolding the enfolded (Bhaskar, 2012), i.e. realising understandings that are embedded potentially in being. Normatively, and especially in relation to policy discourses, educational sites usually refer to nurseries, primary and secondary schools, high schools, further education colleges and universities (and their equivalents).

In addition, this book will certainly consider the family and home, the in-school and out-of-school peer group, places of semi-formal religious education, e.g. churches, mosques, temples and synagogues, and the media and popular cultural outlets such as the internet as educational sites and relationships whose influence has a powerful bearing on the upbringing and developing self and world-understanding of children and young people.[5]

The structure of the book

This book is divided into three parts.

Part I, comprising this Introduction and Chapter 1, sets the argument of the book in micro (personal), meso (contemporary social) and macro (historical trends) context and makes the case for the need for a contemporary educational philosophy of Islam.

Part II, composed of Chapters 2–5, expounds and develops the philosophical position of an Islamic critical realism at its original, dialectical and meta-Real (spiritual) moments. It shows how the application of this interpretative framework to the traditional beliefs and practices of Islam can revitalise the spiritual, social and educational relevance of the Islamic faith for Muslims (and non-Muslims) in multi-faith contexts.

Part III, constituted by Chapters 6–9, turns to the practical educational application of this systemic philosophy. It begins by outlining an ontology of the young Muslim self-in-education on multiple, stratified levels of being. It then shows in detail how the approach to understanding Islam outlined in Part II can be applied theoretically and practically by history, religious education and citizenship teachers to enhance and enrich the education of young Muslims in the humanities in a way that enables them and their peers to take full benefit of the opportunities of life in a multi-faith world. These chapters consider how to enable both Muslim and non-Muslim children to reflect upon the 'new' Western Islamic presence constructively and critically. The book ends with a concluding chapter, Chapter 10, that summarises and pulls together reflectively the systematic philosophy of the book and its application, and relates its argument to the macro-socio-political picture of life in a contemporary liberal democracy.

Readers themselves will best know how they wish to use this book. Those with a philosophical frame of mind and those who want to get to grips with what I believe is a rich, original and coherent contemporary religious and educational philosophy may wish to read Parts I and II before referring to Part III, which is directed at the practical teaching of the humanities subjects. Teachers and other practitioners who do not have the time or the inclination for detailed theory may wish to read the chapters specific to their subjects in Part III and refer back when necessary to the history and philosophy in Parts I and II. My point is that this book and the philosophy that it outlines are designed to be used, and I have tried to structure and signpost the book so that it is as usable as possible.

Notes

1 The Sunna includes 'tacit approval' of behaviour and activities about which the Prophet Muhammad (peace be upon him) purposefully remained silent and his personal habits of hygiene, cleanliness, etc. In the Maliki school of law, founded by Imam Mālik ibn Anas (*c*.711–795 CE), the collective behaviour of the Companions of the Prophet in Madina (called *'amal*) is also, in certain circumstances, considered to be a legitimate source of Shari'a (Dutton, 1999).

2 The Shi'a Muslim Articles of Faith also include *'Adala* – the principle of divine justice – and *Imama* – the principle that God has designated specific religious leaders to follow

the Prophets in the guidance of humankind. I have restricted my consideration to those Articles of Faith in which both Sunni and Shi'a Muslims believe. Both Sunni and Shi'a Muslims adhere to the Five Pillars of Islamic practice.

3 I am aware that 'the multi-faith world' as far as this book is concerned refers primarily in an empirical sense to multi-faith Britain, or even, in fact, multi-faith England. This fact is due to the restrictions in terms of time, space and energy on the research efforts of one man. I do, nevertheless, believe that the philosophical and theoretical approach here outlined is both transfactual and transnational and that Britain provides a useful multi-faith case from which to derive some important general philosophical principles.

4 This is *not* a book of reformation of the basic tenets of Muslim belief and practice, agreed and honed by the traditions of the scholarly Muslim community over centuries. Nor is this a book of Islamic law or jurisprudence for Muslims in the West, of which there already exist some useful examples (Ramadan, 1999). It is a book of theological and educational philosophy which aims to show how the tenets of Islam and the spirit that underlies them can be brought to bear in the service of contemporary human flourishing by means of inspiring humanities education. Its theological positioning and style are, very broadly speaking, *Māturīdite*; that is to say, I attempt to steer a philosophical course on the theological middle ground between extreme rationalist (*Mu'tazilite*) theology, whereby divine revelation can be trumped by human reason, and extreme literalism (e.g. *Ahl as-Sunnah*), whereby far too little regard is given to the role of reason is deriving useful, systematic meaning from revealed religious texts.

5 The book focuses on the (UK) *secondary* (US, middle) phase of education. I have chosen the secondary (middle) educational phase as the empirical focus of the book for three reasons:

1 Educational/developmental. The secondary level, which roughly demarcates the period of adolescence (11–16), is *sui generis* a period of intellectual and spiritual re-evaluation and change during which all types of children, including Muslims, are reflecting on their absolute and contingent values (Feinstein, 2009; Head, 1999). Thus, the secondary period of adolescence is increasingly considered by educationalists, as well as by natural and social scientists, as a distinct developmental phase of singular importance (Baker & Edwards, 2012);

2 Political/structural. The secondary phase in English education has recently (1997 to present) undergone enormous structural change, with first the Labour and then the Conservative–Liberal Democrat academies and free school programmes changing the shape and complexion of state secondary education, possibly for ever. The period 2011–2014 has also seen a root-and-branch review of the National Curriculum. This means that, as well as any negative consequences of these programmes, the secondary level also represents the greatest opportunity for new ideas and positive change.

3 Personal/experiential. My own teaching and research experience over 23 years have focused on humanities education at the secondary level.

However, the focus on the secondary/adolescent phase is, of course, contextually embedded in consideration of the primary and tertiary educational phases and sectors. Also, it is my hope that the philosophy of Islamic critical realism will present reflective opportunities for scholars, teachers and others whose fields of endeavour lie outside secondary education.

1 From sacred civilisation to secular confusion

Why does Islam need a philosophy?

On all sorts of levels – geopolitical, socio-economic, legal, psychological and spiritual – early modernity,[1] modernity[2] and postmodernity[3] have been problematic, even traumatic, for Muslims and the world of Islam.

The period since the near-parallel falls of Christian Constantinople to the Ottoman Muslim Turks in 1453 and the fall of Granada, the last Western European Muslim foothold, to the Catholic monarchs in 1492 has seen seismic geopolitical changes in the Muslim-majority world. This has been structurally transformed from a religious nation (Umma) of heterogeneous peoples variously united to a greater or lesser extent under one or more spiritual and political caliphates ruling, broadly speaking, according to Islamic law (Shari'a), through an expansionist militarised and bureaucratic Ottoman 'superpower' sultanate, followed by debilitating European colonisation, until with the turn of the twentieth century colonised fragmentation gave way to European-style nation-states.

The nation-states of the Middle East and of the Muslim-majority world in general, often created in the crucible of colonial collapse and withdrawal, e.g. Pakistan, Israel and Nigeria, typically cut across and ignored both traditional tribally organised territories and the territorial demarcation of lands, once ruled by the amirs and caliphs of Islam, for example Sokoto in northern Nigeria and Mali. Muslim-majority nation-states and nation-kingdoms, such as Saudi Arabia and Morocco, in themselves had marked the end of Dar al-Islam (the Territory of Islam) – that is, a relatively legally homogeneous territory governed recognisably according to Islamic law (Shari'a) in some form – and the end of the classical Islamic constitution (Feldman, 2008). These Muslim-majority nation-states have usually been characterised by the institutional absence of Islam to such an extent that 'not a single Islamic civilization remains … [Muslim] embeddedness lies always within political and economic structures borrowed from the values and administrative methods of the West' (Winter, 2007, p. 150).

These nation-states were often been governed by oil-dictators (Feldman, 2003) whose power was often untrammelled by the traditional checks and balances on the executive, such as elected Parliaments or a strong class of legal scholars (Feldman, 2008). Nation-states such as the Iraq of Saddam Hussein (1937–2006), the Egypt of Hosni Mubarak (b. 1928) and the Libya of Colonel Muammar al-Gaddafi (1942–2011), while in many senses particular, all evoked both nationalism and socialism to institutionalise socio-economic inequalities and governmental corruption, reducing the public influence and social ethos of Islam.

Of course, the 'Arab Spring' of 2011 and, more recently, the 'Arab Backlash', after half a century or more of political and intellectual stagnation in Egypt and elsewhere, suggests the start of some sort of dynamic process of political and social transformation in the Arab Muslim-majority world and the emergence of the idea of governance according to Islamic with/and democratic principles. But no one can as yet say quite where this will lead and what type of role Islam and those inspired by it will play in the political reconfiguration of the Arab Middle East (Ramadan, 2012). Moreover, the fragility and and volatility of structural change in the Middle East have been graphically illustrated by the recent (2014) territorial gains of the so-called Islamic State. Islamic State is a violent extremist Jihadi group who have taken advantage of the anarchy created by the Syrian Civil War (2011–present) to create an enclave in eastern Syria and northern Iraq governed according to their own brutal interpretation of Shari'a law.

Many factors have been posited as being decisive in the structural decline of the world of Islam, which, for 13 centuries from the migration of the Prophet Muhammad from Mecca to Madina in 622 CE to the abolition of the Ottoman caliphate in 1924, had proved to be one of the most enduringly successful and culturally versatile 'sacred civilisations' the world has yet seen (Feldman, 2008; Winter, 2007). In order to set the contemporary intellectual condition of the Muslim world in historical perspective, it is perhaps worth remembering, briefly, a few of the key intellectual and educational achievements of classical Muslim scholars during the period 800–1500 CE, when, arguably, Muslim civilisation led the world. Thus, from the ninth to the fourteenth centuries Muslim scholars or scholars, often motivated by the demands of their faith, and living within the nexus of diverse, multi-faith Islamic civilisations:

1   adapted the Hindu number system for the advanced arithmetic we use today, including the use of zero;
2   adapted and developed ancient Greek and Persian geometry, trigonometry and algebra for both religious and civic purposes, such as the calculation of inheritance according to Shari'a law;
3   made the earliest studies of the circulation of the blood and infection, and established hospitals based on scientific principles of hygiene;
4   reinitiated the study of scientific history and sociology according to systematic conceptual precepts, categories and principles;
5   developed the systems of sonic harmony that became the basis of Western classical music;
6   preserved and developed both Platonic and, especially, Aristotelian philosophy, in the latter case laying the foundations of Western, empirical scientific method, without which Aristotle and Plato would have been lost to the world.

Moreover, Muslim societies, from the ninth to the nineteenth centuries, made pioneering and lasting contributions to generating a social ethos that would now be considered to bear the hallmarks of a flourishing democracy, including features such as:

- the protection of women's rights to property and right to lead autonomous, fulfilling lives;
- high levels of civic justice;
- the institutionalised tolerance of different faiths (Feldman, 2008; Malcolm, 2013).

However, the institutional fabric that had sustained Islamic scholarship and civic cohesion – courtly patronage, legal schools, mosques and guilds (Allawi, 2009; al-Hassani, 2012) – gradually crumbled as a result of a combination of internal (structural) and external (colonial) pressures from the fifteenth to the nineteenth centuries; and they have never, as yet at least (Feldman, 2003), been adequately replaced.

The collapse of the sacred–civic balance of power that sustained Islamic civilisation

Internally, the increasingly structural and intellectual rigidity and consequent institutional collapse of the semi-autonomous class of religious scholar-jurists ('*ulamā*), who for centuries performed crucial social and religious functions in both legitimising and restraining the role of the executive of the caliphs and of administering daily justice, first hindered an effective response to the changing intellectual and political dynamics of the post-Reformation West (Allawi, 2009) and then set up the conditions for twentieth-century dictatorship (Feldman, 2008).

Despite the often tumultuous political and dynastic upheavals that regularly beset Islamic governance from its earliest days until the Ottoman period, the relative commercial and intellectual stability of the polity (Umma) of Islam was sustained for centuries under Islamic law (Shari'a) in the Sunni and Shi'a Muslim world.[4] This was achieved *inter alia* by the strong relationship of mutual interest between the class of scholar-jurists ('*ulamā*) who embodied the living institution and juridical tradition of Shari'a, and the ruling classes embodied in the person of the caliph or imam, who, although the holder of executive authority, was required to uphold Shari'a and whose position required the legitimacy of the '*ulamā* (Feldman, 2008). However, in the early nineteenth century the necessary bureacratisation of the Ottoman state first brought the '*ulamā* within the orbit of the state and then did away with the need for the scholarly '*ulama* class altogether with the so-called *Tanzimat* Reforms that led to the *Meccelle* – a European-style constitution – in 1876. This disintegration of the '*ulamā* as an empowered legal class and the assumption of law-making into the state fractured and ended the relationship that had sustained Islam for 13 centuries and set up the conditions for post-Islamic twentieth-century dictatorship by reducing and then eliminating the traditional checks and balances on executive Muslim power (Feldman, 2008).

The disintegration of the class of the *'ulamā* in Ottoman Turkey was mirrored in the Indian subcontinent by the gradual waning of the authority of the organic tradition of Shari'a administered by Hanafi *'ulamā* and its replacement under British colonial rule by Anglo-Muhammadan Law. Anglo-Muhammadan Law, like the *Meccelle*, was a European-style legal code administered by civil servants and not an organic tradition of religious law that depended on a trained independent class of religious lawyers (Zaman, 2002). Shari'a under colonial rule thus morphed from a dynamic, living *process* of applying eternal principles of justice to contingent circumstances to rigid, unchanging *content* and fixed rulings that were either followed inflexibly (*taqlid*) and/or administered by non-Muslim colonial authorities.

By the end of the colonial period in the twentieth century, the traditional *Maliki, Hanifi, Shafi'i* and *Hanbali* schools of law (*madhāhib*), once the vibrant institutions that had for centuries acted as the heartbeat of Islamic civilisation in its different forms, were all but moribund in terms of active institutional participation in governance (Feldman, 2008). Increasingly, while individual legal scholars did react creatively to the relative powerlessness of Islam under colonialism (Zaman, 2002), the schools of law became family traditions that were passed on from father to son almost like membership of a religious club, as individual Muslims responded defensively and in an atomised way to the institutional break-up of the Muslim world (al-Azem, 2012).

The Protestant West shapes the conditions of modernity

In relation to the external world, in the early modern and modern period the Muslim-majority world slowly – almost imperceptibly, and despite fertile cultural, aesthetic and intellectual interchange (Norton, 2013) – but surely came to be eclipsed by the post-Reformation Christian West. In contrast to the Muslim world, whose sustainable social and commercial success was predicated upon a close relationship between religion, law and politics, the Christian West, led by the Netherlands and then Britain, embraced the opportunities afforded it by the radical weakening of the temporal authority of the Roman Catholic Church to remove, relatively speaking, the regulation of public activities, such as trade and banking, from religious, Catholic law and structure in order to embark on the commercial and intellectual expansion of early modernity.

Protestantism, and its reform of public canon law, and, in England at least, with its destruction of the institutional power of Roman Catholicism, 'released' increasingly autonomous and self-defining individuals (R. D. Lee, 1997) to prove that they were blessed by God by achieving worldly success, sometimes at the expense of other, 'less blessed' European, e.g. Spanish Catholics, and non-European, e.g. West African, peoples (Tawney, 1926/2013; Weber, 1958/2003). Thus, Protestantism, in its gradual splitting of public legality from personal religiosity, had a shaping hand in creating the dynamic triumvirate of modernity: free-market capitalism, empirical science and liberal democracy (Bhaskar, 1991). These three emergent interrelated forces became the platform for the birth of nation-states out of fragmented and warring European principalities, which propelled Western Europe from being a patchwork of ethnically bound agrarian kingdoms and principalities towards becoming industrialised national demo-cracies (Cannadine, 2013b). This 'new' nationalist individualism drove the age of scientific discovery and commercial expansion, leading to the era of colonisa-tion and the mass exploitation of labour markets by Christian individuals, their corporations and then their national governments, often latterly in the Muslim-majority world.

Difficulties faced by Muslims in the embrace of modernity

The embrace of these individualised, nationalised dynamics of modernity (R. D. Lee, 1997) was much more difficult for Muslim peoples, led during the early modern period by the Ottoman dynasty in Istanbul and the Mughal emperors in Delhi, for three reasons.

First, in the early modern period there was little apparent need for change. At the beginning of the period of European ascendency (*c*.1500) leading eventually to colonisation and hegemony (Gramsci, 1971), the Islamic-Ottoman and Mughal Empires were the superpowers of the day, whose courts astounded Euro-pean diplomats and travellers with their riches and high levels of material and non-material civilisation (Matar, 1998). Muslim peoples could pursue prosperity because they could rely upon political and religious stability and the backing of relatively coherent and fair judicial and legal infrastructures (Feldman, 2008). How, for example, were the Muslim (and indeed the majority Hindu) subjects of Mughal India to know in the sixteenth and seventeenth centuries that the squalid Portuguese, Dutch and then English trading posts (called factories) along their coastline and rights to trade to which their Mughal emperors consented were, in the fullness of time, to sow the seeds of their own colonial subjugation (Fergu-son, 2011)?

Second, the spirit of capitalism, while often taking concrete form in com-panies with monopolies on certain types of trade, was, essentially speaking, one of private individual and material self-advancement. For example, early modern English 'privateers' (or 'pirates' if you were a Spanish Catholic) such as John Hawkins (1532–1595), Francis Drake (1545–1596), Walter Raleigh (1552–1618) and Martin Frobisher (1535?–1594) were adventurers and self-made men who paid their dues to the English Crown because they were forced to. The internal strength of Islam had, to a large degree, been built upon the preservation and transmission of *collective* human capital and on the balance in the interrelationship of autonomous or semi-autonomous collectives such as mosques, religious schools (madrasas), guilds, schools of law (*madhāhib*), charitable endowments and the patronage of the rich and powerful (Gellner, 1983). This was a direct inheritance of the style of Muhammadan teaching of the earliest Muslim community in Madina, which had been accomplished by Muhammad in the company of companions (*Sahāba*) (Sachedina, 2013) in a proto-urban society, rather than to a small group of peripatetic disciples, as in the mission of Jesus.

Third, the foundational intellectual and spiritual premise of modernity – the Reformation–Enlightenment split of public legalism from private religiosity – referred to above remained largely theologically, as well as institutionally, un-Islamic. Although Islamic rulings differentiate spheres of daily action such as governance, trade and marriage (*mu'amalāt*) from the sphere of worship (*'ibadāt*), both these spheres of Islamic law are derived from the primary religious sources of the Qur'an (the Revelation, literally 'the Recitation') and the Sunna (habitual behaviour) of the Prophet Muhammad. Hence, while the Islamic sphere of worship was more overtly 'religious' than the sphere of daily life (Ramadan, 2009), the split between sacred and profane realms of action and experience that became one of the engines of the European expansion, and remains a metaphysical bedrock of Western liberalism, was and is anathema to traditional Islamic understanding. The theological understanding that God is witness to everything that humans do (Qur'an, 10:61) and that the whole of life is, therefore, subject to Shari'a, derived from the Qur'an and the Sunna, allowed only for the slow and uncomfortable accommodation in the classical Islamic constitution of the idea of the sacred alongside that of the separately defined secular realm.[5]

Thus, while the European powers created bureaucratised, legally secular nation-states and forged ahead with their nationalist-individualistic projects of material, empirical-scientific expansion, the Muslim world, in particular in its Ottoman manifestation, struggled for centuries to work out what the best relationship between its ruling classes, in particular the caliph and sultan, its religious legal-scholarly classes (the *'ulamā*) and the daily administration of justice and governance for the people was. While Indian *'ulamā* in the eighteenth and nineteenth centuries came to uncomfortable accommodations with the British Raj that gave rise to the *Barelwi* and *Deobandi* Islamic movements and schisms in Islamic law, belief and practice that still resonate today, the Ottoman regime only started to come to modern, systemic solutions and procedures of creating a modern state with an Islamic complexion through the *Tanzimat* reforms in the mid-nineteenth century (1839–1876).

By the time the Muslim world was forced by the external circumstances of bureaucratised colonial expansion to come to grips intellectually and politically with the modern age, the Ottoman Empire, which had provided its leadership for 350 years, was already regarded as the 'sick man of Europe', and the lands of governed by Muslims according to Islam were already in severe atrophy. The Ottoman Empire, once the military terror of Europe, whose institutional and bureaucratic efficiency was admired (begrudgingly) throughout the Christian West (Malcolm, 2013) and whose sultans had been courted by Elizabethan diplomats (Matar, 1998), was by the mid-nineteenth century reduced to being a useful part of the Great Game of the balance of the European colonial powers. It had become little more than a buffer between the expansionist ambitions of Russia and the imperial interests of Britain in India, which had by now emphatically replaced the Mughal emperors as India's ruling power, and colonial France in the Levant and North Africa (Feldman, 2008).

The theological crisis and the Reformers' response

This meant, crucially, that from the period between 1750 to 1924 the Muslim-majority world gradually shifted, first in the consciousness of non-Muslim powers and peoples, and then in its own self-consciousness, from being the *shaper of* the intellectual and political world, whose influence in matters of the spirit, the intellect and trade spread well beyond the borders ruled according to Islam, to being *shaped by* the intellectual and political world of non-Muslim powers and processes. From setting the global, intellectual, political and military agenda, which the Abbasid, Fatimid, Ottoman and Mughal caliphs and sultans had done with unrivalled imperial wealth, majesty and spiritual confidence for nearly 1,000 years, by the turn of the twentieth century the Muslim world had become little more than a diplomatic plaything in the imperial games and ambitions of non-Muslim Western powers, in particular Germany, France, Russia and, above all, Britain.

Crucially for this book, these institutional changes and a loss of structural coherence towards the end of the Ottoman period (1800–1924) began to generate a theological and intellectual crisis among Muslim religious thinkers, who were now increasingly *not* drawn from the traditional class of the *'ulama* but were often educated in the West in the emerging natural scientific and social scientific secularist disciplines (Feldman, 2008).

This theological crisis ran along these lines. If God had guaranteed Islam and Muslims success in this world and the next when they were following Islam properly (Qur'an, 23), then the loss of success in this world must mean that the Muslim world was not following Islam properly or, indeed, that perhaps God's favour had passed from Islam to the Christian West (Shepard, 2004).

Responses to this crisis came from a group of intellectuals who came collectively to be known as Muslim Reformers (Taji-Farouki & Nafi, 2004). These in themselves represented a paradoxical 'new class' of Muslim person: they were often European-style intellectuals who championed (or criticised) Islam. In the nineteenth and twentieth centuries, as both the power and the authority of the *'ulama* as an effective class waned, the Reformers were hugely influential in setting the intellectual and spiritual agenda of the Muslim-majority world.

Broadly speaking, the Muslim Reformers occupied (and still occupy) three broadly identifiable groups: secularists, Islamic modernists and radical Islamists. All of them were modernists in that they were responding to the challenges of modernity that had been dictated by the processes of Western ascendency that I have already outlined.

The first group, the secularists, might be grouped crudely under the banner: Islam is (or has caused) the problem. For this group, Islam was viewed largely as a monolithic theological-political edifice which, with its conservative class of *'ulamā* and inward-looking rulers, especially in their late Ottoman guise, had prevented the Turkic, subcontinental, Persian and Arab peoples of the Middle East from engaging fully with modernity and reaping the material and intellectual benefits thereof. In particular, they pointed the finger of blame at governance by caliphate and Shari'a. Secularists such as 'Ali Abd Ar-Razaq (1888–1966) in Egypt argued, for example, that Islamic governance by caliphate was not intrinsic to Islam (Shepard, 2004). Others, in particular the Young Turks in Istanbul before the First World War (1914–1918), led a rebellion against the authoritarian rule of Sultan Abdulhamid II in 1908, arguing that persistence of Islamic governance and the caliphate meant that the Muslim-majority world had missed out on empirical science and technology, the infrastructure of banks, capital markets and nationalism, which had given the Europeans their political edge.

Ironically, while bemoaning the relative European ascendency, the secularists often looked for guidance from Europe for its constitutional, legal and educational models to replace those of Islam. For the extreme secularisers, Islam as a means of law and of political organisation had to be rooted out and destroyed, if necessary by force. Famous political exponents of the extreme secularist position came in the form of Kemal Atatürk (1881–1938), an army colonel who, with the groundwork of dissent laid by the Young Turks, founded the Grand National Assembly of Turkey and then the Turkish Republic in the Anatolian heartland of the Ottoman Empire after the Ottoman defeat in the First World War. Another, though very different, secularist political leader was General Gamal Abdal Nasser (1918–1970), who seized power in Egypt in 1956 after a failed Muslim Brotherhood attempt on his life and his imprisonment of the incumbent president, Muhammad Naguib. Nasser envisioned Egypt at the centre of a nationalist, pan-Arab and, indeed, pan-African political and intellectual revival. Both these individuals embarked on programmes of intense political and ideological nationalisation, quasi-Europeanisation of their countries' constitutions (minus full democratic representation) and the further reduction of what remained of the traditional infrastructure of Islam. In the case of Atatürk, this meant the annihilation of what remained of the traditional *'ulamā* and Sufi teachers (*shuyukh*), and in the case of Nasser, a programme of structural reform of the ancient al-Azhar University and the channels of formal education connected with it, and the suppression of the Muslim Brotherhood. Later exponents of the nationalist secularism, again of different political complexions, included Colonel Qaddafi in Libya (1942–2011) and Saddam Hussein (1937–2006) in Iraq.

The secularist nationalists became the dominant political force in the twentieth-century Middle East, who often, as in the case of Saddam Hussein in Iraq, ruled by the principle of might is right and with a one-party state apparatus, together with networks of informers and secret police to stifle dissent, and without an independent judiciary, let alone a scholarly class of jurists to trammel or constrain their power. For this group, Islam, if it was admitted a role at all, was either to be a strictly private, individual faith or a subordinate component in an overriding nationalist ideology, as part of a nationalist cultural heritage (Shepard, 2004).

The second group, the Islamic modernists, might be grouped crudely under the banner: Islam has problems and contains solutions. The Islamic modernists, represented quintessentially by the quixotic al-Afghani (1838/1839–1897), who was Iranian, not Afghan, and the influential Egyptian theologian and jurist

Muhammad Abduh (1849–1905), pointed to gaps and obstacles in the interpretative infrastructure of Islam that had prevented Islam and Muslims from adapting to the challenges of modernity. They held that a deep hermeneutic shift in the interpretation of Islam was required, rather than jettisoning it entirely. Muhammad Abduh, for example, believed that by reintroducing the faculty of deep legal reasoning (*ijtihad*) into the legal infrastructure of Islam and thereby loosening the requirement for the following of legal precedent (*taqlid*) within the four canonical schools of law, Islam and Muslims would be released to respond in an authentically Islamic way to the political, intellectual and spiritual challenges of modernity. Other modernists, such as the Egyptian politician and statesman 'Abd ar-Rahman 'Azzām (1893–1976), argued for the return to Islamic principles of justice, freedom, the brotherhood of man, the value of work, religious tolerance and the redistribution of excessive wealth ('Azzām, 1938/1993), which would bring the 'big picture' of Islam interpretatively into line with the values of Western liberal democracy. This group of thinkers was, and remains, highly influential in thinking about the relationship between Islam and the West throughout the Muslim world.

The third group, the radical Islamists, might be grouped crudely under the banner: Islam is the solution. They brooked no accommodation with either Western values or liberal democracy. This group, often known in Islamic terms as *'Salafi'*, called for a return to what they saw as the pure Islam of the first three Muslim generations – the *Salaf* (Rapoport & Ahmed, 2010). The ideas of this group were presaged in the eighteenth century by Muhammad ibn Abdal Wahab (1703–1792), founder of the eponymous *Wahabi* religious ideology, whose pact with Muhammad ibn Saud (d. 1765) provided the founding pillar of the Saudi Arabian state. They were then given renewed life and vigour in the twentieth century by Abdul 'Ala Maududi (1903–1979), a founding father of Islamism in Pakistan and the chief ideologue of the modernist idea of the Islamic state, and by Hassan al-Banna (1906–1949), who in 1928 founded the Muslim Brotherhood in Egypt. Islamist ideas, which focused around the essential need for a modern Islamic state, were given a further Manichean and divisive edge by the highly influential Egyptian ideologue Sayyid Qutb (1906–1966), whose theological manifesto *Milestones* (1964) (*Ma'alim fi al-Tariq*) was to be instrumental in laying the Manichean world-view that was at the end of the twentieth century to underscore the thinking of violent jihadist groups such as al-Qaedah. Al-Banna was assassinated in 1949 and Sayyid Qutb was executed on the orders of Nasser in 1966.

Broadly speaking, the analysis of the 'crisis' of Islam by these radical Islamist thinkers, while in some ways quite diverse in their particular emphases, held two related internal and external dynamics responsible for the relative decline of Muslim civilisation.

Internally, Muslim society, in particular its class of *'ulamā*, were blamed for the gradual corruption of the religiously pristine and socially egalitarian purity of the Islamic praxis contained in the Qur'an and the Sunna. For centuries, they held, the *'ulamā* had allowed *madhabist* legalistic paraphernalia and a multitude of folk customs and religious innovations (*bida'*) to accrue around the pristine

Islamic praxis of the early Madinan community. To support this claim, radical Islamists drew (and continue to draw), *inter alia*, on the theology of a much-misquoted and seldom understood reforming thirteenth-century jurist called Ibn Taymiyya (1263–1328) (Rapoport & Ahmed, 2010).

Externally, they proposed that this compromised form of the Islamic religion had been further corrupted by the outside influences such as Western democratic ideals and technologies of education, which had further distanced Islam from its pristine, pure and perfect roots (Qutb, 1964/1981). For this group and its latterly jihadist and violent offshoots, such as al-Qaeda and Boko Harām, the solution to decline came in the intellectual and spiritual purification of Islam, a return to its primary textual sources and in the expulsion of the 'infidel' – both the non-Muslim (*kafir*) and the wrong Muslim (also regularly declared as *kafir* through a process called '*takfir*' – excommunication) – from the lands of Islam, if necessary by force.

While the ideas of the two modernist groups – the Islamic modernists and the radical Islamists – were very different in both style and substance, they shared a number of significant methodological features:

1   They were 'protestant' in the sense that they called for a return to the original primary texts of Islam and in the belief that their interpretation of them ought not be confined to a scholarly-priestly class or necessarily follow the precedent (*taqlid*) of the canonical schools of law.
2   Their ideas were couched in terms reminiscent of modern Western political ideologies, with treatises, political agendas and manifestos. Indeed, Qutb (1964), for example, even drew on Nazi political analysis. They had little in common with the traditional model of the transmission of Islamic law and theology from master to pupil; nor were they or their ideas part of a discourse of tradition of Shari'a, within authorised centres of learning that had, as we have seen, for centuries been at the core of the intellectual life of Islam. In fact, they were in spirit so alien to the traditional forms of Islam that some have described radical Islamism as a Western rather than an Islamic phenomenon (Winter, 2007).

Radical Islamism is exacerbated by the political conditions of postmodernity

However, the influence of Islamic modernism, in both its virtuous and its vicious manifestations, might not have been so prevalent, long-lasting and influential had not the underlying theological fear alluded to above that had originally driven it – namely that God had somehow abandoned Islam because Muslims had got it wrong and that the world's geopolitical odds were now stacked against the Muslim world – become even more acute for the Arab Sunni postmodern world (1945–present).

First, the establishment of the State of Israel in 1948 and, in the process, the appropriation of Palestinian land – a chain of events known collectively by Arab

Sunni Muslims as the 'Catastrophe' (*Nakba*) – followed by the failure of repeated Arab Sunni Muslim attempts to peg back the advance and military success of Israel in the Arab–Israeli wars of 1948, 1967 and 1973 severely further dented Arab Muslim confidence and fed into the theological crisis and inferiority complex: the feeling that Islam and Muslims were now, for some reason, on the wrong side of destiny.

Second, and relatedly, the relative failure in terms of standards of living and governance of the Islamic Republics of Pakistan and Iran, compared with the Jewish State of Israel, contributed to the sensation of the moral and infrastructural inferiority of the Umma of Islam.

Third, the incursion of Western armies into Muslim-majority lands in Iraq (2003–2011) and Afghanistan (2001–present) stoked Muslim resentment at the willingness of the West to impose its liberal democratic values on Muslim-majority lands by force. This resentment was aggravated by a realisation that the Muslim-majority world could not get its own political house in order and was, regrettably, still dependent on the post- (or neo-)colonial West for material, military and moral assistance to sort out its own internal political and economic problems.

These geopolitical circumstances, underscored with theological fear and cultural nostalgia for a more glorious Islamic past, clustering, above all else, around the Palestinian question, have sustained and fuelled radical Islamism, especially in young Muslims, for the past 50 years and have meant that the often Manichean and intellectually crude reformist agenda has held sway over the formal and informal intellectual discourse of Islam. In other circumstances, more moderate and intellectually systematic Muslim intellectual voices, such as the Egyptians Muhammad Abu Zahrā (1898–1974) and Shaykh Abdel-Halim Mahmoud (1910–1978), or the Indian independence thinker Husain Ahmad Madani (1879–1957), who grappled with the geopolitical and intellectual circumstances of modernity from within the traditions of Islam and at the interface of Western and Islamic thought, might have come to the fore (Zaman, 2002). Moreover, many contemporary Muslim thinkers who are grappling in a realistic way with the cross-fertilisation of Islamic and Western ideas occupy a liminal and disempowered 'third space' in Muslim society, since they neither fit the more recognisable 'Islamic' package of either reformist or traditionalist Islamic thought, nor conform with the secular assumptions and conventions of the global academy (Kersten, 2011).

Modernity in the Shi'a Muslim world

So far, my analysis has focused on the Sunni Muslim world, which makes up *c*.85–90% of the Muslim world. The response to modernity of the Muslim world dominated by Shi'a Islam was in some ways the exact inverse of that of the Sunni world. In the Sunni world, with the notable exception of Saudi Arabia, politics and power in the twentieth century came to be dominated by secular nationalist governments and dictators with Islamic or Islamist voices protesting from the persecuted margins and calling for a return to an (often imagined) pristine Islamic theocracy.

In the Shi'a world, centred since the earliest days of what became known as the Great Division (*fitnat al-kubrā*) on Persia/Iran, the *'ulamā*, led by Grand Ayatollah Ruhollah Khomeini (1902–1989), wrested power from the secular nationalist monarchy of Shah Mohammad Reza Pahlavi in the Islamic Revolution (1979) and established, in name at least, a Shi'a Muslim theocracy – that is to say, a state with an Islamic constitution governed according to Shari'a law controlled by a hierarchy of *'ulamā*: jurists to whom secular authority in the form of the residency was subservient.

In direct contrast to Sunni Islamism, Shi'a Muslim dissent and protest against theocratic rule and its shortcomings has tended to come in the form of calls for greater secular-style human rights and representational democracy. What both the responses of the Shi'a and the Sunni Muslim worlds share is that they are largely *reactions* to a political, spiritual and intellectual agenda largely shaped from outside the traditional world of Islam. In this respect, the experience of Islamic modernity and postmodernity for both Shi'a and Sunni Muslims has been profoundly different from the classical, medieval and early modern experience. The modern Islamic experience has often been, although of course not uniquely, one of political fragmentation, disempowerment and reaction to non-Muslim intellectual and cultural forms; the original and classical experience of Islam was largely one of gradual spiritual and social transformation and organic institutional empowerment and growth (Feldman, 2003).

The 'new' Muslim diaspora: a significant 'out-group'

Moreover, the structure of the socio-economic world and the de facto relationships between Muslims and non-Muslims has changed again, in the past 50 years in postmodernity, in ways that would until recently have been hard for anyone to predict. The discovery of huge deposits of oil in Muslim-majority countries of the Gulf and Saudi Arabia in the second half of the twentieth century gifted massive wealth to certain Muslim governments and states. These can, as a result, wield great influence on the global political stage. At the same time, the break-up of the European empires after the First and Second World Wars, the Partition of India and labour shortages in the West occasioned in the 1950s by the Second World War created an influx of migrant Muslims into Europe in unprecedented numbers (Schiffauer, 1988). At least 44 million Muslims now reside in Europe (*c*.6% of the European population, excluding Turkey) and 19 million in the European Union (*c*.4% of the EU population) (Pew Research, 2011). In total, nearly a quarter of all Muslims live in Muslim-minority settings (Pew Research, 2011). Moreover, in Britain nearly half of the 2.7 million Muslims (4.8%) are under the age of 25 (UK Gov., 2012). This means that by 2020 there are likely to be at least 5.5 million Muslim Britons (Pew Research, 2011). It is thought that in Britain, as many people regularly attend mosques on a Friday as go to church on a Sunday. This means that Islam is already de facto Britain's second faith, as it is in many West European multi-faith countries (Haddad, 2002).

These 'new' European Muslims live in multi-faith contexts in which Islam exists in almost entirely new legal circumstances that are practically without precedent in the Muslim experience. Islam in the multi-faith West exists as one (minority) legitimate faith among many legally equivalent faiths in a democratic, secular legal framework ruled guaranteed by an international nexus of non-Muslim, humanist rights. In these new contexts, the Shari'a of Islam exists as a code of personal religious conduct rather than constituting the legal framework for the whole, or even part, of society.

Yet no phenomenon can jettison its history, especially not such a powerful and successful one as that of Islam. A strong folk memory of Islam not only as a personal praxis but also as a guarantor of justice persists, both in the Muslim-majority world, where nationalist secularism is widely perceived to have failed (Feldman, 2008), and in the European and North American Muslim diasporas. In the Muslim diaspora, in which ironically it is often easier than in the Muslim-majority world to practise the religion of Islam, Islam and Muslims sometimes live in intellectual tension and often in relative social and economic deprivation compared with their non-Muslim fellow citizens. For Muslims who feel that they are 'on the receiving end', Islam becomes a powerful set of ideals and a potent historical identity through which to resist injustice.

The 'other/counter-other': the hostile reception of Islam by elements of non-Muslim European society

The post-colonial novelty and vulnerability felt by many Muslims in their engagement with the multi-faith world, with its deep and entangled historical roots, has been mirrored and aggravated by a flawed ability of the secularising non-Muslim world to understand, let alone embrace, people who are motivated by faith in general, and the Muslim faith in particular, who are now in their midst.

In this regard, it would be inaccurate to suggest that the stigmatisation of Islam and Muslims in the Christian West is a new phenomenon. Muslims in Europe and Britain, along with other non-Christian religious communities, especially Jews, have been problematised and constructed as the 'other' since the Middle Ages (Cohen, 1973). The 'other', here, is part of a same–other binary (McConaghy, 2000). Islam and Muslims have a history of being conceived of the 'other' in a binary by which white (Christian) Europeans conceive of themselves as 'same' and normal (Sarra, 2011). Moreover, Muslims in multi-faith contexts have often defined themselves as 'same' and non-Muslims as 'other' in a dynamic I will refer to as 'counter-othering'.

Montgomery Watt (Husband, 1994) provides an interesting typography of the medieval Christian conceptions of Islam as the 'other' to be feared and despised, which Said (1978) claims provided the essential backdrop to the nineteenth-century construction of the 'Orient' and to the prevalent modern popular attitudes towards Islam. These conceptions were that:

- Islam is a false and deliberate (on Muhammad's part) perversion of the truth of the Christian Gospels.
- Islam is a religion that is propagated by violence and the sword, in contrast to the peace-loving persuasiveness of Christianity.
- Islam is a religion of self-indulgence and sexual excess.
- Muhammad is an anti-Christ – that is, since Muhammad set himself up as the founder of a religion that was to threaten the claims of Christianity, he must be an agent of the Devil.

Husband (1994) suggests that these historically derived stereotypes persist latently at the root of contemporary 'othering' of Islam and of Islamophobia. In postmodern, less devoutly Christian Britain (59% of Britons identify themselves as Christian but less than 10% of these go to church on a weekly basis; Economic and Social Research Council, 2008), it is probably fair to assume that these theological prejudices no longer resonate strongly with the general British public. Nevertheless, Islam and Muslims are now regularly construed or assumed, especially in popularist media outlets, to be a potent and threatening 'other' to some modern, secular 'normal' (white) liberal beliefs.

The separation of 'church' and 'state': private religion from public secularism

We have seen that one of the hallmarks of the modern Western person is the ability to self-define culturally, politically, religiously and behaviourally in secular, religiously 'neutral', public spaces (R. D. Lee, 1997). The widespread popular fear that Muslims want to resacralise the public domain regularly emerges in the media in connection with issues to do with Shari'a law and the widespread perception that Muslims wish to see Shari'a law implemented in Britain (Gledhill & Webster, 2008). The realignment of religion and politics that is believed to underpin Shari'a law is seen by some as bearing the very hallmarks of religious fundamentalism, with all the associations of violence mentioned above and as a threat to the 'settled' established political order of post-Enlightenment Europe that I referred to above (B. Lewis, 1994).

Notwithstanding these fears of the 'other', which are regularly hyped up in the media, there exist real issues that do need to be addressed by the Muslim community about the relationship between Shari'a law and democratic legal systems such as English common law, given that the Islamic faith does not distinguish in any neat way, as Christianity has done for many years, between private worship and public legality. These issues have become manifest in the emergence of semi-formal Shari'a courts that deal with limited domestic aspects of Islamic law, such as divorce, and in the public domain around issues such as the legalisation of homosexual marriage. Moreover, the 'counter-othering' by elements of the Muslim (usually young male and Islamist) community to the effect that the democratic criminal justice systems are inherently un-Islamic, and therefore not to be respected, also needs to be addressed.

The equal rights and status of women

The arguably disproportionate attention given by the media and popular intelligentsia to women in Islam betrays another foundational 'monolithic' Western, British perception that Islam is essentially a sexist, even misogynistic, religion (Alexander, 2000). Little effort is ever made by commentators to disaggregate the religious from the cultural treatment of women, and the discourse of oppressed Muslim femininity has largely been constructed by non-Muslim journalists without any recourse to the opinions of Muslim women themselves (Modood, 2007).

Notwithstanding this sensationalism, non-Muslim society is often correct in identifying that the Muslim community also has real work to do in re-evaluating, along proper Islamic principles, fair gender relations in a multi-faith context, especially in juxtaposition to the types of roles now routinely performed by women in the West.

Freedom of sexual behaviour

Related to the supposed Islamic oppression of women is the representation of the supposed Islamic suppression of sexuality. In early modern Europe and in the Victorian era, Islam and Muslims were construed as the exotic 'other' by reference to supposed Muslim sexual excess and lasciviousness through orientalist images of the odalisque and the harem (Said, 1978). In our more licentious age, Muslims are equally but oppositely 'othered' by reference to their supposed sexual abstinence and Islam's forbidding of homosexuality and extra-marital sexual relationships (Ramadan, 2010).

In a mirror image of this, in a dynamic of 'counter-othering' as despising (Sarra, 2011), young Muslims in multi-faith contexts often caricature their non-Muslim counterparts, especially girls, as lacking sexual mores and family protection, and therefore as 'available'. The lack of basic respect for white working-class girls shown, for example, by Asian Muslim grooming circles stems in part from the perpetuation of this myth of female Western availability within the Muslim community. It is a myth that is aggravated and perpetuated by highly sexualised representations of femininity in popular Western culture and related phenomena such as the propagation of the idea of 'erotic power' (Hakim, 2011) as a legitimate tool for success in a male-dominated workspace.

Freedom of speech

Of all the rights enshrined in the secular, liberal idea of freedom, freedom of speech occupies the inner sanctum of the holy of holies (Fiss, 1996). It is also the right that Muslims are often presented most flagrantly as violating. The aftermath of the 1989 Rushdie affair left images of Muslims burning books on Nazi-style pyres in the forefront of the popular imagination. The Rushdie affair *inter alia* generated the notion of 'Islamo-fascism', and the belief that Islam does not 'allow' freedom of speech persists among many non-Muslims, fuelling suspicions that the Islamic faith is essentially incompatible with the Western 'way of life' (Huntington, 1996). This powerfully promoted idea ignores a strong and subtle tradition of freedom of expression within the Islamic tradition (Kamali, 1997). It also ignores the fact that Muslims might be raising a legitimate debate about the responsibilities towards others that necessarily accompany individual rights and freedoms.

As such, in the present no less than in the past, Islam and Muslims are construed in the British media and popular intelligentsia as the 'other', as a necessary polarised foil to the idea of the 'enlightened', secular, free European (Birt, 2010; Cohen, 1973). Young Muslims, for their part, are prone to exaggeratedly 'counter-other' non-Muslims as godless, licentious and even, occasionally, subhuman infidels (*kuffar*). They also join in 'othering' themselves (Hopkins, 2004) on the discovery that modern liberal, Western democracies are not the value-neutral, moral level playing fields that they are often purported to be, but are heavily inscribed with very particular (and often awkwardly un-Muslim) totems and taboos that can unfairly limit their life-chances.

These mutually reinforcing dynamics of Muslim–non-Muslim 'othering/counter-othering', as well as the complex socio-cultural dynamics of rural to urban Muslim migration (Schiffauer, 1988), have contributed to the existence of five related social malaises among a significant proportion of contemporary Muslims in the West:

1   *Entrenched political, socio-economic and cultural alienation*, especially in France and Germany but also in Britain. This has been manifest in entrenched, ethno-culturally defined 'ghettoised' communities and a mutual fear of cultural engagement between Muslims and non-Muslims, especially in educational settings. In Britain, among traditional, poor Muslim communities Islam as a faith has been enmeshed with subcontinental cultures and attitudes that are often resistant to cultural and linguistic adaptation and change, for example of language and diet, and to political engagement and educational success, including parental engagement with schools and school curricula. These attitudes have contributed to:

2   *Widespread educational underachievement*, especially among males at secondary level. In England, Muslim young people (73.5% of whom are of South Asian – mainly Pakistani or Bangladeshi – origin) in compulsory state schooling are 'underachieving' compared with white English, Scottish, Welsh, and Northern Irish (ESWI) children and every other ethnic or religious minority group in England, except black African and Caribbean children, in English, Mathematics and Science at Key Stages 1–5 (UK Gov., 2011b). Participation of Muslim females in higher education, although rapidly increasing (Hussain, 2008), currently runs at *c.*% compared with a national average of 54%.

3   *High levels of unemployment*. In 2010, 42% of Muslim males in England and Wales aged 16–22 were NEET (not in education, employment or training). In

particular, in the north of England, competition for decreasing numbers of manual jobs has aggravated racial and religious tensions between poor white English and British Pakistani Muslim youth. These tensions broke out into open rioting in the summer of 2001 in Bradford and Oldham (Ritchie, 2001).

4   *Crime.* British Muslim males, who constitute *c.* % of the male population of the United Kingdom, make up 12% of the UK prison population. This high level of crime is driven, in part, by the high levels of social deprivation and lack of education alluded to above. Nevertheless, the propensity for young Muslim males to get dragged into petty and serious crime is also fuelled by false 'Islamic' teaching – often, although not always, of a radical Islamist nature, disseminated on the internet (Bunt, 2003) – to the effect that it is not incumbent upon Muslims to obey the law of a non-Muslim land (The Religion of Peace, 2014).

5   *Occasional violent extremism*, which in Britain has been largely a 'home-grown' phenomenon: the 7/7 bombers were all brought up in Britain and educated in non-denominational, mainstream state schools. They were not 'imports' from Pakistani madrasas, or even the product of English Muslim faith schools. Extremism is a multi-factored phenomenon driven, in part, by strong perceptions of an unjust Western foreign policy persecuting the global Muslim community, but more potently by lack of opportunity, poverty, the Manichean Islamist view of the world alluded to earlier in the chapter, and the dynamics of 'othering/counter-othering' also alluded to earlier (Moosavi, 2014).

Inadequate school curricula

Moreover, the current school curriculum in England and elsewhere is often inadequate to help young Muslims understand and interpret their faith in its new, multi-faith setting. At present, the humanities subjects, which could potentially help because they interest Muslim young people (Wilkinson, 2014), are not prioritised by governments, schools or, indeed, Muslim parents, owing to a widely held, but mistaken, notion that they do not contribute to national economic efficiency and personal employability. Therefore, history, religious education and citizenship, three subjects that Muslim young people tend to find interesting and feel can be relevant to making sense of themselves and the world around them, are underdeveloped and underused (Wilkinson, 2011a). This leaves a dangerous epistemic gap between the 'presence of the past' (Bhaskar, 1993/2008), the power of religion and the complexity of citizenship in the daily lives of many young Muslims and the adequacy of the humanities subjects to deal with these phenomena in school. We shall explore this further in Chapters 6–9. In addition, complementary after-school Islamic education is often, although not always, inadequate in terms of its meaningful input into the personal development of young people and is rarely, if ever, part of a joined-up strategy that links the various educational environments – formal, semi-formal and informal – where young Muslims are likely to learn.

A 'real, determinate' absence of a multi-faith philosophy of Islam

These inadequacies in formal, semi-formal and informal education have been exacerbated and, in part, generated by the relative (compared with Christian and Jewish theology) *absence* of a contemporary philosophy of Islam for multi-faith contexts. In other words, at present there is an absence of a discourse of systematic meta-theoretical reflection and coherent ethos of the Islamic faith for a multi-faith world (Hart & Maraldo, 1976).

The beginnings of a discourse of contemporary inter-faith Islamic theology, which is drawing on both the primary and the secondary sources of Islam in a critical and creative way (Fadel, 2013; Sachedina, 2013; Shah-Kazemi, 2013), and tapping into the tradition of *kalām* (Mahmutćehajić, 2011), can be observed. However, much of this emerging discourse is restricted, as yet, to the academy; it does not penetrate either mainstream school religious education or complementary Islamic education and has been ignored outright by popularist, often internet-driven, outlets of informal Islam. Moreover, its existence at the theological rather than the systematic philosophical level has restricted both its logical systematisation and its application through education.

This philosophical absence has been accompanied by often restrictive modes of more popular contemporary Islamic scholarship that have often reduced the creative tradition of Islamic philosophical theology – which traditionally linked human beings in a rational and coherent way to a living deity – either to obscure and legalistic quasi-jurisprudential debate or to theologically 'unserious' (see Chapter 2) secular, academic discourse.[6] Neither of these is appropriate for helping Muslim young people to respond to and, when necessary, transform the multi-faith contexts that they increasingly inhabit.

Two default positions of faith set up the Unhappy Muslim Consciousness

This determinate absence (Bhaskar, 1993/2008) of a philosophy of Islam for the multi-faith world, combined with:

- the polarised Islamic scholarship referred to above;
- the aggressive representation of Muslims and Islam as the 'other', together with Muslim 'counter-othering' of non-Muslims and the West;
- the powerfully secularist assumptions of the contemporary political discourse,

has resulted in two default positions being made 'available' in the post-modern world for contemporary Muslims:

1   A *defensive faith* structured psychologically and theologically on a range of false polar opposites to buttress faith, e.g. Islam v. the West, Global Brother/ Sisterhood v. National Citizenship, Science v. Religion, in a way that is

inconsistent with many Muslims' daily lives. In this dichotomised construction of Islam, Islamic piety has become synonymous with anti-Westernness. In other words, the more anti-Western one is, the greater the supposed proof of one's Islamic piety (Ramadan, 2010). This means that a whole range of cultural and intellectual options ranging from full political engagement with democracy to the enjoyment of cultural forms such as theatre and classical music have been often denied, quite unnecessarily, or even 'outlawed', to thousands, if not millions, of young Muslims by ideologues of Islam.

This parlous situation in turn has necessitated a reactionary

2   *abandonment of faith* by many Muslims in order to 'fit in' with a culturally hegemonic professionalised, secularising world-view and its accompanying 'liberal' lifestyle. In this default scenario, so familiar to professional Western Muslims, Islam merely remains as an ossified cultural residue of a once-living parental religion – as an identity that is neither spiritually nourishing nor socially empowering. For this group, Islam is occasionally perceived as a rallying point from which to oppose ethno-cultural discrimination, but seldom as a creative starting point for a coherent social contribution.

As a result, many Muslims today continue to perceive a mismatch between the practice of their professional lives in non-religious contexts and the articulation of their religious beliefs (Imtiaz, 2011). This act of rational compromise with the secular at the expense of the sacred is a process of dialectical disenchantment that has generated in many Muslims in the West a phenomenon closely akin to the Hegelian idea of the *Unhappy Consciousness*. According to this idea, the life of the spirit through connection to God, which is essential to the identity and life-purpose of the Muslim believer (Mahmutćehajić, 2011), is denied expression and even existence, while remaining acutely conscious (or semi-conscious) of its own thwarted reality.

> Itself [the *Unhappy Consciousness*], because conscious of this contradiction, assumes the aspect of changeable consciousness and is to itself the unessential; but as consciousness of unchangeableness, it must at the same time, proceed to free itself from the unessential, i.e. to liberate itself from itself
>
> (Hegel, 1807 trans. 1977, p. 208)

Within this understanding, 'successful' Muslims have often 'succeeded' in life *in spite*, rather than *because*, of their faith by distancing themselves literally and ideologically from the Muslim community, while remaining uncomfortably aware that something important is missing.

The need for a philosophy for Islam in the multi-faith world

As we saw with the vignette of Shazia Saleem in the Introduction, at a practical and intuitive level many young Muslims in multi-faith contexts have now begun to make a successful negotiation of being a Muslim in a multi-faith world *by default*, as well, of course, as making appreciable contributions in a range of walks of life. But these intuitive understandings of Islamic praxis and identity in multi-faith settings have not, as yet, been articulated coherently upon a systematic framework that enables them to be more broadly understood and followed through in the mainstream or complementary educational processes used by Muslim young people.

What is needed, therefore, is a philosophy to communicate between praxis and context and to revitalise traditional Islamic practice and belief in new multi-faith contexts, together with the tools to disseminate that philosophy into educational settings. Such a philosophy would encourage young Muslims to reflect on the meanings of their lives as Muslims in peaceful, productive coexistence and flourishing in partnership with people of other faiths and of none. Such a philosophy might empower the voice of the Muslim faith so that it can be recognised as a legitimate and reasonable 'critical friend' on the debating floor of liberal, multi-faith democracies (and, indeed, other multi-faith political systems). The next part of the book will suggest how the philosophy of critical realism can provide the basis of such a revitalising and cohering theological and educational philosophy.

Notes

1 Here construed as *c.*1500–1750.
2 Here construed as *c.*1750–1945.
3 Here construed as *c.*1945–present.
4 In the Sunni-led Abbasid (750–1258) and Ummayad, Al-Murabit and Al-Muwahid Spain (711–1492) and the Shi'a-led Fatimid (909–1171) and Safavid (1501–1736) periods.
5 It did eventually happen in the form, for example, of Ottoman Canon (*Kānūn*) law.
6 This debate, often played out in popularist and fringe intellectual settings rather than in the institutional heart of universities, is often based around simplistic understandings of things that are either forbidden (*harām*) or allowed (*halāl*) in Islam in an echo of the 'all-or-nothing' mindsets alluded to earlier. In this regard, it is not uncommon, for example, for cultured and traditional Muslim jurisprudential and theological thinking to be dismissed on Islamic blogs as 'orientalist' or (worse still!) as 'Christian'!

Part II
The philosophy of Islamic critical realism

2 Shared meta-theoretical premises

'Underlabouring' and 'seriousness'

In the previous chapter, I argued that the Muslim faith and community are suffering from, among other things, the absence of a coherent philosophical approach to enable young Muslims in particular to relate the timeless principles of their faith to the contingent circumstances of life in multi-faith contexts. In this chapter, I argue that the philosophy of critical realism is tailor-made for this task of spiritual and intellectual 'translation', in that it shares with Islam, as expressed in its primary sources and theological-philosophical traditions, two primary meta-theoretical characteristics: a commitment to 'underlabour' for human well-being and a commitment to philosophical and spiritual 'seriousness'.

A shared commitment to 'underlabouring'

The philosophy of critical realism emerged in the 1970s as a philosophy of science whose primary purpose was twofold: the revindication of ontology (the philosophical study of being) from its reduction to epistemology (the philosophical study of knowing and knowledge), and the establishment of a new ontology of deep structures, causal mechanisms and real change. Also, right from its inception the aim of critical realist philosophy was to 'under-labour' (Locke, 1689 cited in Bhaskar, 2013) for sciences, disciplines and human projects, especially those oriented towards human well-being or emancipation, by bringing conceptual clarity to these sciences and practices by clearing away erroneous and redundant philosophical ideas.

Bhaskar, the originator of the philosophy of critical realism, has written about 'underlabouring' (Bhaskar, 2013):

> 'Philosophical under labouring' is most characteristically what critical realist philosophy does. The metaphor of 'under abouring' comes from John Locke who said, 'The commonwealth of learning is not at the this time without master-builders [...] but everyone must not hope to be a Boyle or a Sydenham; and in an age that produced such masters as the great Huygenius and the incomparable Mr Newton, with some others of that strain, it is ambition enough to be employed as an under labourer in clearing the ground a

little, and removing some of the rubbish that lies in the way to knowledge' (An Essay concerning Human Understanding, 'Epistle to the Reader').

Critical realism underlabours for (a) science and (b) practices of human emancipation.

(p. 1)

The range of sciences and human projects for which the philosophy of critical realism has underlaboured is wide and varied. It has 'underlaboured' for natural science by demonstrating, *inter alia*, the natural necessity of causal laws and deep natural structures for the intelligibility of experimental activity (IEA) and by the disambiguation of the philosophical study of being (ontology) from the philosophical study of knowing (epistemology). It has 'underlaboured' for social science by demonstrating, *inter alia*, that social structures, e.g. languages and education systems, precede and cannot be reduced to individual agency and yet can also be transformed by them (Bhaskar, 1979). It has underlaboured for linguistics by reclaiming, *inter alia*, the referent, the real thing to which words refer, alongside the sign or signifier – the word – and the signified – its meaning (Alderson, 2013). It has underlaboured for environmental studies by showing, *inter alia*, that multi-factored, 'laminated' systems at the sub-atomic, biological, physical, socio-economic, geopolitical and cosmological levels need to be taken into account when considering the impact of humans on the environment, and that human beings exist on the four planes of social being (Bhaskar, 2009). Critical realism has 'underlaboured' for disability studies by showing that reductionism in the understanding of disability has prevented the implementation of proper strategies to ensure the well-being of disabled people (Bhaskar & Danermark, 2006). We will return to some of these specific tasks of 'underlabouring' later in more detail.

This philosophical commitment to 'clearing the ground a little, and removing some of the rubbish that lies in the way to knowledge' and to a comprehensive conception of practices of human flourishing is precisely shared by Islam and its tradition of theological philosophy (*kalām* and *falsāfa*). Islamic theological philosophy was traditionally one tool in the intellectual and disciplinary toolkit of holistic, intra-disciplinary scholars making sense of the Revelation of the Qur'an in conversation with reason and contemporary reality as intimated by the Qur'an (e.g. Qur'an, 59:2). As such, like the edifice of Islamic praxis itself, it was directed towards the recovery of human well-being through knowledge of God (Averroes, 1179/2001).

Indeed, in a situation that is keenly analogous to the contemporary British and European one, the original embrace of Hellenistic philosophy by Muslim scholars was precipitated precisely by the need for Muslim apologists to find a common language in which to describe and defend the Islamic faith in a rational way that would be understood by and would impress the non-Muslim scholars of eighth-century Hellenistic Egypt, Syria and other newly conquered Islamic-Arab domains (Ziai, 2008). Islamic philosophical theology (*kalām*) and theological philosophy (*falsāfa*) developed over the ninth, tenth and eleventh centuries into related disciplines in their own right. Their roots lie in the keen practical necessity to systematise, organise intellectually and apply in new contexts a faith that had been, especially in its first two generations, highly concrete and practical, doctrinally simple, largely imitative of Muhammad himself, and enacted in circumstances of direct correspondence between the injunctions of Revelation and its exemplary context.

The absence of the person of Muhammad as a source of Islamic philosophy

Therefore, Islamic philosophical theology (*kalām*) and theological philosophy (*falsāfa*), like the schools of Islamic law, which emerged in the first two centuries of Islam, were born of circumstances characterised by the *absence* of the person of the Prophet Muhammad and his earliest Companions for reference for exegetical purposes and for understanding the 'ambiguous' (*mutashābihat*) and other verses of the Qur'an and applying them to novel situations. According to Ibn Rushd (Averroes), for example, just as the jurist is permitted to deduce legal positions from sacred texts (*ta'wil*) and by analogy to legal precedent (*qiyas*), the philosopher is justified in his or her attempt to draw conclusions about the nature of reality and the way that it leads to knowledge of the Creator by rational deduction (Averroes, 1179/2001). Thus, theological philosophy was increasingly seen during the Abbasid period (*c.*750–1258) as a tool for 'underlabouring' the Qur'an and the Sunna, as a legitimate and necessary component for arriving at knowledge of God (Ziai, 2008).

Like the gradual emergence of the schools of Islamic law, the genesis of Islamic theological philosophy was occasioned by the need to serve the practical task of cultural translation and systematic codification of Islam in the absence of the Prophet Muhammad and in the presence of entirely 'new' sets of social circumstances. Conversely, it also served the purpose of 'underlabouring' for the thought of the ancients for use in emerging Muslim society. Thus, for example, al-Farabi's (*c.*872–950) *The Virtuous City*, a pioneering work of political philosophy that echoed St Augustine's *The City of God*, was a philosophical response to what the Islamic pursuit of the Good Life might mean in the cosmopolitan and highly urban societies of the newly acquired territories of the former Roman and Persian Empires such as Kufa, Basra, Isfahan and al-Farabi's own Baghdad. These emerging cosmopolitan centres of the Islamic Abbasid Empire were, of course, a far cultural cry from the relatively simple small town of Madina in which Islam had originally taken hold among pious Arab tribesmen, relatively unschooled in systematic, theoretical thought.

This task of Islamic theological philosophy of 'underlabouring' to translate and transfer Islam into new contexts, and the converse task of the translation of systematic contemporary thinking into the Islamic paradigm, are good starting points for the articulation of an Islamic critical realism. Islamic critical realism makes no pretension to rewrite core Islamic doctrine and practice as established and honed by centuries of Islamic scholarly consensus (*'ijma*). Its task is absolutely not to enter, for example, into relatively abstract philosophical arguments about the infinitude of the world or the created or eternal nature of the Qu'ran that exercised al-Ghazāli and Ibn Rushd.

It is designed to 'underlabour' for the meaningful interpretation of Islamic doctrine and practice for the multi-faith contexts of the twenty-first century with particular pertinence to the field of education, but also to the fields culture, economics, law and gender relations (as we shall see in Chapter 9). Its task is to 'clear the ground' of false intellectual and existential dichotomies, 'all-or-nothing' world-views and cultural blocks, literalistic and un-nuanced religious absolutism and inessential cultural paraphernalia masquerading as authentic Qur'anic and Prophetic principle. All these aberrations are 'demi-realities' (Bhaskar, 1993/2008), causally efficacious but essentially false and vicious entities, of which I will say more in Chapter 5. They create blocks to young Muslims' extracting deep, fulfilling meaning from their faith, to their enjoyment of 'normal' relations with their non-Muslim peers and to their enjoyment and transformation of uplifting cultural and artistic forms, and can create hiatuses to the formation of productive Muslim gender relations.

In this sense, in its adherence to the concept of 'underlabouring', Islamic critical realism (ICR) is best described as an educational philosophy. It is not a comprehensive programme of Islamic reform, of which there have been enough failures, or at best only partial and limited successes (Feldman, 2003), in the past 150 years (Armstrong, 2000). It does seek to open pathways into critical Islamic reflection, especially for young people, in the fields listed earlier in order to transform and transcend the types of impasses identified in the previous chapter and to make ever deeper sense of themselves in relation to the world around them. Its task of 'underlabouring' is educational in its effort to reframe, on the one hand, the phenomenon of Western education for Muslims and reframe, on the other, the discourses of Islam for educationalists of the West and in so doing to reopen a pathway from the Unhappy to the Happy Muslim Consciousness.

A shared commitment to 'seriousness'

This Happy Muslim Consciousness will, I suggest, be characterised by a return to philosophical and spiritual 'seriousness'; and it is in their shared commitment to this philosophical 'seriousness' that Islam and the philosophy of critical realism find their second shared meta-theoretical premise.

Philosophical seriousness: seriousness $_{(p)}$

'*Seriousness*' in the critical realist and philosophical sense, hereafter called seriousness$_{(p)}$, means that your practices and behaviour are consistent with your knowledge and belief. It is built conceptually out of a critique of the Enlightenment philosophy of David Hume (1711–1776) as '*unserious*'. Bhaskar has effectively critiqued Humean actualist orthodoxy and thus much modern and contemporary philosophy as 'unserious' in its denial of deep ontological structure in favour of an actualism whereby natural (and social) phenomena are explicable only in terms of constant conjunctions of events. This empiricist actualism in its denial of deep structure took Hume to a position where he could not philosophically sustain the rational belief that to leave a building by the ground-floor door was better than leaving it by the first-floor window because he believed that nature had no underlying causal laws or structures. This was an 'unserious' philosophical position, because if he really believed it, he should have left buildings by the first-floor window on at least 50% of occasions. It also meant that Hume had excluded himself and his philosophy from participating in the totality of the world.

> Similarly, when Hume says that there is no better reason to prefer the destruction of one's little finger to that of the whole world, then again he cannot be 'serious' – because if he were to opt for the destruction of the whole world, then surely he would lose his little finger too! What Hume is tacitly doing, of course, is … extruding himself (and philosophy) from the totality of the world.
>
> (Bhaskar, 2013, p. 1)

This lack of seriousness$_{(p)}$ and the extrusion of philosophy from the world is manifest in much contemporary philosophy and social theory. Postmodern statements that have become commonplace, such as 'There is no such thing as the truth', but which exhibit basic category contradictions are *unserious* because they are themselves categorical truth-statements. Similarly, a social-theoretical statement such as 'There are no grand narratives' is itself a categorical grand narrative. Post-structuralist thinking that denies, for example, the reality of ontological truth presumably operates at least with the desire to be found truthful. Such positions have flouted the hermetic principle of serious$_{(p)}$ philosophy that the theories and principles of philosophy should be consistently applicable in the real world (Bhaskar, 2013).

Seriousness and Islam: seriousness$_{(r)}$

Islam (authentically understood) is 'serious' in this philosophical sense in that it demands an a priori consistency between a statement of belief and a commitment to act in daily life. This type of philosophical seriousness in religion I hereafter will call seriousness$_{(r)}$.

The most elemental characteristic of Islam as a faith and the basic requirement of the Muslim believer is seriousness$_{(r)}$. The moment a Muslim has committed to doctrinal belief – the witnessing that there is no god but God and that Muhammad is the Final Messenger from God – he or she has also committed to a practice of the other four 'Pillars' of Islam – the Daily Prayer (*Salat*), the Social Welfare Tax (*Zakat*), the Fast of Ramadan (*Sawm*) and Pilgrimage (Hajj). All these commitments place the individual squarely and seriously before a

Living God within the natural and social structures imposed by a real world. This is why Islam is so named: it is both 'submission' to God and 'submission' to the way that He has created the Universe.

The outcome of the serious$_{(r)}$ interpenetration of belief/knowledge and practice – this praxis – ought to be a relationship with and guidance from God and peace and harmony with oneself and fellow humankind; in other words, becoming Muslim (Mahmutćehajić, 2011). This is notwithstanding the fact that God's guidance and the signs in the universe and in the self may at times be opaque, and harmony with other humans contingent upon a range of variable factors. In other words, seriousness$_{(r)}$ entails the dialectical movement away from the Unhappy Consciousness referred to earlier to a condition of realised essential (concretely singularised) selfhood in which the individual destiny is in tune with the Divine Decree (*Qadr*) to greater and lesser self-consciousness.

Along with the likes of al-Ghazālī and Hegel, ICR posits the primary characteristic of the Unhappy Consciousness as a lack of 'seriousness'$_{(r+p)}$ in the formation and enactment of the human–divine relationship. It would not, in fact, be overstating the case to claim that 'seriousness' in this profound philosophical sense is Islam's defining characteristic, and the splitting of knowledge–practice unity is the primary source of the Unhappy Muslim Consciousness. This is because seriousness$_{(r)}$ is the foundational principle of both of Islam's core primary sources, the book of the Revelation from God (the Qur'an) and the recorded sayings and behaviour of the Prophet Muhammad (the Sunna), and the pillar of Islamic practice, the Obligatory Prayer. Seriousness$_{(r)}$ also, as we shall see, characterises the classical Islamic philosophical theology of al-Ghazālī and, to a lesser extent, Ibn Rushd.

Seriousness$_{(r)}$ in the Qur'an

Seriousness$_{(r)}$ is evidenced Qur'anically by the fact that belief and practice enjoy an intrinsic and inseparable relationship in the Revealed Text. The phrase used to characterise believers, 'Those who believe *and* do right acts' (e.g. Qur'an, 2:82–83), is the most repeated of all Qur'anic refrains (Sherif, 1995). The Arabic pronoun for 'and' (*wa*) in this characterisation indicates an intrinsic partnership, not an extrinsic relationship ('Iyad, c.1100/1982; Sayer, 1984). That is to say, belief and right action in the Qur'an exist in a relationship of essential mutual interdependence.

The Qur'an backs up this notion of the centrality of seriousness$_{(r)}$ by criticising those who 'play' at religion: 'Leave to themselves those who take their religion for a mere game and distraction and are deceived by the life of this world, but continue to remind them with the [Qur'an] (Qur'an, 6:70). As a further indication of the seriousness$_{(r)}$ of this intrinsic partnership between belief and action in the Qur'an, it needs to be noted that the Arabic root *sad-lam-ha* – to do right – has the sense not only of morally good action, but of also contextually appropriate, sensible action. Appropriate recognition of the transcendent majesty of the Creator is contingent upon the harmonious quality of immanent human relationships (Sachedina, 2013). Indeed, according to the Prophetic tradition, nine-tenths of faith in Islam deals with interpersonal relations – that is, *mu'amalat* (Sachedina, 2013). Thus, the seriousness$_{(r+p)}$ of Islam as faith is objectively determined by the subjective quality of Muslims' inter-human relationships.

> Those who believe *and* do good works shall be the Companions of Bliss, eternally, forever. Remember that We took a covenant from the Children of Israel to worship none but God; to be kind to parents, kin, orphans and the needy; be steadfast in prayer and perform regular acts of charity.
>
> (Qur'an, 2:82–83)

In this Qur'anic verse, the covenant of the Children of Israel with God is contingent upon the respectful enactment of core human relationships to parents, extended family and the most needy in society. Nor is seriousness$_{(r)}$ restricted in its scope by the Qur'an to Muslim believers. It is, Qur'anically speaking, the basic salvational requirement for all those who follow a revealed faith with sincerity.

> Surely those who believe [as Muslims] and those of the Jewry, and the Sabaeans, and the Christians: whoever of them believes in God and the Last Day *and* [my emphasis] behaves righteously – no fear shall befall them, neither shall they grieve in the Hereafter.
>
> (Qur'an, 5:69)

In this verse, it is clear that it is the quality of seriousness$_{(r)}$, rather than the nature of religious affiliation, which sets up the conditions for potential salvation.

The Qur'an (2:177) further explicates the nature of seriousness$_{(r)}$ as consisting in the seamless connection of belief with socially benign and reflective behaviour. In this verse, I have translated the Arabic word *al-Birr* (sometimes read *al-Barr*; Jalalayn, 1505/2013) – usually translated as 'piety', 'goodness' or 'duty' – as 'seriousness' to show how fittingly this concept is applied to interpret the Qur'an:

> Seriousness does not consist in turning your face forwards East or West. Those who are serious about religion are those who believe in God and the Last Day, in the Angels, the Scriptures, and the Prophets; who give away some of their wealth, however much they cherish it, to their relatives, to orphans, the needy, travellers, and beggars, and to liberate those in bondage; those who keep up the prayer and pay the prescribed alms; who keep pledges whenever they make them; who are steadfast in misfortune, diversity, and in times of danger. Those are the ones who are true, and it is they who are aware of God.

Similarly, in chapter 23 the believers are characterised as those who perform or who abstain from performing certain actions rather than as those who know or believe certain things:

> The believers are successful, those who humble themselves in Prayer; those who avoid idle gossip; those who pay the Social Welfare Tax; those who abstain from sexual relations except with marriage partners or those who their right hand possesses (slaves).... Those who faithfully observe their trusts and their contracts, and who perform the Prayer in its time. They will be the heirs of Paradise.
>
> (Qur'an, 23:1–11)

This chapter, perhaps more strongly than any other, shows how belief in and worship of God in the Qur'an is *constellationally embedded* (Bhaskar, 1997) in respect-service-love-justice for humanity. It is impossible to love God without loving His Creation, since, Qur'anically speaking, the purpose of creation is to witness the reality of God (Qur'an, 51:56) (Mahmutćehajić, 2011). This idea will be picked up again when we look at an Islamic philosophy of metaReality in Chapter 5.

Seriousness $_{(r)}$ in the practice of the Prophet Muhammad

The literature recording the actions and words of the Prophet Muhammad is also replete with sayings that reinforce and exemplify the necessary seriousness$_{(r)}$ of the intrinsic Islamic relationship between action and belief expounded in the Qur'an.

For example, a companion of Muhammad, Abu Hurairah (may God be pleased with him), narrated that the Prophet Muhammad, peace be upon him, said:

> Let him who believes in God and the Last Day either speak good or keep silent, and let him who believes in God and the Last Day be generous to his neighbour, and let him who believes in God and the Last Day be generous to his guest.
>
> (narrated in Bukhari and Muslim, Nawawi)

In each phrase, the connection between belief and sound action is seamless; right action is the inevitable outcome, corollary and proof of serious$_{(r)}$ belief. Conversely, wrong action, such as, for example, an absence of practical compassion within this Islamic critical realist understanding, is proof enough that the beliefs underpinning it are 'unserious', flawed and unreal. Thus, Muhammad said, 'He is not one of us who does not show tenderness to the young and who does not show respect to the elder' (narrated in at-Tirmidhi). When beliefs are uncoupled from social responsibility and right action and become 'unserious', they may even at times be categorical false or 'demi-real' (Bhaskar, 1993/2008). Demi-reality consists in a deep or categorial inconsistency which violates the relationship between truth and being.[1] We will explore the concept of demi-reality further in Chapter 5.

Seriousness *(r)* in the Prayer

The seriousness *(r)* of Islamic praxis reaches its zenith in the Obligatory Prayer. The Qur'an says:

> Recite what is sent of the Book by inspiration to you, and establish regular Prayer: for Prayer forbids you from shameful and unjust deeds; and remembrance of God is the greatest (thing in life) without doubt. And God knows the (deeds) that you do.
>
> (Qur'an, 29:45)

The proof of the seriousness *(r)* of the Obligatory Prayer is in its efficacy in preventing wrongdoing; conversely, persistent wrongdoing is indicative of unserious *(r)* Prayer. Indeed, this metaphysical commitment to seriousness *(r)* is reflected in the physical ontology of the Muslim Prayer. The Prayer is not merely a mental act: it is a physical act of surrendering the body to the basic structures of the material and immaterial universe which are also in a state of worshipful submission to God (Qur'an, 62:1). We will consider the Obligatory Prayer in greater depth and detail when we look at the philosophy of metaReality in Chapter 5.

The hermetic principle: the practicality of seriousness *(r)*

Related to the idea of philosophical seriousness *(p)* is what critical realists have called the hermetic principle (Bhaskar, 2012). Since there is only one real, objective world, which we all inhabit and interpret in subjective ways, 'the principles of philosophy should apply to our everyday life. If they do not, then something is seriously wrong. This means that our theories and explanations should be tested in everyday life, as well as in specialist research contexts' (Bhaskar 2013: 12).

Similarly, seriousness *(r)* in Islam consists in the feasibility of doing what you believe and the feasibility that your understanding of the Qur'an and the Sunna can be performed in the world. The hermetic principle of practical daily feasibility is factored into Islamic praxis in the Qur'anic principle 'God wants ease for you. He does not want difficulty for you' (Qur'an, 2:185) and as exemplified, for example, by the Qur'anic permission to shorten the Prayer and not to fast when travelling. Thus, the hermetic principle is an important element of the seriousness *(r)* of Islam.

Seriousness in Islamic philosophical theology

Given the above, it is hardly surprising that this commitment to seriousness *(r)* also characterises classical philosophical theology, in particular the work of al-Ghazāli (1058–1111). For al-Ghazāli, it was the union of knowledge with action that endowed faith with the 'taste' (*dhawq*) of the truth. For al-Ghazāli, in a potent expression of seriousness$_{(p)}$, consistency of knowledge and action was an essential hallmark of truth: 'Knowledge without action is madness and action without knowledge is void' (Letter, 16, cited in Ormsby, 2008). For al-Ghazāli, I think it is fair to say, Humean empirical actualism that could not refute his exiting the building from the first-storey window would be a form of 'madness', akin to the dangerous and 'unserious' rationalism of the peripatetic philosophers. For al-Ghazāli it was seriousness$_{(r+p)}$ (or a lack of it) that entitled (or disentitled) believers to the delights of the Afterlife. Al-Ghazāli gave systematic expression to this idea of eschatological seriousness$_{(r+p)}$:

1   For if one has neither practical nor theoretical virtue (neither virtuous action nor knowledge), one is doomed to perdition;
2   If one has both practical and theoretical virtue … one will attain absolute felicity;
3   If one has theoretical but not practical virtue … one will undergo purgative suffering, but only for a limited period of time;
4   Finally, if one has practical but not theoretical virtue, one will attain safety and salvation from pain, but will not reach perfect felicity.
        (*Tahafut*, Disc. 20, § 19, p. 217, cited in Treiger, 2012, p. 85)

While one might take issue with the hierarchical and judgemental neatness of what must ultimately in Islam be the divine prerogative (Qur'an, 25:25–26), nevertheless al-Ghazāli's commitment to seriousness$_{(r+p)}$ in knowledge/theory–practice consistency is obvious and systematic.

Similarly, for Ibn Rushd (Treiger, 2012) the purpose of philosophy (*falsāfa*) was to lead the believer via the Good Life to the Next Life by pegging the principles of the Qur'an and the Sunna into the circumstances of contemporary life and showing how the meanings of the Qur'an continue to illuminate daily behaviour (Averroes, 1179/2001). In other words, classical Islamic theological philosophy was never merely a conversation between the exponents of abstract principles whose ideas stood or fell on their own inner logic; it was quotidian, practical and biographical, with profound and potentially absolute eschatological consequences for human beings.

In short, the serious marriage of belief and action from the standpoint both of the Islamic primary sources and of their theological-philosophical derivatives is a core hermeneutic axis of the Islamic paradigm.

The implications of seriousness

The consideration that Islam and critical realism share underlying commitments to 'underlabour' for human well-being and to seriousness$_{(r+p)}$ provides the metatheoretical foundation to Islamic critical realism (ICR). Knowledge–practice consistency is the hallmark of authentic Islamic praxis, as it is the hallmark of authentically critical realist thought.

The fact that ICR is stamped with the need and the aspiration for knowledge–action consistency has a number of implications for the rest of this book, in which we will explore further the practical implications of the postulate of seriousness$_{(r+p)}$. For if one is unable to be 'serious' and to act upon one's knowledge, according to the hermetic principle, then either:

1   that knowledge is incorrect – that is, it is not knowledge;
2   or the knowledge is correct and there is (are) an obstacle(s) to putting that knowledge into action; or
3   both 1 and 2 pertain, given that within knowledge there can exist different types of mistake, such as an inadequate understanding of other people and an inadequate understanding of context.

As young Muslims encounter multi-faith society, increasingly as native citizens of Muslim-minority states (Mondal, 2008), the 'underlabouring' task of ICR will be to help them regain seriousness$_{(r+p)}$ by confronting and surmounting these three types of obstacles to knowledge–practice consistency that will be the key to regaining the Happy Muslim Consciousness. The next chapter will articulate the key philosophical framework and methodology for bringing about that seriousness$_{(r+p)}$.

Note

1   An obvious example of demi-reality is Nazism. For a while (1933–1936), the Nazi Party, by implementing a massive programme of public works and armaments manufacture, appeared to be the answer to Germany's economic and social travails. However, because Nazism was, at the level of alethic truth (see Chapter 5), a false racialised ideology driven by a war economy, it led inevitably to war and genocide, and ultimately to the (self-)destruction of the German Reich.

3 First Moment (1M): original Islamic critical realism

In the previous chapter, we saw how seriousness$_{(r+p)}$ is an essential underlying characteristic of both Islamic praxis and critical realist philosophy that set up the metaphysical conditions for the philosophy of Islamic critical realism.

This chapter introduces the core theoretical ideas of critical realism and Islamic critical realism. It explains how the critical realist philosophical fulcrum of ontological realism, epistemological relativism and judgemental rationality provides a comprehensive and enriching interpretative framework that can underscore and nurture a 'serious' approach to Islam and, by extension, other religious traditions. It describes the necessary conceptual tools of original Islamic critical realism at the first dialectical moment of 1M (First Moment) of 'being-as-such' and 'being-as-non-identity'. The chapter claims that this work of 'underlabouring' by the fulcrum of ICR can set up the conditions for young Muslims to develop an authentically Islamic, peaceful and transformatively engaged attitude to life in a multi-faith world.[1]

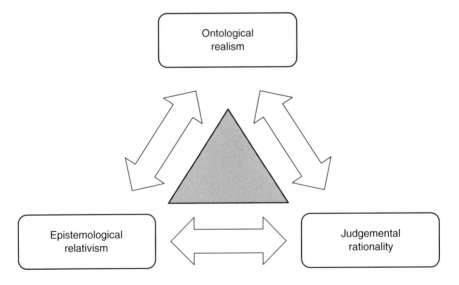

Figure 3.1 The fulcrum of Islamic critical realism (ICR).

Ontological realism

As we saw in the previous chapter, the primary function of original critical realism (OCR) was twofold: the 'revindication' (reclaiming) of ontology (the philosophical study of being) from its reduction to epistemology (the philosophical study of knowing and knowledge) and the establishment of a new ontology of deep structures, causal mechanisms and real change. A basic understanding of critical realist ontology, the philosophical study of being, is, therefore, that being exists independently of our knowledge of it and, in particular, our ability to describe it, so that it cannot be reduced to discourse, nor is it merely contained or constructed in the semiotics of our speech (Sewell, 2005).

For practical everyday purposes, being and knowing are often deeply mutually implicated. For example, the measurement of a mile (knowing) is rarely, if ever, disconnected from the geographical space (being) that it describes. Nevertheless, the fact that being does not equal knowing is shown by the fact that the globe did not suddenly change shape when it was discovered not to be flat, and neither did the experience of living on it (Bhaskar, 2000). Nor did the sun rise, set and shine in a different way once it was discovered to be, and was described scientifically as, the centre of a heliocentric solar system. An extension of this fact of the independence of being from knowing is that beings, entities and phenomena can exist without being known, or even if there is no possibility that they can ever come to be known (Bhaskar, 1975). This is, of course, pertinent to the possibility of the existence of unseen immaterial realms as described in the Qur'an and in the belief systems of other faiths. These are philosophically equivalent to scientific fields, such as gravity, whose effects can be experienced but not directly perceived.

Immanent critique

At the heart of the critical realist revindication or reclaiming of ontology was a critique by critical realists following Bhaskar (1975) of the empirical actualism that has characterised much modern and postmodern philosophy and social science. In the field of the philosophy of natural science, Bhaskar (1975) has demonstrated the weakness of empirical actualism through an 'immanent (insider) critique' focusing on an analysis of the intelligibility of experimental activity (IEA).

Under this immanent critique, empirical actualism is shown to be philosophically at its weakest at precisely the point where one would expect it to be at its strongest, namely a natural scientific experiment. A natural scientific experiment is necessary precisely because the pattern of events forthcoming under experimental conditions would not be forthcoming without it. In a natural scientific experiment, we artificially produce a pattern of events to identify a causal law, but we do not produce the causal law, which, for the experiment to be meaningful, must exist outside the closed system that the experimenter has created. Thus, the IEA presupposes the categorical independence of the causal laws discovered from the patterns of actual events produced in the experiment. Therefore, the IEA presupposes the independent and structured nature of the objects of scientific knowledge and that phenomena are not merely constant conjunctions of superficial events, as described by Hume.

The empirical, the actual and the real

Not only did original critical realism 'revindicate' ontology from its reduction to epistemology, it also posited a 'new' explicit ontology against the old implicit ontology. Rather than constant conjunctions of events, Bhaskar posited a stratified depth-ontology of the realms of the empirical, the actual and the real, and differentiated into 'open' and 'closed' systems. The realm of the empirical is the realm of experience, the realm of the actual is the realm of events and experiences, and the realm of the real includes the underlying causal structures and mechanisms that lie behind or beneath and generate those experiences and events (Hartwig, 2007). Imagine the experience of quenching one's thirst with a glass of water: the event in the domain of the empirical is the subjective experience of drinking the water and the relief that ensues; the event in the domain of the actual is the objective act of drinking water; and the event in the domain of the real pertains to the properties of water which lie in the molecular structure of water in which the experience and the event of drinking water are set.

Stratification and emergence

Furthermore, central to the 'new' critical realist ontology are the ideas that reality is 'stratified' and that most events (outside the laboratory) occur in 'open systems'. To say that reality is 'stratified' is to say that phenomena at one level of reality are scientifically explained in terms of structures or mechanisms located at a deeper level that generate or produce them. To say that most events occur in 'open systems' is to say that they are determined by and, therefore, require explanation in terms of a multiplicity of such mechanisms.

Now, the history of science reveals a multi-tiered stratification of being as deeper layers or strata are successively uncovered: tables, for example, are constituted by molecules, which are constituted by protons and neutrons, which are constituted by quarks, etc. However, not only is reality stratified but some parts of reality are also 'emergent' (Bhaskar, 1975, p. 119) from more basic levels of being through to more complex forms which are irreducible to the more basic levels (Bhaskar, 2013). To give a simple example of the principle of emergence in the natural world, water (H_2O) is dependent on the 'lower-order' existence of hydrogen and oxygen atoms and yet has causal properties and a relationship to the rest of living things that are irreducible to hydrogen and oxygen (C. Smith, 2010).

Emergence in the human and social worlds very often comprises 'stratified and differentiated' layers of being that are closely connected but also differentiated from one another (Bhaskar, 2009). Thus, for example, the physical/subatomic, biological, psychological, social, geopolitical, ecological, cosmological facets of human being are all connected and interrelated, but also taxonomically and causally irreducible one to another. To put this more concretely, the mind at the psychological level is dependent on the chemistry of the body at the level of biology; it could not operate without it. But the mind as ontological cause or epistemological category is not reducible to chemical reactions and the physical activity of neurons at the chemical level.

Laminated systems: four-planar social being

For this 'new' ontology, especially with relation to human being in a social nexus, critical realists also developed the idea of the 'laminated system' (Bhaskar, 1993/2008) to designate both the complexity and the irreducibility of the factors at work in open systems, such as all facets of human society. The context of the emergent human person is, therefore, conceived of by critical realists as existing simultaneously on four 'laminated' planes of social being, to which we will often return in Part III. These planes (Bhaskar, 1993/2008) are:

a   material transactions with nature;
b   inter-subjective (interpersonal) transactions between differently situated human agents;
c   social relations at the irreducible level of structures, institutions and forms;
d   the internal stratification of the embodied personality.

It is not difficult, to look at an example to which we will return in Part III, to see the child in an educational setting as a social being on four planes. The education of the individual child involves simultaneously:

a   material transactions with materials or artefacts ultimately derived from nature: textbooks, PCs, school buildings, food, transport, heating, electricity, etc.;
b   formative interpersonal relations with peers, teachers, family members and community figures by which formal (disciplinary) and informal (inherited-cultural) knowledges and intellectual traditions will be transmitted to the child;
c   indirect involvement via, for example, the level of school management with other institutions and policy-making organisations: the government, local authority, museums, temples, churches, mosques, historical sites, publishers, etc., which will produce powerful regimes of knowledge (Foucault, 1980), e.g. school subjects, into which the child's learning will, at least to a certain extent, be bound;
d   all of which will be brought to bear on the emergent personality of the child in a variety of related dimensions.

A further relevant 'laminated' system to which we shall return is described by Bhaskar (2013) in terms of a 'hierarchy of scale' typically comprising seven emergent, articulated levels:

1   *unconscious motives* as illuminated by psychology;
2   the *individual level* of biography;
3   the *micro level* of small-scale human interactions, e.g. within the peer group, as described by ethnomethodology;
4   the *meso level* of classical sociology, e.g. functional roles within the family, economy or corporation;
5   the *macro level* of whole societies, e.g. the UK economy;
6   the *mega level* of trajectories and spans of time, e.g. feudalism;
7   The *planetary whole.*

Ontological realism when applied theologically to ICR

When applied to theology and spirituality, ontological realism pertains to the essential being of spiritual phenomena. God can be said to exist (or not exist) independently of our knowledge of or belief in Him, or lack of knowledge or belief in Him. Unseen spiritual phenomena, such as the human/divine spirit, Divine Providence, Destiny, Angels, are, for example, part of a spiritual ontology and they can be allowed to exist (or not to exist) independently of our knowledge of or belief in them. Ontological realism about God does not claim that God or other spiritual phenomena exist, but that the fact and realities of His

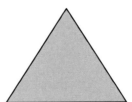

Ontological realism:

God, destiny, angels, resurrection, revelation, etc.

Epistemological relativism:

Islam – Sunni and Shi'a; Christianity – Catholic and Protestant; Judaism – Orthodox and Reformed, etc.

Judgemental rationality:

Exegesis; theology; theodicy; transcendental intuitions; analogy; consensus; logic; textual analysis, etc.

Figure 3.2 The fulcrum of ICR exemplified.

existence and the existence of other types of metaphysical being are philosophically possible and not dependent on our knowledge of Him/them.

The realms of the empirical, the actual and the real apply neatly within this original Islamic critical realist ontology. The realm of the empirical refers to the immediate individual experience of events; the realm of the actual refers to the objective reality of those events within the context of the ongoing development of human social structures; and the domain of the real refers to the understanding of events as produced by the generative mechanisms of nature underscored by a divine plan that is both absolutely transcendentally universal and yet immanently particular.

A wedding ceremony, for example, may be experienced at the level of the empirical by the bride and groom and the wedding guest as the signing of the contract and/or the vows, the first kiss, the exchange of rings, the receipt of well-wishes and congratulations. It may be understood in the realm of the actual as the social contract between two people who are seen to commit to each other in front of witnesses, thus formalising their love in the presence of society and so perpetuating the social institution of marriage. In the realm of the real, it can be understood as the sacramental union of gender/sex opposites, whose creation of one out of two before God both is generated by biological necessity, and, at an ultimate level, enacts a transcendental divine plan of bringing new human life into the world.

Spiritual emergence and false emergence

The idea of emergence is also critical to the Islamic critical realist paradigm in that it suggests how the universal and essential dimension of spiritual being emerges out of other – the physical/subatomic, biological, the psychological, social, geopolitical, ecological, cosmological – facets of human being without, necessarily, being reducible to them.

Although the spiritual dimension of being has emerged over evolutionary time from these 'lower' levels, it is irreducible causally and taxonomically to any of these 'lower' levels. Transcendental and spiritual experience may relate to and be interpreted through the psychological level of the mind and yet it cannot be reduced to human psychology. The dimension of the spirit exists and has real causal effects in both the seen, material and the unseen, emotional-spiritual worlds.

It also follows, of course, that what pertains to be religious experience may be enmeshed in other factors from which spiritual being has not really, in fact, fully emerged. For example, a violent religious fanatic, e.g. a suicide bomber, can be understood as a laminated, emergent 'embodied personality', existing on a variety of ontological levels. These may include, *inter alia*:

- the physical level, i.e. the body as weapon;
- the psychological level, e.g. manifest in the need for peer approval and an absence of social recognition;

- the socio-economic level, e.g. inadequate and unjust distribution of resources;
- the normative level, e.g. false theological teaching…

… all of which masquerade as a spiritual dimension, but out of which seriousness $_{(r+p)}$ and the ability to apply judgemental rationality (of which more later) in consideration of a whole range of theological and human factors has not really emerged. Thus, from being occasioned by an *excess* of religiosity, religious deviation and aberration, such as killing by suicide, represent, in this analysis, an under-realisation of the self in its own faith tradition (Mahmutćehajić, 2011).

My account of ontological realism in both its original and its ICR form has already included such words as 'human' and 'social'. This necessitates a brief explanation of essential differences that critical realists have observed between the ontology of natural and social structures:

1   Social structures, unlike natural structures, do not exist independently of the activities they govern.
2   Social structures, unlike natural structures, do not exist independently of the agents' conceptions of what they are doing in their activity.

(Bhaskar, 1979, p. 38)

In critical realist terms, the structures of society and the conditions and effects of human activity in society really do exist but do so in a different way from structures in the natural world. The essential nature of social structures is that while they have ontological reality, this reality is imbued with value and meaning; and values and meanings, unlike rocks or trees, do not generally exist independently of agents' apprehension of them. Phenomena and events in the social world, of course, happen without our knowing that they happen or without our knowing anything about them, but the processes of coming to know social phenomena necessarily (even if only minutely) change us, as we change them. Thus, society and all types of human structure and activity have an ontological reality that is only relatively independent of epistemology. This connection between human being and human knowing and knowledge brings us to the inseparably connected second element of the Islamic critical realist fulcrum: epistemological relativism.

Epistemological relativism

While ontological realism states that the universe – both material and immaterial – has or does not have reality whether we know (or accept) it or not, epistemological relativism states that the universe – both material and immaterial – is experienced, known and interpreted differently by different individuals and groups (see Figure 3.1).

The contribution of hermeneutics and interpretivist and post-structuralist philosophies and social theories has been to insist on the necessity of disclosing, articulating and, if necessary, deconstructing the contingent, relative positionality of individuals and groups in order to allow a closer correspondence between the nature of the object of research and the truth of the research to be accessed (Gubrium & Holstein, 2003). Critical realism articulates these understandings philosophically by showing that epistemological relativism is distinct from ontological realism and also that knowing is constellationally embedded in being – that is to say, knowing is dependent on being, but being is not dependent on knowing (Norrie, 2010). In other words, things must have real being before they can become either knower or known.

The epistemic fallacy

The taxonomic and causal reduction of being to knowing, prevalent in all manner of anti-realist discourse theory (e.g. Wittgenstein, 1922, proposition 6.25), has been described by critical realist thinkers as the 'epistemic fallacy'. According to Margaret Archer and colleagues:

> Critical realism does not deny the value and theory ladenness of knowledge. What it does is to counter the epistemic fallacy. The epistemic fallacy involves the fallacious inference that because there is no epistemologically objective view of the world, there is no objective world ontologically. Such an inference leads to the extravagant and relativist claim that to the extent that we embrace different world-views, we inhabit objectively different worlds.
>
> (M. A. Archer, Collier & Porpora, 2004, p. 2)

Critical realists have identified the 'epistemic fallacy' in a variety of modernist and postmodern fields. One general form of the 'epistemic fallacy' occurs when Saussurian linguists refer to the 'signified' (the concept), the 'signifier' (spoken or written words) but not the 'referent'; so, they might refer to the idea of the child, to the word 'child', 'enfant', 'niño', etc., but not (sufficiently) to the flesh-and-blood reality of a young human being. Thus, Bhaskar (1979) argues that an extreme tendency of post-structuralism and social constructionism is to reduce 'physical-material being into concepts, as if the limits of language are the limits of the world', to the obvious detriment of understanding phenomena properly (Alderson, 2013, p. 51). Concepts cannot exhaust, contain or even fully describe natural or social phenomena, any more than a description of an apple, however brilliant, could contain the experience of tasting it.

   Extreme examples of the epistemic fallacy may also be found in the field of theology and spirituality. Thus, Don Cupitt, an admired Cambridge-based theologian, describes himself as a Christian non-realist who follows certain spiritual practices and attempts to live by ethical meanings (the signified) traditionally associated with Christianity (the signifier) without believing in the actual existence of the underlying metaphysical realities (such as 'Christ' and 'God') to which these practices and beliefs refer (the absent referent). Such a position ignores the logic that without a spiritual referent – even one whose existence one cannot prove for sure, e.g. God – the 'signified', namely ethics and morality, and the 'signifier', in this case the Christian religion, become ungrounded, nonsensical abstractions. According to the same logic, the Islamic faith as a cultural manifestation without a religious praxis is not only unserious $_{(p + r)}$ but also, according to the ICR fulcrum, hermeneutically nonsensical or without grounding. Likewise, within Islam, Islamic monotheism (*tawhīd*) is often construed to be incompatible with religious pluralism. This is to commit the epistemic fallacy by confusing the realist ontology of One God with the epistemologically relative possibility that He may be known in different ways.

Epistemological relativism when applied theologically to ICR

In the Islamic critical realist paradigm, therefore, epistemological relativism (see Figure 3.2) pertains to our beliefs, knowledge and interpretations of spiritual phenomena, such as God, the Divine Decree/Destiny and Creation. These usually take the form of religious traditions, sectarian positions within religious traditions and doctrinal understandings of religious positions within religious traditions.

To espouse the idea of epistemological relativism (along with ontological realism) is to say that

> a belief about the reality or existence of god [*sic*] is quite consistent with ... the idea that god manifests himself or herself or itself in a variety of different ways or is accessed by different people in different traditions in a plurality of different ways.
>
> (Bhaskar, 2000/2012a, p. 31)

In other words, the fact that God has been known differently does not mean that the God that is known is different.

To claim that it is illogical to believe in God because there are so many religions is to fall into the trap of the epistemic fallacy and to conflate being with knowing. The ontological reality of God's being, if He does exist, would not be altered by any number of diverse religious interpretations, experiences and understandings of It. Thus, it is also important, in the case of Islam, to make a clear categorical distinction between the being of God (*Allah*) and the religion of Islam. While God may (or may not) have decreed that the religion that human beings should follow is Islam (Qur'an, 3:19), Islam is not God and nor can God be exclusively connected, by philosophical or theological necessity, to Islam. This is a first major step towards Islamic intellectual and spiritual humility that does not reject an ontology or theology of God but does not claim a monopoly on authentic religious experience.

Human interpretative fallibility

Crucially, for an Islamic critical realist understanding, the distinction between ontological realism and epistemological relativism makes not only theorising the distinction between God's being and the Islamic religion possible but also theorising the status of Revelation – the Qur'an itself – a genuine philosophical possibility. The revelation of the Qur'an itself, the *matan* – the text revealed to the Prophet Muhammad before any human interpretation – lies squarely in the realm of ontological realism; in the words of classical Islamic theology, it is the uncreated word of God (Saeed, 2006). By contrast, every single act of reading and interpreting the text of the Qur'an falls into the realm of epistemological relativism and is, therefore, potentially fallible. This is crucial to an Islamic critical realist perspective because it allows for the potential fallibility of *all* human judgements and decisions about God and Revelation, including many of those that have traditionally been the most revered, such as the legal judgements and positions of the four canonical schools of law and the various schools of belief (*'aquīda*).

This deep philosophical recognition of human fallibility lies as much at the heart of the Islamic message as the notion of the perfection of God. The Qur'an makes the humanness of the Prophet Muhammad abundantly clear (Qur'an, 3:144) and points to his human (rather than prophetic) shortcomings, which are used as a source of divine teaching (Qur'an, 130:1–6; 3:144). For example, the Companions of Muhammad would question whether his strategic decisions for the Muslim community were a part of the Qur'anic revelation or his own judgement (Ramadan, 2007b). If they were the latter, they were recognised to be human, fallible and therefore prone to refinement or amendment. The Companions of Muhammad understood this core distinction between ontological realism, pertaining to God, Revelation and Prophethood, and epistemological relativism that pertained to the humanity of Muhammad and the shifting vagaries of historical contingency, even if, of course, they did not articulate this understanding as such. Thus, epistemological relativism in the context of ICR embraces the historically conditioned and context-specific nature of all human decisions, including those which are made about Revelation itself.

Judgemental rationality

The quality of the necessary relationship between the philosophical study of being (ontology) and the philosophical study of knowing (epistemology) is dependent upon the quality of the third element of the Islamic critical realist fulcrum, judgemental rationality (see Figure 3.1). This is a process of deciding between the accuracy and validity of competing accounts of phenomena according to sets of religious, scientific and experiential criteria. Judgemental rationality is itself constellationally embedded in epistemological relativism in the same way that epistemological relativism is embedded in ontological realism. Judgemental rationality, like epistemological relativism, is, therefore, grounded in and bounded by our situatedness and our geohistoricity.

Nevertheless, the fact that our decision-making is grounded in geohistoricity does not mean that all judgements, though fallible, are equally unjustifiable or necessarily wrong. Judgemental rationality means that we *can* make judgements about relative, fallible knowledge. Not all perspectives and interpretations are morally or epistemically equal (Collier, 2004). The position of judgemental rationality is that 'human beliefs are potentially true and, second, that there are standards of belief evaluation that permit us to assess the likelihood of any given ensemble of beliefs' (Little, 1993). Judgemental rationality is mediated through detailed attention to the processes of logic, discourse and debate that pertain to any particular field or discipline, the operation of effective and coherent research methods and design, and personal self-scrutiny and reflexivity.

Judgemental rationality when applied theologically to ICR

Judgemental rationality in this ICR context, therefore, pertains to deliberation and deciding about the plausibility of spiritual phenomena and the traditions connected with them according to related exegetical (textual), philosophical-theological, experiential and emotional criteria. According to the principle of judgmental rationality, it is vital for a serious$_{(r+p)}$ approach to faith that aims towards knowledge–practice coherence and consistency that the young person can be prepared to discover and then articulate coherent, rational (doctrinal), emotional and experiential grounds for choosing one mode of spiritual access (religious tradition) as opposed to another, for choosing a religious interpretation while leaving another, and for choosing one mode of religious behaviour as opposed to another. This process of rational and emotional spiritual decision-making is an essential part of the religious experience. (See Chapter 8 for more detail.)

Judgemental rationality is part of the necessarily continual conversation between revealed principles, eternal truths and shifting contingent geohistorical circumstance that we observed in the previous chapter to be a hallmark of Islamic theological philosophy (Ramadan, 2009). It is this interspace (*barsakh*) of ongoing spiritual reflection that is uniquely occupied by humanity which is the realm of judgemental rationality. This interspace necessitates what Bhaskar (2013, p. 12) has called enhanced reflexivity – that is to say, the process of natural human reflection enhanced by appropriate philosophical, exegetic and social scientific tools.

The absence of this sound and sophisticated judgemental rationality has hampered Muslim progress

Many of the problems facing the Muslim community alluded to in the Introduction are the product of a conflation in popularist Muslim thinking of the various elements of the Islamic critical realist fulcrum.

- The epistemological relativist, interpretative elements of Islam – that is to say, all its exegetical and jurisprudential apparatus – have often been falsely attributed ontological reality. This means that fallible, geohistorically particular human interpretations have often been seen in themselves as changeless and sacred. For example, the division of the world into *Dar al-Islam* (the Place of Islam) and *Dar al-Kufr* (the Place of Unbelief) is an interpretative position born of medieval geopolitical circumstance that is often endowed with time-less ontological reality by extreme Islamist ideologues such as Sayyid Qutb (1964/1981). Of course, this fallacy is not unique to Islam or even to religions, to wit the 'sacred', unchallengeable worth attributed to a wide variety of secular values and intellectual positions, such as Darwinian evolutionary biology.

- The processes of judgemental rationality – exegesis (*tafsir*), the 'sciences of the revelation' (*asbāb an-nuzul*), etc. – have generally not kept touch with the broader intellectual contexts of which they inevitably form a part. This means that methodologies and findings of natural and social science that might perfectly well be incorporated into the toolbox of judgemental ration-ality for enhanced Islamic self-understanding and explication have been often been excluded a priori as un-Islamic, or even as part of a system of unbelief (*millat al-kufr*). This has resulted from inadequate appreciation of the fact that the processes of Islamic intellectual development were, and necessarily remain, an organic response to changing geohistorical circum-stance (Winter, 2010).

The Qur'an as a critical realist text

On the basis of the model of the fulcrum of ICR, and following on from the identi-fication of the seriousness$_{(r+p)}$ that characterised the Qur'an that we observed in the previous chapter, it is possible to articulate the second core element of the original Islamic critical realist position, namely that the divinely revealed text of Islam, *al-Qur'an* (the Recitation), can authentically and creatively be understood as a crit-ical realist document. This is not, of course, to claim that God Almighty, believed by Muslims to be its source, is a critical realist! It is to claim that the fulcrum of Islamic critical realism can 'underlabour' interpretatively for the Qur'an in a way that relates its eternal principles to contingent, contemporary multi-faith social realities. That is to say, the fulcrum of ICR provides an interpretative framework for accessing the essence of Qur'anic meaning in a multi-faith world.

The Qur'an is ontologically realist in its references to the real events and natural structures of the created material universe (e.g. Qur'an, 40:61, 64).

> God it is who made the night that you may rest in it, and the day for sight … God it is Who made for you the earth as a [stable (Jalalayn, 1505/2013)] abode and the heaven as a canopy, a ceiling. And He created you and per-fected your forms, and provided you with the wholesome things for nourishment.
>
> (Qur'an, 40:61, 64)

And the Qur'an is ontologically realist in its allusion to the existence of immate-rial, unseen realities such as Angels, Satan and jinn (demons), e.g. Qur'an, 72.

As a necessary corollary of its ontological realism, the Qur'an posits a necessary relationship between the reality of the universe and the interpretative faculties of human beings. Thus, according to the Qur'an, and in line with the critical realist 'stratified' ontology of the empirical, the actual and the real, the universe is both divinely created out of real material and of interpretative significance and benefit for human beings (e.g. Qur'an, 2:164; 3:190). Moreover, both God and creation have an ontology that is real and exists independently of what can be known, and is greater than what can be known or said about them by human beings (e.g. Qur'an, 40:57).

The truth-in-being: Haqq

In other words, in the Qur'anic ontology, knowing is secondary to being. At the same time, the essential knowability of the created universe is constellationally embedded in and intrinsic to the nature of its being. The Qur'an makes the embedded nature of truth within being plain in a notable verse: 'We [God] have created the heavens and the earth and everything between them with Reality (*bil Haqq*)' (Qur'an, 15:85). The Arabic word used for reality, *Haqq*, contains the ideas of real, ultimate being and the epistemic and ethical truth embedded within it (Kamali, 1997), which is suggestive of the intrinsic existential connection of ontology and epistemology posited in the fulcrum of ICR. Moreover, this intrinsic connection between being and knowing, including divine (self-)knowing, is quintessentially characteristic of the non-identity of human being at the level of 1M (being-as-such) (e.g. Qur'an, 2:30–31; 51:56) with the rest of the created order. These twin human abilities of coming to know God and of knowing manipulation of His creation is what characterises the human being as God's representative (*khalifah*) (Qur'an, 2:30), who apparently stands in the place of God in effective dominion over the creation.

Qur'anic emergence and judgemental rationality

As well as the intrinsic connection between being and knowing, the Qur'an (71:13–14) also speaks of the stratified ontological structures and emergence of the human being through different stages (Jalalayn, 1505/2013), of which human beings are the pinnacle (e.g. Qur'an, 2:30). This has been construed by classical commentators to refer to the stages of the development of the human embryo and, while clearly not in itself an endorsement of a Darwinian-style theory of evolution, indicates at the very least that different levels of created form emerge from others.

Indeed, the Qur'an is indicative of, rather than prescriptive of, natural and social scientific answers precisely because it requires of the believer a deep, critical rationality and personal reflexivity, and since it speaks to the level of normative knowledge existent in any particular age. The natural empirical and interpretative-theological signs (*ayāt*) of the universe do not disclose themselves easily and demand of the believer both self-awareness – (self-)reflexivity – and systematic, scientific understanding if they are both to be understood and applied to life. Refrains such as these are the *leitmotif* of the Qur'an: 'There are signs on the horizon and in the self for people who reflect' (Qur'an, 41: 53), and 'In the creation of the heavens and earth and the alternation of night of day … are signs for people who use their intellects' (Qur'an, 2:164; 3:190).

The natural-social signs (*ayāt*) are objectively real – night follows day (Qur'an, 7:54), death follows life objectively for all – and yet the meanings of the ontology of the universe at the level of the empirical, the actual and the real do not disclose themselves without reflection, hard intellectual work and spiritual purification of the eye of the heart, as well as the availing oneself to a range of interpretative possibilities at social and individual, emotional and spiritual levels. The application of criteria of reasonableness and of the probability of truth is a necessary part of understanding the relationship between the universe and the Creator. This process of spiritual judgemental rationality opens up the possibility of transcendental understanding both within the self and in communication with other people and with God (see Chapter 5). Critical rationality is a key component part of Qur'anic belief and sets up the conditions for the living connection of principle with context (Ramadan, 2006).

It follows that faith in this Islamic critical realist understanding is not a 'leap', in the Kierkegaardian sense, into a mode of human apprehension that is different from reason. Critical rationality exists in an intrinsic and necessary relationship with faith. If faith and reason find themselves in contradiction in the Islamic critical realist paradigm, either faith is wrong or reason is deficient, or faith is deficient and reason is wrong. Qur'anically speaking, faith and reason, the rational intellect (*'aql*) and belief (*iman*), are an inseparable generative mechanism of a serious $_{(r+p)}$ relationship with God.

Thus, the Qur'an presents a vision of reality that is consistent with the original critical realist disambiguation of a realist ontology from a relativist epistemology that necessitates judgemental rationality and is consistent with a depth-ontology that is stratified and differentiated, and exists at the levels of the empirical, the actual and the real. Creating and created reality exist objectively for all, but they are apprehended and experienced relatively, differently and unequally through the complex, intersecting prisms of individuality, relationships of power and individual concrete singularity embodying differing properties and tendencies in a way that necessitates a deep, spiritual logic for decision-making.

Establishing the conditions for rational re-enchantment

Therefore, it is possible with these three basic principles of ICR – seriousness $_{(r+p)}$, the fulcrum of ICR and a critical realist understanding of the Qur'an – to claim that God can be said to exist (ontological realism) and can be said to have been accessed and to have revealed His Being through a variety of traditions of faith (epistemological relativism), *and* to choose and commit to one tradition or position within a tradition as opposed to another (judgemental rationality).

The basic principles of ICR set up the philosophical conditions to allow the young person to make a spiritual commitment to a particular faith while still remaining open to and drawing on the insights of other faiths, or other traditions within his or her own faith. Thus, these basic principles allow for the simultaneous sustenance of ontological confidence with epistemological doubt. This is on the principle of one's own human fallibility in the dimension of epistemological relativism coupled with the confidence that the ontological reality of spiritual phenomena are themselves not contingent on human beings' interpretations of them. They commend an educational commitment to submit one's own and others' beliefs and truth-claims to the full gamut of the intellectual, emotional and experiential tools of judgemental rationality in order to check both their intellectual plausibility and their conduciveness to human flourishing. The ICR fulcrum offers the philosophical possibility that God may have granted genuine spiritual insight to those who fall outside one's own religious tradition and that this can enrich rather than threaten one's own commitment to faith and facilitate a genuinely respectful engagement with the 'other'. In other words, the ICR fulcrum potentially, as we shall see in Chapters 7–9, yields a mature and nuanced, rather than a naive and literal, yet still authentically Islamic, spirituality.

This application of the fulcrum of ICR to the Qur'anic world-view can contribute to the process of rational 're-enchantment' (Bhaskar, 2000; Taylor, 2007), which allows that the spiritual realities can be held philosophically to exist in the objective world outside of the mind of the believer, as described in the Qur'an and other religious texts. Yet the spiritual ontology, no less than the ontologies of science, requires the full gamut of reason to check its interpretative plausibility and also requires the believer to concede the deep possibility of human interpretative fallibility when bringing this ontology to bear on the lived, social world that involves him- or herself in relation to others.

At the foundation of this process of rational re-enchantment is a necessary personal commitment to seriousness$_{(r+p)}$ and an understanding that faith and reason underlabour in intrinsic partnership for divine knowledge and human well-being. As we shall see in the next chapter, the model for realising seriousness$_{(r+p)}$ and thereby effecting deep and lasting personal and social transformation can be found for young Muslims in the person of the Prophet Muhammad.

Note

1 This combination of ontological realism, epistemological relativism and judgemental rationalism has been called the 'holy trinity' of critical realist philosophy (Hartwig, 2007), but will here be referred to as the 'fulcrum' of Islamic critical realism to avoid any Christological confusions!

4 Second Edge (2E): dialectical Islamic critical realism

The life of the Prophet Muhammad

Introduction: dialectical critical realism

In the previous chapter I explored at the level of First Moment (1M) – that is, at the original critical realist moment of being-as-such – how the fulcrum of Islamic critical realism can underlabour for Islam by setting up the conditions for rationally re-enchanted understandings of the world, based upon a critical realist understanding of the Qur'an, that are both authentically Islamic and open to the insights of those from other faiths and none. I have also posited both the epistemological non-identity of different religions and the fact that they may be directed towards the same ontological realities, albeit in different ways.

In this chapter I am going to explore how dialectical critical realism (DCR), at the levels of Second Edge (2E) – absence, Third Level (3L) – totality and Fourth Dimension (4D) – transformative praxis, provides the means to continuing this process of rational re-enchantment and personal and social transformation through an understanding of the second source, after the Qur'an, of Islamic praxis: the life and person of the Prophet Muhammad. In order to do this, we will first need to absorb a philosophical understanding of the dialectical moment of 2E (Second Edge) and what critical realism means by 'absence' and its role in generating change.

Second Edge (2E): absence

The philosophical move from understanding being-as-such at 1M to understanding being-as-becoming at 2E is the move towards understanding dialectical change. For this move, Bhaskar, followed by other critical realists, reworked the understanding of dialectic of G. W. F. Hegel, who saw the process of change as the process of the self-realisation of '*Geist*' (Spirit or Mind). For Hegel, this process of self-realisation was primarily an epistemological process that is generated by the positing of identity, which is then subject to negativity in the form of a negative critique, and then incorporated in the resolution of a rational totality; or, put another way, the famous expression thesis→antithesis→synthesis (Norrie, 2010). However, while Hegel understood this process of dialectical change as primarily an epistemological one, Bhaskar (1993), as one might by now expect, places dialectical change squarely in the realm of ontology. He radically alters the phases of dialectic into non-identity→absence→total-ity→transformative praxis in an extension of the 'revindication' of ontology and the positing of a new ontology of original critical realism.

For critical realists, as we have seen in the previous chapter, the opening phase of being-as-such (at 1M) is a phase of non-identity and of being as 'strati-fied and differentiated': men and women are not the same, nations and tribes are different; different religions are not the same and nor are the objects of their ven-eration of worship. All these things exist and can be studied at the level of the empirical, the actual and the real, and at different ontological layers of 'stratifi-cation'. However, DCR adds to the account the fact that stratified, differentiated being inevitably entails gaps, hiatuses and absences which are themselves essen-tial to being.

Being necessarily entails the absence of being. In this regard, critical realist thinkers, e.g. Norrie (2010) and Hostettler (2012), following the lead of Bhaskar (1993), have argued that the tradition of Western philosophy is *ontologically monovalent* in excessively privileging of the positive aspect of being to the exclusion of non-being or the negative aspects of being, which are part of our normal understanding of change. Thus, in our normal understanding, to say that something has changed is to say that something that was there is no longer there and/or that something that was not there is now there. Both these normal under-standings of change involve both absence and negativity.

Critical realists claim that this ontological monovalence has its origins in the resistance of ancient Greek philosophy, initiated by Parmenides, to the idea of real existential change (Bhaskar, 2000). According to critical realist thinkers, absence, negativity and change are essential parts of the duality of presence and absence in being (Norrie, 2010). For example, silence is the precondition of speech, rests are indispensable to musical sound, and, as we know from natural science, empty space is a necessary condition of solid objects. In the experience of selfhood, a sense/knowledge/belief that 'I am this' necessarily entails a sense/knowledge/belief that 'I am *not* that' (Mahmutćehajić, 2011).

In the dialectical critical realist account, 'absence' is not only integral to being; crucially, it is also transformative. Indeed, dialectical change is under-stood by critical realists as the process of the remedying or removal of absence (Bhaskar, 1993/2008), the 'absenting of absence'. Recovery from illness involves, among other things, the removal of the disease. Positive change is often not so much the application of something positive as the removal of some-thing negative. The essential property of political and social freedom is the absence of servitude. Winning freedom is the process of abolishing (i.e. absent-ing) the conditions of slavery.

Real determinate absence

Crucially, therefore, absence has been understood by critical realist thinkers as 'real determinate absence' (Norrie, 2010). Most absence is not indeterminate nothingness; it is causally efficacious, effecting real natural and social outcomes. Clearly, natural absences can effect social outcomes: for example, the absence of natural resources can provoke war. But social and intellectual absences can also effect natural outcomes: for example, inadequate environmental and ethical education can effect climate change. Such absences, experienced as indicative that something is wrong, also contain within them the potential to be positively transformative. A drought may, although it does not necessarily, lead to improved systems of irrigation, better farming techniques and more efficient habits of human water-use. Absence in this positive transformative sense is somewhat akin to the Avicennan idea of created perfection: created being has within itself the power to perfect itself and come into wholeness; the role of human free will, delegated by God, is in bringing this about (Ormsby, 1984).

The removal of absence is, thus, conducive to the development of greater epistemological consistency and ontological wholeness. Thus, the role of absence in a dialectic of social or natural transformation can be described as follows:

> Absence (e.g. omission) → incompleteness → inconsistency (contradiction, etc.) → transcendence → to a more comprehensive and inclusive totality.
>
> (Bhaskar, 2000, p. 55)

According to dialectical critical realism, this process of the dialectical 'absenting of absence' is part of the movement or process of overcoming hiatuses and obstacles to greater ontological wholeness of being, which dialectical critical realism calls 'totality'.

Third Level (3L): totality, partial totality and sub-totality

For critical realists, the idea of totality, which has nothing to do with political totalitarianism, is necessitated by the nature of the natural and social worlds, 'human beings are caught in a structured flow of being and becoming in which the totality of past, present and future relations is implicated.... A sense of totality is central to being' (Norrie, 2010, p. 88).

Totality is also conceived in terms of as 'multiple, overlapping, partial totalities' (Norrie, 2010, p. 88). These are always conceived of in relation to a whole that can never, in practice, be entirely encompassed, but without reference to which partial totalities become meaningless. 'To think of a language, a sentence, a text, a book or even a word is to think of entities where one has to grasp something as a whole as well as [in terms of] its individual parts' (p. 88).

Crucially, and fundamentally different from the Hegelian conception of totality as the 'closed' culmination of a rational, historical process of development, for example the modern state and its legal apparatus, for critical realists totality is 'open' and still in a process of becoming and overcoming hiatus and split. This is a 'realist, emergent sense of open totality' (Norrie, 2010) that is much more grounded in observed natural and social realities than the Hegelian ideal conception. For example, we may think of a language as a 'totality' that is, nevertheless, open to infinite possibilities for modification and change through the mechanisms of changing class relations, ethnic and cultural changes, youth slang, new and revised poetic forms, technological advance, etc. A religious tradition, such as Christianity, would provide another classic example of a 'totality' that is internally doctrinally, intellectually and liturgically related and imbued with a strong sense of tradition and of 'the presence of the past' (Bhaskar, 1993, p. 140). Yet the 'totality' of Christianity is prone to changes in doctrine and attitude, and to internal schism, as a totality that is necessarily open to geopolitical, time-bound contingencies in the form of political parties and their policies, 'secular' social attitudes and the pressures and attitudes of lay Christian congregations.

Again, the ideas of 'absence' and 'negation' are central to the critical realist notion of totality. Every act or instance of becoming more complete also involves the letting go of or removal of something that was absent, which was causing incompleteness and/or a less complete form of completion. For example, the gradual mutual letting go of parent and child provides the impetus for more complete adult responsibility. 'Every becoming is always also a begoing, or passing away, a process of change' (Norrie, 2010, p. 29). For example, in the Islamic tradition we can understand the preparedness of Abraham to sacrifice his son, Ismail (or Isaac in the Old Testament traditions), to God as the fuller becoming of Abraham into prophethood and moving closer to God in his preparedness to let go of the best of this world (Qur'an, 37:101–109). The obligatory Islamic charity, the Social Welfare Tax (*Zakat*), is the act of letting go of wealth for the benefit of others, which is, for the Muslim believer, the door to becoming a purified and more complete human being in a more harmonious society. We will explore these ideas in greater depth in Chapter 5.

Totality, partial totality and sub-totality

In this understanding, a 'sub-totality' is a 'partial totality' from which elements have been omitted to noxious effect. A sub-totality has been defined as 'the site of discontinuities, hiatuses, spaces, binds, barriers, boundaries and blocks between totalities ... the term [used] to denote the splitting, fracturing and broken nature of the whole under the conditions of material diffraction' (Norrie, 2010, p. 91).

Any given national society, for example, may be considered to be an 'open' totality, in which the various different ethno-cultural and/or faith groups may be understood as 'partial totalities'. A 'sub-totality' occurs when a group or groups are systematically excluded from the idea and ontology of the 'total' collective. For example, Jews and Gypsies were partial totalities construed and then excluded as 'sub-totalities' from the 'totality' of Nazi Germany. To give another example, a religious 'sub-totality' occurs when an important dimension of natural-social-spiritual life is excluded from the epistemic and ontic embrace of the praxis of a faith, for example sexuality from monastic Christianity, or multi-faith dialogue from extreme literalist forms of Islam. We will explore the idea of curricular totality and 'sub-totality' in Chapter 7.

Fourth Dimension (4D): transformative praxis

It is in this context of totality as interrelationships of presences and absences, truths and falsities, commissions and omissions, that human agency and the human desire to realise maximal human well-being, flourishing and freedom are constellationally embedded (Norrie, 2010). The ethical manifestation of this transformative impulse to freedom and well-being will be conditioned by geo-historical circumstance and the contingencies of individual concrete singularities. Nevertheless, as an impulse, according to Bhaskar (1993), 'the pulse of freedom' is a universal feature of the human situation, one that plays a discernible and generative role in being (e.g. ontic personal and social transformation), as does our desire to rectify absences and incompleteness in our understanding of being (epistemology). This impulse is the universal desire to be emancipated from 'ills and constraints', which are the ethical equivalents of absences, that lie in the path to freedom and self-realisation.

The pulse of freedom is generated according to the principle of *alethia*, meaning 'truth'. Alethia as truth is not propositional truth; it is ontic truth that is true 'to, for, in and of itself' (Bhaskar, 1993/2008, p. 219). Alethia is close to the Islamic term *Haqq* – truth-and-reality – that we explored in the previous chapter. It is the truth that is both the ontic and the ethical ground that underpins natural-social existence; or, as Bhaskar puts it, 'moral truth or alethia is universal concretely singularised autonomy'. Alethia is the process and product of the type of self-realisation in which, to echo a formula of Marx, the good of each is dependent on the good of all. It is the truth of the free development and flourishing of which each one of us is inseparably a part.

This means that, while ethical transformation is necessarily and primarily a personal transformation, self-realisation cannot fully take place without a more general process of social transformation and the movement of the collective towards alethic truth, however modest and unrevolutionary that may appear to be. For example, Rosa Parks' act of civil disobedience in Montgomery, Alabama, in 1955 to bus driver James F. Blake's order that she give up her seat in the coloured section to a white passenger became a ripple of transformative positivity on a sea of racist negativity precisely because it was a statement of the alethic truth of the equal status of all human beings before God. The transformative power of the action was derived from its transfactuality, in that it was embedded in a universal truth that necessarily affected other people.

An example of dialectical critical realist transformation: a teacher's early career

For a further concrete example of dialectical critical realism in action, we can look at the early career of a teacher.

1   At the level of 1M (First Moment), the undergraduate enters into a state of non-identity with other undergraduates by electing to study a particular subject; and then, as a graduate, he or she deepens the state of non-identity by deciding to become a teacher.

2   This leads at the level of 2E (Second Edge) to the realisation of an *absence* of the necessary knowledge and pedagogical technique to fulfil his or her potential being as a teacher. In order to embark on the removal (or absenting) of this absence, the being-becoming teacher enrols on a teacher training course.

3   This, in turn, leads at the level of 3L (Third Level) to a greater internally and externally related totality of being-becoming-a-teacher as gaps in substantive understanding and pedagogical technique are systematically removed (or made smaller) on the course.

4   Once an appropriate degree of totality – that is, completeness of integrated knowledge and skills – is achieved, the young teacher embarks at the level of 4D (Fourth Dimension) on transformative teaching praxis in order to enrich the lives of his or her pupils and to reach higher and deeper self- and subject-understanding.

Dialectical Islamic critical realism in the life of the Prophet Muhammad

I will now apply this brief account of the universal dialectic of ontological, epistemological and ethical change to interpret the life of the Prophet Muhammad and show how his life provides an intensified historical exemplar of the critical realist dialect of change that can be a model of personal and social transformation for young Muslims and others.

An added transcendental dimension

It needs to be noted at this juncture that dialectical Islamic critical realism (DICR), while fully acknowledging and drawing upon the ontological/Bhaskarian turn in Hegelian dialectics, necessarily adds to it a transcendental, theistic dimension. That is to say, in the language of Paul Tillich (1952/2000), it adds to the dialectical mix God, who is both the transcendent Ground of Being and also, therefore, the immanent Ground of Being-Becoming who intervenes in His Creation.

If we conceive of the dialectical pulse of freedom, as Bhaskar (1993) has, as a ripple of positive becoming on a sea of negative being and absence, then the divine is at once the Ground of both that positivity and (crucially) negativity. Divine intervention and guidance is at once the pebble that sets the ripple of positivity in motion and the pebble that maintains the ripple in motion when it threatens to peter out. Thus, in this metaphor the divine energy is present in the pulse of dialectic change even when it is apparently absent.

In the context of consideration of the life of the Prophet Muhammad what distinguishes prophetic (and, according to al-Ghazālī [Ormsby, 1984] and Ibn

Rushd [Averroes, 1179/2001], inspired) lives from normal human lives is neither that the Ground of Being-Becoming is absent from normal lives (although it may not be recognised) nor that the pulse of dialectical freedom is different. However, in prophetic lives both the regularity and the observability of divine guidance or intervention is intensified in both quality and quantity, and thus so are the pace, depth and breadth of personal and social transformation.

Thus, the Qur'an states that the Prophet Muhammad (and other prophets and religious leaders) exhibit both identity (Qur'an, 68:4; 94:1–11; 53:1–18; 81:15–25) and non-identity (Qur'an, 9:128; 3:144) with the rest of humankind. The life of the Prophet Muhammad has both horizontal (dialectical human change) and vertical (divine revelation/inspiration) axes, and I will consider both as we consider his life as a model of human, social and spiritual transformation. In this addition of the dimension of transcendence, this dialectical consideration of the life of the Prophet Muhammad prefigures the next phase of critical realism and ICR, the philosophy of metaReality and the philosophy of Islamic metaReality that I will turn to in the next chapter.

First Moment (1M): non-identity – Mecca (570–615)

His childhood: difference and separation

The early life of Muhammad (the peace and blessings of God be upon him) and first 13 years of his Prophethood at the level of 1M were characterised by non-identity and difference. In his childhood and youth, he was marked out by signs, unusual events and phenomena. With the onset of Prophethood, he was set apart by the receipt of a message that, in its transcendental cosmology and in the human ethic that was derived from it, marked a radical non-identical shift from the cosmology, theology and human ethic of his society in its particular place and age.

Muhammad was born in the year named 'the Year of the Elephant' by Arabs of the Arabian Peninsula when an ancient house of worship, the Ka'aba in Mecca, in the Arabian Peninsula, was apparently miraculously saved from attack by the Ethiopian Army of Elephants by pebble-throwing birds (Qur'an, 105:1). This date is thought to be 570 CE. He was born into a noble branch, Banu Hashim, of the Meccan-based tribe of Quraysh to a mother named Amina bint Wahb and a father named Abdullah ibn Addul-Muttalib. While pregnant with her child, Amina is said to have had a dream in which she was encouraged to give the child the name Muhammad, meaning 'someone worthy of praise', a name hitherto unknown to the Arabs. She also enjoyed an exceptionally easy pregnancy and birth, which, however, was punctuated by the death of her husband and Muhammad's father, Abdullah. This was a terrible blow to the life-chances of the infant Muhammad in those early medieval days when paternal protection and support was even more determinate of the life-chances of a child than it is today.

Hence, the birth of Muhammad was a joyful new presence intermingled with real existential loss and absence. This absence was also 'determinate' in Muhammad's infancy in the selection of his wet-nurse. It was the custom of the Qurayshi nobility to let out their children to live with Bedu tribeswomen in the desert for a few years in order that they absorb the uncorrupted Arab tongue that was believed to be cultivated by Bedu life. When Bedu wet-nurses came to Mecca came to choose their charges, the absence of a father to guarantee payment meant that none of them would accept the baby Muhammad. Only a latecomer, Halima, who feared the shame of returning to her own tribe empty-handed without a child, finally agreed to take Muhammad home to the desert.

The barren austerity of the desert with its infinite horizons was to colour the outlook of Muhammad (Ramadan, 2007b) and in some ways set up the conditions of heart and mind that were the platform for prophecy. Further, he was distinguished while in the care of Halima, according to Halima's report to Amina, by both the astonishing fecundity of Halima herself and of her date crops and grazing land and by the miraculous visitation of an angel who cut open his torso and removed a black spot from his heart (Ibn Hisham, 1:301, cited in Ramadan, 2007, p. 14). In other words, during this whole formative period the conditions for the prophethood of Muhammad were set up by his external and internal removal and separation from the worlds of temptation and wrong action. In Islamic critical realist terms, in early youth Muhammad was removed from the conditions of urban 'sub-totality' and 'split' that can set up the conditions for wrong action and intellectual misjudgement that block the path to human well-being and freedom.

Muhammad returned to Mecca and to his mother, Amina, when he was four, and when he was six she took him on a journey to the oasis town of Yathrib, 100 miles to the north of Mecca. However, on the return journey Amina was taken ill and died. Thus, at the age of six years the young Muhammad was orphaned and taken into the care of his grandfather, the doting Abd al-Mutallib. In the ensuing years, as a young man Muhammad, like many prophets before him (Ibn Hisham, cited in Ramadan, 2010), became a shepherd in the barren and desolate hills and valleys around Mecca, in which the transcendental and at times brutal splendour of the natural world and the need for human solidarity in order to survive must both have impressed themselves upon him. Moreover, in these years as a shepherd, as in his early childhood, he was set apart from society and lived in conditions of both solidarity with nature and relative non-identity and separation from his peers.

Early manhood: difference-in-identity

As Muhammad progressed into adolescence, his life was increasingly characterised by difference-in-identity. He was integrated once again fully into Qurayshi society, while simultaneously the signs of his non-identity and difference intensified. When he was 12 years old he accompanied his uncle and now guardian, Abu Talib, on a trading trip from Mecca to Syria in order to learn the craft of the merchant. This was a very normal thing to do, as Mecca was a hub of trade owing to the attraction of the Ka'aba, the house of Abraham in Mecca, and the fact that it had become a centre of pagan worship. On the way to Syria, they passed by the hermitage of a Christian monk called Bahira at a place called Busra, who had noted that although the caravan was moving along in fierce sunshine, one part of it had been overshadowed by a cloud offering a deep shade. Bahira asked to be presented to the members of the caravan and finally was introduced last to the young Muhammad, who, as a youngster, was thought to be a person of little consequence. He asked the young Muhammad about his background and lineage and finally requested that he remove his shirt. There on Muhammad's back he found what he was looking for: a mark between the two shoulder blades that was reputed to be the mark of prophecy. Bahira then wished the caravan well on its way, urging Abu Talib to take great care of the young Muhammad and saying that he would face great trials in the years to come.

In the years of his early manhood, Muhammad's growing reputation as a man of his word and an outstandingly successful and honest merchant brought him to the attention of one of the wealthiest and most influential women of the Meccan Quraysh, a widow called Khadijah (may God be pleased with her). After Muhammad had profitably conducted a number of trading expeditions on her behalf, she made enquiries through a mutual friend whether Muhammad, now aged 25, would consider her hand in marriage. Khadijah was beautiful, wealthy and respected, and Muhammad, although (in some traditions) 15 years her junior, accepted her offer. At last, his youth, which had been riven both by the painful and determinate losses and absences that accompany the life of an orphan and by strange, unusual phenomena, culminated in a stable, loving marriage that gave him an honourable standing among his people.

Indeed, Muhammad's impressive social and moral standing in the Quraysh during this period is best illustrated by a famous episode. The Quraysh had long been entrusted with the upkeep of the Ka'aba, the ancient house of God constructed according to tradition by Abraham, and the time had come to renovate it once again. When the work of reconstruction and renovation was complete, the four Qurayshi clans that had organised the work fell into dispute about who should have the honour of replacing the famous Black Stone that was thought to have fallen from Paradise in the time of Adam. The workmen were about to come to blows when Muhammad walked into the precinct of the Ka'aba, and the tribesmen unanimously agreed that al-Amin, the Trustworthy One – as Muhammad was nicknamed – should decide how to resolve the issue. Muhammad placed the Black Stone on a thick covering, gave each tribe a corner to lift up and then replaced the Black Stone himself. Thus, he satisfied the honour of all the Qurayshi clans and in the process showed a knack for 'man management' that was to be a hallmark of his later prophethood and political leadership.

However, increasingly as he reached his late thirties, Muhammad was finding the life of trade and the city irksome. He longed for the wide open spaces in which the transcendent was less veiled, and was apparently one of a small group of believers in God, the Hunafa, who secretly shunned the all-pervasive idol worship that took place in Mecca and on which the wealth of Mecca depended. It became his custom every month of Ramadan to set himself apart from his peers and to retreat into a small cave on the top of Mount Hira, just outside

Mecca, from the back of which in the distance only the Ka'aba was visible. Perhaps he yearned for the freedom from responsibility that had characterised his youth and sought answers to the 'big questions': why am I here and for what purpose was the universe created?

The first words of the Revelation: a moment of transcendental unity

It was in this small cave, in these conditions of real physical separation and radical, ethical non-identity with the mercantile and idolatrous values of Mecca, that one night in Ramadan, 610 CE, the Angel Gabriel appeared to Muhammad and said in the darkness, 'Read.' Muhammad, who was illiterate and formally uneducated, replied in astonishment, 'I am not one of those who read!' Twice more the same command to 'read' was issued. Twice more Muhammad made the same reply, until the angel, holding Muhammad in a fierce clench, recited, 'Read! In the name of your Lord who has created humankind out of a blood-clot. Read! Your Lord is the most Noble who has taught humankind what they did not know before by means of the Pen!' (Qur'an, 96:1–3).

Muhammad, desperate to flee from this appalling apparition and these terrible words, abandoned the cave, but wherever he turned outside the cave there was the awesome figure of Gabriel filling the horizon, repeating the same words. He fled down the mountainside and into the arms of his wife Khadija with the words, 'Cover me! Cover me!', fearing that he had been possessed by a demon that threatened his sanity.

Khadijah comforted Muhammad and reassured him that God Almighty would never bring insanity and ruin to a man of his palpable goodness, truthfulness and fairness. Following these calming words and their sentiments, which were confirmed by Khadijah's Christian cousin, Waraqah ibn Naufal, the Prophet Muhammad received the second verses of what was to become the Qur'an (which means 'the Recitation'): 'O You [there] wrapped up in your mantle! Arise and deliver the warning! Glorify your Lord! Purify your garments! And shun abominations!' (Qur'an, 74:1–4)

These initial revelations of the Qur'an were accompanied by apparitions of Gabriel assuring Muhammad of his prophethood, sometimes in human form and sometimes as an angelic being (Ramadan, 2007b). The revealed verses themselves would come after a bell-like sound and would require suffocating concentration (Ramadan, 2007b). The message of these early Meccan verses of the Qur'an was clear and oft-repeated: that God is One, transcendent in His majesty, worthy of worship alone and without partner, Creator and Sustainer of the cosmos, and that all men will be judged in both on the quality of their obedience and devotion to God and on the quality of their interactions with other human beings.

Gradually, by painful and exciting degrees, Muhammad surrendered to the terrifying responsibility of his prophetic calling and, initially in great secrecy, began calling both the poor and the elite of Mecca to the Qur'anic message of divine unity and human solidarity. Early converts, after Khadijah, to this renewed form of the ancient Abrahamic faith (Qur'an, 98) included large numbers of Mecca's disenfranchised poor and enslaved classes, such as the Ethiopian slave Bilal ibn Rabah al-Habashi, who had a beautiful voice and was to be honoured by Muhammad as the first official caller to the Islamic prayer (*Muathin*), for whom the Qur'anic message of basic human equality had obvious emancipatory appeal. The early converts to Islam also included, however, influential figures of the Qurayshi nobility such as Ali ibn Abi Talib, Muhammad's cousin, and Abdullah ibn Abi Qhulafa, popularly known as, Abu Bakr, his long-time friend, a wealthy and respected merchant and community leader. These men in terms of social standing and wealth had nothing to gain and everything to lose by adhering to the message that Muhammad brought; and the fact that the new message and its bearer were beginning to attract the wealthy and influential, as well as the poor and disenfranchised, began to be a matter of deep concern for the leaders of the Meccan Quraysh.

Second Edge (2E): absence – Mecca to Madina (615–623)

Persecution: setting up the conditions of absence

Thus, at the level of 1M – being-as-such – the non-identity both of the person of the Prophet Muhammad and the difference of the ethical substance of his message began to generate at the level 2E (Second Edge) conditions of loss, split and absence.

The message of the Meccan verses of the Qur'an of the radical equality before God of men and women and of different races, nations and tribes (e.g. Qur'an, 49:13), and of uncompromising monotheism (*Tawhid*) that entailed shunning pagan idolatry and the abolition of social malpractices such as the murder of infant girls (e.g. Qur'an, 17:31), was a statement of deep cosmological, social and personal non-identity between the new faith and the Qurayshi tribal world. Indeed, the Qur'an itself testified to the growing religious and ethical gap between the polytheism of the Meccan majority and the Islam of the Muslim minority (Qur'an, 109) (Friedmann, 2012).

This message and the attractive way that Muhammad embodied it, for example by refusing to curse or threaten those who violently opposed the new message, such as his uncle Abu Jahl, by refusing to dishonour kinship bonds and by honouring and recognising the human value of society's weak, including slaves, women and children, threatened a society that depended on racialised slavery, trade generated by pagan worship, blood-feuding, infanticide and the social inferiority of women. The vast majority of Meccan women had virtually no legal rights and in marriage were considered to be the property of men. Indeed, some Qurayshi men 'owned' up to 40 women as wives. Moreover, by forbidding infanticide, especially of infant girls, which was a common Qurayshi practice, the Qur'an (17:31; 81:8–9; etc.) reinforced this message of equality between the sexes in respect of the sanctity of all life.

Moreover, Muhammad was now making public his call to rich and poor alike. He performed the new prayer which had been prescribed in the Qur'an

(17:78–79) and demonstrated to him by the Angel Gabriel (Ibn Hisham) in rotation in his followers' Meccan houses. The Qurayshi nobility feared that the word of a new religion with a significant following among people who 'mattered' would get out and that this would deter their trading partners and allies on whom their very survival was dependent in the fragile desert economy. They first tried to bribe Muhammad to abandon his mission with promises of wealth and tribal leadership, and when this failed, they took more vicious steps to stop the new message from spreading. Poorer Muslim followers of Muhammad such as the slave Bilal, who enjoyed no powerful tribal protection, were tortured and other poor Muslims such as Ammar, and his father Yassir and mother Sumayyah, were beaten and then murdered in broad daylight. Muhammad himself was taunted and physically threatened whenever he ventured out, although, unlike many of his followers, he enjoyed the protection of powerful family members, such as his uncle Hamza, who intervened to prevent the worst of their excesses.

Nevertheless, the deep existential non-identity between, on the one hand, the Islamic message and its enactment by Muhammad and his Companions and, on the other, the ethos of its social context meant that Muhammad lost all his social status and much of his tribal protection. He had become a social 'untouchable' who was regarded by much of Meccan society as a hapless delinquent.

Absenting the conditions of absence: the first emigration

These extreme conditions of absence and split generated the first Islamic Hijra (emigration): real physical movement in order to bring about real existential change, which we can describe in critical realist terms as the 'absenting' by Muhammad of his community from the conditions of absence. In 615, about 100 Muslim men and women were chosen by Muhammad to leave Mecca and make for Abyssinia, where the Negus of Abyssinia was noted for his fair treatment of all people. These Muslim émigrés found a sympathetic protector in the Christian Negus, who was struck by the strong parallels between the Qur'anic verses surrounding the lives of Jesus and Mary and the Christian Gospels. The Muslims of Abyssinia settled and served the Abyssinian state until they were recalled by Muhammad to Mecca many years later, following the conquest of Mecca (630 CE), thus becoming a model of the correct Muslim practice for Muslims living in peaceful coexistence under the protection of non-Muslim authority (Michot, 2006).

Boycott: absent and outcast

Back in Mecca, Muhammad and his followers were soon to be subject to further persecution and loss. Sometime around 617, the Qurayshi leaders instigated the ultimate sanction on an errant clan in tribal society: a ban on all social intercourse, e.g. trade and marriage, between the tribe of Quraysh and Muhammad's clan, the Banu Hashim, and the clan of his uncle, the Banu Muttalib. This was total intra-tribal ostracism, which meant that Muhammad, his family and his followers were stripped of the basic tribal rights of protection and forced for their own safety to set up camp in one of the desolate, rocky, infertile valleys outside Mecca and survive on scraps of food smuggled out of Mecca by friends and sympathisers. The privations of this three-year period took a terrible physical, economic and social toll on the group. For example, Abu Bakr, a wealthy merchant before this period, lost the majority of his fortune, wealth that had been instrumental in supporting the new faith.

The Year of Sorrow

Then, shortly after the ostracism was lifted in 619 and the clans returned to Mecca, both Muhammad's uncle Abu Talib, his tribal protector, and his beloved wife Khadijah, his closest companion, soulmate and first religious follower, succumbed to ill health as a result of the ostracism and died. By the end of the Year of Sorrow, as 619 was afterwards named, Muhammad had lost the two human beings who had sustained him as close companions, protectors and advisers through the difficult periods of non-identity and absence. Moreover, death had brought an end to the mutually devoted marriage between Muhammad and Khadijah, which had provided the Muslim community with a model of a faithful collaborative partnership between a man and a woman based on worship of God and mutual trust and support. This was in stark contrast to the Arabian norm of uncontrolled polygamy of one man with multiple wives.

To add insult to injury in 619, Muhammad's overtures to the neighbouring town of Taif for protection for himself and his community met with a humiliating rejection, as the leaders of the Thaqif tribe poured scorn on his claims to be a prophet of God and he was chased out of the town by children throwing stones. Despite Muhammad's deep faith in his mission and his trust in his Lord, to whom he repeatedly turned in prayer and supplication, these losses, setbacks and his rejection by his own people must have seemed total; his situation was one of perilous vulnerability (Ramadan, 2007b) and noxious absence. The general outlook for the new faith appeared bleak.

The Night Journey: transcendental intervention

However, in critical realist dialectics, as we have seen, the conditions for onto-logical renewal and greater wholeness of both being and understanding lie in conditions of absence. Absence is generally not indeterminate nothingness; it is itself 'real, determinate' and potentially positively transformative for natural, social and personal circumstances. In line with this understanding, it was during this period of deepest social and material absence and want that Muhammad received the most profound spiritual confirmation of his prophethood in the form of the Night Journey. One night, the Angel Gabriel awoke the Prophet Muhammad, who had fallen asleep after praying in the precincts of the Ka'aba, and bade him mount a white horse-like, celestial animal called the Buraq. Muhammad, with Gabriel in attendance, then journeyed from Mecca to the Dome of the Rock in Jerusalem, from where he ascended through the seven heavens meeting and greeted the prophets Jesus, John, Idris, Aaron and Moses and, finally, led them as their imam in the Prayer.

Also on the Night Journey, Muhammad is said to have reached the furthest limit of the lote tree (Qur'an, 53:1) – that is, the nearest that the human being can reach to the presence of God. In other words, the conditions of deep absence and loss had emptied the being Muhammad of everything except the will of his Lord (Mahmutćehajić, 2011). From 'there', Muhammad negotiated the number of obligatory prayers in the Muslim day as five at the instigation of Moses, and from 'there' he received the verses of the Qur'an (2:285) that codified the basic elements of the Muslim creed:

> The Messenger has believed in what was revealed to him from his Lord, and [so have] the believers. All of them have believed in God, His angels, His books and His messengers, [saying], 'We make no distinction between any of His messengers.' And they say, 'We hear and we obey. [We seek] Your forgiveness, our Lord, and to You is the [final] destination.'
>
> (Qur'an, 2:285)

On his return from Jerusalem to Mecca, Muhammad is said to have observed in detail a trading caravan that arrived in Mecca some weeks later, thereby confirming the reality of the Night Journey to those Muslims who were almost startled into disbelief by its other-worldly and miraculous nature. By contrast, the Companion Abu Bakr famously said to Muhammad after hearing the account of the Night Journey for the first time, 'I believe you, as you have always spoken the truth' (Ibn Hisham, 2:256) Abu Bakr, who was later to be the first successor to Muhammad as leader (caliph) of the Muslim community, was thereafter known by the epithet As-Siddiq, meaning the one who confirms the Truth. Others of the Companions were similarly minded, remembering that Muhammad had been called al-Amin – the Trustworthy One – in the days before Islam. His Qurayshi opponents, by contrast, now had more fuel for the narrative of Muhammad's insanity and the threat that he posed to their iniquitous social order.

The Hijra (620–622): absenting the conditions of absence

Nevertheless, in the quotidian world of empirical-material forms, the absence of recognition among the tribes local to Mecca, the loss of wealth and social status, and the loss of his wife and uncle forced the Prophet Muhammad to look further afield for support of and opportunities for his prophetic mission. In 620, among the annual pilgrims to Mecca, Muhammad encountered softer-hearted people from the northern Arabian town of Yathrib of the tribe of the Khazraj, who found the message of divine unity and human equality and solidarity attractive, given that at that time Yathribi society was being torn apart by violent inter-tribal disputes.

In 621, the same group returned to Mecca, accompanied by two members of the other major Yathribi tribe, the Aws tribe, and the Yathribi delegation pledged allegiance to the Prophet Muhammad at a place called Aqaba. The two parties entered into an understanding that in the near future, when the appropriate moment presented itself, Muhammad and his followers would join them in Yathrib. They hoped that the combination of the Qur'anic message of divine mercy and human solidarity embodied in the person of Muhammad would unite their city and bring them peace.

So, between the years 620 and 622 the early Muslim community that had remained in Mecca, numbering less than 100, began slowly but surely to slip out of Mecca and make the 100-mile journey north through the desert to Yathrib. Thus, they began to remove themselves from the conditions of absence that had blocked their path to freedom and full human and spiritual fulfilment for 13 brutal years. Almost the last to leave, on 16 June 622, were Muhammad himself and his closest companion, Abu Bakr, who first doubled back south to throw off their Qurayshi pursuers, who were by now alive to the threat of the Muslim exodus – or Hijra (emigration), as it was to be known – and the threat that Muhammad might pose them were he able to establish a stable base for himself and the new faith. The pursuers caught up with Muhammad and Abu Bakr, who were forced to seek refuge in the tiny cave of Thawr. When the pursuers arrived at the cave, a spider's web across its mouth and a dove nesting close by persuaded them that no one was inside and they turned away. Thus, when they were at their most vulnerable, divine intervention in the order of nature had saved Muhammad and Abu Bakr, who journeyed on to a rapturous welcome at Yathrib. Yathrib was thereafter to be known as Madinat al-Munawara, which means 'the enlightened place of total religion'.

Third Level (3L): totality – Madina (622–632)

Thus far, we have seen how the Qur'anic message and its embodiment by Muhammad and the Muslim community in Mecca was a 'partial totality'. The Qur'an had spoken of divine unity, the need for human being to worship and surrender to divine command, the sanctity of all human life, the brotherhood of humankind and of a mighty Day of Reckoning when all human beings would be judged for eternity on the quality of their lives and the way that they had treated others. This 'partial totality' was primarily theological and eschatological in nature, and did not as yet guide Muhammad and the Muslim community as to the conduct of their daily lives in matters to do with marriage, trade, warfare, day-to-day governance and justice. In Islamic parlance, in Mecca the Qur'an and the Prophetic example had prescribed and illustrated the *'ibadat* (rulings connected with worship) without the *mu'amalat* (rulings connected with daily life). This 'partial totality' was, of course, occasioned by the constrained social context and the values and the pagan cosmology of the Quraysh onto which the Qur'anic message was being brought to bear.

In Madina, the absence of just governance faced by the tribes of Yathrib, together with the presence of Muhammad and his Companions and the continuation of Revelation, generated the conditions of 'totality' whereby the totality of the Islamic paradigm – *'ibadat* (rulings connected with worship) without the *mu'amalat* (rulings connected with daily life) – could be revealed and practised. In recognition of this opening up of the more total Islamic expression, the Hijra year, 622, from then on marked the official beginning of the Islamic period, the Year 1 AH (meaning 'after the Hijra'). 'Totality' denotes the official beginning of the Islamic paradigm.

This not to say that the Prophet Muhammad did not have intense spiritual, social and political obstacles to overcome and challenges to meet. The latent conditions of 'totality' had to be realised out of conditions of tribal hiatus and split between the Aws and Khazraj tribes and the competing demands of the Christian and Jewish communities of Madina, many of whom were naturally lukewarm about the arrival of the new 'prophet' and his followers. Jewish groups, in particular, had potentially a lot to lose, as traditionally on the Arabian Peninsula their religious textual knowledge, ancient heritage and authentic religious traditions had conferred on them a certain intellectual and spiritual status that compensated for their relatively powerless position as an ethnic and cultural minority group among the majority of pagan tribes.

Among Muhammad's first actions in Madina, after he had bought a plot of land for the construction of a mosque and his family's adjoining dwelling, was the drawing up of a legally binding contract of mutual assistance for a local community (Umma) that recognised the religious and tribal rights of the different groups in Madina: the Muslim émigrés (*Muhajirun*), their native Madinan Muslim hosts (*Ansar* – literally, 'helpers'), the rest of the Aws and Khazraj tribes, and the Jewish residents of Madina. This agreement guaranteed the rights to life, property and safe passage of all the 'citizens' of Madina and was a pact of mutual assistance (*'ahd al-Umma*) in the event that any party come under attack from hostile outside forces. In effect, Muhammad had drawn up one of history's first political constitutions. This created a multi-faith community of Abrahamic believers (*Ummat al-muminīn*), including a small (*c.*100) but growing group of Muslims, a large population of Jews, and some Christians, whose rights to freedom of religious worship were guaranteed.

Thus, the 'totality' of a community was created contractually on the social four-planar level (c) of irreducible institutions and social forms in a way that transcended different individual beliefs and yet guaranteed their protection, in the process initiating the transformation of Islam from a personal religious to a religio-social and political ethic. The Qur'an also made the social solidarity of the brotherhood of Abrahamic faiths plain and the fair treatment of all different types of human being obligatory (Şentürk, 2002). The constitution of Madina enshrined the Qur'anic principle of religious freedom (Qur'an, 2:256) into proto-civic law and activated legally the common-sense notion that 'compulsion in religion' is most unlikely to achieve a serious$_{(r+p)}$ commitment to faith.

This principle of religious freedom in the four social planes was to become a hallmark of Islamic governance in the early and later periods of Islam. At the level (c) of irreducible institutional forms, for example, when the second caliph of Islam, 'Umar ibn al-Khattab, conquered Jerusalem, he refused to perform the

Obligatory Prayer in the Church of the Holy Sepulchre for fear that his army might take this as an indication to turn it into a mosque, thus compromising Christian religious freedom. Christian diplomats and even prisoners of war in sixteenth-century Ottoman Istanbul were regularly impressed by the relatively high degree of religious freedom and protection afforded the People of the Book (*Ahl al-Kitab*) – that is, Christians and Jews – by the Ottoman state (Malcolm, 2013) at a time when in Reformation and Counter-Reformation Christian Europe individuals were regularly executed for quite minor 'deviance' in their religious praxis.

Regrettably, the *ideals* of multi-faith Abrahamic brotherhood, thus codified, were not to survive the actual conditions of seventh-century tribal life in the Hijaz unscathed. Eventually, and after many acts of leniency, repeated acts of political and then military treachery by the Jewish Banu Qurayza led to the Prophet's ordering the execution of their males and the expulsion of other Jewish tribes, such the Banu Nadir, and some Christian tribes from Madina and its sur-roundings (Friedmann, 2012). Nevertheless, it is vital to note that it was acts of *political* treachery rather than *religious* affiliation that led to these terrible hia-tuses and absences of peace in the more generally harmonious 'totality' of the Madinan period (Friedmann, 2012; Ramadan, 2007b). The Banu Qurayza had thrown in their lot with the Madinan multi-faith community's enemies and suc-cumbed to political and military treason in a brutal time and place characterised by a complete absence of law enforcement (Friedmann, 2003), by a complete absence of a criminal justice system, and the lack of any coherent means of polit-ical protection other than force of arms. It was the Banu Qurayza's political treachery, and absolutely *not* their Jewishness, that Muhammad could not afford to let go unpunished. These events show that in the fight for survival the Proph-et's humanity and mission were conditioned, as much as anyone else's, by the norms, expectations and concrete limitations of his geopolitical circumstances.

The emergence of the institutional and collective out of the personal and indi-vidual was also reflected in the change in the religious life of the Muslim com-munity. In the first years of life in Madina, the five obligatory daily prayers were instituted in the new mosque, which itself became a focal point of community life in which the Prophet himself taught his Companions to reflect upon the meanings of their religion. The Social Welfare Tax (*Zakat*) was instituted for the first time in an obligatory legal capacity, contributing to the upkeep of Madina's poor and to the emergence of a more equitable society which strengthened the formal ties of religious brotherhood established by the Prophet. The fast (*Sawm*) during the month of Ramadan was also formally instituted. This provided an annual space for the collective act of spiritual reflection and purification from the grosser, though utterly normal and necessary, appetites of eating and sexual intercourse. (See Chapter 6 for further details of the meanings of the Five Pillars of Islam.)

It is instructive from a critical realist perspective to reflect on how the fol-lowers of Muhammad in Madina were called not his 'followers' but his 'Com-panions' (*Sahāba*): the prophetic teaching of Islam was enacted in the setting by

Muhammad of an ethical example of divinely attuned behaviour through the quotidian business of living in community and through collective acts of transcendental solidarity in surmounting the human and material challenges that faced this heterogeneous multi-faith and multi-cultural society. Although, as we have seen, the Qur'an made the special status and non-identity of Muhammad as God's Prophet and Messenger undeniably clear (e.g. Qur'an, 4:80), it also pointed unequivocally to his identity with the rest of humanity (Qur'an, 9:128). Muhammad acted as a first among equals, heeding sound advice, learning from his and his Companions' mistakes and appealing to them to understand the revealed truths of the new religion in the light of rational inquiry and the lessons of their lived experience (Ramadan, 2007b).

It is vital to understand Muhammad's critical realist approach to his teaching of Islam as a route to the establishment of Islam in two ways.

First, Muhammad actively discouraged any 'cult of personality' surrounding his person. He refused to be treated like a king ('Iyad, *c*.1100/1991), although this was a common and 'natural' response to his charismatic and often awe-inspiring person. He ate and drank moderately and was clothed humbly and simply but with great cleanliness, always aiming to find the middle ground between ostentatious wealth and conspicuous, ascetic poverty.

Second, the legal injunctions that started to emerge in Revelation as part of the totality of Islam, for example to do with divorce and trade, were principles that might have appeared forbidding 'on paper' but were given a flexible, realistic and compassionate enactment by Muhammad in practice. For example, if someone was too poor to pay the compensation for having intentionally broken one of the days of obligatory fasting, Muhammad simply waived the fine. If someone came to him to confess a sin, even quite a heinous one such as adultery, he asked that person to remain silent if at all possible and to keep it between him- or herself and God, so that he would not be required to enact the punishment that the crime would require once it was witnessed in society. Indeed, the level of proof for the *hudud* (corporal and capital) punishments of Shari'a was so high (for example, four male witnesses to the act of adultery were required) that the threat, rather than the normal reality, of severe punishment represented how destructive these actions were for both the believer's vertical relationship with God and his or her horizontal relationship of trust with other humans. In practical terms, the *hudud* were almost only ever enacted as the result of voluntary confession, and Muhammad even tried to avoid these where possible (Feldman, 2003; Ramadan, 2007b).

Increasing hostility leads to all-out war

In short, in their new situation in Madina, removed from the conditions of Meccan absence, Muhammad and his Companions were now emancipated for the establishment, as opposed to merely the practice, of the totality of the Islamic faith. However, their increasing strength and influence at the heart of the Arabian Peninsula was deepening the resentment, jealousy and hostility of those who were either outright opponents of the Muslim faith community, such as the Meccan Quraysh, or allies and converts only on account of political expediency, such as a group of Madinan Helpers (*Ansar*) who came to be known as the 'Hypocrites'. The hostility of the Meccans in particular to the totalising effects of Islamic establishment and the fact that the new, more equitable practices of trade were beginning to 'infect' their own trading partners was gradually intensifying. Soon this hostility started to transgress the bounds of honour that was acceptable to any Arabian group on the Peninsula if they were to survive with their respect and livelihood intact. The goods and property of the Muslims who had left Mecca were now routinely confiscated and sold off, and those Muslims who had been unable to emigrate were subject to intensified persecution.

This is the context of the so-called Qur'anic permission to fight (22:39–40) and the first full-scale battle between the Madinan Muslim community, which was fought at the Wells of Badr on 13 March 624 CE (17 Ramadan, 2 AH in the Islamic calendar) between a Muslim army numbering *c*.300 and a Meccan army of *c*.1000. This engagement began as an attempt by the Muslim community to intercept a large Meccan trading caravan that its members believed was laden with their own property. However, it became a statement of the increasing power of the nascent Muslim community. After a full-scale engagement, the Meccan army was routed, with over 70 dead compared with the Muslim community's 14 dead. The Meccan dead included some of the leading society figures, including 'Amr ibn Hisham, known as Abu Jahl, meaning 'the father of ignorance', one of the Muslim community's fiercest Meccan opponents. The engagement was also marked by powerful signs of the new religion's spiritual status. A small handful of dust thrown by Muhammad in the direction of his enemies to mark the start of the battle became a blinding force in the Meccans' eyes. After the battle, the Revelation confirmed, 'You did not throw, when you threw; God threw' (Qur'an, 8:17). In other words, the actions of Muhammad and his community were so aligned with the Divine Will as to be annihilated by it in a moment of immanent–transcendent identity (see Chapter 5). To use our original Islamic critical realist framework, at the level of the empirical Muhammad threw a handful of dust at the Meccan host; at the level of the actual, this act marked the start of the battle and was a statement of intent; at the level of the ultimately Real, this was the expression of the Divine Will working in and through His creation.

The Battle of Badr marked the deepening identity between the actions of the Muslim community and the Divine Plan. By contrast, the Battle of Uhud a year later, which was intended as a revenge attack by the Meccans on the Medinan community, was a lesson in how the abandonment of the higher purpose aligned with Divine Destiny for a lower one motivated by individualistic greed can have catastrophic results. When this battle, which was fought at the foot of Mount Uhud, just outside Madina, was almost won by a much larger Muslim army than at Badr, the Muslim archers who were protecting the rear of the army abandoned their elevated positions in order to rush down the slopes into the mêlée and claim their share of the spoils of the battle. This act, which Muhammad had specifically warned against, allowed the Meccan cavalry under Khalid ibn Walid to outflank the Muslims and thereby nearly inflict defeat on them. In the desperate defensive fighting, Muhammad had a tooth smashed, with the rings of his helmet being driven into the flesh of his cheek, and had to be carried from the battle on horseback to be tended in the shelter of a nearby cave.

Although the battle eventually petered out into a stalemate and the Meccans did not gain access to Madina itself, the Muslim community lost 70 dead to the Meccans' 22, including Muhammad's beloved uncle Hamza, whose corpse was viciously mutilated at the instigation of Hind, the wife of the Meccan leader, Abu Sufyyan. The lesson of the Battle of Uhud for the Muslim community was clear: it was the Muslim alignment, both individual and collective, with the Divine Purpose through prayer and acts of human solidarity that was the source of their strength; not force of arms, nor even the presence in their midst of the Prophet Muhammad himself.

The Battle of Uhud also taught the fledgling multi-faith community of Madina that war was only to be fought for the preservation and restitution of political justice and not personal gain. Indeed, nine-tenths of Shari'a, which existed only in proto-legal form in Madina in the form of the Qur'an and the Sunna, looks to provide justice to the complexity of worldly affairs (*mu'amalāt*), rather than dealing with the relative simplicity of Islamic worship (*'ibadāt*) (Sachedina, 2013). Thus, for example, at the height of the hostilities between the Muslim community and the tribe of Banu Nadir, who had betrayed the Muslim intentions to the Quraysh, a Jewish member of the Banu Nadir accused a Muslim of stealing his shield. After careful consideration of the evidence, Muhammad ordered that the property of the truthful Jew be returned and the Muslim criminal be punished. In this 'totality' of Islamic expression, to be Muslim did not mean to be the member of a special-interest cultural club, but to be responsible for the witnessing of truth, the upholding of justice and the universally applicable rule of law (Mahmutćehajić, 2011).

Moreover, the emergent Madinan totality nurtured multiple dimensions of human being; it was not merely a legal expression. As well as marriage and trade, Muhammad respected and encouraged the taste of the Madinan Ansar for music and poetry, especially on festive occasions, and reprimanded the more culturally austere *muhajirun* when they wished to curtail such activities (Ramadan, 2007a). The Prophet Muhammad recognised that if faith was to be spiritually nourishing of the whole human being, it required creative, culturally appropriate expressions and needed to be grounded in the cultural life of the community (*'Urf*).

The Qur'an (7:32) itself backed up such licence to enjoy beauty and the fine things of this world; and Muhammad himself declared that his loves in this world were women, sweet scents and the spiritual peace occasioned by the Prayer. Thus, although the unfolding of the Madinan totality was punctuated by momentous tests and challenges caused by hiatuses, absences and splits in the greater tribal fabric of the Arabian Peninsula, it was in the day-to-day exigencies of social life lived to the full in society that the Islamic totality promoted full human flourishing.

Fourth Dimension (4D): transformative praxis – the Hijaz (629–633)

We have seen that according to dialectical critical realism, conditions of totality and ontological wholeness, generated by the radical absenting of absence, lead dialectically to more general transformative praxis. This is clearly observed in the early Islamic paradigm. During the month of Ramadan in 629, after a decisive Muslim victory over the confederated forces of the Meccans and their allies, Muhammad dreamed that he was entering the sanctuary of the Ka'aba with his head shaven, holding the key to the Ka'aba in his right hand. He took this as a sign that he was called by God to make the Lesser Pilgrimage (*Umra*) to the Ka'aba in Mecca. After consulting with senior Companions, about 1,300 unarmed Muslim pilgrims left Madina for Mecca intent on completing the Lesser Pilgrimage. The band of Muslim pilgrims was intercepted by a Meccan force at the pass of al-Hudhaybiyya some way outside Mecca. The Meccans did not attack the pilgrims, as it was the sacred month of Dhu al-Qi'dah; nor, however, did they allow the Muslims to complete the pilgrimage. Rather, Muhammad and the Meccans led by Suhayl ibn Amr negotiated what became known as the Covenant of al-Hudhaybiyya: that the Muslims would be allowed to complete the Pilgrimage the next year; that a 10-year truce would be observed by both sides; and that the terms of the agreement would apply to any clan that entered into alliance with either side. Finally, it was agreed that Muslims leaving Mecca for Madina would be returned to Mecca, while Muslims leaving Madina for Mecca would be allowed safe passage.

Some of the Companions protested, notably the irascible and fearless Umar ibn al-Khattab, later the second caliph of Islam, at what looked like the unfavourable terms and conditions of the Covenant of al-Hudhaybiyya. However, the Qur'an affirmed the covenant as a 'clear victory' (48:1) that in reality, far from being a defeat, paved the way for the transformation of the whole Arabian Peninsula. For by means of this agreement, the Arabian Peninsula was being opened up by default to the Islamic ethic of peace, non-violent social transformation and the inevitable pulse towards freedom and more comprehensive well-being that was bursting out of the totality of Madina. It was an agreement that would initiate the transformation of a fractious, poor tribal society into a united, wealthy faith community.

Yet in the contingent reality of the eighth-century Hijaz, riven by deep tribal rivalries, social anomalies and the relative absence of coherent governance, the Covenant of al-Hudhaybiyya was bound to be broken, and so it was by the allies of the Meccans on multiple occasions. Finally, in 630 the Banu Kab of the Khuzaah tribe, who were allies of the Muslim community, were treacherously attacked at night by the Banu Bakr, allies of the Quraysh, with innocent loss of life. Muhammad realised that if he was to retain the trust of his allies, that breach of the Covenant of al-Hudhaybiyya could not go unpunished.

Muhammad prepared a large army for a secret all-out assault and set off for Mecca. On the way, he was met by Abu Sufyan, leader of the Meccans, who, tipped off by spies, realised the seriousness of the situation and had come to beg

Muhammad not to attack Mecca. Muhammad received Abu Sufyan, for some many years his implacable and merciless adversary, in the Muslim camp with firm courtesy, but, rather than call off the assault, he bade him to enter Islam and return to Mecca to advise the Meccan Quraysh to do likewise. At first, Abu Sufyan demurred, saying that while he could accept that there was no god except the One True God (*Allah*), he could not except the prophethood of someone whom he regarded as his social equal or even inferior (Ramadan, 2007b). Muhammad suggested that he remain in the camp and reconsider his position. Having being treated to the gentle and well-mannered conduct of Muhammad and his Companions overnight, and having observed the sincerity of their worship, Abu Sufyan had a change of heart in the morning and accepted both components of the Muslim declaration of faith that there is no god except the One True God and that Muhammad is the Messenger of God.

The Prophet, mindful both of the embodied personality and the institutional relationships of Abu Sufyan as a proud leader of the Quraysh, charged him with the task of suggesting and organising the surrender of Mecca to the Muslim army to avoid unnecessary loss of life. Abu Sufyan returned to Mecca to the jeers of his wife, Hind, and the disbelief of other Meccan leaders, such as Ikrimah ibn Abi Jahl, the son of Muhammad's great enemy Abu Jahl. Neverthless, the conversion of Abu Sufyan from enemy and disbeliever in Islam to believing ally demonstrated to many of the Meccan Quraysh the transformative power of the totality of Islam in praxis – the collective enacted unity of practice and belief. It also demonstrated to the Muslims the necessity and efficacy of treating each individual as a concrete embodied personality (Bhaskar, 1993/2008) with his or her own particular characteristics in four-planar being (Ramadan, 2007b).

After some light skirmishes that did not result in loss of life, Muhammad and the Muslim army finally entered Mecca as its conquerors and masters on 20 (some say 21) Ramadan, 630 CE. The dialectic of absenting absence, generating totality into transformative praxis, had turned a fugitive band of religious refugees into a disciplined, conquering army. However, in direct contravention of the norms of war of the day, Muhammad forgave all his former enemies who gave themselves up either to him or to a Companion – even those such as Wahshi ibn Harb, who had murdered his uncle, Hamzah. Not only were the Meccans forgiven, but also Muhammad forbade them to be insulted or to be made to feel like second-class citizens.

Muhammad's only act of destruction in the whole conquest of Mecca was of the idols in the House of God, the Ka'aba. Muhammad smashed these, uttering the following words from the Qur'an (17:81): 'The Truth has arrived, and falsehood perished: for falsehood is bound to perish.' Thus, he exemplified the dialectical critical realist principle that the act of making truth present also necessarily entails the absenting of the false. He recognised in this statement that the demi-reality (Bhaskar, 1993/2008) of pagan idol worship, which had dominated the life of the Arabian Peninsula for centuries, affecting events and creating unjust social structures and ethical norms, had inevitably crumbled before transformative, collective *alethia* and the majestic, transcendent reality-truth of God.

The lessons of Muhammad: the dialectics of re-enchantment

Given that the logic of dialectic demands both an ontological and an epistemological transformation (Norrie, 2010), and since the Qur'an (33:21) encourages Muslims to bring about such a transformation, what are we to learn from this dialectical critical realist understanding of the life and mission of the Prophet Muhammad? Or, to put it another way, what are the lessons that can be learned from this narrative by contemporary Muslim young people that will help them to negotiate a multi-faith world of competing truth-claims that is often characterised by the apparent absence of the Real and Transcendent breaking in on world affairs, especially Muslim world affairs.

The first is that a serious$_{(r+p)}$ approach to Islam, in which belief/knowledge and religious practice/personal-social behaviour are brought into ever-closer alignment, in the way that was enacted by the Prophet Muhammad with his Companions, is naturally and inevitably accompanied by a process of change and transformation of the individual and then the collective through the phases of non-identity, absence, totality and transformative praxis. This process takes patience and perseverance (Qur'an, 2:45–6), and is inevitably and rightly accompanied by the necessity to transcend and transform heteronomy, hiatus and split. Yet as a process it is a part of the inevitable 'pulse of freedom' (Bhaskar, 1993/2008).

Second, this seriousness$_{(r+p)}$ does not only, or even primarily, refer to an other-worldly transcendent relationship with the divine, although this relationship, developed through prayer, fasting and voluntary and obligatory acts of charity, is important. Seriousness$_{(r+p)}$ is to be enacted and found in the day-to-day relationships with other people of all human types through good manners, the keeping of one's word and contracts, and fulfilled engagement with life. It is through the persistent attention to the spirit and detail of rich, respectful and other-regarding human relationships, rather than victory on the battlefield, that the early Muslim community's life was transformed from one of non-identity and absence to one of totality and transformative praxis.

Third, part of the seriousness$_{(r+p)}$ of the Prophet Muhammad was that, in the language of ICR, his ethical outlook was determined by a divinely enchanted ontology viewed through the purified, prophetic lens of a merciful and flexible epistemology, mediated by sensitive judgemental rationality, in dealing with particular people's issues in specific sets of circumstances. This is why his were the dialectics of re-enchantment and realignment of the ethics of the world with their divine ontological ground. The fact that Muhammad knew God as the Most Merciful and Most Compassionate required hum to adopt such a compassionate and merciful ethical outlook if he was to be in tune with the nature of his Lord; and this 'fine tuning' was effected through the daily transcendental practice of the obligations of Islam. So it is to these obligations of Islamic praxis 'underlaboured' by the philosophy of metaReality that I now turn.

5 Islamic metaReality

The Articles of Faith and Pillars of Islam

In the previous chapter, we examined the dialectical process of how Islam in Mecca was manifested as a 'partial totality' constrained by the noxious absences (of rejection) and heteronomous splits occasioned by the vicious behaviour of Meccan society; how it developed into a 'totality' in Madina that was conducive to its full expression and the full(er) flourishing of its adherents; and how, following the conquest of Mecca in 630 CE, this full(er) flourishing burst out to transform the tribal praxis of the Arabian Peninsula through the transcendence of tribal ties of blood by the addition of an extra dimension of shared faith and humanity. We also explored some of the meaning that might be derived from this dialectical critical realist interpretation of the life of the Prophet Muhammad by young Muslims (and those educationally associated with them) today in terms of a serious$_{(r+p)}$ approach to the rational re-enchantment of reality offered by Islamic praxis.

In this chapter, I want to explore some of the possible inner meanings of this transformative and emancipatory praxis in the form of the six (consensually agreed) Articles of the Islamic Faith and the five basic obligations of Islamic practice – the so-called Five Pillars of Islam. I will do so by applying the critical realist insights gained so far, together with insights from the next moment of the philosophy of critical realism, known collectively as the philosophy of metaReality (PMR). By this exposition I do not intend to provide the be-all and end-all of Islamic 'esoteric' interpretation, but to offer a creative suggestion as to how young people can extract the juice and the pulp from the fruit of their faith by diving into the Islamic tradition and 'underlabouring' for it with a systematic, coherent philosophy. Or, to put this another way, I aim to suggest how the obligatory beliefs and acts of Islamic worship (*'ibadat*), by constraining the outer human person to some immanent obligations of behaviour, liberate the inner self for engagement with transcendental emancipatory meaning. Thus, I intend to follow the traditional spiritual structure of Islamic praxis – *Iman* (belief), *Islam* (outer obligatory worship) and *Ihsan* (the derivation of inner spiritual meaning) – from the point of view of the philosophy of metaReality, as well as describing the philosophical grounds, as I understand them, of Islamic ethics and law (Shari'a), of which the Five Pillars of Islam form an important part.

The philosophy of metaReality from difference to identity

We have seen from my exploration of original Islamic critical realism at the moment of being-as-such (1M) that the initial starting point of critical realist thought (Bhaskar, 1975) was the vindication of ontology, the philosophical study of being, and a critique of its reduction to epistemology, the philosophical study of knowledge and knowing. Original critical realism claimed both (1) that ontology was a necessary precondition for an adequate natural and social science; and (2) that this 'new' ontology was one of differentiated and stratified structures and causal mechanisms and real difference. As we have seen from our ICR approach in Chapters 3 and 4, this means, for example, that different religious traditions in general are not the same, although they may pertain to the same or similar spiritual realities.

Dialectical critical realism, as we have seen in the previous chapter, thematised being-in-process and change as involving absence, with action characteristically as the removal or 'absenting' of absence or lack. Within the context of the life of the Prophet Muhammad, we have seen that Islamic belief as it emerged from Revelation and was enacted in the life of Muhammad was not the same as pagan unbelief and that it was the difference between the beliefs and social mores of the pagan Quraysh and the fledgling Muslim community that created the conditions of radical existential absence that led, historically, to dialectical change and structural social transformation.

However, while original and dialectical (Islamic) critical realism thematise difference, non-identity, real change and duality as being real and necessary features of the natural and social worlds, the philosophy of metaReality (PMR) thematises unity as the necessarily prior substratum to duality. This is because while unity can exist without duality, duality cannot exist without unity. 'Thus concepts of identity, unity, etc. are ontologically, epistemologically and logically *prior* to concepts of non-identity, etc.' (Bhaskar, 2002/2012c, p. xlv). Translating this into the terms of ICR, we might claim, for example, that the unity of God can exist without the multiplicity of the world but the multiplicity of the world cannot exist without the unity of God.

Non-duality and transcendental identity

Bhaskar (2002/2012a) has described three ways in which the world of duality and difference is ultimately underpinned by the world of non-duality and transcendental identity:

1 *As the constitution of everyday life.* That is to say, unity and transcendental identity are essential to the ordinary 'constitution, that is the reproduction and transformation, of everyday life' (Bhaskar, 2002/2012a, p. xi).
2 *As a basis of being and of the human self or soul.* This refers to the unified ultimatum or 'ground-state' (Bhaskar, 2002/2012a) out of which the stratified layers of all being, including human being, emerge.

3   *As the deep interior of the cosmos.* At this level, unity and transcendent identity are experiential rather than proven by argument and akin to mystical intuitions as to the all-pervasive presence of the Absolute, i.e. God.

Non-identity and transcendence as constitutive of everyday life

In the previous chapter, I suggested that a dialectical Islamic critical realist understanding of the life of the Prophet Muhammad entailed the idea of divine transcendence breaking in upon the natural and immanent process of dialectical change in the form of the Revelation of the Qur'an and other acts of guidance. Crucially, however, for a metaReal understanding of transcendence and non-identity, transcendence and non-identity are not limited to, or even primarily experienced as, an other-worldly notion of divinity, but are posited by natural necessity in our daily actions on the hermetic principle referred to in Chapter 2. That is to say, transcendental identity is quotidian and essential to the operation and reproduction of daily life. The 'transcendence of duality is a pervasive reality in human action and social life and "the process of enlightenment is a natural extension" of this always-already quotidian transcendence' (Hartwig, 2012, p. xiii).

In order to substantiate these claims about the quotidian nature of transcendental identity, PMR draws upon the idea of transcendence in a variety of different modes.

1   *Transcendence into* – that is the retreat of a being from objectivity, back into self-identity with his or its own subjectivity. [*This the transcendental self.*]

2   *Transcendence onto* – that is the advance of a subject's consciousness into total absorption into objectivity, something outside himself [or herself]. *This is transcendental identification in consciousness.*

3   *Transcendence at, in or on* – total focus or attention on an act, or an act which is spontaneously performed. This is transcendental or non-dual agency.... Note it has the two forms of complete mindfulness or attention and complete spontaneity or mindlessness. In fact these are the only two forms of activity in which ideally one should ever be engaged ... [*This is known as transcendental agency.*]

4   *Transcendence with* – this is transcendental unity in activity, involving teamwork or holistic transcendence. This is exemplified by teamwork in sport, cooking a meal or turn-taking in conversation. [*This is known as transcendental holism.*]

(Bhaskar, 2002/2012c, pp. 4–5; my emphasis)

Thus, for example, the most basic example of oral human communication, the conversation, necessarily involves acts of repeated transcendental identification because it involves the mutual transcendence of the separate consciousnesses of two embodied personalities in the creation of a shared context of meaning. Were transcendental identification in consciousness not a possibility at the level of interpersonal relations, a conversation could not take place. To give another effective, quotidian example of transcendental unity, without the existence of transcendental holism, one would not be able to

> steer one's way around the pavements of a busy London street unless some kind of almost miraculous holistic, synchronicitous performance was taking place. Otherwise one would be bumping into people all the time. One could easily show this by simulating on a computer the chances of crashes or accidents, which are in actual life extremely rare.
>
> (Bhaskar, 2002/2012c, p. 5)

Transcendence in education

Indeed, one can properly analyse a quotidian educational event, such as participating in school class or an academic seminar, as necessarily involving all four modes of transcendental identification.

The act of objectified absorption in what the speaker/teacher is saying is necessarily an act of *transcendental identification in consciousness*. The act of internalising what the speaker is saying, and understanding it in terms of what has already experienced or come to know, is an act of the *transcendental self*. The act of mindfully and respectfully formulating a question for the speaker or preparing a critique is an act of *transcendental agency*. The act of entering into the seminar conversation with that question or critique and moving its collective meaning forward can be an act of *transcendental holism*.

As a basis of being and of the human self or soul

Thus, it is fair to say that a realm of transcendental unity and identification is a necessary precursor that creates the conditions for normal, everyday life. This is the realm identified by PMR as the basic constituent of created being and the ultimate ground of the Self. This Bhaskar (2000) has named the 'ground-state'. The ground-state

> embodies the qualities necessary to bind the universe together as a whole and at the same time is always specifically differentiated in the species or being concerned.... The ground-state qualities of human beings consist *inter alia* in their energy, creativity, love, capacity for right-action and the fulfilment of their intentionality or will in their objectifications in the natural and social world.
>
> (Bhaskar, 2002/2012a, p. xiii)

The ground-state is akin to the religious idea of the soul and the essence of the human being – to quote Dupree in *You, Me and Dupree*, 'That Carl-ness ... that you can't put a price-tag on' (LeSieur, Russo, & Russo, 2006). It is what defines the essential nature of the individual embodied personality when it is released from the illusory ego, of which I will say more later.

As the deep interior of the universe

According to the metaReal account, the ground-state itself is only possible as a result of the existence at the level of the deep interior – what Bhaskar (2000) in secular terms has called the 'cosmic envelope'.

> There is a third level, only slightly more recondite, in virtue of which non-duality can be said to underpin the world of duality and dualism ... if you go deeply enough into any aspect of being you will find buried in its fine structure or deep interior qualities which can only be described in terms of such quasi-metaphorical language as emptiness (*sunyata*), suchness (*tathata*), the void or the Buddha-nature, pure unbounded love or *sat-chi-anand*, that is the bliss consciousness of being.
>
> (Bhaskar, 2002/2012a, p. xiv)

This is the level that comes close to and can enrich and inform the Islamic conception of God that we shall explore later in the chapter when we look at the articles of the Muslim faith. For now, suffice it to say that, because of the existence of the ground-state and the Ultimatum of Ultimata, acts of transcendental identification that underlie daily life are not limited to quotidian experiences of conversation, a class or negotiating a busy street. They may be found in the 'bliss experience' (Bhaskar, 2000) of, to give one of an almost infinite number of possible examples, listening to a sublime piece of music or looking at a wonderful landscape or a piece of art. Indeed, according to this analysis, the pleasure that is gained, for example, from listening to a great orchestra playing a beautiful piece of music, by those who enjoy such things, is not merely due to the harmony of the sound. It also occurs because that sound is the result of, and therefore represents and reminds us of, the unity-in-difference that is the true 'bliss-like' transcendental substratum of existence (cf. Qur'an, 10:19)

During these transcendental experiences of identification, feelings of non-identity, separation and 'otherness' become translucent or are suspended and/or vanish in a moment of identity with some being, state or reality that is greater or 'higher' than our normal selves. Thus, 'In the purest form of [transcendental activity], ground-state is speaking to ground-state' (Bhaskar, 2002/2012c, p. 9).

In terms of ICR, we might call the ground-state the divine spirit (*ruh*) that is the essential life-force of every human being that is 'borrowed' from God as the ultimate honour bestowed on humankind (Qur'an, 15:29; 38:72; 32:8). The ground-state is the divine substratum that sustains at the level of the Real, the human self (*nafs*) at the level of the Actual and the Empirical.

> So when I have proportioned him, completed him, and breathed in him, [when I have] caused to flow [therein], My spirit, so that he becomes a

living [being] then fall down in prostration before him!' – a prostration of salutation [that is actually] a bow.

(Qur'an, 38:72; commentary in brackets by Jalalayn, 1505/2013)

Islamic critical realist transcendence: a hierarchy

Embracing this idea of transcendence from the quotidian to the celestial, we are in a position to posit a hierarchy of transcendence that is particular to the Islamic critical realist perspective:

1   At the bottom of the 'pyramid' are a host of the everyday transactions that necessarily require a transcendental aspect for their effective operation: conversation, work and trade among them.
2   At a 'higher' level are acts of mutual transcendent enrichment through education and the sharing of coherent ideas; through the experience of the sublime via aesthetic transcendence in art, music, sport and other forms of transcendental holistic activity; and through scientific intellectual discoveries that involve the epistemological transcending of received knowledge.
3   At a 'higher' level still is the transcendence of human love and of altruistic acts of solidarity, trust and devotion in which one human spirit or ground-state 'speaks' directly to another in service or sacrifice.

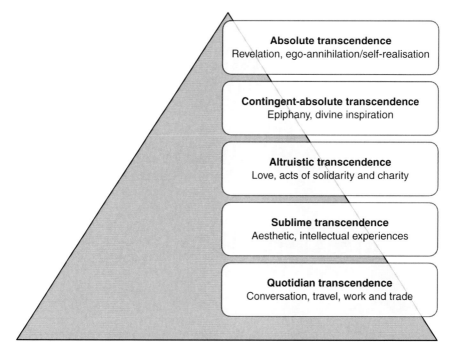

Figure 5.1 Stratified levels of transcendence.

4   At a 'higher' level still comes the experience of divine epiphany and inspiration when the Divine Ground-state communicates directly with the human ground-state.
5   At the pinnacle of transcendence is the obliteration of the human ego and the assumption of the ground-state in the unity of God and similar acts of religious unveiling (Bhaskar, 2000), including the receipt of meaning directly from the presence of the divine, Revelation.

The metaphor of 'height' in each case denotes the extent to which duality is transcended and the illusory separate ego with its 'demi-real' tendencies (see what follows) suspended in order that both the real embodied personality of the human being and its god-like spirit, the ground-state (*ruh*), are unveiled. It is a metaphor of the purity with which one ground-state, including the Divine Ground of all ground-states, speaks to another.

Demi-reality, unbelief (*kufr*) and the meanings of *Jihād*

Central to this claim to the primacy of unity and identity over duality and difference are two related notions. The first, as we have seen, is the idea that the basic conditions of daily life-in-duality (normal duality) are dependent on unity. The second is that the conditions of modernity have given rise to a characteristically individualistic, sharpened and exaggerated form of duality which critical realism has called a *demi-reality*. This gives rise to three essential realms in the philosophy of metaReality:

1   The realm of duality is the 'normal' condition of created being in the form of embodied concrete singular personalities, individual human beings, animals and all other forms of the multiplicity of natural life.
2   Underlying this 'normal' condition, we have posited a necessarily prior and transcendental unity which at a variety of levels from the quotidian to the celestial sustains the diversity/duality.
3   The third realm is the realm of demi-reality. This is the realm of illusory separateness, schism, wrongdoing, discord and split, and of the embodied personality that is at loggerheads with the ground-state/spirit (*ruh*). 'The *dualistic* world of demi-reality [is one] in which the dualities of the world … sharpen into antagonistic, oppositional splits, proliferating into gaping contradictions and producing profound alienation at all the planes of social being' (Bhaskar, 2002/2012a, p. x). It is called *demi*-real since phenomena that are *essentially* illusory and unreal with no grounding in alethic truth-in-being (*Haqq*) may still effect real experiences, changes and outcomes in the world.

For example, a social class or caste structure typically masks the fact that every human being is uniquely a concrete universal existing in four social planes in the same way and to the same degree, each endowed, according to ICR, with a purpose in life to fulfil his/her life's purpose (*qadr/dharma*) to exactly the same extent. Yet social class or caste structures are 'demi-real' because they mask or undermine this essential truth. Nevertheless, these demi-realities will, in a very real and fully experienced way, constrain and limit the possibilities of millions of individuals to fulfil their life's purpose (*qadr/dharma*) and to lead prosperous and happy lives.

Demi-reality on four planes of social being

The reader will remember from Chapter 3 that all social events are conceived of by critical realists as occurring simultaneously on four 'laminated' planes of social being:

a   material transactions with nature;
b   inter-subjective (interpersonal) transactions between differently situated human agents;
c   social relations at the irreducible level of structures, institutions and forms; and
d   the internal stratification of the embodied personality.

(Bhaskar, 1993/2008)

Like any social phenomenon, therefore, *demi-reality* also exists on these four related 'laminated' social planes:

a   At the level of material transactions with nature (a), demi-reality occurs when individuals or collectives through selfishness and/or ignorance and/or greed prevent a just and sustainable distribution of material resources for responsible custody of the planet.
b   At the level of personal interactions (b), demi-reality consists in the barriers and blocks, be they superficial (e.g. personality clashes) or deep-set (structural or educational), to harmonious transcendental *with* forms of communication and interaction generally, including altruistically transcendental love.
c   At the level of irreducible institutional forms (c), demi-reality consists in all that sustains inequitable class structures, e.g. oppressive master–slave-type relations, symbolic violence, and blocks the dialectical social tendency to identity-in-difference and collective recognition of the transcendental and the Transcendent.
d   At the level of the embodied personality (d), demi-reality consists in the illusory ego that incites the embodied personality to actions that belie the existence of the transcendental unity-in-diversity with other human beings and that take the embodied personality into antagonistic inconsistency with its ground-state/spirit (*ruh*) and, therefore, further and further from God.

This metaReal understanding of the idea of demi-reality, and the illusory ego that is principally responsible for it, is close to the related Islamic ideas of *nafs* (ego/self), *Iblis* (the Devil) and Unbelief (*kufr*). Indeed, ICR can extend and enrich the epistemic embrace of these three related concepts. *Nafs* is the infantile and self-absorbed ego that prevents the *ruh* (spirit/ground-state) from transcendental witnessing (Bhaskar, 2002/2012c) of its own essential Reality, because the embodied personality gets trapped in worldly duality or even demi-reality (Qur'an, 79:40; 59:9).

Iblis (the Devil), which is derived from the Arabic verb *balasa*, means 'the one who causes despair'. Thus, in this ICR interpretation the Devil is the intense demi-reality that on the social plane (d) of the individual embodied personality causes despair by dividing the ground-state from a transcendental connection to its own essential ground in the mercy of God and on social planes (a), (b) and (c) drives societies and nations into conditions of antagonism and war, and causes and perpetuates environmental degradation.

Demi-reality as unbelief *(kufr)*

Likewise, *kufr* (unbelief) comes from the Arabic word *ka-fa-ra*, meaning to 'cover up'. Unbelief in the ICR understanding is conceived of, therefore, as a particular form of demi-realitythat consists in covering up the truth – ethical and alethic – in four related 'laminated' social planes:

a   At the level of material transactions with nature (a), *kufr* is covering up our creaturely dependence on nature and its Source. It is a form of ingratitude which manifests as greed, unnecessary waste and persisting in habits of material consumption that threaten the future sustainability of the planet.

b   At the level of personal interactions (b), *kufr* consists in covering up our essential interdependence with other people at the level of the actual and at the level of the real, covering up the truth of every other person's destiny with God (*qadr/dharma*). It manifests at the level of the empirical in rudeness, dishonesty, avoidable unpunctuality and anything else that suggests that one believes oneself and one's life to be *essentially* more important than someone else's.

c   At the level of irreducible institutional forms (c), *kufr* consists in social and governmental institutions that have abandoned the idea that they are answerable to and need to be transparent before both humanity *and* God. It is manifest in political and legal corruption and wrongdoing, and can lead to the ultimate destruction of the grounds of all institutional social life: the preservation of justice.

d   At the level of the embodied personality (d), *kufr* consists in covering up the alethic connection of the human ground-state/spirit (*ruh*) to the Ground of all Being, God. It is manifest both in acts of heedlessness to calls to godlike activity and worship and in the types of action that homeostasise the contingent as eternal and the eternal as contingent, e.g. the accumulation of wealth for its own sake and the pursuit of material luxury.

Combating demi-reality: the true meaning of **Jihād**

It is in the struggle between the realm of normal duality, the essential realm of unity and the illusory realm of demi-reality as *kufr* that the true meaning of *Jihād* resides. *Jihād*, which in Qur'anic language means 'struggle in the path of God', is the struggle to remove (absent) everything that prevents the embodied personality from acting consistently with the ground-state/spirit (*ruh*) and witnessing (of which I shall say more later in the chapter) the reality of God. *Jihād*, just like demi-reality and unbelief, exists in four social planes:

a   At the level of material transactions with nature, *Jihād* is the struggle to ensure the equitable and sustainable distribution and use of the world's resources and the struggle to resist individual and collective selfishness and/ or greed that lead to environmental degradation. These demi-real (*kāfir*) characteristics jeopardise the chances of basic material satisfaction for some and bloat the consumption of finite resources by others to levels way beyond their human needs. *Jihād* at this level includes, *inter alia*, the practical daily struggle to use only such material resources as are necessary, to recycle as much as possible, to travel in fuel-efficient ways, to insulate one's house and to struggle to protect the natural world for the enjoyment of posterity and in support of biodiversity.

b   At the level of personal interactions, *Jihād* is the struggle to effect transcendental unity with other people by identifying and removing the obstacles of the ego and those heteronomous elements and splits in embodied personalities that sully and throw up obstacles to harmonious interaction between individuals. It is the struggle, for example, to be polite, to keep one's word, to honour one's contracts, to respect elderly people and to show tenderness and love to the young.

c   At the societal level of irreducible institutional forms, *Jihād* is the struggle against the realm of the demi-real as it blocks or obscures the tendencies within societies to move towards greater harmony, unity and identity-in-difference. *Jihād* at this level is manifest in the form of diplomacy, conflict resolution, community activism and peacemaking, and standing up for the truth when faced with institutional or quasi-institutional corruption. This *Jihād* may occasionally take the form of a just war, when, as we have seen in the life of the Prophet Muhammad or, for example, the Second World War, the very survival of the tendency of collectives to seek the god-like and just social conditions is violently threatened by a regime in which demi-reality predominates on all social planes. The Prophet Muhammad described this as the 'Lesser *Jihād*' because it is in some ways easier both to identify and to propagate than the 'Greater *Jihād*' of opposing and unveiling the illusory ego – *Jihād* of the fourth level.

d   At the level of the individual and concrete embodied personality, *Jihād* is the lifelong daily struggle, which Muhammad called the 'Greater Struggle', against the insinuating and vicious ego that is propelled towards the illusory pursuit of self-interest in ignorance (*'jāhiliyya'*) of the interdependence of all human being and nature, and of the ultimate dependence of all life on God. It is the struggle of the ground-state/spirit (*ruh*)/Transcendentally Real Self against the ego that incites (*nafs-al-ammara*) the embodied personality to reprehensible acts, including speech and thought-acts of pride, greed, envy, lust, backbiting, stinginess and malice. This ego must be fought and purified (Qur'an, 79:40; 59:9) as, unchecked, it serves the function of perpetuating the realm of demi-reality (*kufr*) by separating the embodied personality from the ground-state (*ruh*).

The dialectics of transcendence: the exemplar of marriage

In order to chart how the levels of transcendent identity-in-difference and unity-in-duality fit with and extend the dialectical development of Being (Moment, Edge, Level, Dimension, MELD) explored in the previous chapter, the philosophy of metaReality has posited three further levels of ontology in addition to those that we have explored in the life of the Prophet Muhammad. These (Bhaskar, 2002/2012c) are:

- the Fifth Aspect of Inwardness (5A);
- the Sixth Realm of Re-enchantment (6R);
- the Seventh Zone of Non-duality (7Z).

These represent the stages of return of the transformed self or community at the level of 4D to the condition of initial primordial unity-in-duality with God and of more complete, transformed and grounded identity-in-difference with other human beings.

One can illustrate this complete schema, MELDARZ, which includes the three levels of ontology described by the philosophy of metaReality, in an ICR exposition of the development of a relationship between a man and a woman in marriage and the role of that relationship in the creation of new life:

- *First Moment (1M): being-as-such/man and woman/duality-in-oppositional unity*. There exist between a man and a woman both identity (as the basic building-block of the human species; cf. Qur'an, 49:13) and, crucially, difference (as the 'opposite' sexes with both essential biological and constructed social differences). It is in both the identity and the difference that the potential for dialectical change and development in the relationship of a man and a woman resides.
- *Second Edge (2E): being-as-process/courtship and engagement*. This process of the dialectical movement of difference towards identity involves moments of quotidian, sublime and altruistic transcendence. Conversations and shared intellectual, emotional and aesthetic experiences, for example, may lead to moments of identity and the transcendental mutual recognition of similarity of embodied personality and potentially of shared *qadr/dharma*

(individual destiny within the divine plan). During this phase the removal of heteronomous elements within the personality and the transcendence of ego-hood can lead to…

- *Third Level: totality of commitment/partnership and marriage.* Individual difference is subsumed in a commitment to share a life and to live by the consequences of shared acts of sustained mutual commitment. This leads to…

- *Fourth Dimension: the necessity of a transformed/transformative and more transcendental daily praxis.* The act of life-sharing entails the necessary and repeated transcendence of illusory ego-hood and mutual approximation to the ground-state and to a more god-like condition through conversation, compromise, negotiation, repeatedly transcending heteronomy and repeated altruistically transcendental acts of love.

- *Fifth Aspect: intercourse and lovemaking.* These other-regarding acts of love lead to or entail spiritual and sexual union, which both expresses and increases the dialectical tendency towards deeper unity. This releases…

- *Sixth Re-enchantment: orgasm/conception.* The space/moment of pure creative non-duality when new life may (or may not, as God wills) emerge. This is the moment when the complete release of immanent human control can occasion transcendental intervention. This space has physical, biological, emotional and spiritual manifestations that are stratified, ontologically united and distinct. This repeated process of re-enchantment in the fullness of time leads to…

- *Seventh Zone: the family.* A new life-space/experience is created and the potential for the further replication of human life is opened up. This life-space involves a transformed adult embodied personality, especially and unavoidably in the woman, since her embodied personality and ground-state during pregnancy and at birth are completely implicated. In this transformation, the illusory ego-hood of the adults is permanently unveiled (to some extent) to reveal the transcendentally real self – that is, if the family is to function and if the parents are to nurture and protect children with other-regarding acts of altruistic transcendental solidarity and love. Of course, this phase may also happen through adoption or guardianship, which merely means that the physical and biological mechanisms at the level of 5A and 6R are replaced by social mechanisms.

At any stage in this relationship, absences, hiatuses, psychological 'sub-totalities' and splits, in the form of infidelities, unresolved issues from childhood, the pressures of the workplace, etc., may arise in either or both parties. These may arrest the movement towards unity or derail it entirely, requiring transcendental outside intervention in the form of psychotherapeutic advice, spiritual guidance or other types of help. Nevertheless, this is an adequate exemplar of the basic model of transformation of being from (relative) non-identity to (relative) identity or unity-in-difference that the philosophy of metaReality holds to be the alethic (*haqqīqī*) condition of all human being.

Such a type of schema or similar might be used by a teacher of young Muslims, for example, to expound the rationale of the Islamic obligation for marriage and to show why the Prophet Muhammad said that marriage comprised half of the life-transaction (*deen*). It suggests that marriage manages a powerful dialectic inherent in human being that, at best, can result in purified embodied personalities that exist in a condition of more mindful unity-in-duality and consistency with the ground-state/spirit (*ruh*).

The philosophy of metaReality, Islamic ethics and Shari'a

This concrete framework for understanding the moments of dialectical change that may be embedded within the relationship – potential and actual – between a man and a woman provides a useful starting point for reflecting on the nature of Islamic law (Shari'a) and ethics in Islam.

For just as the nature of being, as described by the philosophy of metaReality, tends to movement and change from non-identity and difference to unity and identity, so the nature of Islamic ethics and law (Shari'a – Arabic for 'pathway') is to delineate the journey of the human being from the moment of separation from spiritual unity with God and physical unity with the mother at birth to the moment that the ground-state/spirit (*ruh*) sheds its body and everything that is attached to it at death.

In other words, Shari'a describes and provides a framework for the human being at all levels as it moves from non-identity with God and difference from all other human beings as a concretely singular self to identity with all other human beings, at least in the form of dead matter, and eventually spiritual return to God (Qur'an, 2:156). That is to say, in critical realist language, Shari'a in Islam is constellationally embedded in the alethic nature of human being (*ādamiyya*).

The Qur'anic tetrapolity

This idea of Shari'a as constellationally embedded in the nature of human being can be neatly contained by the critical realist idea of four-planar social being brought into line with a Qur'anic world-view that naturally necessitates the existence of Shari'a:

1   *The concrete universal nature of human being (at plane (d)).* All human beings are of the tribe of Adam (*banu Adam*) – that is, they share a basic humanity, sharing properties, needs, tendencies, etc. But they are particular, *inter alia*, in sex, nation, specific tribe, wealth, age, historical moment, the form and arrangement of physical features and historicity, family background and particular abilities (Qur'an, 49:13).
2   *The personal interactions (at plane (b))* into which all humans are thrown (Norrie, 2010) by natural necessity for survival are both benign (e.g. Qur'an, 49:13) and also potentially damaging (Qur'an, 49:11), and therefore require regulation by . . .

3   *Universally recognised parameters of behaviour and a nexus of axiomatic*
     rights (at plane (c)) and entitlements (Şentürk, 2002). The Arabic word for
     rights – *haqq*, pl. *huqquq* – is again suggestive of the fact that ethical and
     alethic truth are embedded in the nature of being. These axiomatic rights
     and duties together comprise a Path (Shari'a) that is conducive to collective
     human well-being in the consistency of the embodied personality with the
     ground-state and…
4   *Protective of the created material universe (at plane (a))* over which God
     has delegated unconditional stewardship to humanity as an act of trust and
     recognition (Qur'an, 2:30–34).

In other words, in this Qur'anic metaReal understanding, the duality of the universe in its diverse constituent pairs of opposites at the levels of the empirical
and the actual is trumped by Identity and Unity at the level of the Ultimately
Real. Created reality is described by the Qur'an as series of interwoven dualities
which are themselves intrinsically related in such a way as to indicate their
source in Absolute Unity: Life–Death, Night–Day, Male–Female, This World–
Next World. 'He brings the living out of the dead and the dead out of the
living …' (Qur'an, 3:27). We manage, exist in, are tested by the realm of
immanent duality (Qur'an, 67: 1–2); we yearn for, and are healed and nourished
by, experiences of transcendental unity (cf. Bhaskar, 2002/2012c). Non-identity/
duality, as have have seen, is very real: men and women, and nations, are different and live in dualities that often sharpen into a state of demi-real enmity and
antagonism (Qur'an, 2:35–36). Identity, however, is more real and more essential to human life (Qur'an, 49:13).

Understanding particular Islamic requirements for modesty and the
prohibition of intoxicants

This idea of Islamic ethics being constellationally embedded in the nature of
being also helps explain the rationale for some of the particular rulings of
Islamic law (Shari'a) that regulate, for example, relationships between men and
women, which may be understood as having the potential to exist, broadly
speaking, in the dialectical relationship described above. The requirements for
modesty both of dress and behaviour, which involve, *inter alia*, avoiding clothes
that accentuate the contours of the body for both sexes and extra-marital sexual
activity or actions that might lead to sex outside marriage (Qur'an, 23:5–7;
24:30–33; 70:29–31) can be understood as a recognition of the innate physical,
social, spiritual structure of human being. The powerful tendency of the
'opposite' sexes to move dialectically from non-identity and difference into
union of all different types entails the need for that tendency to be actualised
within parameters that protect the axiomatic rights (to life, property, religious
freedom, safety and nourishment) of both men and women (Şentürk, 2002).
   Far from being an attempt to keep men and women apart, the requirements
for modesty of both dress and behaviour in Shari'a exist to facilitate the coming

together of men and women in a way that is realistic about the innate *and* socially formed structures, properties and tendencies of human being. As we have seen, human beings not only can exist in 'normal' difference as the duality of different embodied personalities, but also can be trapped in the realm of the demi-real, in the zone of the nightmarish self-perpetuation of error, heteronomy, sharpened antagonism and violence, of which the twentieth century was replete with ghastly historical examples. Shari'a is meant to regulate and avoid the perpetuation of the demi-real on the four planes of social being.

Similarly, the fact that Shari'a forbids the consumption of intoxicants of all types (Qur'an, 2: 219; 5, 93–94) is not an ethical imposition of a Being beyond being, but an act of existential recognition of being by Being that intoxicants are, for the most part (Qur'an, 2:219), prejudicial to the health and well-being of human life. In other words, this prohibition can be understood as an act of divine mercy or of *al-Latif*, the One who is Subtly All-Aware.

Crucial to this Islamic critical realist approach to ethics, and an intrinsic corollary of the above, is that while things that are forbidden by Shari'a are inimical *sui generis* to the health and welfare of human being, so it is also inimical to human well-being that people should be unnecessarily prevented from doing things that *are* allowed by God and whose nature is to be conducive to stimulating positive dialectical change and human flourishing (Qur'an, 5:87). The ethics of Islam promote the recognition of God-recognition and human-flourishing in balanced and equal measure. We will revisit this idea when discussing an approach to culture in Chapter 9.

Understanding Islamic ethics in non-Islamic environments

This principle of the priority of ontology in Islamic ethics also sustains philosophically the correct Islamic attitude to living in non-Muslim lands. The Muslim living in a non-Muslim land is required to obey the law of that land as if it were Shari'a unless the law of that land explicitly forbids the believer from obeying Shari'a. An example would be if British law forbade marriage (al-Qadah, 2014). In such a case, the Muslim is required either to emigrate or act peacefully to have a law changed. Thus, by recognising as legal the contingent circumstances of the believer, Shari'a makes it easy for the Muslim believer to act godfully and in tune with his or her ground-state/spirit (*ruh*), and to integrate authentically with the contingent customs that surround him or her. Indeed, in certain circumstances, custom and tradition ('*Urf*) may become a source of Shari'a. So, Shari'a enables the believer to belong, legally as well as emotionally, in circumstances, such as those of contemporary Britain, that are not overtly 'Islamic'. In adopting this attitude of integrative and transformative lawfulness, Muslims in non-Muslim lands can, perhaps, learn from Judaism and its rabbinic teaching of *dina d'malkhuta dina* ('the law of the land is the law'), which allowed Jewish communities to establish themselves and flourish in medieval Christian Europe, often in the face of acute discrimination and hostility (Kessler, 2013).

Thus, obedience to the law in (and of) Islam can be understood not as compliance with a set of injunctions that are extraneous to the structure of human and natural being but as a critical and realistic submission to the nature of Being-Itself. Ethical obedience in Islam is one important means of both unveiling and restraining the realm of the demi-real (*kāfir*) ego-hood and for allowing the human being to exist healthily in four-planar social being in increasing approximation to the ground-state and to God. This is why, returning to a theme of the introduction, Islam is referred to as a *deen* (or life-transaction), as every act or lived moment is understood as an opportunity for the believer to attune him- or herself more closely to the ground-state/spirit (*ruh*) or to become less attuned to it and further from the presence of God.

So far, I have alluded to types of ethical consideration that in Islamic parlance are known as *mu'amalāt*, or actions connected with daily life. This was appropriate, given my starting point of the quotidian nature of unity and transcendence. However, given that the criterion of seriousness $_{(r + p)}$ requires that right action is hand in glove with right belief, I now wish to consider, from a metaReal point of view, matters that pertain to divine worship – in Islamic parlance, *'ibadāt*. First, I will consider the six Islamic Articles of Faith that are stipulated by the Qur'an and the Sunna: God, His Angels, His Messengers, His Books, His Decree and His Day of Reckoning. Then I will consider the five obligatory pillars of Islamic worship: Witnessing (*ash-Shahada*), Prayer (*as-Salat*), the Social Welfare Tax (*az-Zakat*), the Fast (*as-Sawm*) and Pilgrimage (*al-Hajj*).

The Islamic Articles of Faith

God

God (Arabic *Allah*, the One worthy of Worship) is uniquely the heart and focus of Islamic worship and belief. God is described in the Qur'an as follows: 'Say [Muhammad]: He, God is One; God is the Eternal, Absolute; He does/did not give birth, nor is He begotten; And there is no being like Him' (Qur'an, 112:1–4).

The Qur'an has been thought traditionally to describe the Supreme Being as Supremely Transcendent and, following the lead of the Qur'an and the Sunna, a traditional codification of belief (*'aquīda*) about God that was formulated, for example, in the School of Abu al-Hasan al-Ash'ari (874–936) runs as follows:

1 God is One, undivided in His Essence. His Unity is Absolute.
2 There is no second with Him in His Divinity. He is uniquely worthy of worship.
3 He is Living and Self-Subsistent and sustains all other being without diminishment.
4 He is neither diminished by time nor does sleep overtake him.
5 He is God of everything and its Creator.
6 He has power over everything.

7   He knows what is outwardly apparent and inwardly hidden.
8   He wills every created being and event.
9   He hears, sees and speaks without bodily parts and without instrument.
10   There is nothing like Him.

('Iyad, *c*.1110/1982)

This tradition, which emphasises God's transcendent power and knowledge *over* His creation, and His ineffability,is complemented in the Qur'an and in the Sunna by an Islamic tradition of divine immanence, intimacy and knowability. For example, the Qur'an declares,'When My servants ask you [Muhammad] about Me, say that I am always near. I answer their prayers when they pray to Me. The people shall respond to Me and believe in Me, in order to be guided' (Qur'an, 2:186).

The proximity of God's Being to human being, the Ground of All Being to the ground-state, is described in the Qur'an not only epistemically in terms of His knowledge and guidance (Qur'an, 34:50), but also ontologically in terms of His closeness to the very structure of being and to the core of the human self: 'It is We who created humankind, and we know what dark suggestions his/her soul makes to him/her: for We are nearer to him/her than his/her jugular vein' (Qur'an, 50:16). In other words, the Being of God, in this Islamic critical realist understanding that takes account of both transcendence and immanence, is both:

i   *absolute* – independent (self-sufficient autonomous) being, and
ii   *alethic* – the ultimate ground or deepest categorical truth of all other things, and thence of all beings, i.e. totality. God is both the self-grounded ultimatum and the inner categorical core structure of reality; the existentially and essentially constitutive basic truth and ground of all grounds of the rest of it.

(Bhaskar, 2000, pp. 41–42)

In this conception of God, which is true to the tradition of Islam and the core understandings of critical realism, the immanence of God must necessarily be apprehended in a mode of transcendence, and the Transcendence of God must be manifest and recognised immanently from the point of view of contingent being. Transcendence and immanence are both necessarily characteristics of a God who (1) at once creates *and* sustains the universe, and (2) is known and worshipped by those He[1] has created.

The names and attributes of God

God is said in the Islamic tradition to have 99 attributes, with corresponding names. These names are divided into names of Majesty – e.g. the Compeller (*al-Jabbār*), the Abaser (*al-Khāfiḍ*), the Avenger (*al-Muntaqim*), the Bringer of Death (*al-Mumīt*) – and the names of Mercy – e.g. the Intensely Merciful (*ar-Rahim*), the Ever-Forgiving (*al-Ghaffār*), the Ever-Providing (*ar-Razzāq*), the

Subtly Aware (*al-Latif*). In a Prophetic tradition, God has said, 'My Mercy prevails over my Wrath', and every chapter of the Qur'an bar one (9) begins with the phrase 'In the name of God, the Universally Merciful, the Intensely Merciful.'

Mercy is, therefore, the characteristic that is most appropriately connected with God, and His other names can be considered as a subset of this general attribute. For example, His bringing of life is a Mercy, in that He perpetuates the universe by it and new life brings joy and hope to humankind and the chance of knowledge of Him. His bringing of death is a Mercy, in that it releases the spirit/ground-state/spirit (*ruh*) from the embodied personality and the illusory ego, and opens up the possibility of Paradise and witnessing God directly (Mahmutćehajić, 2011). His bestowing of gifts is Merciful because it brings increase, and in other circumstances His withholding of the gifts is also a Mercy as it stimulates gratitude, life-skills and spiritual calling on God; every gift and opening has its correct moment. Even a natural disaster from the perspective of those who have moved from a less forgiving to a more forgiving realm of existence may be viewed as a Mercy. Indeed, those who die in natural disasters in Islam die as martyrs.

In our ICR understanding, there is a strong indication of the primacy of the divine aspect of Mercy in the fact that all human activity, even the most apparently iniquitous, is necessarily sustained by god-like and virtuous behaviour (Bhaskar, 2000): the pirate crew bent on rape, pillage and plunder only functions through obedience to the captain, harmonious social relations and knowledgeable sailing; a unit of soldiers operating in a vicious war only functions effectively through acts of transcendental holism and even acts of altruistic sacrifice and love. Everything that happens is grounded somehow in Mercy and Love: the task of the Transcendentally Real Self is to discover how this is and to transform the demi-realities (*kufr*) that are obscuring the Merciful Alethic Ground of any given phenomenon. This has traditionally been the task of what Christian thinkers have called 'theodicy'.

His Angels

The Islamic belief in Angels is a statement of the Muslim refusal to yield to a disenchanted (Taylor, 2007) ontology that excessively privileges the seen, material and measured over the unseen, immaterial and immeasurable. In fact, Angels both symbolise and enact the connection of the seen with the unseen and the unseen with the seen (Mahmutćehajić, 2011). Angels in the Islamic cosmology are beings of pure light that exist in the unseen and are dedicated exclusively to the worship of God (Qur'an, 21:20; 41:38). They relay the commands of God from the divine presence to earth and carry them out, as well as recording the actions of humankind. The most important of them perform vital cosmological functions:

- Jibra'il (Gabriel) is the angel responsible for human–divine communication. In the scheme of the ICR hierarchy of transcendence, Gabriel is the vehicle of Absolute Transcendence, e.g. Revelation, and Contingent-Absolute Transcendence, e.g. prophetic inspiration. Gabriel is the archangel who was responsible for revealing the Qur'an to Muhammad, verse by verse, and who was responsible for announcing the miraculous birth of Jesus to Mary.

- Israfil (Raphael) is an archangel in Islam who will blow the trumpet twice at the end of time. It is said that the first blow will end all life, while the second blow will bring all human beings back to life again to meet their Lord on the Day of Reckoning.
- Mikail (Michael) is charged with the distribution of material provision and natural resources. Michael is often depicted as the archangel of mercy who is responsible for bringing rain and thunder to earth. He is also responsible for the rewards given to good people in this life and in a relationship to the universe that is akin to the Hindu idea of *karma* in the Vedanta tradition, i.e. 'what goes around comes around'.
- 'Azrael (Azrael), also known as *Malak al-Maut*, the angel of death, is responsible for removing the Transcendentally Real Self/ground-state/spirit(*ruh*) from the embodied personality upon death (Qur'an, 79:1–2). For some, for whom the embodied personality has acted in consistency with the ground-state, this extraction will be smooth and painless; for others, for whom the ground-state has been obscured by demi-reality (*kufr*) and wrong action, this extraction will be painful and harsh (Qur'an, 79:1–2).

It is perfectly possible to understand Angels, thus conceived, as a rational component of the cosmos – as, in effect, the agents of transcendental communication between the realm of Unity and the divine command and the realm of duality at the level of the Ultimately Real, before the divine command is enacted sensibly and materially at the levels of the actual and the empirical. Importantly, they are a statement of the Islamic belief in the unseen realm that is inaccessible to empirical testing, although there are human beings, such as prophets, whose ground-state/spirit is in such a condition of purity (Averroes, 1179/2001) that they have been granted glimpses into the unseen.

As we saw in Chapter 1, according to the criteria of ontological realism the empirical unknowability of the realm of the unseen is not a decisive factor in either its existence or its non-existence. We know from the history of science that ontology exists independently of epistemology: things that we do not know about or understand at any given moment may indeed exist, such as gravity, cells, protons, quarks and the Higgs boson particle, and things that are believed fervently to exist at any given moment may, in fact, have no reality, e.g. geocentricity, phlogiston and the four humours.

His Messengers

Similarly to the Angels, the Prophets (*anbiyyā*) and Messengers of God (*rusul*) are agents of transcendental communication who mediate between the Ground of All Being, God, and the human ground-state/spirit. They convey the means to their mutual alignment through acts of worship, obedience and patterns of healthy behaviour (*Sunna*). Thus, they are the human intermediaries from the realm of Absolute Unity and the Divine command to the realm of duality at the levels of the real, the actual and the empirical.

Islam distinguishes between a few Messengers (*rusul*) who are 'major Prophets' and have been given a divinely revealed book – Noah, Abraham, Moses, David, Jesus and Muhammad – and thousands (124,000) of prophets (*anbiyyā*) who have been charged throughout human history with communicating the message of Divine Unity and ethically sound behavior, but who do not transmit a book. Messengers and Prophets are beings in whom the Ground of All Being is permitted to shine through a purified ground-state as the moon at night reflects the light of the sun. They are, nevertheless, in all respects human beings.

His Books

The Books of Revelation that are communicated by the Angel Gabriel to the Messengers for the guidance of humankind are the Torah, the Psalms of David, the Gospels (in a pre-Pauline form) and the Qur'an. They are descriptions by the Ground of All Being of Himself and the relationship between Him and humans in four-planar natural-social being. They emerge from the realm of Absolute Transcendence. The Books present the nature of a covenantal transaction (*deen*) between the Creator and the creature that is sacred, and they describe in some detail some of the history of this covenantal transaction and its eschatology. They also describe the cosmos in a way that transcends the contingencies of individual epochs and, as such, is alethically truthful (although open to wrong interpretation). It is in their nature to require careful exegesis and interpretation in order that timeless principles can be applied justly in time-bound circumstances (Ramadan, 2009). Thus, if we apply the framework of ICR, the Books are ontologically real and apprehended by humans who are positioned, epistemically relative beings. This means, therefore, that the Books require diligent, exegetical judgemental rationality to determine their best possible, though still fallible, contingent interpretation.

His Decree

Every event and phenomenon in the world, both good and bad, happens as a result of the preordained will of the Creator (*al-qadā wa'l-qadar*) (Qur'an, 9:51) which has been written on the Preserved Tablet (*Lawh al-Mahfudh*) of the universe from before endless time. This preordination exists at the level of Absolute Unity and is occasionally apprehended by the human ground-state (in the heart) in a moment of contingent–Absolute transcendence. This apprehension may come in the feeling of deep cosmic inevitability of chains of apparently unconnected events and of the mutual unfolding of one's individual life-destiny in relation to the life-destinies of countless others and other events – that is, in the apprehension of an individual's unique and particular place in the mosaic of cosmic coincidence.

At the level of the Ultimately Real, all events and phenomena are held by Islam to be preordained. At the level of the empirical and actual, quotidian circumstances of life, human free will exists and is necessarily an element of the moral accountability that is a necessary precondition of the final Article of Faith: the Day of Reckoning. That is to say, we are free agents of all our actions within the contingent circumstances of being time-bound creatures and we are free to judge the ethical and legal value of our actions both before, during and after we undertake them.

The Day of Reckoning

The Day of Reckoning is the day, according to Muslim belief, when every embodied personality will be reconstituted to account before God for what each of us has done in this earthly life (Qur'an, 99). Thus, the Day of Reckoning is the portal to the next life, either to eternal bliss, as the ground-state is freed to approach its Ultimate, Absolute Source by degrees through the spiritual delights of Paradise, or to eternal separation and alienation, as the now-disembodied personality, enmeshed in demi-reality, is removed from its ground-state/spirit (*ruh*) by degrees for eternity (Qur'an, 79; 99). Nevertheless, the Prophet Muhammad said that only the most heinous of wrongdoers will be removed from the Divine Presence for ever. In other words, the impulse for the identification of the ground-state with the Ground of All Being is so foundational and essential to every human being that once the necessary purification of split and wrong action has taken place, this dialectical tendency of non-identity and difference towards Unity and Identification cannot be resisted, except for those in whom the demi-real (*kufr*) has, like aggressive ivy, permanently overgrown and choked them now-disembodied personality.

The Qur'an (99:8) states that on the Day of Reckoning, each limb will make an account before God of what it has done. In other words, every part of the embodied personality will declare heteronomous acts that were driven by the illusory ego, consequences of which will be 'stuck' to the self in the form of absences, gaps and splits as proof of the consequences of demi-reality (*kufr*). In the presence of the Ground of All Being, these small and large absences and incompletions will speak for themselves (Qur'an, 91:20–22). In short, the belief in the Day of Reckoning is a further statement of an rationally enchanted worldview in which the material, measurable and seen (empirical) is not the be-all and end-all of the moral ontology of the universe.

The Five Pillars of Islam

So far, I have given an account of the traditional Islamic articles of faith in a way that does justice, I believe, both to the primary sources of Islam – the Qur'an and the Prophetic tradition (Sunna) – and to the principles of transcendence and the primacy of existential unity over duality that characterise the philosophy of metaReality. This account shows how the philosophy of metaReality underlabours for

Islamic doctrine in a way that can unveil its internal philosophical coherence and ontological depth.

However, as we have seen from Chapter 1, belief/knowledge is serious $_{(r + p)}$ only if it is partnered by right and appropriate action. The most basic form of appropriate right action in Islam that is the necessary corollary of right knowledge/belief is the so-called Five Pillars of Islam. These are prescribed in the Qur'an and the Sunna and explicitly linked together in a famous Prophetic saying (*hadith*):

> On the authority of Abu 'Abd ar-Rahman 'Abdullah, son of 'Umar ibn Al-Khattab, who said: I heard the Messenger of God say:
>
> Islam has been built on five [pillars[2]]: Witnessing that there is no divinity but God and that Muhammad is the Messenger of God, establishing the Prayer, paying the Social Welfare Tax, making Pilgrimage to the House of God, and fasting the month of Ramadan.
>
> (Related by al-Bukhari and Muslim)

The Witnessing

The Witnessing (*ash-Shahadah*) that *there is no divinity but God* (Allah) *and that Muhammad is the Messenger of God* aloud in front of two adult Muslim witnesses is the gateway to Islam; it is the declaration of faith. It is also repeated after the ritual ablution with water before the Obligatory Prayer, during the Obligatory Prayer and at other pivotal moments in the Muslim day. Thus, it is a speech act (Austin, 1962) by concrete, embodied personalities (*nufus*) of witnessing the alethic truth of God, the Ground of All Being, as revealed to the most purified of all ground-states/spirits, Muhammad, and the other Messengers. In order for it to be a serious $_{(r+p)}$ speech act rather than an empty ritual, the witnessing requires transcendental mindfulness *in* its declaration and *with* other believers if it is to be efficacious in preparing the embodied personality for consequent acts of worship/unification, e.g. the Obligatory Prayer.

The Obligatory Prayer

The Prophet Muhammad described the Obligatory Prayer (*as-Salat*) as the 'foundation' of the Muslim's transaction with God and the act that separates the Muslim from the non-Muslim. The word *as-Salat* is derived from the related word *as-silat*, meaning 'a connection'. In other words, the Obligatory Prayer represents in itself a commitment to seriousness $_{(r+p)}$ that binds together action and belief, the servant with the Lord, the ground-state/spirit with the Ground of all Being.

The Qur'an describes the Prayer as forbidding immorality and wrongdoing (29:45). In other words, it is a transformative act that embodies seriousness $_{(r+p)}$. The Obligatory Prayer is the embodiment of seriousness $_{(r+p)}$ since is it described in the Qur'an not only as 'prescribed activity' (4:103) but also as an 'establishment' in the daily life of the believer (e.g. Qur'an, 2:43; 5:55; 31:4). 'Establishment' means that its prescribed moments before dawn, at midday, in the mid-afternoon at sunset and at nightfall demarcate the Muslim day and give the day a transcendent–immanent rhythm of the tightening and loosening of the grip of the realm of normal duality (including demi-reality [*kufr*] and the illusory ego) on the embodied personality (*nafs*) and reconnection with the ground-state/spirit and God.

The Obligatory Prayer is constituted by cycles of movements – standing and reciting the Qur'an, bowing, prostrating and sitting – that both represent and enact different modes of the relationship of the human being with God, the creature with the Creator, the servant with the Master, the ground-state with the Ground of all Being. These movements also represent the cyclical interrelationship of creation–life–death–resurrection and enact before God the dynamic ontology of the human being, who is both God's representative and master over creation (*khalif*) and the servant of God ('*abd*) who is absolutely dependent on God and interdependent with society and nature (Blackhirst, 2003).

As the worshipper enters into the Prayer, he or she calls out, 'God is greatest', and with a complementary movement of the arms puts the world of vicious demi-reality (*kufr*), including the illusory ego, behind him or her. As the worshipper stands (*quiyyam*) and recites the Qur'an, he or she acknowledges the natural, healthy realm of duality and apparent separation of the creature and the Creator, the exhaustible embodied personality standing before and in relation to its inexhaustible alethic, constituent Ground. In the standing position, he or she is the *khalif* who connects, as the only upright animal (Blackhirst, 2003), heaven and earth, Creator and creation, the Being of God with the knowledge and worship of God.

The bowing (*ruku'*) is the recognition of dependence on God, which is, ultimately, independence from everything that is not God. It is the movement of the embodied personality towards the ground-state away from duality and demi-reality. It is the beginning of the humbling of the ego and the relinquishing of the status of *khalif*-hood and the acknowledgement of servanthood ('*abdiyya*) in the face of a Majestic Lord.

The prostration (*sajda*) is the bodily and spiritual enactment of unity – the unity of the ground-state with the Ground of all Being and the unity of the material substance of human kind with the earth from which it has emerged and to which it is returning (Qur'an, 36:7–8). It is the obliteration of the outward differences of the embodied personality, represented by the visible face, in recognition of our ultimate sameness as servants of God. It is the 'dive to the ground-state' (Bhaskar, 2002/2012b, p. 19), a moment in which the trappings of illusorily ego-hood are eradicated in order that ground-state/spirit can re-emerge to reconnect and communicate with the Ground of All Being, God. It is a condition in which the wrongdoings of the ego and gross categorical error that obscure the Divine Source from the embodied personality and generate demi-reality (*kufr*) on four-planar social being can be presented in a fitting state of abasement to God and released. The prostration also represents the position of the Adamic birth when the spirit of God was lent to humankind (Blackhirst, 2003); thus, it is a moment of spiritual renewal and realignment when the world is momentarily shed in order that it may be more wholesomely and transformatively re-embraced.

The prostrations are interposed by sitting (*julus*) on the floor in a return to duality in order to take stock of the weaknesses and flaws in the embodied personality in humility before in the presence of Absolute Purity (*al-Quddus*), before the worshipper returns to the prostration for further purification and release. The act of spiritual purification of the Obligatory Prayer is reinforced by the third Pillar, the Social Welfare Tax.

The Social Welfare Tax

The Social Welfare Tax is the acknowledgement of the fact that the spiritual health of the individual is constellationally embedded in the health and equity of society and that the good of all is dependent on the good of each (Bhaskar, 1993/2008, chapter 3). As we have seen, according to Islamic seriousness$_{(r+p)}$, remembrance of God entails responding to the needs of one's fellow humankind. The Social Welfare Tax has two components (Qur'an, 9:60): an obligatory element comprising 2.5% of the savings of those who have reached a certain threshold of wealth (*nisāb*), to be paid to an Islamic authority for the upkeep of the poor, the destitute, travellers and those who are struggling in the path of God, and for the easing of those in debt; and a voluntary component, consisting of regular alms-giving to charity or those who may need help at any given moment (Qur'an, 2:215). Thus, the Social Welfare Tax is an act of transcendental solidarity *with* humanity. It is an expression of solidarity that acknowledges our interconnectedness on the four planes of social being, grounded in the ultimate level of the real at which we are all equally (though differently) creatures before God. Thus, the Social Welfare Tax is both an expression of and transformative of natural-social reality. It is an act of giving up and the removal (absenting) of material excess in order to encourage the immaterial transcendental solidarity that sets up the conditions of human flourishing. This is reinforced by the next Pillar of Islam, the Fast.

The Fast

The Fast is instituted in the month of Ramadan every year so that, in the words of the Qur'an (2:183–185), humans may learn self-restraint and increase in awareness of the presence of God. Outwardly, it is to refrain from all solid and liquid nourishment between before dawn and sunset and then, according to the Sunna, to consume these things only in moderation at night. Inwardly, it is to refrain from speech, action and thought that is displeasing to God and which therefore creates illusory distance between the ground-state/spirit and the embodied personality. The Fast awakens the awareness of our dependence on the provision of God and gratitude to Him for the day-to-day sustenance that we receive from Him which strips away the illusion of secondary causes (Averroes, 1179/2001) and generative mechanisms. True to the spirit of Islamic serious-ness$_{(r+p)}$, the Fast is also designed to awaken solidarity with the poor (Abdalati, 1975) in contemplation of feelings of hunger and basic material want that in turn lead to spontaneous and transformative giving. Thus, acts of voluntary charity in the month of Ramadan are believed to be particularly conducive to the well-being both of the giver and of the recipient. At the level of unity-in-duality, the Fast weakens the grip of the ego on the ground-state/spirit that is liberated to sense deeper identity-in-difference with other human beings and the potential to draw near to God (Qur'an, 2:146).

The Hajj

The Hajj is the embodiment of death and the stripping down of the human being to the bare essentials of our contingent creatureliness before the Absolute, the Almighty. It is the ritual recognition of the fact that we are naked before the Truth of God and can hide nothing from him. Thus, it is the completion of the surrender to God (*deen al-Islam*) by human beings in ritual enactment of the reality that death and the present moment are the life's only certainties (Mahmutćehajić, 2011).

On entering the zone of the Hajj, both men and women don the *ihram*, which is the white funeral shroud in which they will be buried and in which they are permitted to kill no living creature. The rites of Hajj involve, *inter alia*, the entry into Mecca and the first sight of the House of God, the Ka'aba, where God was first worshipped by the Prophet Abraham. This is a moment of powerful tran-scendental agency, the objectification of the ground-state/spirit (*ruh*) together with embodied personality in reflection on the house and its centrality to millen-nia of monotheistic worship. This is resolved into transcendence *in* the circum-ambulation (*tawāf*) of the House, which represents the ground-state, located in the heart, revolving around its source, stripped of the trappings of the ego or the embodied personality, in an echo of the Angels' circumambulation of the throne of God (al-Ghazāli, *c*.1090/1983). Next, the pilgrim runs or walks between the promontories of Safa and Marwa in remembrance/re-enactment of Hagar's des-perate search for water for her baby, the Prophet Ismail. The pilgrim needs to be mindful of the fluctuation of the balance of his or her actions on the Day of Reckoning and his or her utter dependence of the grace of God for the most basic source of life, water.

On the Day of Hajj (*Arafa*) itself, after nights spent under canvass, i.e. in the bare minimum of shelter, at Mina, the pilgrim travels, preferably on foot, i.e. in a condition of humility, to the plain of Arafa, where Adam, Abraham and Muham-mad were all supplicants before the mercy of God. Thus, the pilgrim enters a condition of contingent–Absolute transcendence, begging forgiveness and acknow-ledging the condition of surrender to being human-before-God. This means being at once a microscopic human part of an immense divine plan and thus almost completely insignificant, and at the same time, as a concrete singular individual, being of integral and indispensable significance to the divine plan. Thus, the Hajj is an acknowledgement of finitude in surrender to the Infinite, the equality of human-kind and solidarity of human being with the living matter of the whole of creation.

In summary

The Prophet Muhammad was asked whether, if the believer were to complete the Five Pillars of Islam and performed no other act of worship, he or she would enter Paradise. He answered, 'Yes.' In other words, the Five Pillars of Islam delineate the necessary transaction (*deen*) of the Muslim believer with God, to which nothing more need be added for him or her to effect a serious $_{(r+p)}$ rela-tionship with God. The Five Pillars reflect the existence of the believer on the four social planes described by the philosophy of critical realism. They also express the fact that these four social planes are permeated and made possible by the quotidian transcendence and by the fifth plane: that of the celestial tran-scendent realm of Ultimate, Unified Reality.

Notes

1 The Arabic pronoun used for God is '*Huwa*', which translates as 'He'. This does not preclude the inclusion of the feminine within the divine, as in Arabic the default pronoun used for phenomena with masculine and feminine aspects is always '*Huwa*' – he – rather than '*Hiyya*' – she. Thus, He in this Qur'anic sense is non-gendered. Equally, the Qur'anic word for mankind, '*Insān*', should be considered as non-gendered and to refer to humanity.
2 The Arabic word for 'pillars' (*arkān*) does not appear in the Arabic transmission. The word 'pillars' is generally accepted to convey the meaning of the hadith most appropri-ately in this context.

Part III

Generating success with humanities education

6 Towards an ontology of educational success

Muslim young people in humanities education

Introduction: from theory to research to practice

Part II of the book represented an attempt to show how the philosophy of Islamic critical realism can 'underlabour' for the re-emergence of the coherent, spiritual rationality of the Islamic faith in multi-faith contexts. I have attempted to show the young Muslim and his or her educators how the Islamic *deen* (life-transaction with God) can embrace and be enhanced by a systematic engagement with contemporary philosophy. This part of the book applies that approach to the education of Muslim young people in multi-faith contexts. It suggests that the practical philosophy of Islamic critical realism can 'underlabour', for the generation of multidimensional young Muslims, success through education, with a focus on the humanities subjects: history, religious education and citizenship. It aims to show how these subjects can facilitate an informed, integrated and transformative engagement of young Muslims with the contemporary multi-faith world.[1]

Consistent with the critical realist approach outlined so far, Part III begins in this chapter at the dialectical moment of 1M (First Moment – being-as-such) with questions of ontology: *what* is the nature of young Muslims in humanities education and what facets of the human being do, and can, the humanities subjects educate? It will discuss the nature of young Muslims in education both from the point of view of previous empirical research analysed through the lens of ICR and then through a discussion of original research into Muslim youth in history education that presents a contrasting point of view.

In subsequent chapters, I will address at the levels of 2E (Second Edge – absence), 3L (Third Level – totality) and 4D (Fourth Dimension – transformative praxis) questions of epistemology alongside ontology: *how* can the different humanities subjects be brought to bear to bring about this education for productive engagement of young Muslims with the multi-faith world? The empirical case focus of this ontological inquiry is British Muslim youth in humanities education, especially history, in English schools, but I believe that the model of the learner and the insights derived from the case study will be transferable to other, non-British multi-faith settings. The introduction of an empirical, research focus at this point represents a deductive drilling down from the theory of the previous part at the level of the real to the actual and empirical-practical realities of the contemporary humanities classroom.

1M: who are young Muslims in education?

The reductive contemporary educational policy context for young Muslims

Pring (2010) has suggested that, traditionally, in European educational models the humanities subjects were concerned with the development of individuals' humanity: in other words, subjects such as literature, history and religious education nurtured the development of the young human being's ability to respond to the world and other people informatively and humanely. By contrast, young Muslims' humanity in Britain and elsewhere has been subject in recent years to a reductive and often inhumane educational policy agenda that has increasingly, since the terrorist attacks of 9/11 (2001) in New York and 7/7 (2005) in London, come to view young Muslims in education through the prism of national security (K. E. Brown, 2010).

Since the early 2000s, when Asian British Muslims became the topic of intense academic interest, a broad characterisation of Muslim young people as 'believers' whose powerful religious identities 'trump' a commitment to 'secular' education, in contrast to Sikh and Hindu 'achievers', who have higher educational aspirations, has often informed educational attitudes to Asian youth in British schools (Alexander, 2000; Archer, 2003; Hussain, 2008; Shain, 2010).

These stereotypes of Muslim youth as driven by one-dimensional religious or quasi-religious fervour have been reinforced, post 9/11 and 7/7, by the War on Terror and the Preventing Violent Extremism policy agenda, which has percolated into the school and higher educational environment (Shain, 2010). Teachers and lecturers have been increasingly required to spot any propensity in their Muslim charges to radicalisation and violent extremism, and educate them away from these tendencies (Sayyid & Vakil, 2010). For Muslim boys, these stereotypes have clustered around both a real and an imagined vulnerability and a propensity for radicalisation and violent extremism, while for girls they have focused intensely on Islamic dress codes such as the wearing of the *hijāb* (modest clothing, including the Islamic headscarf) and the *niqāb* (full veil). All of these stereotypes have been supposed to evince a distancing from or rejection of both liberal, secular values and national belonging, in our case 'Britishness' (Mirza, Senthilkumaran & Ja'far, 2007).

At the same time as these overwhelmingly negative stereotypes surrounding Muslim youth were solidifying and intensifying (1997–2013), it is well documented that first the 'New Labour' and then the Coalition Conservative/Liberal Democrat UK governments embarked on a targets-driven agenda to raise 'standards' in British schools. This, according to a substantial body of research (Ball, 2003; B. Francis, Skelton & Read, 2009; Wilkinson, 2011a), left many teachers reluctant to think of educational success in any terms other than measurable attainment in public examinations such as GCSE or the targets and markers of measurable attainment on the way to these public exams. This targets-driven shift, which has been described as a shift from the 'personal' to the 'functional' (Fielding, 2000) understanding of the role of schools, has been observed to have contributed to the creation of risk-averse teaching and learning cultures (Pring, 2013).

The targets-driven school culture has intensified over the past 17 years in the United Kingdom and has been mirrored internationally by the increasing value placed by governments on comparative Programme for International Student Assessment (PISA) scores (Scott, 2011). At primary school level, an increasing premium has been put on relatively abstract literacy and numeracy measured by SATs scores, while perspectives derived from the humanities subjects have become increasingly marginal. At secondary school level, it has meant the privileging of English, maths and science at the expense of other subjects in terms of school timetables and budgets. This means that the humanities subjects, apart from English literature, have been driven to the margins of the compulsory educational process in English secondary schools. The much-vaunted and repeated ideals of 'Educating the Whole Child' and 'Every Child Matters' enshrined in the Children Act 2004 has increasingly been overtaken by a demireality – that is, an unrealised ideal that is in actuality squeezed out of the classroom by the 'terrors of performativity' (Ball, 2003).[2]

This reductive educational policy context at the level (c) of irreducible institutional forms in which the humanities subjects have on the whole been downgraded and marginalised has been characterised by the relative curricular absence of Islam (Wilkinson, 2014). This is manifest both in the absence of the contribution of Islamic civilisation and the role of Muslims in history of humanity, and in a lack of in-depth investigation of Islamic praxis (and, indeed, the praxes of other faiths) in religious education (Wilkinson, 2011a). Islam and the Muslim contribution have often constituted an 'absent curriculum' in humanities subjects at each of the levels of national policy, school management and the classroom, which causes some Muslim young people to disengage from their humanities education. It can even insinuate the idea of Muslims in Britain as second-class citizens (Wilkinson, 2014).

Religious identifications

In contrast to the relative institutional absence of Islam, the Muslim faith has consistently been shown to be of high emotional and intellectual significance in the lives of young British Muslims. Islam as a faith and an identity has in recent years typically been observed to be important to $c.90\%$ of Muslim young people (Alexander, 2000; L. Archer, 2003; L. J. Francis & Robbins, 2005; Mondal, 2008; Shain, 2010; Wilkinson, 2011a). This persistent prevalence of faith-based identity 'appear[s] to confound social psychological and social cognition theories of ethnic identity …, which assume that adherence to minority belief and practices, such as language and religion, declines with each new generation' (L. Archer, 2003, p. 48).

These identifications with Islam are for many Muslim young people the result of a serious$_{(r+p)}$ engagement with their faith that leads to an aspiration towards and a commitment to educational achievement. Shain (2003), for example, used her observations of Muslim girls at secondary school to construct the category of the 'Faith Girls'. These were Muslim girls who prioritised the importance of their Islam in their search for academic success and used it as a platform for their relatively good (compared with the Gang Girls') relations with their teachers. The 'Faith Girls' were 'actively creating positive identities and possibilities for themselves through religion. They drew on residual elements of their respective cultures and reworked them in the English context so that they operated in their favour' (p. 124).

The strength of identifications with Islam and a Muslim identity may also be generated by the 'determinate absence' (Bhaskar, 1993/2008) and/or the uncertainty of other types of identity. For example, the shifting uncertainties of Muslim young people's ethnic and national identifications as non-white, post-migrant Britons may, in part, be compensated by a strong identification with Islam and a Muslim identity. For example, Archer described her young people's Islamic identifications including the fact that many of her cohort placed themselves squarely within the context of the global Islamic brotherhood – the Umma, as relatively 'strong', in contrast to their shifting and uncertain allegiances to ethnic and national identifications (L. Archer, 2003, p. 50).

ARCHER: Are you more proud of being Pakistani, Bangladeshi or being Muslim?
GUFTER: Muslim
IMRAN: Muslim
GUFTER: It's like a *religion* … It's … like *strong* and it's like
JAMIL: Cos like if we all Muslims like you're all *one* … like they don't [say we're] Bangladeshi or we're not Pakistani
GUFTER: Yeah, plus ethnicity is just where you're *born* … whereas this is religion and it's *important*.

(cited in L. Archer, 2003, p. 49; original italics)

However, in a dynamic of the intersection and interplay of different facets of identity at the ICR four-planar level (d) of the embodied personality, the young people's religious identities also need to be understood in part as articulations of gender and race. For example, Archer identifies in the young people's idealisation of the united global brotherhood a challenge to the contemporary Western ideal of 'white', individualised masculinity (p. 50). An apparently strongly 'religious' and highly aggressive identity as evidenced by some of her young people's responses to the infamous 1989 *fatwa* of Ayatollah Khomeini against Salman Rushdie can be interpreted, in part, as the performance of the new 'hard' forms of Muslim masculinity that the Rushdie affair 'made available' and that superseded the 'malleable' Asian model. This hypothesis of a highly gendered performance of religious identity is supported by the fact that the majority of

Archer's cohort barely practised their Islam in any obviously discernible way. For example, they did not perform the obligatory Prayers or fast during the month of Ramadan.

Thus, for large numbers of British Muslim young people in education, Islam constitutes an *identity* from which to resist 'white', 'Islamophobic' oppression rather than a daily practice that forms a platform for educational engagement and success (Ramadan, 1999). Thus, the religious identifications of young Muslims can, in different circumstances, both promote and impede their educational achievement and productive integration into society through employment. Their religious identifications can enhance a productive engagement with education and the 'other' in four-planar social reality or contribute to the 'us' and 'them' dynamics and the Manichean world-view that I first identified as a stumbling-block to Muslim educational progress and social integration in the Introduction to this book.

Muslim youth in education: low educational attainment and 'hegemonic' masculine 'resistance' to school and the humanities subjects

Given the gap, therefore, between the official lack of educational recognition of Islam in foundation and core subjects[3] and its seminal importance to the lives and identities of many young British Muslims, it is perhaps unsurprising that both national statistics and qualitative academic research suggest that young British Muslims are not fulfilling their educational potential. When taken in comparison with non-Muslim boys and Muslim girls, Muslim *boys* can be viewed as part of an (albeit contested; D. Epstein, Elwood, Hey & Maw, 1998; B. Francis, 2000) trend of comparative male educational failure in which girls are identified as outperforming boys in public exams on a regular basis, especially in English and the humanities subjects (L. Archer, 2003; Head, 1999; Richardson, 2011).[4]

Muslim *girls* tend to perform significantly better than Muslim boys both in education generally and in the humanities subjects in particular at primary and secondary levels. Indeed, their measurable attainment runs only slightly beneath national averages for girls (UK Gov., 2008, 2011b). However, although many Muslim girls *are* actively encouraged by their parents to attend university (Tryer & Ahmad, 2006), there still remain significant cultural obstacles to the participation of Muslim girls in higher education (HE): *c.*30% fewer Muslim Bangladeshi and Pakistani girls than Muslim boys attend university, in an inversion of the national picture of higher female than male HE participation.

The factors in the educational under-attainment of young British Muslims

The factors in the relatively poor educational attainment of young British Muslims are complex (Hussain, 2008). Researchers have referred variously to overcrowded housing (P. Lewis, 2002), the relative absence of parental English language skills in some Muslim communities (Hussain, 2008), low levels of parental engagement with mainstream schools (Wilkinson, 2011a), low teacher expectations, the curricular removal of Islam from the school learning environment (Wilkinson, 2011a), racism and anti-Muslim prejudice (L. Archer, 2003; Shain, 2010), and low cultural expectations of higher educational achievement for girls (Haw & Shah, 1998) as contributory factors. The picture is further complicated by the fact that the attainment of some Muslim groups, e.g. Bangladeshi-origin boys and girls, is improving relative to other cultural groups, while that of others, in particular Pakistani boys, is relatively static and even in decline (UK Gov., 2013a).

In addition to the studies just referred to, which have tended to focus on the structural and social obstacles to young Muslim success at the four-planar level (c) of irreducible institutions and social forms, previous research focusing on Muslim young people in education by researchers interested in gender in education (e.g. Alexander, 2000; L. Archer, 2003; Shain, 2010) foregrounded the agency and attitudes of Muslim youth themselves to their schooling at the four-planar levels (b) of interpersonal relations and (d) of the embodied personality. These researchers identified the tendency of working-class British Asian Muslim young people to mobilise around the dominant 'hegemonic' (Connell, 1995) gender forms, such as the 'gangsta' and the 'lad' (L. Archer, 2003). These 'hegemonic' gender forms, enacted in the context of the peer group, are often sites of cultural survival in racist school environments that manifest themselves as resistance both to academic achievement and to British national identity, which are construed as 'feminine', 'white' and even 'un-Islamic' (Alexander, 2000; L. Archer, 2003; Shain, 2010).

Hegemonic masculinities and femininities

Connell (1995) introduced the concept of 'hegemonic' masculinity as referring to the most powerful forms of masculinity operating within a culture at any one time. Masculine models compete for dominance, and therefore hegemonic masculinity describes 'those dominant and dominating modes of masculinity which claim the highest status and exercise the greatest influence and authority' (Skelton, 2001, p. 50 cited in L. Archer, 2003, p. 15). Hegemonic masculinities are not fixed, nor are they asserted consistently by all men. They can endure over the course of a week, a year or even a generation in different contexts and times (L. Archer, 2003, p. 15). As Gramsci (1971 cited in L. Archer, 2003, p. 15) proposed, hegemony is never 'complete or absolute' but needs to be 'defended' and constantly reasserted against 'competing alternatives'.[5]

Hegemonic 'laddishness' in schools, to which Muslim boys have been observed to be prone (L. Archer 2003), involves the performance of 'hardness', 'coolness' and an indifference to academic achievement (Frosh, Phoenix & Pattman, 2002). In L. Archer's (2003) qualitative study, Abdul, for example, declared his total 'laddish' indifference to the prospects of 'the girls' getting good GCSE grades:

'I'm really not bothered … nah, I couldn't give a damn, it's all about marks, innit? As long as I, as long as I get my GCSEs as well I'm not really arsed what they [the girls] get … I don't give a fuck if they get A stars or A moons!'

(p. 67)

As well as manifesting itself as an aggressive indifference to school work, 'laddish' behaviour also manifests itself as being predisposed to 'messing about' (B. Francis, 2000), which some boys in Archer's study attributed to the 'natural' biological disposition of boys to be less hard-working than girls. As with the hegemonic form of 'the effortless achiever' of the upper-class public school boy (Mac an Ghaill, 1994), the 'lad' is perceived by some Muslim young people to be a 'naturally' male form (L. Archer, 2003, p. 44).

A close relation of the 'laddish' hegemonic form is that of the 'gangsta', the principal difference being that, while the 'lad' is underpinned by white working-class assumptions of the shop floor (Willis, 1977), the 'gangsta' is associated with 'black' resistance to the forms of 'white' career-oriented, middle-class authority (Alexander, 2000). The 'gangsta' identity is visibly represented by the symbolic trappings of street-based power, for example the wearing of trainers and tracksuit, which become symbolic of escape from unwanted police attention, and of the 'hoodie', as a protection against surveillance and therefore as a sub-version of authority.

Working-class Muslim boys have been found to draw strongly on the 'gangsta' type of hegemonic masculinity, which is closely connected with the notion of being 'black'. However, the Asian Muslim young man is 'precariously positioned' (Alexander, 2000) in aiming for acceptance within the black African-Caribbean group as someone whose opposition to whites cannot be relied on. Asian young people tend to be marginalised within 'discourses of blackness' as 'not black enough' (Modood, 1994). Asian Muslim young people may be forced to negotiate (unconvincingly) between competing discourses around 'skin colour' (biological blackness) and 'resistance to whites' (political blackness). For example, two of the young people in Archer's study criticised African-Caribbean young people for mixing with white young people – in other words, not resisting the whites on the grounds that 'they should [know better] cos they more blacker than us!' (L. Archer, 2003, p. 59).

Hegemonic femininities

In a study parallel to Archer's research into working-class Muslim boys in education, Shain (2003) identifies hegemonic forms around which Muslim girls in secondary school tend to mobilise in order to 'resist' both racism and the stereotypical characterisation of Muslim girls as 'passive, controlled and vulnerable' (p. ix). She identifies four 'hegemonic' femininities from analysis of the responses of a sample of 44 girls from schools in Greater Manchester and Staffordshire to their compulsory schooling: 'Gang Girls', 'Survivors', 'Rebels' and 'Faith Girls'.

- The 'Gang Girls', like the male 'gangsta', drew strongly on a strategy of 'us' and 'them' in resisting the authority of the school and compulsory school learning as 'white' and racist. Thus, in order to assert non-passive, non-white Asian Muslimness, they participated in creating a vicious circle of mutual suspicion and rejection between them and their teachers, which inevitably meant that they underperformed academically in school. The Gang Girls' hostility to the learning culture of the school was aggravated by the cultural expectations at home that girls should not progress to further or higher education. Thus, the Gang Girls 'played an active part in the repro- duction of the conditions of their oppression' (Shain, 2003, p. 76).

- 'The Survivors' were engaged in *active*, rather than passive, conformity with the school's processes because they recognised the long-term value of getting a good education for their employment and other prospects. They were described by teachers as 'good workers' and 'nice girls' (Shain, 2003, p. 77), and tended to have positive relationships with both white teachers and white pupils. This made them objects of mistrust for the Gang Girls. Although they might appear to epitomise the stereotype of the timid, passive Asian girl, in fact they tended to have made conscious, active decisions to use education as a means to getting on and were 'playing for potentially positive future consequences' (p. 92).

- 'The Rebels' rejected uneven gender relations in their experience of their own Asian Muslim families and communities, and found comfort in the rel- ative freedoms (as they saw it) of school. They often admired their white teachers and distanced themselves from both Asian teachers and the 'Gang Girls'. They sought out white friends and, even, romantic white boyfriends, which put them at odds with other Asian Muslim girls, for whom such behaviour was considered 'forbidden'. They were, therefore, selective about the Islamic religious practices that they chose to adopt, ignore or reject and were in the process both of transforming Asian Muslim culture and being transformed by white majority culture.

- As we have seen above, the fourth group – the 'Faith Girls' – prioritised the importance of their Islamic faith in their search for academic success and in their relatively good (compared with the Gang Girls') relations with their teachers. They were 'actively creating positive identities and possibilities for themselves through religion. They drew on residual elements of their respective cultures and reworked them in the English context so that they operated in their favour' (Shain, 2003, p. 124).

Moreover, the relative exclusion of Muslim girls from higher education (HE) can itself be understood as partly generated by 'hegemonic' patriarchal mascu- line forms (Haw & Shah, 1998) that become entangled in and/or are disguised as religious principles interacting with 'hegemonic' feminine expectations not to participate in HE. These 'hegemonic' cultural obstacles in many respects run directly counter to Islamic principles of the need to make knowledge available by and for all regardless of gender, class or ethnicity (Qur'an, 49:11; 20:14;

Mernissi, 1975). Similarly, Muslim girls may reject HE as a masculine entitlement to which their male relatives have privileged access.

Hegemonic demi-reality: self-exclusion from the humanities subjects

Furthermore, these 'hegemonic' forms have been observed to encourage a highly instrumentalised understanding of education and an exclusive perception of the role of formal schooling for improving their chances of getting a job (L. Archer, 2003; Shain, 2010). Within the context of this instrumentalised attitude to education, subjects such as the 'hard' natural sciences and mathematics, which have more obvious instrumental value, also have had greater 'masculinised' appeal to male British Muslim young people than the arts and humanities. These have often been construed as 'feminine' and less appealing, because they are perceived to offer a less clear-cut route into traditional 'masculine' (i.e. manual) working-class employment (L. Archer, 2003, pp. 135–136).

This lack of appeal of humanities subjects has been manifest, for example, in a significantly low uptake of GCSE History by British Muslims, both girls and boys. The national rate of GCSE uptake in History in recent years has been 33%, compared with a national average of GCSE uptake of History by Muslim girls of 28% and by Muslim Bangladeshi- and Pakistani-heritage boys of 22% (Vidal Rodeiro, 2009; Wilkinson, 2011a). This significantly low uptake of history at GCSE suggests that neither Muslim young people nor their families believe that history can significantly help them improve their life-chances and that their schools and teachers have not managed to disabuse them of this negative and false idea, a caricature of the truth.

Thus, these 'hegemonic' gender forms can in the terms of ICR be described as 'demi-realities' (see Chapter 5, pp. 154ff.). That is to say, they are non-essential, illusory (for the most part) constructions of gendered selfhood, antagonistically sharpened against educational and spiritual achievement, which, nonetheless, have a significant and keenly felt bearing on the lives of Muslim young people. Nevertheless, this picture from previous research does not represent the whole picture; my own experience of Muslim young people in education and the original research that follows will strongly challenge the notion that Muslim young people cannot and do not take great personal, academic and social benefit from education in general and from the study of the humanities subjects in particular.

The context of this research: why the humanities and why in particular history?

In contrast to the research background described above, my own experience as a history, citizenship and Islamic studies teacher of Muslim young people (mainly middle-class and working-class Muslim boys but also significant numbers of middle-class and working-class Muslim girls) in three school years over the period 1992–2009 suggested to me, anecdotally, that Muslim young people often respond positively to their humanities provision both in terms of measurable academic achievement and in terms of the impact of the humanities on their identities as learners and citizens. The exploration of historical narrative at a national, local and personal level in history, discourses of citizenship and critical belonging in citizenship and the truth-claims of religion in religious education all seemed to have an important joined-up role to play in engaging Muslim pupils with their Islamic faith, their ethno-cultural heritages and the civic history of their nation, Britain. My experience as a history teacher, for example, resonated to some degree with the claim of the National Curriculum for History, hereafter called NCH (Qualifications and Curriculum Development Agency, 2009), that history as a school subject can promote the success of pupils on a variety of intellectual and emotional levels, and 'helps pupils develop their own identities through an understanding of history at personal, local, national and international levels' (p. 92).

History, identity and Muslim young people

Thus, my own teaching experience and the aspirations of NCH both suggested a significant role for the humanities subjects and, in particular, school history in the internal integration of British Muslim identity and external engagement with the 'other' and the 'world'. With regard to the connection of narrative to identity, Bruner (1997, p. 159) also notes that it is in the 'narrative mode' that the self is understood and articulated to others 'retrospectively' after the forward encounters with life. Personal narratives articulate who we are, who we perceive ourselves to be, and who others perceive us to be at any given moment (Cronon, 2000). National narratives, especially when presented as school history curricula (Wegner, 1990), provide one of the core building-blocks of nationhood and express what a nation perceives itself to be (Barton, 2012). If a group or individual can find moments or points of self-identification with the 'grand narrative' of the school history curriculum, they can imagine themselves, and be imagined as, parts of the national historical community as a whole (Ahonen, 2001, p. 190). 'These narratives … are interventions in the present since they shape the self-understanding of individuals and communities' (Chapman, 2011, p. 96).

Owing to the power of school history both to reflect and to generate national identity, history curricula have in recent years generated intense political media and political debate, especially as national identities in Europe have become more publicly contested with increasing immigration (Grever, Haydn & Ribbens, 2008). For example, in England, both with the formation of the National Curriculum in 1989–1990 and with the root-and-branch National Curriculum Review in 2011–2013, the reform of school history has generated more intense public debate than in the case of any other school subject (Cannadine, 2013a; Phillips, 1998).

As we saw in the Introduction and Chapter 1, young Muslims, especially young Muslim males, have loomed large in this public debate about national identity, citizenship and their connection (or lack of it) to school history. 'Home-grown' British cultural separatism in girls and radicalisation and violent extremism in boys, according to some, evidences both a lack of connection to Britain, particularly in Muslim males, and the need for school history to effect this connection and to bring about a sense of common citizenship (G. Brown, 2006; Freedland, 2005; Garton Ash, 2006).

I was therefore keen in the context of this empirical research to explore the impact of school history on the educational success and the lives of members of this low-achieving, often socially disadvantaged and often demonised group (Alexander, 2000; L. Archer, 2003; Hopkins, 2004; Shain, 2010) and to see whether my hunch that the humanities subjects have a lot to contribute to Muslim young people's development withstood the test of rigorous academic research.

The sample of Muslim young people

My sample of British Muslim young people that represented this group was, in terms of its schools, ethnicities and class, indicative of the general population of Muslims in England.[6] All 307 British Muslim young people came from four secondary state schools in Muslim-dense areas of English inner cities. All their schools had a high proportion of male Muslim students. Of the students at each school:

- Technology School – (*n*) 52 – 63.4% were Muslim;
- Faith School – (*n*) 67 – 100% were Muslim;
- Community School – (*n*) 49 – 63.6% were Muslim;
- Specialist School – (*n*) 139 – 98.6% were Muslim.

All the sample schools were state comprehensive schools and, with the exception of the Islamic faith school, were non-denominational. All the schools followed the National Curriculum both for History and for other foundation and core subjects. For comparative statistical purposes, 60 non-Muslim British young people were also sampled as the Muslim pupils' classmates and peers. These young people were also broadly indicative of the population of inner-city English schools in terms of ethnicity, class and religion.[7]

Methodology: the fulcrum of ICR underlabours for social science

Coming from a critical realist theoretical perspective, I was keen that the nature of my object of inquiry, my Muslim young people's relationships with the NCH, should determine the methodological approach deployed for its study rather than a priori decisions about the respective value of quantitative or qualitative research methods or a personal preference for either numbers or letters (Sayer, 1984; Scott, 2010). Thus, my research design was consistent with our recurrent theme of the primacy of ontology over epistemology and was generated by the meta-theoretical framework of the fulcrum of Islamic critical realism, ontological realism, epistemological relativism and judgemental rationality, which we examined in detail in Chapter 3.

Ontological realism here meant the full recognition that the Muslim young people's experiences of NCH were real, were mediated by real teachers, in real classrooms, in real schools quite independently of my researching them or not. In other words, my research subject was there to be discovered. It also meant recognition of the fact that it was in the nature of my object of inquiry to have both an 'intensional', personal-experiential, vertical axis and an 'extensional', national, horizontal axis dimension, which meant that it was important that my research strategy embraced both 'intensionality' and 'extensionality' (Scott, 2010).

Epistemological relativism meant being reflexive about my relationships with, and positionality in relation to, my research subjects and recognising that once I was engaged with the process of the research, the Muslim young people's experiences of NCH were only relatively independent of me, the researcher. My values, thoughts and feelings would inevitably be brought to bear to some degree on their experiences of NCH, their understanding of them and the ways in which they conveyed them to me. It was relevant that I was a 41-year-old white British, upper-middle-class male Muslim convert to Islam who has taught Muslim pupils history and religious education over a period of 20 years, often, although not exclusively, in the context of secondary Islamic faith schools.

This meant that in this research I was 'situated' (Haraway, 1988) as an insider-outsider, sharing, as a Muslim male, a number of faith positions and gender identifications with my respondents. However, as a white British, upper-middle-class 41-year-old (at the time of the research) I was largely a stranger to the experiences of ethnic minority, largely working-class, teenagers. I was also strange-familiar to the research context in respect of being a history teacher not teaching but observing in history classrooms (Coffey, 1999). Nast (1994) refers to these types of insider-outsider/emic-etic positions of similarity-in-difference and difference-in-similarity as positions of 'betweenness', in that neither similarity nor difference between researcher and researched is ever absolute. Of course, I was more of a stranger to the worlds and experiences of the 12 Muslim girls whom I interviewed in a focus group, and I compensated for this loss of familiarity by conducting these interviews in collaboration with a female Muslim colleague.

I consider myself to have been in an appropriate 'position' from which to undertake research into Muslim young people in history education: I had enough of an 'insider' about me to generate authentic feelings of empathy for the young people and trust in me by them, and enough of an 'outsider' to generate appropriate levels of critical research distance from my research subject.

Judgemental rationality involved the selection of the appropriate research tools to embrace the breadth of the impact of NCH nationwide *and* the depth of the generative mechanisms of success (or failure) brought about by that provision on individual learners and to take account of, and compensate for, my own positionality. Therefore, I designed a mixed-methods, qualitative-quantitative research strategy to garner both an 'extensional' breadth and an 'intensional' depth of understanding of the educational success of my sample of Muslim young people with NCH. I deployed quantitative attitudinal surveys to get an 'extensional' picture of the Muslim young people's responses to their history provision nationally. I then conducted qualitative semi-structured interviews in order to attempt capture some of the complexity of the young people's 'intensional' responses to NCH. Thus, the questionnaire was designed to reflect the broad, objective 'there-ness' of my subjects' responses to their education, and the interviews were designed to access the 'mediated' quality of their experience and help to describe the causal relationships between NCH and their experience of it. The observations were intended to contextualise and to test, in a limited way, the young people's responses to both the surveys and the interviews in order to compensate for the effects of my own positionality on the interview process. The 23 male Muslim interviewees also completed a research diary during the period of the interview process, which added longitudinal texture to the reports of their experiences of NCH. Thus, there was an element both of 'alignment' of my data collection methods, which were used sequentially, and of 'triangulation' of the data collected in my research strategy to corroborate, confirm or problematise data collected by another method (Scott, 2010).[8]

From the total sample of 295 Muslim young people who completed a quantitative attitudinal survey about their history provision, 23 of them with their corresponding 10 teachers were sampled for interview using a sampling strategy that took into account the history class or set that they were in, their interest in the subject of history and their measured NCH Level. These factors had been shown by the statistical data of a pilot study to be significant predictors of success with the subject (Wilkinson, 2007).[9]

A laminated ontology of educational success

My analytical framework for an ontology of the Muslim history/humanities learner by which I intended to frame and understand my sample's responses to NCH was underscored by concepts adapted and applied to educational theory from the philosophy of critical realism and Islamic critical realism. We saw in Chapter 1 that critical realism emerged in the 1970s as a philosophy of science whose initial primary aim was twofold: the revindication of ontology (the philosophical study of being) from its reduction to epistemology (the philosophical study of knowing and knowledge), and the establishment of a new ontology of deep structures, causal mechanisms and real change (Bhaskar, 1975). This notion of deep causal structures and generative mechanisms, applied in this case to a human educational setting, was important, as it opened up the philosophical possibility that the generative mechanisms of success lay deep in the structure of a history curriculum within a more general humanities education.

Stratification and emergence

Central to the ontology of the Muslim history/humanities learner were two further ideas that I introduced in Chapter 3: that reality is 'stratified' and that most events (outside the laboratory) occur in 'open systems'. It will be remembered that to say that most events occur in 'open systems' is to say that they are determined by and, therefore, require explanation in terms of a multiplicity of such structures and mechanisms. To say that reality is 'stratified' is to say that phenomena at one level of reality are scientifically to be explained in terms of structures or mechanisms located at a deeper level that generated or produced them. Moreover, reality is not only stratified but also '*emergent*' (Bhaskar, 1975, p. 119) from more basic levels of being through to more complex forms which are irreducible to the more basic levels (Bhaskar, 2013). To give a simple example of the principle of *emergence* in the natural world, water (H_2O) is dependent on the 'lower-order' existence of hydrogen and oxygen atoms and yet has causal properties and a relationship to the rest of living things that are irreducible to hydrogen and oxygen (C. Smith, 2010). To remind the reader of the example of emergence in the human world given in Chapter 3, the mind at the psychological level is dependent on the chemistry of the body at the level of biology; it could not operate without it. But the mind as cause or category is not reducible to chemical reactions and the physical activity of neurones at the chemical level.

This idea of emergence has also been applied by G. L. Brown (2009) to education. Slightly expanding Brown's schema (to include socio-economic mechanisms), this emergence in education entails comprises a formation that includes:

- *physical mechanisms*, e.g. size and quality of classrooms;
- *biological mechanisms*, e.g. adequate nutrition;
- *psychological mechanisms*, e.g. student motivation and parental expectation;
- *socio-economic mechanisms*, e.g. class and wealth;
- *socio-cultural (including moral and political) mechanisms*, e.g. language and peer-group attitudes;
- *normative mechanisms*, e.g. as determined by curricula.

With reference to this schema, the metaphor of 'articulation' is also useful. It suggests that changes at one level may have either intended or unintended knock-on effects at a different level or levels of being. To give examples from the system above applied to history education, an overheated classroom at the physical level may have a knock-on, articulated effect at the psychological level on a child's concentration and at a cognitive level in his or her ability to remember 'the facts'; poverty at the level of class may reduce a child's ability to engage with the normative level of the history curriculum by diminishing, *inter alia*, his or her chances of travel to places of historical interest.

Laminated systems in history and humanities education

We can also see how the 'laminated system' of four-planar social being introduced in Chapter 3 can be applied neatly to describe the child in the child in a historical educational setting. The education of the child in history involves simultaneously:

a   *material transactions with nature* or artefacts ultimately derived from nature – textbooks, PCs, school buildings, food, transport, heating, electricity, etc.;
b   *formative interpersonal relations with peers, teachers, family members and community figures* by which formal and informal historical narratives and traditions will be transmitted to the child;
c   *indirect involvement via, for example, the level of school management with other institutions and policy-making organisations* – the government, the local authority, museums, historical sites, publishers, etc. – which will produce powerful regimes of knowledge (Foucault, 1980), e.g. school subjects, into which the child's learning will, at least to a certain extent, be bound;
d   all of which will be brought to bear on the *emergent stratified personality of the child.*

A further relevant 'laminated' system is described by Bhaskar (2013) in terms of a 'hierarchy of scale' typically comprising seven emergent, articulated levels which I also thought had a bearing on the complex, multi-tiered context of Muslim young people in humanities education:

i   *unconscious motives* as illuminated by psychology;
ii   the individual level of *biography*;
iii   the *micro level* of small-scale human interactions, e.g. within the peer group, as described by ethnomethodology;
iv   the *meso level* of classical sociology, e.g. functional roles within the family;
v   the *macro level* of whole societies, e.g. the UK economy;
vi   the *mega level of trajectories and spans of time*, e.g. feudalism;
vii   the *planetary whole.*

Using the above levels, the intense and often negative geopolitical (vi, above; the War on Terror, etc.), economic (poverty and employment; (v), above) and social (peer group; iii, above) and religio-cultural ((i), (ii), (iv), above) contexts identified in the literature above in which Muslim young people find themselves all needed to be taken into account.

These theoretical considerations made in conversation with the four-planar situation of Muslim young people in Britain as described by previous research led me to develop a laminated ontology of educational success for Muslim young people in history education in a variety of different dimensions. These dimensions were multiple, and 'articulated' and loosely emergent from or with each other, as will be evidenced by the analysis of my empirical findings. These dimensions of success were to be outlined extensionally through the young people's responses to their attitudinal surveys and 'filled in' with an understanding of the causal relationships between the 'articulated' dimensions through the interview data, non-participant observations and the interviewees' diaries. These dimensions were 'stratified' and 'laminated', in that they were layered almost imperceptibly over each other. However, unlike the hierarchical 'emergence' in the natural world, they were not hierarchically arranged but, rather, connected in a form of 'mutual emergence'.

Thus, I conceived of the dimensions of the success of the Muslim learner in history as constituted by:

- *The intellectual dimension of success (IDS)*. This was success understood both as 'objective' academic attainment as assessed by the sample of Muslim boys' teachers according to NCH Levels and in terms of pupils' own assessment of their basic historical understanding of the history of England, Britain and the rest of the world. It was also the dimension of success delineated by the ability of the Muslim young people to understand and articulate the understandings of the history that they had learned in relation to their own lived experiences.[10]

- *The spiritual dimension of success (SDS)*. This was the dimension of success at which the Muslim young people reflected on changing historical values and apprehended ethical, moral and religious significance. This was a vital level, given the importance of religiosity and strong religious identifications for Muslim boys recorded in all the literature and exemplified in the sample, 89% of whom strongly agreed that 'my religion is very important'.[11]

  Using the categorisations outlined earlier, both the intellectual and spiritual success related primarily, although not exclusively, at the level of biography (ii) to the emergent embodied personality of the individual child (d).

- *The affective-cultural dimension of success (ADS)*. This was the emotional, identity-related and motivational dimension of success, which was connected to the level at which NCH helped, or did not help, the pupils reflect upon and understand their home cultures and their relationships with majority British culture. It was also related to the types of negotiations of masculinity and femininity within the peer group identified earlier in the chapter. The dimension of affective-cultural success was connected at emergent levels (i), (ii) and (iii) to the embodied personality of the child (d).[12]

- *The instrumental dimension of success (InDS)*. This was the dimension at which NCH provided, or did not provide, life skills that Muslim young people recognised would be useful in post-school contexts of work. This was also a vital dimension, given the heightened instrumentalised attitudes to schooling of Muslim boys, in particular, identified in previous research and the general perception noted in the literature that Muslim male pupils, in particular, tend not to regard the humanities subjects as useful for their chances of gaining employment (Adey & Biddulph, 2001). It was also related, as we will see, to levels of uptake of GCSE history.[13]

- *The civic dimension of success (CDS)*. This was the dimension at which NCH nurtured, or did not nurture, Muslim pupils' desire and ability to participate socio-politically and belong emotionally to British society and to relate to the international community, including the Muslim-majority world. This was important, given the significance of the political context of history education and its connection with the Britishness agenda that was established by former UK prime minister Gordon Brown and continued by the succeeding Conservative–Liberal Democrat government during the period of research. It was also important to test the potential role for school history to promote the informed social integration of Muslim young people identified or postulated by academics and journalists as we have seen earlier in the chapter.[14]

Both instrumental and civic success were connected at levels (iii), (iv) and (v) of micro-, meso- and macro-social relations to social relations and structures generally at the non-reducible level of structures, institutions and forms (c).

- *The overall holistic dimension of success (OHDS).* This corresponded to pupils' overall assessment of the impact of history on their complete development as a human being, which was measured as a factor called *awareness of myself and my world.* The overall holistic dimension of success took into account the successful emergence of the embodied personality of each individual child (d) considered as a whole. It was the most important facet of success, and was used as a dependent variable in statistical regressions. It was meant to correspond to feelings of deepening integration, both internally related to self and externally related to society, for each child through the process of history education.[15]

This model enabled me to investigate the impact of the boys' history education at multiple, discrete ontological levels and as a whole, and it helped me to avoid reducing success to measurable academic attainment, which was nonetheless accounted for as an important component of *the intellectual dimension of success.*

The dimensions of young British Muslims' success at history

In terms of the generation of success conceived of at the 'laminated' dimensions listed above, the study suggested that Muslim young people were succeeding (albeit to differing degrees) in each of the 'articulated' intellectual, spiritual, affective, instrumental and civic dimensions posited by the theoretical model. It also suggested that history as a school subject has great potential to contribute to the holistic development of Muslim youth, for whom faith, civic knowledge and participation and success in the world are all important.

The intellectual dimension of success

In terms of extensional, measurable academic attainment and the development of basic historical understanding according to core curricular objectives, the

Muslim young people in my research achieved significant *intellectual success* at the NCH both in absolute terms and relative to the non-Muslim sample.

There was no significant difference between the Muslim and non-Muslim responses to any of the three *basic historical understanding* variables, which gauged the extent to which the NCH had provided a basic historical understanding of England, Britain and the rest of the world. Of the Muslim sample, 52.3% had either 'above average' or 'considerably above average' basic historical understanding according to the NCH criteria, and there was no significant difference in this between the Muslim and non-Muslim samples. Moreover, in terms of basic measurable *attainment* according to National Curriculum levels, as reported by their teachers, there was no significant difference between the Muslim sample of 295 and the comparative non-Muslim sample of 60 young people, with 42.5% of the Muslim sample gaining either 'good' (NCH Level 6 or 7) or 'excellent' (NCH Level 8) attainment at NCH. Furthermore, the Muslim sample's mean level of attainment at 6.15 was in line with national averages and governmental expectations for the end of Year 9 (Qualifications and Curriculum Development Agency, 2009) and slightly above that of the mean score of the non-Muslim sample at 5.93.

The fact that NCH had contributed to the IDS of Muslim young people in terms of knowledge and understanding was corroborated 'intensionally' (Scott, 2010) at interview in the informed enthusiasm of 12 of the 23 young people when talking about their historical learning. Of particular note were the feelings of engagement and understanding of current affairs evoked by connecting classroom learning about the English Civil War with visits to the Houses of Parliament by two young people in the Community School (Levstik & Barton, 2011).

For example, the testimony of Rami (Community School, middle-achieving, British-Pakistani) showed the loose 'articulated and laminated' emergence that was more generally apparent throughout the sample (see Table 6.1) between the civic and the intellectual dimensions of success.

MATTHEW: So tell me a bit more about that, how have you learned about how Parliament developed?

RAMI: Been learning about the Royal side and the Parliament side, and the way [...] they hated each other and [...], how it all come together and how King Charles I, his head got [...] chopped off [...] we visited Parliament as well [...]. We went in the House of Commons and the House of Lords and seen ... where, when like the Queen gave a message, 'cause she can't go in the House of Commons ... yeah, and how [...] the guy knocks [...] and you can see the marks and everything. Like if you look up Parliament, yeah, and all the things which have been happening, you could see.... Why ... 'cause of the past.

Rami's and other young people's reflections suggested that IDS was particularly stimulated when the Muslim young people were gaining a 'history of the present' (Dewey, 1916) and understanding the ongoing 'presence of the past'

(Bhaskar, 2013) through their curricular history. Thus, IDS promoted their success at the levels of the social relations at the four-planar level (c) of irreducible structures, institutions and forms, in articulation with the internal stratification of the embodied personality (d).

The spiritual dimension of success

Given that 89% of the young people in my sample had 'strongly agreed' that *my religion is important to me*, in line with other research (L. Archer, 2003; Shain, 2010; Singh Ghuman, 1997), it was clear that an adequate ontology of Muslim success could not omit the spiritual impact of the NCH on the sample's religious identities and on their processes of ethical and moral reflection. This was doubly the case given the stated aspirations of the NCH to provide a consideration of the values of people in the past (Qualifications and Curriculum Development Agency, 2010).

Extensionally speaking, 47.3% of the Muslim sample rated the impact of the NCH in terms of how much it had helped them think about their religion as 'strong' or 'quite strong', and there was no significant difference in this between the Muslim and non-Muslim sample. This might be considered a finding of only modest levels of SDS. However, it was clear from the interviews and diaries that the religious, moral and ethical dimension involved in the study of the past was a significant component in their finding history interesting and worthwhile. For example, Benyamin (Technology School, middle-achieving, British-Algerian) summarised the general value of history for the Muslim boys for promoting ethical reflection in the SDS eloquently, using the specific example of the 1919 Treaty of Versailles:

MATTHEW: So do you think […] history does have a … purpose for helping young people to make their mind up about things, decide, and make moral judgements?

BENYAMIN: Yeah, I think it is […] you have to make moral judgements; you can't just make judgements like what you hear or like you can't just follow other people; you have to be yourself and you have to think about what you're going to do, what's your decision, what's your conscience telling you to do […] when there was the Treaty [of Versailles] between the French, the British and the Germans, and the French […] wanted revenge but the British wanted peace and the Americans wanted them to be punished but not too harshly and I decided that peace was like, would be the best option. So that's what I went with and other people went with the revenge and other people went with the punishment but not too harshly. But I made my decision to the fact I thought that was the best outcome. […] Peace, like no killing, no revenge … it's not the German people's fault what happened in the war, it's the Parliament, the government's fault, so the German people shouldn't be punished for what they haven't done, so peace is always the best option.

Benyamin eloquently cited the crucial general role of history in developing the ability to make autonomous moral judgements, which in his own case led to the transfactual decision that 'peace is always the best option'.

The ethical and moral benefits that the young people consistently said that they enjoyed deriving from the study of history included the folllowing

Gratitude for the social, medical and technological privileges of the present though acknowledgement of the achievements and the sacrifices of people in the past

The most frequently cited ethical reflection, referred to by 10 of the young people at interview, was that of gratitude for the relative comforts enjoyed by those alive today compared with the relative material and social hardships suffered by people in the past.

For Ahmad (Technology School, middle-achieving, Afghan-British), this feeling of gratitude was connected to awareness that the technological and medical progress of the past 100 years meant people lived longer, which he had found 'inspirational'. Samir (Specialist School, middle-achieving, Bengali-British) compared and contrasted the hardships endured by child labourers in the past with his own privileged situation of receiving an education compared to some children in the world who still do not.[16]

And while the tenor of the majority of these reflections was one of confidence in the stability of the present, 'progressive' (Cronon, 2000), even at times 'Whiggish' (Booth, 1993), Amir (Community School, high-achieving, Pakistani-British) reflected on the necessity of not taking things for granted, owing to the fragility of present gains and the often unexpected nature of war:

AMIR: [History] made me a bit grateful that it [war] doesn't happen any more but in some situations it might come up. [...] Might repeat itself if things get out of hand.

It is interesting to note that these boys' positive outlook on their relatively peaceful and prosperous circumstances situated them very much as citizens of Britain in the West rather than of the more obviously Islamic world, much of which, of course, is at present in political, social and religious turmoil (Allawi, 2009). This correlated with findings about the Muslim young people's strong ties of citizenship with Britain, which we will explore further in Chapter 9.

Challenging stereotypes and countering discrimination, including challenging Islamophobic, anti-Semitic and anti-Western/Christian prejudice

Five of the Muslim young people interviewed and three of their teachers thought that history in school had a significant role to play in the SDS by challenging the Manichean 'us' and 'them', Muslim (good)/non-Muslim (bad), world-view that we have already identified in the Introduction and earlier in this chapter as being a feature of the post-colonial Muslim worlds and its diaspora. They thought that this history could perform this function by challenging the stereotypes underpinning this divisive world-view.

Ahmad cited a critical role for history in combating Islamophobia if the achievements of Islamic civilisation and the Muslim contribution were a feature of classroom learning. He also recognised the value to Muslims of acknowledging the achievements of notable Westerners, including Christians, to the general patrimony of humankind.

MATTHEW: And how about the other way round? Do you think if Muslims knew more of the history of Western countries they might show more respect for Western countries as well?

AHMAD: Yeah, it would be like some Muslims, yeah, the extremism and the terrorism they would, it's more like good, but if they know about Western people like [Isambard] Kingdom Brunel, they wouldn't do that stuff [terrorism].

It was, therefore, noticeably important to Ahmad that Muslim–non-Muslim respect should be a mutual commitment and that history might play a role at the level of SDS in helping this happen.

ANTI-SEMITISM

Both teachers and Muslim pupils noted that a small minority of Muslim pupils brought anti-Semitic views into the history classroom. Three of the boys' teachers in two different schools (Specialist School and Community School) expressed the opinion that anti-Jewish feeling was a feature of the out-of-school culture of some Muslim pupils in their schools. This corresponds with views of other teachers in the United Kingdom and Scandinavia of the presence of anti-Jewish sentiment among Muslim boys, often generated, in particular, as alluded to in Chapter 1, by the real and perceived injustices suffered by Muslims in the Palestinian–Israeli conflict (Axelrod, 2010; Siddique, 2010).

While teachers' views of Muslim pupils are certainly not unproblematic and may be prone to racism (Willis, 1977) and Islamophobia (van Driel, 2004), the fact that three of the boys themselves 'owned up' to anti-Jewish feeling indicated that these teachers had identified a real issue. Three of the boys themselves (two from Technology School, one from Community School) acknowledged without a direct question that both anti-Jewish and anti-Western sentiment existed among their peers and posited the role that NCH in general, and the study of the Holocaust in particular, had to play in creating empathy with the suffering of Jewish people and thereby addressing this anti-Jewish sentiment.

The Holocaust and the way it had been presented by a teacher, David (white British,Technology School), had created an emotional response in Muslim (Technology School, middle-achieving, Afghan) of 'feeling a bit sad' since 'they

[Jews] didn't do anything wrong, they just got killed for nothing'. Ahmad (Technology School, middle-achieving, Afghan-British) recognised the fact that study of the Holocaust had 'changed the way I thought'.

Providing lessons in teamwork and serving others

At the level of SDS, three of the Muslim young people interviewed had drawn spiritual sustenance from NCH about the superior value of working collaboratively and as a team.

For Waleed (Community School, middle-achieving, Pakistani-British), the pre-eminent lesson that he had taken from his study of the English Civil War and the mistakes of Charles I was the need 'to listen to advice' and to work with other people. Uthman (Faith School, middle-achieving, British-Indian) thought that NCH in general could contribute to people wanting to work together as part of 'Team England'. In a related way, the life of William Wilberforce had impressed on Amir (Community School, high-achieving, Pakistani-British) the value of having empathy for other people's situations and the importance of looking beyond the trappings of wealth and status to observe and respect people's true character.

MATTHEW: You said something very nice here [in your diary]: 'I think he was a good man because he had feelings for others rather than for himself...'

AMIR: Yeah, because I seen ... in the film that we watched it gave me a decent opinion of why, how he felt, because he was just looking at the slave being sold to rich people and he wanted to buy it, buy the slave, to free him from his sadness [...]. He was different. He was unique to others because people that have money think about themselves only. It's better to be poor and look at other people.

It was clear that for Amir, William Wilberforce had surpassed the status of a mere historical personality to become something of an ethical and moral role model.

Becoming a better, more reflective person

In short, nearly half the sample of boys reckoned that the study of history in general and their NCH provision in particular had the power in some way to help them and others become better people and lead 'better' lives at the level of SDS. The ethical and moral reflections provoked by NCH had suggested to these boys, *inter alia*, gratitude for material comfort and education, the value of peace, teamwork, empathy for the suffering of others, the need not to abuse positions of authority and the possibility of transforming the world for the better.

AHMAD: It's like [...] it can actually help ... 'cause if you're learning, if you're learning about the history, what's good, what happened in the world, you might change the way you live or help like how the way you treat people around you [...] if you think of that, it actually helps you like live as a better person.

This was why for Benyamin (Technology School, high-achieving, Algerian-British), not only did history provide ethical lessons, but the study of history itself was accompanied by an ethical imperative in a way that Walsh (1992) has referred to as history as 'piety':

BENYAMIN: I think that's just how life should be: you should understand what was before you [...] I just think ... you should know how life was before you. It'll help you like when you get older and all that and you should just have a general understanding of it.

The absence of the Muslim contribution

However, 49% of the sample suggested that the spiritual success of the NCH was restricted by the absence of any teaching on the history of Islamic civilisation at any of the research schools, even though there were modules of the history of the Muslim contribution available on the formal curriculum of the NCH for teaching in the classroom. This was a real, determinate absence (Bhaskar, 1993/2008) that we will be exploring more deeply in the next chapter at the dialectical level of 2E (Absence). This fact also indicated that the moral and ethical power of history for the *examination*, rather than the inculcation (Slater, 1992), of values was under-realised by the young people's teachers (Barton & Levstik, 2004).

SDS as an explanatory factor in other types of success

We have examined the spiritual dimension of success in some detail since, in terms of its explanatory importance for other facets of success, the spiritual dimension was a core significant factor in both the intellectual and the overall holistic dimensions of success (see Table 6.1). This importance of spiritual success in other types of success shown up by statistical analysis was confirmed at interview with the young people, where it was suggested strongly that *the more that the NCH had challenged the young people to examine ethical or moral issues, the more historical facts and information they remembered.* This was particularly the case with lower-achieving pupils. For example, for one lower-achieving boy from the Technology College, who by his own admission had very little taste for history, a process of ethical reflection about the Holocaust – 'How could a civilised nation have done this?' – was complemented by a surprisingly detailed recollection of Nazi racial policy and the grisly technology of the Holocaust.

This last observation bears out the heuristic utility of the 'articulated' element of my theoretical model of success: the spiritual dimension of success for some

Table 6.1 Significant factors in different types of Muslim success with the English National Curriculum for History (linear regression)

Success factors	Intellectual success ($R^2 = 0.356$)	GCSE uptake ($R^2 = 0.268$)	Overall holistic success ($R^2 = 0.419$)
Civic success	$\beta=0.262$****	$\beta=0.300$***	$\beta=0.322$****
Overall attitude to history (= interest + perceived importance)	$\beta=0.212$**	$\beta=0.323$****	
Spiritual success	$\beta=0.171$***		$\beta=0.296$****
Out-of-school history	$\beta=0.125$**		$\beta=0.236$***
Teaching	$\beta=0.112$*		

Notes
* $p<0.5$.
** $p<0.05$.
*** $p<0.05$.
**** $p<0.005$.

young people had a knock-on, articulated effect of promoting the intellectual dimension of success without these being reducible to each other. Conversely, if spiritual success was not achieved, the intellectual success and the absorption of core historical knowledge of some young people also suffered: two young people at the Faith School said that the NCH 'bored' them in general because they could find no space within it to reflect upon their own Muslim heritages. Thus, the spiritual dimensions and success and intellectual dimensions of success existed in a relationship of non-hierarchical, mutual emergence.

The affective-cultural dimension of success

The value of the NCH on the affective-cultural dimension of success was the least appreciable in terms of its impact on the Muslim young people. This meant that the NCH was found wanting in terms of the NCH's stated aspiration: 'It [history] helps pupils develop their own identities through an understanding of history at personal, local, national and international levels' (Qualifications and Curriculum Development Agency, 2009). The interview data suggested that the young people's ethnic and cultural identities were rarely engaged by the NCH. Indeed, two Community School boys articulated the belief that ethnic minority history had no place in the mainstream National Curriculum and instead thought that the NCH ought to focus exclusively on a British national story. This in itself suggested that some of the sample had already digested a hidden message about the relative lack of historical worth of their own cultural and ethnic heritages, both as discrete entities and as part of the shared history of England, and Britain. The recommendations of the Ajegbo Report (2007) that the history curriculum should be instrumental in teaching about diversity of different types would appear to have been largely lost on my sample of history teachers.

The family factor

Extensional and intensional data both suggested that on the affective-cultural dimension of success, parents and families were highly significant factors in helping young people motivate themselves to study (cf. Wilson & Corcoran, 1988), to deepen and clarify understanding and to negotiate identity through historical narratives. Indeed, *out-of-school history* comprising:

- exposure to historical conversations at home about the family;
- conversations about curricular learning with siblings; and
- the history of Islam that some young people received as part of their mosque-based education

was a significant factor in overall holistic success (see Table 6.1).

However, despite its intensional significance, parental involvement in the NCH was extensionally significantly less available for the Muslim boys than for the non-Muslim sample of boys: 32.6% of the Muslim sample either 'strongly' or 'mainly' agreed that they talked about history with their families at home, compared with 56.7% of the non-Muslim sample. The reasons for this 'real determinate' (Bhaskar, 1993/2008) absence will be explored in depth and detail in the next chapter.

The female experience of ADS: 'we are not oppressed'

It was noticeable that the only significant differences between the female and the male Muslim young people's responses to NCH were located at the level of ADS. While the boys wanted NCH to reflect the fact that they belonged in English, and British, society, the idea that history in classrooms should send out a strong message to society that Muslim women were 'not oppressed' emerged four times in the one focus group with the 12 Muslim girls.

In this respect, the girls were particularly keen for people to know the history of Muslim women who had achieved great things. For example, a tenth-century maker of astrolabes, Miriam al-Ijli (d. 967), had particularly caught their imagination as the Muslim woman whose work, they thought, was a precursor to Sat-Nav. The history of Miriam al-Ijli encapsulated what the girls wanted history to say about them: that Muslim women had achieved great things as independent agents and that those things had a contemporary value and use to society.

The girls did not dismiss the idea that the history of the daily, ordinary and domestic was also part of the important contribution of women, but, above all else, they wanted people to know that they could do great things and that they were 'not oppressed'. This tallies with the findings of Shain (2003) in that the Muslim girls wanted history to help them develop their Muslim femininity as agentic and dynamic, not as timid and passive.

Another important difference between the male and female Muslim cohorts at the level of ADS was in the quality and quantity of their interaction with parents around history curriculum. Both the quality and the quantity of parental interaction of the girls around history were superior for the girls as compared with the boys. Unlike the boys, the girls used curriculum topics as a focus for discussion with parents and siblings on a regular basis and agreed strongly with the proposition that their parents worked hard to help them with their history learning by taking them to museums and on 'historical holidays'. This interaction was rich, and often, they claimed, in-depth, and it involved 'loads of debates'. The girls were not surprised to hear our findings that the boys' interaction with parents had been as important to the quality of their learning as the input of teachers, since this parental quality time had, in their own experience, given them 'space to reflect' and internalise the curriculum. The difference in this finding between the girls and the boys may, in part, be accounted for by the fact that hegemonic 'laddishness', perhaps, would not 'permit' adolescent boys to 'own up' to a meaningful relationship with their parents!

The instrumental dimension of success

In line with the findings of other researchers in history education, history as a school subject was perceived by the Muslim young people to be of limited instrumental use in terms of getting a job (cf. Adey & Biddulph, 2001). Moreover, the findings also concurred with those of other researchers (e.g. L. Archer, 2003) of Muslim young people as to the heightened need for Muslim young people to derive instrumental value from their education compared with other groups, as discussed earlier in the chapter.

The perceived instrumental irrelevance of history was a significant factor that accounted for the fact that the Muslim sample considered it significantly (χ^2 (4)=11.008, $p=0.026$) and greatly less *important to learn history at school* than did the non-Muslim sample. Only 59.2% of the Muslim sample either 'strongly' or 'mainly agreed' that it was *important to study history at school*, compared with 80% of the non-Muslim sample. By contrast, there was no significant difference in *interest in history at school* between the Muslim and the non-Muslim sample (69% for both samples). In other words, the Muslim young people had found history interesting but relatively irrelevant to their chances of getting a job. This finding was echoed by interviews with three young people who suggested that a perceived lack of instrumentality was a severe stumbling-block to GCSE uptake. Ishaq (Faith School, middle-achieving, British Malawi/Indian), for example, linked the possibility that he was not going to take history for GCSE directly with its perceived lack of instrumentality.

MATTHEW: You're undecided if you're going to take GCSE history … but what would make you choose it if you did?
ISHAQ: Like if it was more important […] to do history […] if you could get more jobs if you'd done history […] it doesn't really help you in the future.

Furthermore, at none of the schools had any teacher (or any outside guest) explained how history might be helpful for getting a job in terms of transferable skills or critical habits of mind (White, 1992) that are likely to be of value to prospective employers (P. Lee, 1992). Thus, in some ways the instrumental dimension of success, like ADS, existed as much as a 'determinate absence' (Bhaskar, 1993/2008) as a significant presence, which will need addressing in the future, given that overall holistic dimension of success and the intellectual dimension of success were emergent out of it. This lack of perceived instrumentality limited the potentially great impact of history on the social planes of intersubjective (interpersonal) transactions between differently situated human agents (b) and social relations at the irreducible level of structures, institutions and forms (c).

The civic dimension of success

The fact that the NCH should help them reflect on and deepen their understanding of their British citizenship was a core reason for studying history at school for my sample of Muslim pupils. Moreover, *civic success* was a key explanatory predictor of intellectual and overall holistic success for the Muslim sample of young people (see Table 6.1). In other words, the ability of school history to promote civic understanding (Barton, 2012) had a knock-on, articulated effect in the dimensions of intellectual success and the emergent totality of the whole person in history education.

On the whole, the Muslim young people tended strongly to think that history had a role in developing the types of mindset and attitudes that characterise the 'critical patriot' (Ramadan, 2010). The 'critical patriot' feels a sense of attachment to his or her country and pride in its achievements, which entails a duty to criticise and challenge national attitudes that have been, or are now, responsible for injustice or wrongdoing. The NCH had suggested to six of the young people interviewed that England, or Britain, was a country that had together achieved great things (as one boy put it, 'as team England') and also that the country had participated in considerable injustices and mistakes that it should learn from and avoid repeating, e.g. slavery.

Muslim (Technology School, middle-achieving, Iraqi) had been given an historical insight into both the good side – 'Like they fight for their country always, didn't ever give up' – and the bad side – 'they used to be racist. Did the slave trade' – of the British character, which he regarded as valuable practical knowledge about his compatriots. Indeed, there were a number of generic civic outcomes that the Muslim young people thought that history at school should have. They thought that history should:

- Inform them about the institutional history of England. In this regard, the study of the English Civil War had been illuminating for four of the interviewees concerning the contemporary constitutional relationship between Parliament and the Crown.
- Tell them about acts of political and social transformation that had improved society. NCH topics such as the suffragettes (cited by 17 young people as

their favourite topic) and slavery (cited by 61 young people as their favourite topic) were among the most popular because they had suggested to some of the young people that democratic political participation can change social life for the better. In this respect, *civic success* for the young people contained an element of history for 'social action' (Banks, 2006).

- Help them understand the nature of political power. The NCH topics slavery and the Holocaust had suggested to three of the young people interviewed that political power can be used and abused.
- Give them the critical skills of mind to help them to decipher information. Adil (Community School, high-achieving, Bengali-British), for example, had been brought to a recognition of the importance of respect for evidence and the role of examining evidence to determine whether events 'actually happened'.

ADIL: ... Since it's the evidence that actually teaches us. We learn from the evidence and got all the information from the evidence we find.

Adil cited the ability to use evidence properly as the most important of the skills he had developed through the study of history. In particular, the NCH module History KS3 *Unit 7: Images of an Age – what can we learn from portraits 1500–1750?* had alerted him to ways in which powerful people edited and manipulated their images through portraiture – a useful civic lesson for the Photoshop age.

Moreover, the *transformative* impact of the NCH for increasing a sense of belonging in England had been significantly greater for the Muslim sample than for the non-Muslim sample, with 50.9% registering either 'strong' or 'quite strong' *transformative citizenship history* compared with 41.2% of the non-Muslim sample. In other words, the Muslim sample felt more strongly than the non-Muslim sample that history at school had an important role to play in connecting them with the country. This significantly high level of *transformative* civic success suggested the potentially great impact of history in terms of Muslim young people's external integration and engagement at the level of social relations at the irreducible level of structures, institutions and forms (c).

The overall holistic dimension of success

The study indicated that the NCH had made an appreciable and significant overall contribution to the overall holistic success in the Muslim sample in terms of *awareness of myself and my world* (measured by variables **8c** and **8d** and principal component factor analysis). That is to say, the NCH was significantly important in the development of the totality of their emergent persons in an educational process. This was evidenced by the statistical analysis, which showed that 61.3% of the Muslim sample believed that they had developed a 'strongly' or 'quite strongly' increased *awareness of myself and my world* as a result of NCH compared with 42.9% of the non-Muslim sample – a significant difference (χ^2 (4)$=8.429, p=0.077$).

Ordinal logistic regression suggested that *spiritual success*, *civic success*, *out-of-school history* and *quality of teaching*, in that order of explanatory power, were all significant factors in the *overall holistic dimension of success* (see Table 6.1). That is to say, overall holistic success was loosely emergent to varying degrees from these different types of generative mechanisms of success. This result again suggested that the stratified, laminated model of success, considered as an articulated totality, has heuristic value, as without consideration of these different emergent facets of success, the overall impact of the NCH would have been more or less unaccountable.

In short, the significantly high levels of success in the intellectual and overall holistic dimensions of success enjoyed by the Muslim sample with NCH in absolute terms and compared to the non-Muslim sample, together with the more qualified value of the NCH in the other spiritual, affective-cultural and civic dimensions of success, suggested strongly that history has the potential to be an important subject for Muslim young people on all four planes of social being described by the philosophy of critical realism. History at school can help Muslim young people succeed in a way that does some justice to the totality of their personhood on a holistic, multidimensional model of a human being inspired, in this case, by the philosophy of critical realism.

From theorised evidence to evidenced theory: an ontology of the learning self in humanities education and the role of the humanities

Now that the learning self in history in its various dimensions has been theorised and grounded empirically with the evidence from Muslim youth in history education, we are in a position to posit a more general ontology of the Muslim learning self in the humanities from an Islamic critical realist perspective. This, as I mentioned at the start of the chapter, will be a prerequisite for a discussion in subsequent chapters of the modalities of nurturing that multidimensional self in humanities education.

We have seen in the previous chapter how the self, including the learning self in humanities education, in the model of ICR is made up of transcendentally real self/ground-state/spirit, embodied personality and illusory ego. We have also seen that in humanities subjects such as history, the engagement of the agency of the embodied personality with the structure of the subject discipline happens, *inter alia* and in a non-hierarchical way, in intellectual, spiritual, civic, instrumental and affective-cultural dimensions. All of these dimensions act as the mechanisms of the successful emergent personality by drawing the embodied personality away from its epistemic connection with falsity and false, partial accounts of the world, including Manichean, dichotomous world-views that are buttressed on culturally inherited prejudices. These dimensions, if engaged coherently by the humanities, can, I propose, act in 'articulated', stratified connection to restrain the illusory ego and loosen its epistemic connection with demi-reality, while strengthening the ontological connection between the embodied personality and the ground-state/spirit (*ruh*). This greater internal consistency ought to nurture the ability of the self to operate truthfully and effectively in four-planar social being.

Indeed, each of the humanities subjects can be understood as providing a different emphasis to the goal of the greater realisation of more internally integrated and externally engaged embodied personality on one or more of the four-planar levels of human being as described by the philosophy of critical realism:

a   At the level of *material transactions with nature* or, in ICR terms, custody of creation, geography will pertain most intensely to helping the human being understand the relationships between human being and the material and natural world (see Chapter 8). This understanding will have a physical, a social and an ethical dimension (Matthews & Herbert, 2008), which are themselves likely to occur on stratified local, regional, national, international and planetary levels (Jackson, 2006).

   Geography is essentially the study of 'the relationship between human activity and the environment, describing and explaining the significance of location, *distance, direction, spread, and spatial succession*'.
                                    (Cohen, 1988, p. 248 cited in Gregg & Leinhardt, 1994, p. 350)

b   At the level of *inter-subjective (interpersonal) relations and transactions* between different human agents, religious education predominantly pertains. In religious education, the fulcrum of Islamic critical realism can, as we saw in Chapter 3, set up the conditions for the development of mindsets that engage in an informed and respectful transcendental relationship with differently embedded 'others' and the Transcendentally Real 'Other' (or absence of Him, Her or It). Religious education can nurture embodied personalities that are enabled to commit to faith (or lack of it) in a way that acknowledges the human epistemic fallibility and the diversity of religious insight. We will explore in depth and detail in Chapter 8 how these knowledgeable and flexible mindsets can be fostered by religious education.

c   *At the level of irreducible structures, institutions and forms*, history in a past-oriented mode and citizenship in a present-oriented mode (Barton, 2012) can complement each other to develop less alienated and more internally and externally integrated Muslim young people. We have seen how history can be both highly informative and highly transformative of the ability of the Muslim young person to find a place for him- or herself in multi-faith society, if necessary by the transformation of Muslim–non-Muslim perceptions. We have seen that *at the level of irreducible structures, institutions and forms* (c), the overall holistic dimension of success developed from the relationship of mutual emergence between civic and intellectual dimensions of success. We also saw that for Muslim young people the spiritual dimension of success was essential to the development of the intellectual and overall holistic dimensions of success. This suggests that history and citizenship in close partnership with religious education can promote the intellectual engagement and success of the Muslim child across the school curriculum.

d   At the level of *the internal stratification of the embodied personality*, all the humanities subjects can contribute together to the success of Muslim learners so that internal gaps and absences in self-understanding and being are reduced and the strength of connection with and recourse to the ground-state/spirit by the embodied personality is increased. At this level of internal integration and the coming into being of healthy self-understanding, we have seen above how the co-ordinated home–school approach in the humanities is critical and that it can be highly detrimental to the development of the child if he or she exists in isolated, unconnected home, school, peer group and out-of-school/mosque learning cultures.

In summary: who are Muslim young people in humanities education?

Muslim young people in humanities education exist in multiple 'laminated' dimensions of mutually emergent being that exist in articulated and complementary tension. The ontology of the young Muslim learner is also shot through with absences in being and understanding derived, in part, from illusory 'hegemonic', 'demi-real' gender forms and absences of the Islamic faith at the normative/curricular level of school life. These absences and demi-real aspects of their being can pull the young Muslim away from a healthy approximation to the ground-state/spirit through a full engagement with humanities education and away from productive engagement with the non-Muslim 'other'. Muslim young people are simultaneously and constantly engaging internally with their embodied personalities in the intellectual, spiritual, affective-cultural, civic and instrumental dimensions of their being. In this struggle (*Jihād*) for authentic selfhood, serious $_{(r+p)}$ engagement with Islam is generally conducive to greater ontological wholeness and educational success. Highly gendered, unserious $_{(r+p)}$ Islamic identities, while sometimes providing sites of resistance to discrimination, tend to be counter-productive.

The study of the impact of history education on Muslim young people in England presented in this chapter has suggested:

1   the a priori necessity of a non-reductive ontology of the Muslim learning self in humanities education in order that Muslim pupils can fully access educational success via each of the humanities subjects;
2   that this success will necessarily exist on four-planar social levels and in intellectual, spiritual, affective-cultural, civic and instrumental dimensions if it is to nurture the development of the whole Muslim child;
3   that the different humanities subjects can be brought to bear as mechanisms of success as a holistic package with different disciplinary emphases.

I will now turn to how these different disciplinary emphases can nurture the multidimensional, articulated success of Muslim young people.

Notes

1 Geography is also a crucial part of this transformative package of humanities subjects, but it is not covered in depth in this book, partly because of the author's lack of research and practice-based knowledge of geography, and partly because it is not believed to be of *specific* significance to the development of Muslim young people in the way that history, RE and citizenship are. Nevertheless, it is my opinion that the ability to 'think geographically' (Jackson, 2006) is a crucially important dimension of the educated young person.

2 As a result, the deeper aims and purposes of education in general and of the role of particular subject disciplines, including history, in the holistic education of the child have been inadequately considered or systematically ignored (Pring, 2013). This absence of an in-depth policy and meta-curricular consideration of the purposes of history education in the twenty-first century contributed, for example, to the February 2013 Draft National Curriculum for History for English schools (UK Gov., 2013b). In this draft, prepared supposedly for the education of British children who will need to access a globalising world after two years of public consultation, there was barely a mention of the world outside Britain and a total absence of any mention of the historical contribution of Islamic civilisation to the development of humanity (Wilkinson, 2013). The question of who are we educating and what are we educating *for* in a humanities subject such as history, in the policy context, has remained a real, determinate absence in the debate about the History curriculum that has generated much heat but little light (Cannadine, 2013a).

3 In English schools, English, maths and science are called 'core' subjects and enjoy large amounts of curriculum time. History, geography, religious education, citizenship, art and design, and music are called 'foundation' subjects and are compulsory, although they are given less curriculum time than the core subjects.

4 Within the Muslim community this measurable outperformance by girls of boys is even more pronounced than in majority white British society. For example, in 2010 the average difference between British Muslim boys and girls (8.25%) who achieved five A* to C grades at GCSE (with English and Mathematics) was even greater than the considerable difference between white British young people and girls (7.1%) (UK Gov., 2011b). Therefore, relative not only to girls from Muslim ethno-cultural groups but also to boys from other ethno-cultural groups (UK Gov., 2011b; 2013a), Muslim boys fairly can be said to be achieving poor academic results.

5 At a macro-historical level, these types of hegemonic construction can be interpreted as falling within macro-historical types of hegemony. For example, Hoch (1979) postulates a historical oscillation between 'puritan' and 'playboy' types of masculinity. At a micro level, masculinity may be hegemonic and relational within highly localised space and timeframes and in relation to different types of people (Archer, 2003). Patriarchal, 'racialised' hegemonic masculinities may be enacted by Muslim boys and men differently in relation to Muslim girls and women as compared with to white women.

6 The young people were defined as Muslim rather than by their ethnic identifiers, as both in the literature (e.g. L. Archer, 2003; Shain, 2010) and in the background quantitative pilot study the young people themselves clearly identified most strongly with their Muslimness over and above their ethnicities and British nationalities, which were, nonetheless, important to them. Moreover, in Britain there are clear demographic differences, in particular in terms of employment and education, between Asian Muslim Britons and Asian Sikh and Hindu Britons, which meant that the

identification of the young people by their religious background, as opposed to their ethnicities, was sociologically sensible.

The ethnic make-up of the sample of Muslim young people was broadly indicative of the generality of the population of UK-based Muslims ($n=1,546,626$). In the sample, 81.1% were of South Asian origin (either Bangladeshi, Indian or Pakistani British); 7.5% were 'white' of both European and Arab origin; 9% were either African-Caribbean British, African or Somali; and the remaining 2% were of mixed ethnic heritage.

When calculated on the official, governmental index of poverty, namely, eligibility for free school meals (FSM), the sample of Muslim young people was considerably poorer than both the comparative non-Muslim sample and the national average of children in state schools. In the Muslim sample, 47.5% were eligible for FSM compared with 30% of the non-Muslim sample – a statistically significant difference (χ^2 (2)$=6.327$, $p<0.042$). The national average of FSM in English schools is 14%. Thus, the Muslim sample could be characterised, broadly speaking, as belonging very much to the poorer end of the working class, as is characteristic of British Muslim communities generally (Platt, 2001).

7   The findings in this chapter are taken from the sample of 295 Muslim boys who completed the survey and were interviewed, and 12 Muslim girls who were interviewed together in a focus group lasting one hour. The result from the focus group of Muslim girls suggested that the attitudes and feelings to NCH of the girls mapped very closely onto those of the boys, with two important exceptions, as is discussed in my analysis of the affective-cultural dimension of success (ADS). I therefore decided that it was unnecessary to conduct a separate survey with Muslim girls and I take the findings reported here to be representative of both Muslim boys and Muslim girls.

8   I analysed the statistical data using chi-square tests to show differences and correlations for similarities between the Muslim and non-Muslim samples' responses to NCH. Where variables were indicative of an underlying factor, I deployed principal component factor analysis (PCFA) to identify it. All this was done using the Statistical Package for the Social Sciences (SPSS). All responses to the variable statements were ranged on a Likert scale: 'I strongly agree'; 'I mainly agree'; 'I am uncertain'; 'I mainly disagree'; 'I strongly disagree'. The variables were grouped into clusters by themes that were intended, where possible, to be linked to an underlying factor which I then used as an explanatory mechanism through linear regression.

9   The qualitative interview data were gathered at one-to-one interviews, undertaken and recorded on a digital voice recorder in school time at the young people's schools. They were transcribed and then analysed through the combination of a 'grounded'-style and a more thematic approach (Glaser, 1992). I interviewed each of the 23 young people twice, and each interview lasted between 25 and 35 minutes. I observed all 23 young people in their history classes twice.

10 This was measured through each pupil's National Curriculum Level and survey independent variables **3a**, *The history I have studied at Key Stage 3 (KS3) has given me a good understanding of the history of England*; **3b**, *The history I have studied at KS3 has not given me a good understanding of the history of the rest of Britain*; **3c**, *The history I have studied at KS3 has helped me understand the history of other countries*; and **8d**, *The history I have studied in Years 7, 8 and 9 has helped me think more deeply about the world I live in*, and related principal component factor analysis (PCFA). Intellectual success was further explored in interview data and through classroom observations.

11 It was measured by independent variables **5d**, *The history I have studied at KS3 has helped me think about my own religion*; **5e**, *The history I have studied at KS3 has not helped me to think about what is right and what is wrong*; and **5f**, *The history I have studied at KS3 has taught me important lessons for life*, and related PCFA. The spiritual dimension of success was further explored in interview data and through classroom observations.

12 It was measured by independent variables **5c**, *The history I have studied at KS3 has not helped me to think about my own cultural background*; and **9k**, *I talk about history with my family at home*, and related regressions and PCFA. The affective-cultural dimension of success was further explored in the interview data.

13 It was measured by independent variables **7a**, *I am going to take history at GCSE*; and an open-ended variable **7b**, *I am going to take history at GCSE because …*, and related PCFA. The instrumental dimension of success was further explored in interview data and through classroom observations.

14 It was measured by independent variables **4a**, *The history I have studied at KS3 has helped me understand how Parliament developed*; **4b**, *The history I have studied at KS3 has not helped me to understand the changing role of British kings and queens*; **4c**, *The history I have studied at KS3 has helped me understand what a democracy is*; **4e**, *The history I have studied at KS3 has helped me think about what it means to be a British citizen*; **4f**, *I am more likely to vote when I am old enough as a result of the history I have learned*; and **5b**, *History lessons have helped me feel more at home in England*. PCFA identified two citizenship-related factors in these variables which I named Basic Citizenship Success and Transformative Citizenship Success. I then combined these as an aggregated variable, civic success. The civic dimension success was further explored in interview data and through classroom observations.

15 This was derived as an aggregated factor from *dependent* variables **8c**, *The history I have studied in Years 7, 8 and 9 has helped me think more deeply about myself*, and **8d**, *The history I have studied in Years 7, 8 and 9 has helped me think more deeply about the world I live in*, and explored more deeply in the interview data.

16 In four of the 10 cases, the ethical response of being grateful for the relative comfort of the present was accompanied by the reflection that these things should not be taken for granted.

In Tariq's case (Faith School, middle-achieving, Pakistani-British), his NCH had acted symbiotically with the Islamic history he 'had learned at madrasa' to create the impression of the 'hardness' and violence of the past compared with the ease of the present, which 'we should not take for granted'.

7   History education

From absence to emancipation

Introduction: ontological monovalence in education

In the previous chapter, I posited at the dialectical moment of 1M (First Moment – being-as-such) an ontology of the Muslim learner in humanities education as existing in four-planar social being and in intellectual, spiritual, affective-cultural, civic and instrumental dimensions. On the basis of this model, I highlighted that the humanities subjects brought different disciplinary emphases of knowledge to bear on the different social planes of human being. We also observed en passant how the positive impact of history in terms of the internal and external integration of understanding of the self and the world, especially on the four-planar level (c) of social relations at the irreducible level of structures, institutions and forms, is limited by significant absences in the spiritual, affective-cultural, civic and instrumental dimensions of success. This means that while the potential of history in and out of school to help Muslim young people make sense of themselves and the world around them is great, its benefits are currently woefully under-realised.

This chapter looks in greater theoretical and empirical depth at the impact of different types of educational absence on the learning experiences of Muslim (and other types of) young people in history and how the removal of these absences can lead to a more emancipatory experience of history. In the first section of the chapter, the concept of the 'absent curriculum' is articulated at the dialectical moment of 2E (Second Edge – absence) and illustrated through analysis of the responses of the same 307 Muslim young people in four state secondary schools in England to absences in their compulsory history provision, as identified in the previous chapter. This idea of the 'absent curriculum' is complemented by a look at other 'real determinate' absences in the young Muslims' experience of history: the absence of educational visits, the relative absence of parental input, and the absence of connection between in-school and out-of-school mosque-based history.

The chapter then proposes a strategy of the 'retotalisation' of history at the moment of 3L (Third Level – totality) by which teachers and educators of young Muslims could engage their charges more fully in their study of history by using the full ontological breadth of historical events available to them on national curricula in general and the new English National Curriculum for History in particular.

It finishes at the dialectical moment of 4D (Fourth Dimension – transformative praxis) by showing how the effects of the history curriculum, once it is emancipated from 'sub-totality' and parochialism, can help re-energise the broader Muslim community more broadly construed with a love of learning about and from the past.

2E: the absent curriculum

Ever since the Swann Report (1985), *Education for All*, in the United Kingdom, and as a result of scholars' identification of hidden curricula of unarticulated social messages delivered to pupils in schools (M. Apple & King, 1983; Vallance, 1973), it has been recognised that gaps and absences in educational experience and provision affect the educational engagement and achievement of pupils. Nevertheless, this chapter contends that the study of the educational experience has been prone to a philosophical oversight identified in Chapter 4 known as *ontological monovalence* by focusing on what is present at school to the exclusion of what is absent. By contrast, this chapter, consistently with Chapter 4, argues that both presence and absence are part of an adequate account of schooling, including the duality of an adequate ontology of curriculum.

Gordon L. Brown (2009), drawing on the philosophy of critical realism, has made an insightful typology of the concept of curriculum as comprising:

- the *formal curriculum*, which consists in the published syllabus together with related policy documents;
- the *enacted curriculum* that is actually taught;
- the *hidden curriculum* of unintended learning;
- the *null curriculum* of what is not included in the formal curriculum but could have been.

To this typology this chapter adds both the *selected curriculum*, which is the formal curriculum as selected by school management for their school-based departmental schemes of work, and the *absent curriculum*.

The *absent curriculum* is the totality of the curriculum that could have been, but has not been, taught. It has three component parts, which will be conceived and illustrated by this chapter (see Figure 7.1):

1   The absent *null curriculum* at the level of national policy comprises those topics that could have been included on the formal curriculum but are omitted by policy-makers and curriculum planners.
2   The absent *unselected curriculum* at the level of school management comprises those topics that are available for selection from the formal curriculum for school departmental schemes of work but which are not selected for the school-based curriculum.

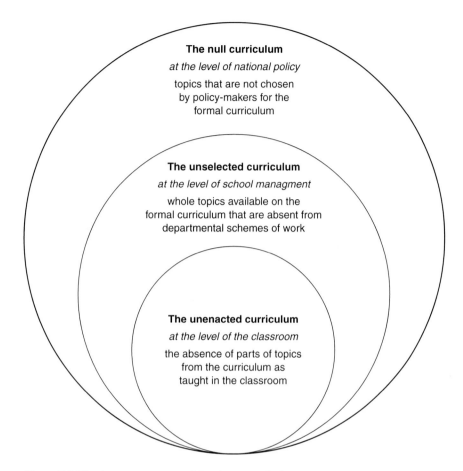

Figure 7.1 The three components of the absent curriculum.

3   The absent *unenacted curriculum* at the level of the classroom comprises of those topics or elements within topics that are available for teaching from school departmental schemes of work but in practice are not taught by teachers in the classroom.

This chapter will articulate and illustrate the concept of the absent curriculum in its three component parts and demonstrate that the absent curriculum as well as the present curriculum affects the lives of children in a variety of ways by looking at the impact of elements that were absent from the National Curriculum for History in England at Key Stage 3 (ages 11–14) on our sample of 307 Muslim young people in English schools (aged 13).

Theoretical framework: the philosophy of critical realism and its theory of absence

The conceptualisation of the educational experience in general and curriculum in particular as a duality of presence and absence and its three particular component parts is undertaken using the critical realist concepts of 'absence', 'totality' and 'sub-totality' that I have already theorised and applied to the life of the Prophet Muhammad in Chapter 4.

We have seen in Chapter 4 that critical realist thinkers such as Norrie (2010), Hostettler (2012) and Alderson (2013), following the lead of Roy Bhaskar (1993/2008), have argued that the tradition of Western philosophy is *ontologically monovalent* in the excessive privileging of the positive aspect of being to the exclusion of non-being or the negative aspects of being. According to critical realist thinkers, absence, negativity and change are essential parts of the duality of presence and absence in being (Norrie, 2010). For example, silence is the precondition of speech, rests are indispensable to musical sound, and, as we know from natural science, empty space is a necessary precondition of solid objects. A historical narrative will also be shaped as much by what is left out as by what is recorded.

It will be remembered that in this critical realist account, absence is not only integral to being, but also transformative. Indeed, dialectical change is understood by critical realists as the process of the remedying or removal of absence (Bhaskar, 1993/2008). In education, the path to knowledge is as much the removal of ignorance and the unblocking of obstacles to understanding as it is the learning of positive 'new' things. Likewise, the reform of a curriculum is as much a removal of significant absences and making its hidden ideological drivers visible (M. W. Apple, 1993; Vallance, 1983) as the modification of what is more obviously present.

Thus, it will be remembered that absence has been understood by critical realism as '*real determinate absence*' (Norrie, 2010), and the removal of absence is conducive to the development of greater epistemological consistency and ontological wholeness. Thus, the role of absence in a dialectic of social or natural transformation can be described as follows:

> Absence (e.g. omission) → incompleteness → inconsistency (contradiction, etc.) → transcendence → to a more comprehensive and inclusive totality.
>
> (Bhaskar, 2000, p. 55)

According to critical realist thinkers, this process of the dialectical 'absenting of absence' is part of the process of overcoming hiatuses and obstacles to greater ontological wholeness or totality of being, which critical realist thinkers call 'totality'.

Totality, partial totality, sub-totality and history curriculum

For critical realists, the idea of totality, which has nothing to do with political totalitarianism, is necessitated by the nature of the natural and social worlds … human beings are caught in a structured flow of being and becoming in which the totality of past, present and future relations is implicated … a sense of totality is central to being.

(Norrie, 2010, p. 88)

Totality is also conceived of as 'multiple, overlapping, partial totalities' (Norrie, 2010, p. 89) which are always conceived of in relation to a whole that can never, in practice, be entirely encompassed, but without reference to which partial totalities become meaningless. 'To think of a language, a sentence, a text, a book or even a word is to think of entities where one has to grasp something as a whole as well as in its individual parts' (p. 88).

In this understanding, we have seen in Chapter 4 that a *sub-totality* is a partial totality from which elements have been omitted to noxious effect. A sub-totality has been defined as 'the site of "discontinuities, hiatuses, spaces, binds, barriers, boundaries and blocks between totalities" … the term [used] to denote the splitting, fracturing and broken nature of the whole under conditions of material diffraction' (Norrie, 2010, p. 90).

The concepts of 'totality', 'partial totality' and 'sub-totality' can be neatly illustrated using the case example of a history curriculum. In a history curriculum, historical periods and great events can be considered to be 'totalities' (within greater 'totalities'), in that any particular part of them makes no sense without reference to the whole. In this analogy, a 'partial totality' would be one particular contained historical episode within a greater 'totality' of a period or event. For example, the Somme offensive in 1916 might be considered a 'partial totality' of the hostilities on the Western Front, which are in turn a 'partial totality' in relation to the 'totality' of the First World War. No 'partial totality' makes sense without reference to the greater 'totality' of which it is part, and yet it can almost be considered and studied as a discrete and independent episode.

Within this understanding, *a curricular 'sub-totality' emerges when a 'partial totality' is constructed as curriculum and taught as if it were a complete curricular 'totality'.* Using the First World War example, a curricular sub-totality would emerge if the Western Front were taught as the 'totality' of the First World War. Such a sub-totality creates a block or a hiatus to gaining an understanding of the nature of the whole event or phenomenon. Of course, it can be argued that it is impossible to construct 'total' curricular representations of historical events: historical accounts are always highly selective collections of related facts driven by a host of ideological, narrative and empirical considerations (M. W. Apple, 1993; Cronon, 2000). Nevertheless, partial curricular totalities become 'sub-totalities' when key or core elements of the total picture are omitted from officially endorsed narratives for either practical or ideological reasons and then presented by authorised educators as the complete 'partial totality', or even as the complete 'totality'. The idea of curricular 'sub-totality' and concrete examples of it in action in a history curriculum will be explored more fully later in this chapter.

Towards a critical realist ontology of curriculum

Applying these concepts from the philosophy of critical realism to the concept of curriculum, we can describe a curriculum as a totality that has ontological (material, social, economic, educational and psychological) reality for those who design it (policy-makers), for those who mediate it (teachers) and for those who participate in it (pupils), and, indirectly, for society more generally construed.

The ontology of this totality is an interrelationship of both presences (the formal curriculum at the level of policy, the selected curriculum at the level of school management and the enacted curriculum at the level of the classroom) and absences (the null curriculum at the level of national policy, the unselected curriculum at the level of school management and the unenacted curriculum at the level of the classroom) (see Figure 7.2).

Both present and absent curricula have ontological reality as effecting real epistemological (learning) and ontological (social, economic and psychological)

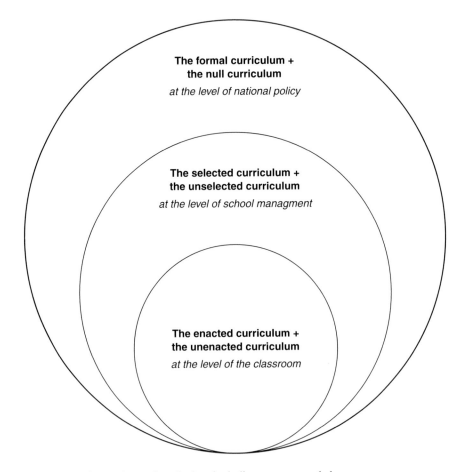

Figure 7.2 The ontology of curriculum including presence and absence.

outcomes, and are conveyed in both overt and hidden ways. This statement of ontology with regard to the present curriculum should be uncontroversial; teachers, parents and researchers know that the curricula and syllabuses that curriculum-planners design and that teachers bring to bear in the classroom affect the lives of children in a variety of ways, both intended and unintended (Vallance, 1973). That which is omitted or otherwise excluded from the curriculum, the absent curriculum, which may have significant effects on the learning outcomes of pupils, has often been ignored.[1]

The focus on three elements of the English National Curriculum for History

For the purposes of illustrating the *absent curriculum* at its three different levels and discovering its impact, this chapter focuses on three elements of NCH at Key Stage 3 in England (ages 11–14). These elements were available on the formal curriculum of NCH for study by my sample of Muslim young people at the time of research. They were chosen as they might all have reasonably been expected both on paper as the *selected curriculum* and in delivery as the *enacted curriculum* to include the history of the Muslim contribution in some appreciable way.

The first focus: an important optional module of international scope

The first focus was a module on the formal curriculum of NCH, *Unit 21. From Aristotle to the atom: scientific discoveries that changed the world?* This optional module might, given its subject matter, reasonably have been expected to include something of the contribution of Islamic civilisation to the progress of natural scientific understanding in the Islamic 'Golden Age' (*c*.700–1450), at least within the context of an international historical consideration of 'the world'.

The second focus: optional modules on the history of the Muslim contribution

The second focus was on whole modules of NCH that were available for selection by school management from the formal curriculum of NCH that specifically foregrounded the history of the contribution of Muslims and historical involvement of Britain with the Muslim world. These were *Unit 6. What were the achievements of the Islamic states 600–1600?* and *Unit 13. Mughal India and the coming of the British, 1526–1857. How did the Mughal Empire rise and fall?* These modules existed on the formal curriculum of NCH under the Key Concept of 'Diversity', but unlike the two other topics for study organised under this concept, slavery and the Holocaust, they were optional. The formal curriculum of NCH also provided detailed non-statutory schemes of work to facilitate their delivery in the classroom.

The third focus: important mandatory modules of history of international significance

The third focus was on two historical episodes of significant international scope that had an undoubted impact on the Muslim-majority world and that were taught compulsorily as part of the enacted curriculum of NCH at the four research schools. These were the First World War and the Independence of India.

We shall now observe the absent curriculum in its three component parts.

The absent, null curriculum: the absence of the Muslim contribution at the level of national curricular policy

The analysis of the first topic focus – *Unit 21. From Aristotle to the atom: scientific discoveries that changed the world?* – enables illustration of the absent curriculum at the level of national policy as the absent null curriculum. That is to say, at the level of national curricular policy the history of the Muslim contribution had been omitted by curriculum planners from the formal curriculum of NCH at places where it might naturally and easily have been included.

In this module, the history of the Muslim contribution to scientific progress was a particularly obvious null curriculum that would have fitted naturally and appropriately into the non-statutory NCH Programme of Study – *Unit 21. From Aristotle to the atom: scientific discoveries that changed the world?* – and yet was completely absent.

Not one mention on the formal curriculum of NCH was made of the seminal contributions of Muslim scholars of the Abbasid dynasty in Baghdad (c.762–c.1258) or of the Umayyad dynasty in Spain (c.756–c.1031) to the preservation and development of classical learning. The pioneering progress made by al-Khwarizmi (Latin: Algoritmi [hence algorithm], c.780–c.850) in mathematics, by Ibn al-Haytham (Latin: Alhazen, 965–c.1040) in the science of optics, by Ibn Sina (Latin: Avicenna, c.980–1037) in medical knowledge and practice, to name but three out of many possible examples, was simply airbrushed out of history. The grand narrative of the unit of work moved 'seamlessly' from Aristotle (384–322 BC) via Copernicus (1473–1543) and Galileo (1564–1642) to Newton (1642–1726) and Darwin (1809–1882) without any reference to the scientific developments of the Muslim world between 700 and 1450. The preservation and development of the learning of ancient Greece, Persia, India and China by scholars working within Islamic environments before its transferral into Renaissance Europe was entirely missing. The omission of the work of Arab Muslim scholars in preserving and expanding upon Aristotle's empiricist materialism was of particular note given the fact that the rebirth of European natural science relied upon this Muslim contribution for theoretical purposes (Masood, 2009).

Thus, the absent null curriculum represented a damaging gap both in terms of the quality of *all* pupils' historical learning of the development of empirical science and, as we will see, in terms of the feelings of self-worth and intellectual participation of our Muslim young people. In this case, the null curriculum was damaging, above all else, because it did an injustice to a coherent narrative of the history of science itself (cf. Whitburn, Hussain & Mohamud, 2012).

The absent, unselected curriculum: whole modules of history of the Muslim contribution on the formal curriculum were absent at the level of school management from departmental schemes of work

The analysis of the second topic focus – whole modules of NCH that were available for selection by school management from the formal curriculum of NCH that specifically foregrounded the history of the contribution of Muslims – enables illustration of the absent curriculum at the level of school management as the absent *unselected curriculum*.

Despite the presence of the history of the Muslim contribution – *Unit 6. What were the achievements of the Islamic states 600–1600?* and *Unit 13. Mughal India and the coming of the British, 1526–1857. How did the Mughal Empire rise and fall?* – on the formal curriculum of NCH, this available history of the Muslim contribution was not selected for departmental schemes of work in any of the four schools researched, even the Islamic Faith School.

Only one of the four research schools, the Specialist School, had *ever* taught either of these two possible full-length units (about 10 lessons) of the history of the Muslim contribution. Even the Specialist School had abandoned Unit 13 after one year, according to one teacher because of its poor reception by pupils. In other words, at the time of research (2009–2010), both modules of the Muslim contribution to NCH were completely absent from my research schools, even though the schools had on average an 81.4% Muslim intake. These modules were, therefore, an archetypical case example of an absent *unselected curriculum*: they were whole curricular topics that were available on the formal curriculum but were not selected for departmental schemes of work by school middle-management.

Teachers' rationale for this unselected curriculum: a cluster of real, determinate absences

This unselected curriculum was itself, as the boys' teachers explained, generated by a cluster of interrelated real, determinate absences. The teachers' rationale for this component part of the absent curriculum also suggested that the unselected curriculum bore the character of a hidden curriculum. It was both unobserved by pupils and parents and perpetuated by the unarticulated, barely perceived cultural capital (and lack of cultural capital) of educational actors. As we shall see, it also conveyed a hidden socio-cultural, ideological message of the relative cultural insignificance of Islam and its civilisation (M. W. Apple, 1990; Bourdieu & Passeron, 1977).

ABSENCE OF TEACHING RESOURCES

Mike (Community School, male, mid-thirties) alluded to the absence of relevant curricular resources from which to teach the two modules and to possible 'teacher laziness' in the failure to create them as factors in generating this unselected curriculum: 'It's a case of why reinvent the wheel?'

Along similar lines, Mary (Technology School, white British female, early thirties, Head of Humanities) alluded to the fact that at the Technology School they did not have the resources for the curriculum to keep pace with the 'changing demographics' of the school.

ABSENCE OF THE RIGHT CULTURAL CAPITAL

Mike also suggested that the absence of the necessary 'cultural inheritance' that a typical history teacher brought to the classroom might serve to exclude the history of the Muslim contribution available on the formal curriculum from its delivery in the classroom.

MIKE: I think you tend to lean towards your background, don't you, and both me and him [another teacher] would've been brought up with parents who would have told us lots about World War I and World War II.... And therefore it's second nature and that's what we have.... I mean.... It's a cultural inheritance, you know, and you know, maybe it's a damnation on me and my ignorance of Islamic history, you know, that I don't include it [the history of the Muslim contribution] in a curriculum or that it hasn't been thought about.

It was clear that the history of the Muslim contribution fell outside both teachers' cultural 'comfort zone', a fact that contributed to its being an unselected curriculum item.

PERCEIVED ABSENCE OF PUPIL INTEREST

Mary also cited the absence of student demand as a main reason for the absence of the history of the Muslim contribution, as 'none of the students have ever requested or put forward any kind of specific interest in it'. The theme of the absence of pupil interest also came up again at the Community School and the Specialist School. At the Community School, Paul (Community School, white English-British) had specifically designed a module on the history of Pakistan in response to pupil pressure, which had not, on delivery, appealed to the boys.

PAUL: [I] planned six lessons on Pakistan, and after lesson 2 they were, 'Oh, this is boring, Sir; this is rubbish.'

Similarly, a module on the history of Bangladesh had been a failure in Anthony's (Specialist School, white British, mid-thirties) opinion, as it had not resonated culturally in any way at all with British-Bangladeshi pupils:

ANTHONY: And we went through, a couple of years ago, of actually having a topic on Bangladeshi history, right from the Mughals all the way through to the British, through to Sheikh Mujibah Rahman, War of Independence 1975 [...]. Fascinating and irritating how little interest the students had. They <u>really</u> had no interest. I found it harder to get them engaged in that topic than any other topic we do [...] I had no idea why this was.... And we've now binned the Bangladeshi [module].

By contrast, Mike (Community School, white English-British) spoke of the 'passion' of pupils for his teaching of the Arab–Israeli conflict and that fact that the module had a connection to some students' political boycott of Israeli produce. Hence, the Arab–Israeli conflict had 'made it' onto the selected curriculum of Mike's history department even though it was not, in theory, available on the formal curriculum of NCH itself. Here was a good example of the selected curriculum 'trumping' the null curriculum because an individual teacher had realised that good practice entailed teaching a controversial historical episode which *really mattered* to pupils (Barton & McCully, 2007).

ABSENCE OF UNDERSTANDING WHERE THE HISTORY OF THE MUSLIM CONTRIBUTION 'FITTED IN'

All these absences were connected to a greater, more total absence of knowing how the history of the Muslim contribution 'fitted in' within the broader themes that the teachers were covering on the curriculum.

Paul (Community School, white English-British) explained:

And so Year 8 and Year 9, the Year 8 one for me is more about power and parliaments, democracy, and Year 9 is kind of the empire, world wars, and so the traditional approach. So, again, it probably stems back to my knowledge as well, that I don't feel [...] I'm not sure where that fits in, in Year 9 for instance or within Year 8 where I could weave it in.

The key issue here appeared to be the absence of a harmonious relationship between the agency of teachers and the structure of the curriculum. In the structure of the formal curriculum of NCH at Key Stage 3, the history of the Muslim contribution 'fitted' under the core objective for 'Diversity' (Qualifications and Curriculum Agency, 2009) but it did not fulfil any clear logical or historical function that enabled it to be turned into the selected or enacted curriculum of the school. Although the history of the Muslim contribution reflected 'Diversity', the discrete modules did not facilitate the agency of teachers to 'weave' the two modules into the broader themes of their schemes of work and therefore into the Big Picture and Big Questions that they were addressing across the curriculum. This observation bears out the findings of the influential Parekh Report (2000), which suggests that the guidelines offered to teachers by teacher training providers and schools as to the modalities of creating a diverse curriculum are as yet inadequate.

Moreover, the lack of enthusiasm of pupils appeared to suggest that the modules on the history of the Muslim contribution were regarded as 'tokenistic' and 'bolt-on', and sent out the message that history of Islam and Muslims was not part of the mainstream story of Britain, the world and humanity as presented by NCH. While slavery and the Holocaust were statutory, and large amounts of classroom time were dedicated to them, the history of the Muslim contribution was optional and absent. The history of the Muslim contribution belonged on the formal curriculum of NCH in such a way as to suggest to some pupils that Muslims and their history are not connected in any meaningful way to Britons and the history of Britain.

In fact, of course, the history realities of events such as the Crusades, early modern trade and diplomacy between England and the Mughal and Ottoman Empires, the British Empire, and post-colonial migration and settlement, to name but three obvious examples, mean that the histories of Islam, Muslims, Britons and Britain are in many ways deeply connected with each other. This interpenetration of historical narratives might have enriched and brought inter-cultural British–Islamic engagement to the history classroom had any of the teachers seen fit to explore it (Barton & McCully, 2005; Gilliat-Ray, 2010).

In short, this absent, *unselected curriculum* at the level of departmental management was historically unnecessary and might have been remedied by enriched teacher training and other mechanisms that promote good teaching practice.

The absent, unenacted curriculum: the absence of the history of the Muslim contribution from topics that were taught the classroom

Analysis of the third topic focus – two historical episodes of significant international scope that had an undoubted impact on the Muslim-majority world and that were taught compulsorily as part of the enacted curriculum of NCH at the four schools, namely the First World War and the Independence of India – enables illustration of the absent, unenacted curriculum at the level of classroom delivery.

This absent, unenacted curriculum took the form of curricular 'sub-totalities', as described in the theoretical section. That is to say, selective parts – 'partial totalities' – of great historical events – 'totalities' – were packaged as curriculum and presented 'officially' by teachers as if they represented the full totality of events, to the exclusion of the Muslim (and other) contributions.

Example of the absent, unenacted curriculum: (1) the First 'World' War

The First World War was the second most frequently cited favourite topic at 20.7% ($n=55$), after slavery at 22.9%, of the Muslim young people. It was also significantly more cited in the questionnaire survey by the Muslim sample than by the non-Muslim sample as a 'favourite topic'.

At interview, five out of the 23 Muslim young people interviewed mentioned the First World War as their 'favourite topic', citing the role of the Alliance system, the development of weapons technology, trench warfare and the contribution of women on the home front as reasons for their interest, thus alluding, in their own way, to the appeal of this particular topic when considered as a 'totality'.

However, given the popularity of this topic an opportunity was missed at all four of the schools to create links between the pupils' religio-cultural Muslim heritage and their civic heritage as Britons. This was a significant omission considering that the contemporary Muslim-majority world was shaped in large part by outcomes of the First World War: the demise of the Ottoman Empire and the creation of European-style nation-states across the Middle East (Bentley & Ziegler, 2006). At all the research schools, the First World War was taught as if the entire conflict was played out on the Western Front, and thus the First World War was taught as a 'sub-totality'. That is to say, the 'partial totality' of the European Western Front was constructed in the delivery of the curriculum as if it represented the 'totality' of the First World War.

At the Specialist School, the history teacher, Anthony (white British, mid-thirties) recognised that his teaching of the First World War was packaged in this way:

MATTHEW: So I'm wondering, when you're teaching the First World War, given the background of these kids, do you sort of open it up to include, you know, the war in the Middle East or the war on the Eastern Front...?
ANTHONY: No, we're ... we're very much the former [the focus on the Western Front].

Anthony justified his construction of this curricular 'sub-totality' in terms of captivating the students with the archetype of the 'classic fighting Tommy'.

ANTHONY: You've got to do the trenches, you've got to do the British, British soldier, you know, the classic Tommy fighting in the trenches ... you know, because that captivates the students, you know, they love that, the grittiness, the mud, the guns, the rats, the filth, the horror, right, you know, it gets them into it, so you've got to do that. And, yeah, it'd be, it'd be perfect to do all the other elements as well, but then you're spending a term or over a term on what, on a four-year part of history when you've got all these other things to think about as well.

It was clear from my observations of Anthony's class that the vividness of trench life and of the 'fighting Tommy' *did* captivate the students. Nevertheless, how much more meaningful might this captivation have been had his 100% Muslim class also learned about the lives of units of Indian Muslims who fought with Sikhs and Hindus alongside 'the classic Tommy' (white, British and Irish working-class) and dealt with trench warfare through Prayer (*Salah*), Supplication (*dua'*) and other Islamic means while fighting for the British Empire (Cowling, 2009)? Moreover, even granted the undoubted and continuous pressures of time faced by history teachers, a focus on the Western Front surely ought not to have precluded at least a passing mention of the impact and prosecution of the Great War in other parts of the world, such as the Eastern Front or the Middle East, without which the war on the Western Front becomes meaningless and 'de-totalised'.

Given the critical role of the First World War in generating the political structures under which the Muslim-majority world now labours, this omission meant that a great opportunity both to construct a 'history of the present' (Dewey, 1916), to reflect in an inter-cultural way on the role of Muslim agency in world affairs and non-Muslim agency in Muslim-majority affairs (Barton, 2012) and to link the young people's British and Islamic identities went begging at all the schools. This absent, unenacted curriculum was clearly an obstacle to the young people gaining a comprehensive and useful understanding of an important historical totality of which today's present in Europe, the Middle East and elsewhere is at least in part a product.

Example of the absent, unenacted curriculum: (2) Gandhi and the Independence of India

Similarly, the Independence of India was being taught at all the schools, even the Islamic faith school, without any mention of Partition and the creation of Pakistan.

For Pervez (Faith School, high-achieving, British-Pakistani), this absence of the history of the formation of Pakistan from the curricular account of Indian Independence was a source of disappointment and confusion. Moreover, his description of the fact that the story of Gandhi was taught at the Faith School as the totality of Indian Independence, without mention of the creation of Pakistan, shows the emotional impact of a 'sub-totality' being taught as a 'totality' on some pupils.

PERVEZ: [T]o learn about Gandhi is not exactly something that's very exciting. If it was more like how the Pakistan started then it would be exciting but Gandhi … I don't mind learning it but it would be better about … I'm not exactly excited about it.

MATTHEW: …So would I be right in saying that if, let's say, Gandhi … you were learning about Gandhi and Mohammed Jinnah and the whole sort of movement to start Pakistan … as sort of together … then that might be more interesting?

PERVEZ: Yeah […] 'cause I wasn't even aware of that, you know, because we haven't learned it, I haven't even heard of that, so yeah, that's quite new to me so it would be better if we can learn things like that.

Pervez was reluctant to ask for the Pakistani side of the matter to be addressed as he was under the strong impression that his classmates and his teacher were not interested in the Pakistani component of Partition – 'even though the teacher is

Pakistani' – and believed that Pakistan had been 'forgotten' by his classmates and by the school. Furthermore, he situated his classmates' 'forgetting' about Pakistan within the broader national context and the feeling that Britain had also 'forgotten' about Pakistan now that it was no longer a part of the British Empire. Here the absent, unenacted curriculum can clearly be seen as creating a false impression as, in reality, Britain has not forgotten about Pakistan and retains a large diplomatic presence there as well as contributing to the country through aid (UK Gov., 2013e).

Equally importantly, as with the First World War, an opportunity to discuss contentious issues (Barton & James, 2010) surrounding the nature and the status of a religious state in the modern world, which is a part of the necessary religious reflection of British Muslim young people, went begging. This situation might have been resolved had Partition been included as part of the 'totality' of the Indian independence and had not the 'partial totality' of Gandhi's life – important and inspirational though it is – squeezed out all other important elements of this particular curricular 'totality'.

The impact of the absent curriculum

This example of the negative emotional impact of the absent curriculum was symptomatic of a more widespread negative impact of the absent curriculum in terms of weakening some of the sample pupils' connection to the subject of history in general and to British history in particular.

For example, 11 out of the sample of 24 students (45.8%), who came from all the schools except the Community School, noted *unprompted* the absence of the history of the Muslim contribution from their curricular learning. All 11 boys alluded in some way to the real determinate, negative impact of this absent curriculum, which ranged from feelings of 'boredom' and frustration to more keenly felt feelings of alienation and rejection.

For Haider (Faith School, Pakistani-British, low-achieving), for example, the absence of history of the Muslim contribution at school contributed to his 'boredom' with the subject, to his finding it unimportant and to the feeling that he was 'not learning the right stuff'.

Pervez (Faith School, Pakistani-British, high-achieving) said that without the history of the Muslim contribution, history at school was 'a complete waste of time'. Notwithstanding the adolescent hyperbole of this statement, Pervez's testimony suggested that something that would have been seminal to his potential engagement with the subject was missing. This was reinforced by the fact that both Pervez and Haider said that the inclusion of some element of the history of the Muslim contribution would have rendered other topics, such as the compulsory study of the changing relationship between the British monarchy and Parliament, more interesting – even, said Haider, 'all those Henries!'

Thus, the absent curriculum had a negative effect, preventing some of the young people from finding history as a school subject generally meaningful, relevant and useful. Importantly, it prevented some of them from relating to, remembering and understanding the 'normative' history of England and other statutory parts of NCH that delivered a basic historical understanding of the young people's nation: in this case, Britain. In this regard, my statistical data showed that the Muslim sample felt that they had gained a significantly (χ^2 (4)=15.498, $p=0.004$) poorer understanding of the basic civic history of England than the non-Muslim sample: 50.8% of the Muslim sample felt that they had a good understanding of the core civic history of England as a result of NCH, compared with 68.9% of the comparative non-Muslim sample of 60 young people. In this sense, it would appear that the recommendations of the Ajegbo Report (2007) that all pupils need to be able to relate to Britishness in a concrete way through connection to the British national story remain very much unrealised and that the absent curriculum is part and parcel of this unsatisfactory situation.

The absent curriculum is a real determinate factor in pupils' learning and emerging identities

We have seen that the absent curriculum is a real, determinate part of a duality of presence and absence in a balanced ontology of curriculum. It has been conceived of in this chapter at three levels: the absent *null curriculum* at the level of national curricular planning; the *absent unselected curriculum* at the level of school departmental curricular planning; and the *absent unenacted curriculum* at the level of classroom delivery. In the case example explored in this chapter, the absence of the history of the Muslim contribution, whether it was a *null curriculum* missing from the formal curriculum of NCH, or an *unselected curriculum* of entire topics available on the formal curriculum that were ignored by school management, or occurred as an *unenacted curriculum* when topics were taught as 'sub-totalities' in the classroom, constituted an absent curriculum that had a real, determinate impact on some of my sample of Muslim young people's experience of the National Curriculum for History. The negative impact of the absent curriculum was particularly evident in the dimensions of spiritual and affective-cultural success, which, as we have seen in the previous chapter, were dimensions that had strong knock-on effects in the dimension of intellectual success.

This absent curriculum was for some young people demotivating in itself and acted as an obstacle to their more general engagement with the rest of the history curriculum, including 'standard' English and British national history. This failure to connect with the 'historical community' of the nation, as the result of an absence of engagement with school history, may have great negative consequences in terms of aspirations for life for the excluded group. As Ahonen (2001) notes,

> As history is used for identity building, any grand narrative diffused through a school curriculum tends to reinforce a uniform identity. Those with no place or role in the grand narrative will be excluded from the historical

community. They either face a sense of double consciousness or lack of resources to face up to their past.... Those who are excluded lack an important asset for the building of future expectations.

(p. 190)

In other words, the absent curriculum in a National Curriculum for history merely comes to be perceived by pupils from groups whose histories have been unnecessarily absented from the formal, selected and enacted curriculum as an official statement of their relative ontological and civic insignificance.

2E: the absent pedagogy

We have seen how both absences and presences in the curriculum determine the learning outcomes of Muslim young people (and, of course, other types of young people) in history. Similarly, absences, as well as presences, in pedagogy were determinate of Muslim young people's experience of NCH.

Positive presences in pedagogy

With regard to the positive presence of pedagogy, pupils at the Faith School and Community School in particular expressed a link between good classroom and behaviour management and good subject knowledge and powers of explanation. They liked history teachers who controlled the class and explained things well. Other features of effective teaching practice cited by pupils included:

- good organisation;
- making history fun and interesting through varied teaching strategies;
- having detailed subject knowledge;
- giving pupils the opportunity to talk about their own experiences;
- showing 'kids' 'respect' by listening to them'.

All of these tally with some of the generic qualities of good teachers observed by other researchers (R. Smith, 1995).

Particularly cited by the Muslim sample compared with the non-Muslim sample was 'the use of evidence and investigation' as explanatory of their 'interest in history'. By contrast, 'no fun trips and activities', 'too much writing' and 'disrupted lessons' were cited significantly more by the Muslim sample than by the non-Muslim sample as reasons for 'boredom with history'.

In line with the generic findings of other researchers into effective pedagogies (Conroy et al., 2013), multi-media teaching strategies that involved audio-visual, as well as oral and written, presentation were more effective at promoting interest and the retention of information than oral or writing-based strategies alone, in particular for pupils from lower sets.

Abdul Qadir (Technology School, low-achieving, African-Caribbean) had noted in his diary, for example, rich detail that he had remembered from class about the Nazi persecution of Jews in 1930s Germany, which he said he had remembered and understood ''cause he [his teacher, David] put PowerPoint presentations up as he was explaining at the same time as well: that's how I understood'.

In the same vein, Muslim (Technology School, middle-achieving, Iraqi) cited the same lesson on the Holocaust as the most interesting and memorable owing to a teaching strategy that involved a combination of 'pictures and information', which was not like 'normal lessons [when] you just have writing and everything [and] you don't understand'. In general, and in common with other young people, the Muslim sample liked 'active', multi-modal pedagogies such as preparing for debates by sourcing data online and writing down their arguments, and disliked mono-modal strategies that were just 'copying from the board'.

The absent pedagogy

However, it was as much the absence of a pedagogy that the Muslim pupils liked and which was missing, as the presence of pedagogies from which they took regular benefit, which really stood out from my data. Of the sample of Muslim young people across the schools, 28.5% cited 'we don't do any fun trips or activities' as a reason why they found history 'boring', compared with 19.3% of the non-Muslim sample, a significant difference of 9.2%.

The absence of historical educational visits, as an integral part of the young people's experience of history, was particularly keenly felt at the Faith School, where three out of the eight pupils referred to either the complete absence or the relative absence of trips compared to other schools they had attended. For example, I asked Ishaq (Faith School, middle-achieving, British-Indian) if there was anything he would change about history:

MATTHEW: [I]f there's one thing you could change about history, what would you do?
ISHAQ: I'd make more trips.

The interviews revealed that the Faith School history department had not laid on a single history trip during the entirety of the boys' Key Stage 3 history. A sense of trips as an integral part of their experience of history (DeWitt & Storksdieck, 2008) and one that was a missing feature in their history provision was expressed by three Faith School boys, who were all quite specific about the benefits that they felt were forgoing.

History trips were important to Ishaq (Faith School, middle-achieving, British-Indian) as he felt they helped him empathise with a historical event or situation in order to 'feel it [history] more' in a way that might help him plug gaps in his classroom understanding. In a related way, Haider (Faith School, low-achieving, British-Pakistani) believed that history trips helped him get a 'more detailed explanation' of what had happened in the past, in a way that was 'not boring'. Furthermore, Ayyub (Faith School, low-achieving, British-Indian) and Ishaq both thought that this absence of educational visits reflected badly on history at the Faith School when the boys compared it to their experience of history at primary school.

The Faith School was not alone in having offered no educational visits during the whole of Key Stage 3 history. The Technology School – the other school where the boys had significantly less positive attitudes to the study of history – had offered no educational visits in the previous year either. This suggested to me that at the Faith School and the Technology School, a poor attitude to history was not confined to pupils but was shared by the school management!

The other schools had offered at least one trip a year, which at the Community School had taken the form of a recent very popular trip to visit the Houses of Parliament. This trip had had a great impact on a number of the Community School boys, in terms of the strength of the imprint of their classroom learning and on their motivation to learn more (DeWitt & Storksdieck, 2008). Thus, either the presence or the absence of educational visits as part of NCH learning was, to my mind, a strong indicator of the status of the subject within the schools and the willingness of staff to connect pupils through NCH to the world outside the school gates. In this regard, I saw it as no accident that at the Technology School and the Faith School, NCH had made significantly less impact on pupils' overall holistic dimension of success, compared with the Specialist School and the Community School, where school visits were embedded in the curriculum.

2E: the absent parent

As well as the absent curriculum in its three component parts and the absent pedagogy, the relative lack of parental input and involvement in the Muslim sample's experience of NCH was a 'determinate absence' that hampered their progress. We saw in the previous chapter how out-of-school history, comprising parental input, out-of-school historical visits and sibling assistance, was a highly significant factor in the intellectual and affective-cultural dimensions of the success of the Muslim young people.

Yet out-of-school history was significantly less available for the sample of Muslim young people, especially the boys, than for the non-Muslim sample. Of the Muslim sample, 32.6% either 'strongly' or 'mainly' agreed that they talked about history with their families at home, compared with 56.7% of the non-Muslim sample who either 'strongly' or 'mainly' agreed that they talked about history with their families at home – a significant difference. This suggested strongly that Muslim parents and families were less involved with their sons' history education than non-Muslim parents, even though their involvement, when it happened, was an even more significant factor in their intellectual and affective-cultural success.

The qualitative importance of history at home

Both the relative *importance* and the relative *absence* of the Muslim parental input into the young people's learning of history emerged strongly at interview. In line with the literature, which indicated the significant positive impact of parental involvement on the schooling of adolescents in general (Wilson & Corcoran, 1988) and in the specific area of achievement and motivation (Gonzalez-DeHass, Willems & Holbein, 2005), the positive impact of talking about history with the family in terms of understanding and enjoyment of the subject was clearly observable from the qualitative data from pupils at all the four schools. From these data, I could discern quite specific ways in which family involvement both in the formal mechanisms of NCH, such as homework, and more informal discussions about, for example, family background had impacted positively on the boys' success at NCH, especially in the affective-cultural dimension, as we saw in the previous chapter.

Amir (Community School, high-achieving, British-Bangladeshi), for example, gave an account of the positive contribution that his mother in particular made to his history learning in terms of understanding, motivation and enjoyment:

AMIR: .[S]he [my mother] encourages me to keep it up with my progress […] she helps me. Like I tell her to read my essay, see if it makes sense and she would tell me to correct things on it […] I enjoy it more when she helps me because then I learn from my mistakes and what I've done wrong.

Amir seemed to indicate two crucial facets of his mother's contribution: first, her contribution to his overall motivation 'to keep up with my progress'; and second, her contribution to specific educational tasks such as essay-writing by being Amir's critical academic friend. Amir's identification of his mother as this pillar of support for his learning in history in the intellectual and affective-cultural dimensions resonated with the findings of other researchers (Rogers, Theule, Ryan, Adams & Keating, 2009).[2]

The positive potential impact of the involvement of parents on academic self-concept at the four-planar level (d) of the embodied personality in particular (Rogers et al., 2009) was shown by Umar's (Faith School, middle-achieving, British-Indian) account of how both his parents, who were from different ethnic backgrounds, each made a distinct contribution to his out-of school learning.

UMAR: .[I]t's just like my mum tells me more about history but more in England, she says about more like, more of … the days that she used to live in, like in her time. And my father tells me more about the Islamic history and all that, about different countries.… For example, India, he tells me about how India is different to this country and all that.
MATTHEW: And […] does the history you talk about at home in any way affect the way you study history at school, or motivate you to study it?
UMAR: […] [S]ometimes my parents talk about history in England, it does like

affect me in school 'cause you talk about the same country and it just type of matches you [...]

MATTHEW: And is that helpful for you in your mind?

UMAR: It is, because I learn in school and then I get help at home as well so it's like, if I don't understand it properly in school I can ... go home and just like go over it and [..]. It makes it easier because I've like different people telling me about history, first at school and then at home.

The 'division of historical labour', with his father talking to him about Islamic and Indian history and his mother talking more about life in England in the recent past, has clearly reinforced and deepened Umar's formal NCH learning by providing him with a greater general contextual awareness of the past. The phrase 'it just type of matches you' would appear to indicate a clear example of affective-cultural success brought through the balance between the school and the home that makes Umar's experience of the past make sense, as well as filling gaps in the understanding he has gained at school. His testimony showed the great importance of parental 'emotional work' with history (Crozier, 2005) to nurture both the intellectual and the affective-cultural dimensions of success.

It was not only parents and older adults in the family who were a source and a sounding-board for boys' historical reflections: three boys (one Technology School, two Faith School) referred in passing to siblings as another fruitful resource for deepening their understanding of the past. For example, Waleed (Community School, middle-achieving, British-Pakistani) gained greater 'depth' of information in conversation with his brother, 'who had helped' him learn about the Holocaust.

Interestingly, this finding about sibling assistance runs contrary to much research on the impact of siblings on academic success. This has tended to focus on sibling relationships as a source of *distraction* from home-based study rather than as a source of support (e.g. Eccles, Early, Fraser, Belansky & McCarthy, 1997; Xu & Corno, 2003). This, in turn, suggests that the close and extended family ethos that has typified Muslim communities (P. Lewis, 2002) and that is emphasised in Islamic teaching (e.g. Qur'an, 2:215; 4:36; 58:22) might be a particular source of affective-cultural capital that Muslims can draw on to contextualise and improve their history learning and their academic achievement more generally (Bourdieu & Passeron, 1977).

Indeed, the broader, extended family as a context for discussing history informally was important to three of the Muslim interviewees. For Salman (Specialist School, middle-achieving, British-Bengali), talking about history was a regular feature of family life, and first-hand family accounts of the past had the effect of bringing history alive for him.

SALMAN: Yeah, I talk [...] about it [history] with my older sisters, my dad and my mum.

MATTHEW: And [...] do you think that that makes you more motivated to study at school?

SALMAN: Yeah. It's 'cause then [...] I witness history events from my uncles and aunts that were around in the Bangladesh Independence time and I get to take on ... the stuff that they saw with their own two eyes, and I get to pass that on as well, and I get a better understanding.

What is important about Salman's account is the idea that he was learning from first-hand family accounts of important historical events, which both gave him 'a better understanding' and situated him educationally as a significant part in an ongoing historical family tradition, 'taking on' and 'passing on' these eye-witness accounts.

The impact of home–school communication: the teachers' views

The young people's teachers' accounts strongly support the pupils' views about the great value of the input of parents and family. Three out of the four teachers who expressed an opinion on the subject of parental involvement confirmed both the relative importance and the relative absence of communication over NCH between Muslim boys' and their parents, as well as between their homes and the history classroom at school.

Mike (Community School, male, white British), for example, was adamant about the 'massive progress' a partnership between history at home and history at school effected both in the intellectual and affective-cultural dimensions of Muslim success.

MIKE: .[Y]ou can tell instantly pupils who talk about history and historical events with parents, and the progress that they seem to make is massive compared to those where you're kind of coming in and basing everything they get in is almost being, coming from you ... you get some [pupils] who clearly have read up on things and they're eager to tell you things and ... I don't know, maybe it's because they have more of an interest and they're more gripped by it in the first place [...] there are pupils who come to me say in Year 7 who I've barely taught or not taught at all, and yet they come to lesson and they're like, 'Oh yeah, I was chatting online, I know about this', or 'Over Christmas I went to the Imperial War Museum and saw the Holocaust section of the museum ...' and stuff like that, and they already know about this, this and this, you know.

MATTHEW: So can you feed off that, then, when you ... can you use that?

MIKE: [with enthusiasm] Yeah, definitely, yeah, yeah.

Mike's observations on the positive impact of involved parents in the intellectual and affective cultural dimensions of the Muslim young people's success tally with research that shows the consistent benefit of educational parental involvement on the effective educational development of their children. For example, Oyserman, Brickman and Rhodes (2007) conclude from a controlled study of the effects of parental involvement on the learner identities of 239 mainly African-American students:

Taken together, parent school involvement behaviors are likely to connect with children's belief that school is an important context to engage in efforts to attain positive and avoid negative possible selves ... highly school-involved parents provide the youth with a sense that doing well in school is possible for them and therefore is worth investing in and that becoming off-track can be avoided via engagement with school.

The quantitative absence of history-at-home

Nevertheless, despite this ample evidence as to the particularly significant benefit of parental and family engagement with history for the Muslim young people, the home learning environments of 46% of the Muslim boys in the sample were characterised by an almost total absence of historical talk. Therefore, one can infer that these boys existed in home cultures that did not articulate their connections with the past in regular, meaningful ways, or at least in ways that the boys recognised as 'history'.

Haider's (Faith School, low-achieving, British-Pakistani) allusion to a lack of talk about history at home was typical of six out of my eight interviewees at the Faith School:

MATTHEW: [A]nd how about at home; do you ever talk about history at home?
HAIDER: No.
MATTHEW: Not at all?
HAIDER: Nah.
MATTHEW: But I don't necessarily mean, you know, about Henry VIII or about, you know, or the life of the Prophet, but it may be about your family history, about where you come from.
HAIDER: Um, no.
MATTHEW: Nothing at all?
HAIDER: Nah.

Pervez's (Faith School, high-achieving, British-Pakistani) home talk was characterised by cultural but not historical references to Pakistan:

PERVEZ: No, I don't really talk about it [history] ... I don't really talk about it but I am proud to be who I am and sometimes I would say that 'We Pakistanis do this and that', but no, I don't talk about it [history].

Ishaq (Faith School, middle-achieving, British-Indian) claimed to talk about family history, but not about school history.

MATTHEW: Do you talk about history with your family at home?
ISHAQ: Yeah, our family's history but not the stuff that we do in school.

Contained within this allusion to 'the stuff that we do in school', which was said somewhat dismissively, was the feeling that it was distinctly less valuable to Ishaq than 'our family's history'.

The reasons for this absence

The reasons given by the boys for this 'determinate absence' of parental input were varied and connected to:

- the adolescent life stage of the boys;
- the life circumstances of parents;
- the perceived lack of importance by the parents of history as a school subject.

The sample's responses were indicative of a more generally observed decline in adolescence of the parent–pupil relationship (Eccles & Harold, 1996; Head, 1999; Oyserman et al., 2007). Haider (Faith School, low-achieving, British-Pakistani), for example, regarded it as 'not hip' to talk about school with his parents, and as a result his parents had lost interest in talking about his school life. Haider's disinclination to talk about school, including history, appeared to be connected with an adolescent desire to distance himself from the authority both of the parents and of the school, and therefore might be construed as an example of the 'hegemonic, demi-real' 'laddishness' that we observed in Chapter 6 as characteristic of some Muslim boys' attitudes to school life (L. Archer, 2003; B. Francis, 2000).

In Uthman's (Faith School, low-achieving, British-Indian) case, this absence of parental input might best be described as a collusion of silence.

MATTHEW: Would you have talked about it [the history lesson] with them [if they had been at home]?
UTHMAN: Maybe if they asked.
MATTHEW: Maybe if they asked. But you wouldn't have offered to tell them.
UTHMAN: No.

In this regard, Thompson (2004) has observed the difficulties involved in the question 'How was school today?' and the ineffectiveness of this question unless it is posed sensitively and strategically. The complexity of the school experience for children and its apparent separateness from the home, as a place where they are developing independently of their parents, may render the experience of school difficult to articulate to parents.

Furthermore, in the case of the Muslim sample an often intense programme of after-school commitments, e.g. at the mosque, in addition to their parents' professional commitments, had sometimes crowded out conversations with family members that might have helped consolidate classroom history learning. This finding corroborated findings by Epstein and Becker (1982) and Xu and

Yuan (2003), who note the impact of pressures of time on parental involvement in children's homework at both elementary (primary) and middle (secondary) school.

Finally, the perceived relative lack of importance of history as a subject on the part of parents was another root cause of the absence of their involvement in NCH. For example, Ishaq (Faith School, middle-achieving, British-Indian) put the absence of his parents' involvement in his NCH learning down to their 'not finding history as important as other subjects [...]. Like maths and English are important'. This finding was suggestive of the fact that the heightened instrumentality that we observed as characteristic of Muslim attitudes to school in Chapter 6 was, perhaps, 'inherited' from the pupils' parents.

This perceived lack of 'importance' was also related to the absence curriculum that we analysed earlier. The absent curriculum was mentioned by Waleed (Community School, middle-achieving, British-Pakistani), for example, as prohibitive of family discussions.

MATTHEW: So how about this thing, 'I don't learn anything about my background.' Why did you highlight that one?

WALEED: 'Cause like we don't learn anything like about the history between Pakistan, like the Independence from India, we never learned about that.

MATTHEW: And why is that important to you?

WALEED: 'Cause ... you could talk to family at home, like they could help you and that.

This, I believe, may also have been an important factor in the significantly higher absence of history at home among the Faith School boys. The Faith School parents, who had specifically chosen an Islamic educational environment for their children, were likely to have been particularly alienated by the absence of the Muslim contribution on the curriculum delivered at the school.

OTHER OUT-OF-SCHOOL SETTINGS FOR HISTORY: THE MOSQUE AND ISLAMIC HISTORY

As well as history discussed in the context of the family, it was clear from the boys' interview accounts that the types of religious history that the boys had studied in the mosque had been important to them. It had also often thrown NCH that they had studied at school into somewhat negative relief, as the 'scientific, forensic' style of history in the classroom sometimes existed in epistemic tension with the heroic, inspirational type of religious history in the mosque.

For example, at the Faith School four of my eight respondents alluded both to the importance to them of the history of Islam and to the fact that they received this facet of their historical education in the mosque rather than at school. In this regard, Uthman's (Faith School, low-achieving, British Indian) learning about the history of the Prophets was 'the main thing' to do in history and he had only done this in the mosque. In a similar vein, both the history of Islam in madrasa and the fact that it was told 'as stories' had appealed to Umar (Faith School, middle-achieving, British-Indian).

> UMAR: See I enjoy history in mosque, in madrasa, is that they tell you about the history of the Prophets and all of the people and like more interesting I find is the stories and about … how, like how they suffered in those days and all that stuff.

Pervez had found inspiration from his study of Alexander the Great (who is regarded as a Prophet in some Islamic understandings) in madrasa as an example of someone who showed 'true knowledge of something that you should implement in your life'. Likewise, Ayyub felt that the delivery of Islamic history in the curriculum would provide pupils with role models that would act positively on their behaviour.

Furthermore, it was clear that there was a complete absence of a historical connection between the mosque and the school. Only one boy out of the 24 interviewed suggested that his history at school had helped him in any way to reflect about his religion or about the message of Islam. Conversely, Islam had not helped the boys think about classroom history. In spite of the fact that the Qur'an indicates the benefits of looking at and reflecting on the past (e.g. Qur'an, 30:9; 83:13), and despite the fact that in Islamic traditions the past is regarded as a fertile source of both living historical lessons and enduring values and truths, the young people appeared never to have been guided to reflect on the religious implications of the past (Hussein, 2003).

> Have they not travelled through the earth and observed what fate befell those [civilisations] before them? They were greater than them in power, and they ploughed the earth and built it up more than they have built it up, and their messengers came to them with clear evidences
>
> (Qur'an, 30:9)

This indicated a clear and evident absence of any communication between the mosque and the school as to the purposes of history for Muslim boys. This was a particularly glaring absence at the Faith School, where after-school Qur'an classes happened in the school mosque on-site and where I noticed that a number of my interview sample themselves studied. This parallels the findings of Green (2009) in a Christian faith-school context about the lack of coherent penetration of faith values through the curriculum that characterises many faith schools. This means that faith schools, despite embracing the trappings of faith, such as modest uniforms, gender separation and the performance of prayer, often replicate the strict, often unserious$_{(r+p)}$, compartmentalisation of knowledge into sacred and secular spheres in a way that mirrors the educational culture of non-faith educational settings. This absence of the mobilisation of the boys' Islamic religious and home-cultural values meant that the impact of NCH in both the intellectual and the spiritual dimensions of their success was, as we have seen, greatly under-realised.

3L: the ontology of inclusion

So far, we have seen how a constellation of 'real, determinate' educational absences – the absent curriculum, absent pedagogy and the absent parent – limited the benefits of school history for our Muslim young people, especially in the spiritual and affective-cultural dimensions, with additional articulated 'knock-on' effects in the intellectual and overall holistic dimensions of success.

The question for this section of this chapter becomes, therefore, 'How can National Curriculum History help Muslim boys succeed?' by 'absenting' the absences and shortcomings of NCH and by bolstering and modifying the positive features of the historical pedagogy identified in the previous chapter. This will happen at the dialectical critical realist moments of 3L (Third Level – totality) and 4D (Fourth Dimension – transformative praxis) of envisioning a 'totalising', transformative praxis of history teaching and learning (Bhaskar, 1993/2008). It will include a consideration of the implications of these suggested modifications for teaching practice, curriculum planning and the future of the ongoing debate about the aims of compulsory school history that have re-emerged in a timely way with the publication by the UK government of the new statutory framework for History (UK Gov., 2013c).

Addressing the question *how* can history education help Muslim young people succeed in all of the intellectual, spiritual, affective-cultural, instrumental and civic dimensions of success will involve a joined-up strategy of 'retotalisation' in four particular areas. These areas are all applicable to the new statutory framework of the National Curriculum for History. They would, if implemented in ways that were appropriate to the specifics of local school situations, transform history for Muslim young people from a subject at which they can have success but is of limited instrumental value into a subject that could be at the core of their future overall holistic success. The areas to address are:

At the moment of 3L (Third Level – totality):

- retotalising NCH by incorporating more international and Islamic history into the core substance of NCH at all the Key Stages;
- forging a history of the present for the future, which includes reimagining an intrinsic History-for-Citizenship;

and, at the moment of 4D (Fourth Dimension – transformative praxis):

- forging shared curriculum: creating communities of historical learning.

Together these represent a totality of a reinvigorated approach to history.

Retotalising history by incorporating more international and Islamic history into the core substance of NCH

We have seen how success in the spiritual and affective-cultural dimensions of success had significant knock-on effects in the intellectual dimension of success for the Muslim young people. We have also seen, however, that NCH had had little or no bearing on their religious identities or sense of themselves as religious agents. This was unsatisfactory both in terms of the intrinsic value of religious reflection for Muslim young people in the spiritual dimension and because it established a split whereby Islamic mosque-based history was perceived as a purveyor of useful, relevant historical lessons for life and NCH often was not.

We have also seen that the young people's and their teachers' views on the value of the history of the Muslim contribution in the curriculum were in tension, even in contradiction, with each other, perhaps because of differing conceptions of what Islamic history meant. The boys on 11 occasions bemoaned the absence of the history of Islam from the curriculum and speculated that its presence would be of great benefit to them in terms of making NCH 'important' and motivating them to study. Teachers, by contrast, pointed out that neither pupils nor parents ever requested to be taught the history of Islam, and when they had taught Islam-related topics, these had not been popular.

I have suggested from analysis of the data that the source of this contradiction was connected with two things. First, Islam is presented on the curriculum through two discrete modules as a 'bolt-on' phenomenon that has little bearing on the 'big' curricular themes of NCH, such as political and social change and technological innovation. Second, the way teachers had presented the history of Islam in their own informal curricular constructions was as an ethno-cultural history of 'back home' – in other words, of Pakistan and Bangladesh – whereas many of the Muslim boys were struggling to discover the meaning of an Islamic present in Britain, not an ancestral ethnic past 'back home' (cf. Mondal, 2008).

In response to this situation, and in the context of the National Curriculum Review (2011–2014), I would suggest that teachers need to 'retotalise' the National Curriculum for History by the incorporation of relevant elements of the history of Islamic civilisation and the Muslim contribution into the thematic heart of the teaching of the revised National Curriculum, and by re-'totalising' the curricular partial totalities that are currently delivered as curricular 'sub-totalities', e.g. the First World War and Gandhi. This would be of benefit to Muslim and non-Muslim students alike and would present a truer, fairer and broader version of the 'national story of the United Kingdom' (Gove, 2010 cited in Vasagar & Sparrow, 2010). The structure of my suggestions is based around a tripartite division of history teaching as a necessary balance of three modes of engagement (Nietzsche, 1876 cited in Davison, 2000):

1   the 'heroic' mode, which is the mode in which history inspires and provides role models (and cautionary tales);

2   the 'antiquarian' mode, which is the mode of gleaning factual information and evidence;
3   the 'critical' mode, which is the mode of deconstructing and getting under the skin of the past and of received truths or half-truths.

These modes of engagement would neatly complement a framework suggested by the fulcrum of ICR: ontological realism, epistemological relativism and judgemental rationality (Figure 7.3).

Key Stage 1: ontological realism in the 'heroic' mode

At Key Stage 1, ontological realism would indicate the simple fact that events in the past happened and had (lasting) consequences, and would appropriately be engaged in the 'heroic', inspirational mode, appropriate for five- to eight-year-olds. At this Key Stage, teachers' selections of significant historical figures ought to include at least one 'significant' Muslim thinker who has made a significant contribution to the intellectual progress of humanity. Miriam al-Ijli (d. 967), a

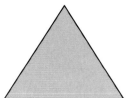

Ontological realism (heroic mode):

Events in the past

Epistemological relativism (antiquarian mode):

Constructing narratives and interpretations of events in the past
Narratives and interpretations involve both what is present and what is absent from selections of events

Judgemental rationality (critical mode):

Deploying the tools of historical plausibility, criticism, 'crap-detecting' and 'myth-busting' to narratives and interpretations of events in the past, including consideration of what is present and what is absent

Figure 7.3 The fulcrum of ICR for history education.

pioneer of navigation, or Ibn al-Haytham (d. *c*.1040), the father of the science of optics (al-Hassani, 2012), would be extremely appropriate 'heroic' figures of study for the following reasons:

1 The phenomena that they pioneered are still relevant today and used by the whole of humanity.
2 This sends out the message to all pupils that history is a relevant subject for understanding the present.
3 Muslim thought has served humanity as a whole.

Miriam al-Ijli (d. 967), as a Muslim woman scientist, would, perhaps, be pre-eminently appropriate and send out a strong message that women in general and Muslim women in particular are 'doers and achievers', as my sample of Muslim girls had suggested they wanted to be portrayed. In other words, Miriam al-Ijli has a proven track record for 'inspiration'.

Key Stage 2: ontological realism and epistemological relativism in the 'antiquarian' mode

At Key Stage 2, children, including Muslim young people, begin to nuance 'heroic' history with a more 'antiquarian' approach. That is to say, as well as being inspired by figures from the past, they start to learn the skills of history – gathering and presenting facts – and start to become aware that facts require interpretation, which is a subjective pursuit and open to multiple, sometimes conflicting, claims. In terms of ICR, ontological realism in the heroic mode is supplemented by epistemological relativism in the antiquarian mode. This would also represent a move towards a critical approach to history, and the development of judgemental rationality, without losing that unique characteristic of the past to be 'heroic' – that is, to inspire and provide role models.

Therefore, at Key Stage 2 a 'civilisational' approach would tie together, nuance epistemically and totalise the different 'Dark Age' and ancient civilisations that are statutorily to be taught, according to the new framework for history. For example, the ancient civilisations of Greece and Rome could be used to identify the core features and dimensions of the nature of a civilisation, and the 'Dark Age' civilisations to illustrate the idea of civilisational continuity, collapse and rebirth. When the Anglo-Saxon and Viking peoples are taught, specific curricular reference would need to be made to the broader Islamic commercial and monetary environment of early medieval Europe. As proof of this, pupils might do a case study of the Offa dinar and travel to examine it in the British Museum and explore the reasons why the Mercian Anglo-Saxons were minting an Islamic-style currency. They might also examine why Baghdad represented the 'El Dorado' of Viking civilisation (Oliver, 2012). This will set the history of these British peoples in truer, richer, more interesting context, and integrate Islam, as a central political and cultural force in the 'Dark Ages', into the national story by suggesting a narrative of constructive Muslim–non-Muslim exchange. To build up this critical, epistemically relative understanding of comparative civilisations, embedded in a realist ontology, tenth-century Abbasid Baghdad might be studied, for example in comparison with tenth-century Viking Jorvik (York), and this study ought to include a visit to the Jorvik Viking Centre. As a plenary to Key Stage 2, a module or project of work entitled 'The Dark Ages: were they really so "dark"?' would problematise received meta-theories and ideas about the past and would initiate pupils in the more critical phase that is to be the flavour of Key Stage 3, and begin to develop their historical judgemental rationality.

Key Stages 3 and 4: ontological realism, epistemological relativism and judgemental rationality in the 'critical' mode

At Key Stage 3, international events, which are currently taught as 'sub-totalities', would need to be retotalised. As regards the medieval past, the Crusades can be taught through narratives of conflict *and* cultural cross-fertilisation of material civilisation (e.g. carpets and tapestry), social habits (e.g. the use of cutlery) and ideas (e.g. chivalry) to suggest the epistemic porosity of religions and cultures even when they are locked in conflict. For the early modern past, a national story such as the defeat of the Spanish Armada can be taught in the context of the global struggle of the international superpowers Spain and Ottoman Turkey. This will give all pupils the chance to understand how power has operated on the international stage and how empires ebb and flow, and will begin to provide them with meta-historical tools of evaluative analysis associated with judgemental rationality.

A more complete, accurate and integrated history means at Key Stage 3 teaching the First World War within the broader international context of the collapse of the Ottoman Empire and the creation of nation-states in the Muslim world (Allawi, 2009). This would address 'whitened' narrations of empire-building and the contribution of empires' people (Wemyss, 2009), and might in practice include archival online work researching the letters sent home by Sikh, Hindu and Muslim soldiers fighting on the Western Front (Omissi, 1999). This retotalisation also means, for example, including the history of the creation of Pakistan and Partition within the story of Indian Independence, even if there is a 'case' focus on the personal contribution of Gandhi. This is essential knowledge for young Muslims for understanding ongoing struggles in and for Kashmir, and more generally tensions between Pakistan and India that affect young British Muslims at a community level on a daily basis. It is vital knowledge for them to be able to decode uncritical, skewed accounts on the internet of Partition-drive radicalisation (Wilkinson, 2011b).

At Key Stage 4, the accent of history teaching ought, I believe, to fall squarely on critical history, without abandoning both the antiquarian and the heroic modes of the previous Key Stages. Again, totalising dynamics and the idea of a history of the present for their future will be crucially important for attracting Muslim pupils to History at Key Stage 4.[3]

At Key Stage 4, pupils need to deepen their judgemental rationality and be empowered by more advanced tools of historical analysis to deconstruct and evaluate highly contested historical accounts. In this regard, although the complexities and tensions that surround the Arab–Israeli conflict for teachers, pupils and parents are to be accepted and recognised, the removal of the Arab–Israeli conflict as a topic of study at KS4 in 2008 was a mistake.[4] The Arab–Israeli conflict is a thorn in the flesh of many young Muslims and, as we saw in Chapter 1, one-sided, extreme narrations of it undoubtedly fuel Islamist radicalisation (Wilkinson, 2011b). Schools provide the only controlled environment for them to discuss and debate their views in a responsible, relatively impartial and informed way. This research showed that Muslim children tend to be both passionate and, according to one teacher, 'remarkably well informed' about the Israel–Palestine question. But their passion and views need to be set in deep historical perspective, and the history classroom gives them the opportunity to scrutinise the issue in depth and from different points of view. I would, therefore, recommend the optional reinstatement of a unit of study entitled 'The Arab–Israeli conflict, 1896–2012: do the roots of the conflict provide a clue to the solution?' or similar, that places the conflict and its causes in as deep a historical context as possible, stretching back at least to the First Zionist Congress (1897) and the situation of Palestine in the Ottoman Empire.

I would also recommend that such a module be designed in consultation with a variety of different Jewish, Muslim and Christian members of staff to incorporate a variety of different perspectives and sources. Such a module might, if properly designed, perform a critical historical function and suggest the transformative socio-political possibilities of the study of the past, which, as we have seen, is a feature of history that is vitally important to Muslim children.

Of course, history teachers are under enormous pressures of time, and it will be reasonably argued that both curriculum planners and teachers will always need to have their own focus on particular topics, that they will select events on the curriculum according to their own 'local' criteria and that they cannot be expected to impart knowledge, even superficially, of the full totality of enormous historical events (Cronon, 2000). Nevertheless, even passing mention of the salient features of the broader international and, where appropriate, the Islamic context will boost the affective-cultural and intellectual dimension of young Muslims' engagement with the past. Moreover, the recognition of the contribution that Muslims, among all the other groups, have made to the story of Britain and humankind, for better and, sometimes, for worse, will make quite simply for more complete, less biased, truer history. Hence, all pupils have a right to know some of the salient features of the history of Islam, and the presence of Muslim young people in the classroom occasions the opportunity of a broader, deeper, truer history for all.

Thus, importantly, this retotalised approach means that the agenda for inclusion of the histories of ethnically or culturally minor groups is not driven so much by a multicultural or the newly awakened anti-multicultural ideology (Bunting, 2011), but by the desire to represent as fully and accurately as possible the nature of the historical topic under discussion. If this totalising perspective is borne in mind by curriculum planners and teachers, 'inclusion' ought to become more a matter of accurate historical representation, even if it comes in 'national narrative' form, and less subject to the shifting ideological tides of any given political moment. Thus, history education can become a genuine conversation between a carefully conceived ontology of young learners and a broad and fair epistemology of historical events, mediated by the wise judgemental rationality of teachers and parents.

Forging a history of the present for the future

We have seen how in terms of the delivery of 'instrumental' success, the Muslim young people tended to be of the opinion that history was 'no use in life'. In terms of the delivery of skills, we have also seen how the subject was regarded as overly literate and 'boring' by many of the boys, not necessarily because they did not like writing but because the types of exercises in historical literacy that teachers used were often based on uncreative teaching strategies, such as excessive copying from the board and sections from textbooks (cf. Loewen & Deininger, 1997). When written tasks were used in the context of educational games, investigative tasks using ICT, creative presentations and well-structured essay tasks, the boys realised that historical literacy could be fun, fulfilling and useful precisely because they were mobilising skills that they recognised would be of use in the future beyond the confines of the classroom. 'ICT can help to persuade some learners to engage with historical activities, particularly if they struggle with conventional written work' (Haydn, 2003, p. 22). In this respect, NCH needs to become a 'history of the present' for the future. By researching the deep layers of history underlying contemporary affairs using investigative ICT and, for example, writing them up for presentation to their peers, as had happened at the Specialist School, young people can develop technological, written and oral skills of communication that will be of clear use to them in the future world of work. These skills, derived from a critical engagement with live knowledge, will help them develop the inquiring attitudes of mind and character that they will often need in order to find or create work. History is an ideal subject in which to incorporate the critical, coherent use of ICT, given the quantity and quality of historical resources and databases now available on the internet.

> In 'The Information Society', learning to handle information intelligently is an important skill, and given the nature of history as a subject discipline, and the attributes of ICT, few, if any subjects are better placed to equip pupils with this skill.
>
> (Haydn, 2003, p. 20)

Moreover, history teachers themselves need to recognise and explain the instrumental value of these cognitive and technical skills. A history that more deeply enriches and enlightens boys' understanding of their present, while giving them more obvious access to some of the core skills needed to master their futures, can situate history as a core subject in the National Curriculum Review in order to enhance the dimension of overall holistic success of Muslim, and indeed all, young people.

Reforging an intrinsic history-for-citizenship

Part of this history of the present for the future involves reforging an intrinsic history-for-citizenship. We have seen that many Muslim young people saw the pre-eminent value of history at the *social level (c) of irreducible institutional forms* as a route to the civic dimension of their success. The idea that NCH should provide that route was one of its most important *raisons d'être* in the eyes of many of them. NCH was regarded as a bridge to majority culture and knowledge of society at large with which many boys, especially at the Faith School and Specialist School, had little contact in their daily lives. Within this general sense of history as a legitimate route to informed citizenship, the narratives of civic and political empowerment and change and the achievement of social justice appeared to be particularly poignant for Muslim young people as offering the historical hope and the possibility of changing attitudes and social circumstances. We have also seen that some of the boys appreciated and valued the skills of weighing up evidence, judging between contested accounts and, in general, the skills of 'crap detection' (Postman & Weingartner, 1969) and selecting and prioritising information that are vital civic skills for Muslim boys if they are to succeed in deciphering the authentic codes of an information-saturated age (Haydn, 2003).

Hence, as far as Muslim young people were concerned, uncomfortable though it may be for some academic historians (P. Lee, 1992), the idea of NCH as an effective and appropriate means for discussing, instilling and nurturing civic participation and belonging was a powerfully positive one. The implication of this ought not to be thrusting 'Britishness' down Muslim boys' throats. But it does mean that teachers need to be aware as part of the strategy of totalisation that many Muslim young people want to know about the political and social development of Britain and the relationship of that development to the wider international world in order to situate themselves within it and to be able to challenge injustices and wrongdoing. In this sense, NCH ought to be considered not as a tool for making Muslim young people 'feel more British' (G. Brown, 2006) or 'adopt muscular liberal British values' (Cameron, 2011), which are nebulous ideas anyway, but as a tool for Muslim boys to discover ways in which they can connect being authentically British to being seriously $_{(r+p)}$ Muslim and to participate fully in the civic life of Britain. In short, all of the above means transforming history in school from a subject that is viewed by many Muslim young people as an 'interesting' but relatively unimportant study of the past into a subject which contributes to their overall holistic success in intellectual, spiritual, affective-cultural, civic and instrumental dimensions.

4D: transforming communities of learners

A shared curriculum: creating communities of historical learning for pupils, teachers, parents and out-of-school practitioners

We have seen at the level of 3L (Third Level – totality) how the absent curriculum and the absent pedagogy can be addressed by a strategy of retotalising school history to embrace the history of the Muslim contribution in a way that delivers a useful 'history of the present'. To address the issue of the absent parent and, relatedly, the situation of the lack of connection between school and out-of-school history, history departments in schools with a large Muslim pupil base might consider a range of options to promote the involvement of Muslim parents in both the construction and the delivery of NCH at a local school level. These options might, at the dialectical level of 4D (Fourth Dimension – transformative praxis), be transformative of the whole relationship between local Muslim and school communities, and might include the following.

Creating parent–teacher–community partnerships through curricular workshops and conferences

Although the idea of parent–teacher partnerships has been problematised as demanding 'unreasonable' shifts in parent–teacher power relations (Katyal & Evers, 2007), Becher (1984) has identified the active situating of schools as part of broader learning communities as performance-enhancing for all connected parties. Sheldon and Epstein (2002) have also noted the positive impact of curricular involvement of parents on classroom behaviour of students in inner-city US junior and middle schools. Brighouse and Woods (1999) indicate the effectiveness of developing teacher–parent partnerships through curricular workshops that 'draw the community together within learning' (p. 112). In this regard, community cultural studies workshops have also been shown to have at least moderate success in creating cultural bridges between teachers and ethnic minority parents (Bloch & Tabachnick, 1994).

Curricular workshops intended to draw on the resources of the broader learning community would be particularly appropriate for the development of history curricula, as everybody has a significant relationship with the past underscored by truth, 'myth' and by ideological biases (Cronon, 2000). The experience of multicultural and bilingual educators shows that the direct involvement of parents in the school curriculum would confront teachers with a whole range of different historical and cultural perspectives. This, in turn, would help them understand where, historically speaking, their pupils are coming from and challenge some of their own historical prejudices and assumptions (Nieto, 2006). Moreover, since some Muslim boys appear to be exposed to some quite extreme biases, and even rank prejudice, outside school, parent–teacher conferences or workshops might be a forum for discussion of and, where appropriate, negotiation of 'beneficial', 'acceptable' and 'unacceptable' differences between in-school and out-of-school historical perspectives.

Within this community of historical learning, the place of local imams and mosque-based teachers would also be significant. Mutual discussions about the purposes of history between school-based and mosque-based practitioners that uncover and construct some shared understandings as to the aims of history would signify to the boys 'goal consensus' and that history as a subject was meaningful and valued to different types of interested adults (Ziegler, 1987). These workshops might take the form, for example, of an annual history curriculum review to which parents and local religious teachers would be invited that would provide the context for more meaningful collective Muslim-community input than the 10–15 minutes often allocated to each child's parents at school academic review evenings (Becher, 1984). Of course, it needs to be recognised that the epistemic basis of religious history and academic history may turn out to be very different, at times perhaps contradictory. Nevertheless, in the adult negotiation of contested epistemologies it is always worth remembering the goal of the child's integrated ontology.

Overcoming obstacles to teacher–parent partnerships

Epstein and Becker (1982) have noted that encouraging more proactive and institutionally structured parent–teacher relations can run up against a number of obstacles, such as:

- consumption of teacher time;
- parents feeling that home time and 'down time' is being intruded upon;
- the failure of parents to follow through on undertakings made in partnership with teachers, due to busy schedules.

They also have noted, however, that the use of parent–teacher co-ordinators can alleviate the first two of these problems. Given the fact that the absence of overlap noted between the cultural experiences and expectations of some Muslim parents and NCH that lay at the root of a lack of parental interest in NCH, especially at the Faith School, parent–teacher curriculum conferences would be a starting point for raising awareness about NCH among Muslim parents and religious leaders and encouraging greater parental involvement. Moreover, we have also seen how for some of the boys the family itself was a rich source of history, and these conferences might provide the arena in which to explore how family history might be developed more fully in the classroom (Palloff & Pratt, 2007).

Other initiatives might include specific guidance to parents over curriculum-appropriate educational visits to historical sites that would link-up school and home-based learning and, as we have seen, provide extra-curricular contextual resources for boys to enrich their classroom discussions. The indication by teachers of specific homework tasks that require parental input has been found to be a particularly effective way to engage parents from low-income backgrounds, which are typical of many Muslim parents (Hoover-Dempsey, Bassler & Brissie, 1987).

Finally, on the evidence of this study, schools might encourage some Muslim parents themselves to consider finding more time, energy and, if necessary, more knowledge to become involved in the historical education of their children. This might take the form of:

- taking a more hands-on role in the completion of written homework;
- talking more regularly to teachers;
- organising formal and informal educational visits to sites of historical relevance in Britain and in the Islamic world;
- initiating regular history-oriented family conversations;
- just keeping in touch orally and emotionally with what pupils are doing in history.

At the level (c) of irreducible institutional structure, organisations such as the Association of Muslim Governors (AMG) might explore how to drive forward the implementation of curricular material related to the Muslim contribution that is deemed important through participation on schools' governing bodies, PTAs and through other formal and informal parent–teacher–pupil channels. This type of responsible direct action was in part instrumental in raising the profile of black history to the level of the formal curriculum in the 1980s and 1990s (Hewer, 2001). Thus, the 'retotalising' approach to history in school can become at the dialectical moment of 4D (Fourth Dimension – transformative praxis) a mechanism for transforming the mutual engagement of the large sectors of the Muslim community with their children's schools and drawing the two together as a united learning community.

Conclusion: reimagining the nation through history education

In any curriculum, there is always a tension between what policy-makers and teachers choose to transmit to the next generation as part of the inherited stock of cultural knowledge and what needs to be revised, added or removed in order to respond to novel circumstances, new understandings and possible future challenges that the coming generation will face (Goodson, 1990).

This is particularly the case with history curricula, which are perceived to transmit the building-blocks of national cultural identity (Phillips, Goalen, McCully & Wood, 1999). The types of history that make up 'official' school curricula are powerful statements about what a nation perceives and does not perceive itself to be. Significant challenges to an inherited stock of national histories become a challenge to a range of acceptable inscriptions on the narratives of national identity and thereby a challenge to the class, gender, race and faith-based structures of society (Goodson, 1990). On the basis of the evidence of NCH at my four state schools, the English part of the British nation has yet to integrate into its national self-understanding the notion that a small but significant and growing (*c*.5%; IK Gov., 2012) part of its national constituency is Muslim.

In the context of history as an ongoing, shifting narrative of national identity, accommodating, investigating and celebrating the history of Islam that accompanies British Muslim boys is complex. For centuries, Christendom and the histories of its peoples and nations were, as we saw in the Introduction, construed in direct response to the challenge of the Islamic 'other' (B. Lewis, 1994; Kisby Littleton, 2009)). In recent, less overtly Christian, times, powerful elements in the political and intellectual establishment of the secularising 'West' are in the process of defining themselves in direct contrast to the religious 'other', most obviously represented by highly visible forms of Islam (Birt, 2010).

However, responding to the particular curricular needs of Muslim young people is not only, in some ways, a challenge to national British identities as traditionally (and implicitly) developed in the crucible of school history classes, but also an opportunity to build fairer, broader national identities built on broader, fairer and truer histories, for which there is also evidence of a national appetite (Equality and Human Rights Commission, 2010). A national history (or histories) that reflects the real interconnected internationality of much of British history and that acknowledges the historical contribution of Muslims and the Islamic world will help prepare all British pupils emotionally and intellectually for life in an unavoidably multi-faith society in an inevitably globalising world (Ramadan, 2010).

In this way, by addressing the particular needs of Muslim young people history education can not only help this poorly represented, underachieving group succeed, but also help the British nation and other Western nations successfully embrace the multi-faith and globalising challenges of its present and future through a fair and frank recognition of the contribution of Muslims and other minority groups to the successes of their past.

Notes

1 The sample, rationale and methodology are the same as given in Chapter 6, pp. 127–129.
2 For example, Rogers et al. (2009) conducted a quantitative study of the effects of parental involvement on the achievement and academic self-concept (learner identity) and global self-concept (equivalent to overall holistic success) in maths and literacy on 110 fifth-grade (47 boys, 63 girls) and 121 sixth-grade (63 boys, 58 girls) children sampled from four elementary schools in a small Canadian city from a mixture of white families from middle- to upper-middle-class backgrounds. They concluded:

> All aspects of maternal involvement had a direct relation with children's personal characteristics. Mothers' active management of the learning environment had a positive association with all four child characteristics: academic competence, self-concept in reading, self-concept in math, and global self-concept. Maternal encouragement and support for learning was associated with higher levels of academic competence, higher self-concept in reading and a higher global self-concept. Maternal participation with homework was associated with higher

academic competence, higher self-concept in reading, and a higher global self-concept.

(pp. 44–45)

Rogers et al. (2009) also identify that maternal 'pressure', as opposed to encouragement, to achieve was correlated negatively with achievement and academic self-concept. In this case, it would appear likely that Amir's mother has judged her academic relationship with her son well by 'encouraging' him in his formal tasks but also being available as a critical sounding-board to point out his 'mistakes'.

3 At the time of writing (February 2014), the content of GCSE History remains unfinalised.

4 This belief is shared by the prominent Jewish scholar Dr Edward Kessler, Executive Director of the Woolf Institute, Cambridge.

8 Religious education

Learning about, from and for religion-for-life

Introduction: delineating the spiritual dimension of Muslim young people

In the previous two chapters, we have seen that religion (in this case Islam) is a significant presence in the lives of the great majority of British Muslim young people. Indeed, 89% of my own sample of Muslim young people identified their religion as 'very important' to them. This strength of identification with Islam is consistent with the high levels of religiosity in young Muslims observed by researchers in recent years (L. J. Francis & Robbins, 2005; Hopkins, 2009). We saw that this persistent prevalence of a faith-based identity in Muslim young people 'appears to confound social psychological and social cognition theories of ethnic identity ... which assume adherence to minority belief and practices, such as language and religion, declines with each new generation' (L. Archer, 2003, p. 48).

We have also observed in Archer's study of Muslim boys at secondary level that this Islamic religious identity was often 'performed' as an identity rather than practised as a faith in a posture of resistance to educational structures and authorities that were perceived by some Muslim young people as oppressive, racist and Islamophobic. Therefore, for some Muslim young people an Islamic religious identity acted as an obstacle to educational success and engagement, particularly if it was mediated through other, often demi-real, aspects of the their identities, for example 'gangsta', 'laddish' or 'Gang Girl' hegemonic gender constructions.

By contrast, we also saw from Shain's (2003) study of Muslim girls that a practice-based, serious$_{(r)}$ connection to Islam can, and often does, nurture a healthy approach to academic achievement and engagement with the life of the school. This finding complements those of other faith traditions which show that a reflective grounding in the life of the spirit can be especially beneficial for the educational development of adolescent girls (Baker & Edwards, 2012). Therefore, paradoxically, so far we have seen that a connection to Islam can both help and hinder educational achievement in Muslim young people, depending on how it is mobilised in relation to other factors and other facets of Muslim identity, such as gender, class, ethnicity and nationality.

Finally, we have also seen how the dimension of spiritual success was a core component in Muslim achievement in history and how its absence significantly weakened the positive impact of the history curriculum in the intellectual and civic dimensions of success in a knock-on and 'articulated' way. The dimension of spiritual success was the ability of young Muslims to engage in autonomous moral and ethical decision-making through engagement with the past, and their ability to put the values of their faith and their fellow countrymen in deep historical perspective.

Given the importance of the spiritual dimension and the Islamic religion for young Muslims, it is the contention of this chapter that a well-conceived, engaging religious education (RE) needs to form an essential part of the holistic education of the young Muslim. This serious RE needs to take place on various educational sites, including the school, the madrasa, the home, the internet and the peer group. A serious RE is especially important for Muslim young people at secondary school, who, as we have seen, not only have a propensity for religious meaning-making of different types but also are in the throes of a period of life – adolescence – which is *sui generis* given up to the re-evaluation of values and intense reinterpretation of the self in a variety of different dimensions (Head, 1999; Kroger, 1996).

Therefore, this chapter will explore the education of the spiritual dimension of young Muslims in greater focus by examining their religious education through the prism of the dialectical critical realist framework MELD as follows:

At the level of *First Moment* (1M – non-identity/being-as-such), the chapter will explore the nature of young Muslims in RE and the nature of their relationships with their teachers, using the empirical ethnographic work of Ipgrave (2006) and others. This section of the chapter also makes the case for RE as an exploration of the ontology of the spirit in the light of the absence of a clear rationale for RE in English schools.

At the level of *Second Edge* (2E – absence), the chapter will explore how RE in England and Wales is characterised by a lack of what I term 'seriousness-in-education', seriousness$_{(e)}$; that is to say, there exists a lack of consistency between the importance of religion in the world today and in the lives of young people and its value as a school subject. At present, RE in England and elsewhere in the West is hampered by a lack of seriousness$_{(e)}$, which is a contributory factor in an absence of respect for RE from pupils and an absence of support from Muslim parents and the Muslim community. These absences create a particularly testing structural environment for RE teachers.

At the level of *Third Level* (3L – totality), the chapter argues that these absences can be overcome transformatively by teachers using, as part of their teaching toolkit, the fulcrum of ICR and the ICR idea of transcendence, as presented in Chapter 3–5. These tools can be part of a totalising approach to RE that can help to bring to multi-faith religious education the necessary theological height and philosophical depth, as well sociological breadth, to make the subject engaging and useful for young Muslims and other pupils. The section discusses the possible practical implementation of the fulcrum of ICR and the ICR idea of transcendence in what I call the extra-faith, inter-faith and intra-faith modes.

At the level of *Fourth Dimension* (4D – transformative praxis), the chapter argues that serious RE in school needs to be part of a transformative and communicative nexus of RE to inform and nurture the spiritual dimension of Muslim young people that includes the educational sites of the school, the home, the peer group, the internet and the madrasa and mosque.

1M: who is the Muslim learner in religious education?

Consistent with the ontological approach that has characterised our understanding of Muslim young people in education thus far, before we address questions of how to create an effective RE provision for Muslim young people, we must ask the ontological questions at the level of First Moment (1M – being-as-such): what is the nature of religious education and what is the nature of the Muslim learner in religious education?

What is religious education? The shaping influence of British Islam on RE provision

Ipgrave (forthcoming) makes the point that contemporary RE 'has been shaped in response to a number of images of British Islam: Muslims as victims of racism, as community activists, young Muslims rioting on the streets of northern towns ... [and] that of the Islamic extremist and terrorist'. The seismic and continual changes in the aims and substance of RE since the 1970s have been shaped in no small part by the increasingly visible and vocal presence of Islam and the Muslim community in British public discourse, and the increasing numbers of Muslim children in mainstream British RE classrooms. These Muslim presences have signified the 'new' presence in the British national consciousness of a whole community of British people that specifically self-identifies and is mobilised by its faith, possibly for the first time since the pioneering presences of Christian Victorian Evangelicals and mass Jewish migration to Britain in the nineteenth and early twentieth centuries.

The 'new' Muslim presence has contributed to a landscape of shifting aims and purposes of religious education in England that has intensified, though not necessarily clarified, since the 1988 Education Reform Act. Since the 1944 Education Act made RE compulsory in England and Wales, RE has been conceived in policy (Qualifications and Curriculum Authority, 2004) and delivered in the classroom around three dynamics that have existed in epistemic tension, with different components holding the balance of power at different times: knowledge *about* religion, knowledge *from* religion and knowledge *for* religion (Conroy et al., 2013; Wright, 2007).

Although the 1944 Education Act specified that RE was to be 'non-denominational and non-catechistic' (Ipgrave, forthcoming), in its early post-Second World War days the subject was entirely Christian and predominantly biblical. This was to change radically in the 1970s and 1980s as RE policy and practice began to respond to the presence of large numbers of British children in the RE classroom whose religious background was not Christian. To place multicultural RE in its more general educational context, the birth of multicultural education in the late 1970s and early 1980s was occasioned by a growing consensus of activist-led educational opinion that the assimilationist model of education, whereby children from migrant communities were expected to slough off their home languages, culture and religion at school and become absorbed into white-majority cultural norms, had damaged the educational and life chances of children from minority culture British groups. A sense of urgency was injected into the shift from the assimilationist to the multicultural model by the race riots in Brixton (London) and Birmingham, and following the influential Bullock (1975), Rampton (1981) and Swann (1985) reports, which sent out a unified message to the effect that

> [n]o child should be expected to cast off the language and culture of the home as he crosses the school threshold, nor to live and act as though school and home represent two totally separate and different cultures which have to be kept firmly apart.
>
> (Bullock Report, 1975, para 20.5)

This general shift from the assimilationist to the multicultural model of education contributed to a shift in the view of RE from a subject whose default task was one of instructing and enriching the Christian religious backgrounds of the majority to a recognition of a crucial role that RE had to play in 'acknowledging the diversity now present in British society, and also in discussing fundamental "moral" issues such as racism' (Swann, 1985, pp. 487–488 cited in Ipgrave, forthcoming). The Swann Report and the influential Schools Councils Project specifically endorsed Ninian Smart's phenomenological approach to world religions for school RE, and itself derived from the phenomenological approach to religion and its related philosophy, as 'the best and only means of enabling all pupils, from whatever religious background, to understand the nature of religious beliefs, the religious dimension of human experience and the plurality of faiths in contemporary Britain' (Swann, 1985, p. 518 cited in Barnes, 2001, p. 445).

> Previously RE had worked on the assumption that the majority of students were from Christian families and that what they were learning was part of their religious culture; now pupils would study religions as things other people believed in and practised.
>
> (Ipgrave, forthcoming)

Thus, the multicultural turn in RE education might, broadly speaking, be labelled as a move towards the respect for and study of the phenomenon of religious experience both in universal essence and manifest in diversity. It was based upon the underlying philosophical and phenomenological assumption, itself derived from Hegel's distinction between the essence (*Wesen*) of a thing and its manifestations (*Erscheinungen*) to consciousness, and influential texts such as Rudolf

Otto's *The Idea of the Holy* (1923/1950). This approach, broadly speaking, was premised on the idea that all religions share an underlying essence and that religious experience and religious knowledge often transcend conceptual knowledge and linguistic articulation (Barnes, 2001). It was largely, although not universally, as we will see, welcomed by Muslim community groups, such as the Muslim Council of Britain, since it appeared to afford greater epistemic and ethical parity between Christianity and the other major UK faiths such as Islam.

This multicultural, phenomenological approach to RE was enshrined legally in the landmark 1988 Education Reform Act, which stated that the new agreed syllabuses for RE must 'reflect the fact that the religious traditions in great Britain are in the main Christian whilst taking into account the teaching and practices of the other principal religions represented in Great Britain'. Thus, for the first time, locally agreed RE syllabuses had to take a statutory inclusion of Muslims and Islam within their embrace. As a result, the 1990s saw increasing opportunities opening up for Muslims to contribute to locally agreed RE syllabuses at the behest of government or, increasingly, as a result of Muslim community activism. This activism included an increase in Muslim parents becoming school governors in order to protect their children's religious interests and to determine what the teaching about their own faith in school should entail. Less positively, an element of the Muslim community, led by certain more conservative or hard-line mosques, was active in encouraging parents to exercise the right to withdraw their children from collective school worship (Hull, 1998; Ipgrave, forthcoming). This activism culminated in a significant input from the Muslim community into the government-controlled Schools Council Curriculum Authority model syllabuses (Ipgrave, forthcoming).

Criticism of the phenomenological approach and backlash

However, both the official endorsement and the philosophical grounds of phenomenological RE were soon to suffer a backlash. Philosophers of RE, such as Philip Barnes (2001), critiqued the phenomenological approach's 'liberal Protestant' privileging of the interior, emotional experience of religious essence over the truth-claims and forms of religion and, using the philosophy of Wittgenstein, reinstated the indivisibility of the outward forms and symbols of religion from the inner experience of it. Barnes also claimed that the notion that religious experience was essentially opaque to linguistic expression had facilitated a lazy sidestepping of the controversial, but essential, aspect of religious literacy: 'that of assessing religious claims to truth and adjudicating between rival (conceptual) claims to truth' (2001, p. 455). Others criticised the phenomenological approach to RE criticism as taking a *smörgåsbord* approach to religion that had privileged learning *about* a smattering of the major world religions. This *smörgåsbord* approach had all but eliminated the possibility of learning *from* the wisdom of different religions *for* empowering children to be able to make up their own spiritual minds and to lead religiously literate lives in which they were able to develop a coherent religious world-view (Ellis, 1997; Wright, 2007). In the view of such critics, there was now an inappropriate power imbalance in favour of knowledge *about* over knowledge *from* religion and knowledge *for* religion.

The fact that the multicultural turn in RE had allowed the incorporation of the views of 'religionists' and a fear that the input of 'religionists' had both compromised the necessarily non-confessional secularity and constrained RE within a world religions approach also resulted in a policy backlash for the RE educationalist community led by John Hull. This backlash contributed to the 2004 non-statutory National Framework for Religious Education, which acknowledged a range of possible RE pedagogies above and beyond the phenomenological world religions approach that had underpinned multicultural RE.

Before the RE community had been able to respond effectively to this body of opinion, events in the Muslim world or related to it had once again forced RE policy-makers, thinkers and teachers to reassess the role of RE. The race riots of 2001 in Oldham, Bradford and Birmingham involving Muslim Asian and white British opponents, followed by the attack on the Twin Towers in New York on 11 September 2001, followed on 7 July 2005 by the attacks on the London Transport network, prompted a growing and vocal reaction against multiculturalism and its educational initiatives. This was generated by an increasingly consensual belief that multiculturalism had untied the necessary bonds of community cohesion, built on shared values and a shared public culture, which meant that, in the evocative words of Sir Trevor Phillips, then chair of the Equality and Human Rights Commission (EHRC), Britain was 'sleep-walking into segregation' (Casciani, 2005).[1]

Where once multicultural policy-makers had co-opted RE to celebrate 'diversity', policy-makers now co-opted RE to create 'community cohesion' in a way that, according to some, implicitly focused on the Muslim community as the source of the problem. A series of high-profile television programmes between 2005 and 2010 also reinforced a national suspicion that the Muslim community and, in particular, its faith school 'system' was among the principal culprits in undermining British social cohesion (Ahmad, 2011; Siddique, 2010). The 2007 government inspection (Ofsted) report on RE announced: 'RE cannot ignore its role in fostering community cohesion ... current changes in society give this renewed urgency' (Ofsted, 2007, p. 40 cited in Ipgrave, forthcoming). The problem here was that everyone 'knew' that the 'current changes' and the 'renewed urgency' referred above all else to the possible threat of 'home-grown' violent Islamist extremism, for which the 'doctrines' of multiculturalism were often blamed (Ipgrave, forthcoming). This reaction ignored both the fact that 96% of British Muslim children were and are educated in mainstream non-faith state schools and the fact that these mainstream state-educated non-faith schools had educated all the 7/7 bombers, none of whom had been educated in Muslim faith schools.

This community cohesion approach in RE placed increasing emphasis on developing the 'healthy' horizontal axis of RE of relating positively to others as social beings, but increasingly ignored or problematised the vertical metaphysical dimension of religious beliefs and truths. Religious beliefs and absolute religious truth-claims were, as the source of 'the problem of Islamist extremism', to be subjected to the light of intense rational criticality rather than be considered as a possible source of wisdom in their own right, within a paradigm of RE that was increasingly in the 2010s described as Philosophy and Ethics, rather than Religious Education (Conroy et al., 2013). The Religious Education Council (REC), for example, put forward a 'problems and issues'-based approach (Ipgrave, forthcoming), and the problems and issues that increasingly appeared in classroom discussion and on examination papers appeared to some to have Islam and Muslims increasingly in mind. Children are now exposed to a range of highly complex and emotive issues before they have the necessary religious knowledge or literacy to answer them with any properly critical depth or sophistication. Ipgrave (forthcoming), for example, draws up an interesting list of these types of GCSE examination question:

> 'Faith schools are inappropriate for the twenty-first century.'
> 'Anyone who takes their religion seriously has got to be a fundamentalist.'
> 'Religious believers should be involved in politics.' Do you agree?
> 'Religious identity should be more important than national identity to a religious believer.' What do you think? Explain your opinion.
> 'Religious believers should marry someone their parents approve of.' What do you think? Explain your opinion.

In all these questions, Ipgrave feels that the Muslim is quite clearly the archetype of the stereotypical and 'problematic' religious believer.

This critical rational, 'philosophy and ethics' approach, underpinned by a strong liberal secular hidden curriculum (Wright, 2007), and which avoids the study of religion qua religion (Conroy et al., 2013), is likely to be detrimental to the spiritual and religious education of Muslim young people and other young people of serious faith. For, as we have also seen in Chapter 3, the Islamic religion as *deen* – the complete life-transaction – necessarily also exists at the level (c) of irreducible institutions and forms in that its rulings are part of a totality pertaining to the civic and institutional life of the believer, as well as at the levels (b) of interpersonal relations and (d) of the embodied personality. Furthermore, the recent shift towards philosophy and ethics underpinned by a critical orthodoxy, driven in part at least by a securitisation agenda post 9/11 and 7/7, can unwittingly create a dangerous environment in RE for young Muslims, for whom the faith of their family may be one of the few stable elements of their lives. There is a danger that with both 'social cohesive' and 'philosophical' RE, Islam may become unwittingly synonymous with backward-looking and illiberal forms of faith.

At a conference that I attended at the University of Cambridge in October 2012, there was a robust debate about what was the true object of religious education. What, in Hirst's (1974) conception, is the form of religious knowledge to be addressed by RE? What is the most basic element to which the study of religion pertains? While the form of mathematics is numbers and everything related to them, the form of English and modern foreign languages is letters and the meanings derived from them, the form of history is the past and everything related to it, the form of geography is the earth and the relationships of human beings to it, the form of religious education was not immediately apparent. Is the form of religious education simply 'religion'? In that case, what does religious education mean for those who have no religion, and what counts and does not count as religion?

It is the contention of this chapter that the most basic form of knowledge of religious education is the life of the ground-state/spirit/soul and the ultimate religious and spiritual concerns, doctrines, practices and forms related to it. In other words, what distinguishes RE at the level of 1M – non-identity/being-as-such – from other humanities subjects is the study of the metaphysical/spiritual qua metaphysical/spiritual, rather than the metaphysical/spiritual as an implied element in other aspects of life, as is the case, as we have seen in Chapter 6, with history. The chapter will examine how this form of the spirit can be addressed by RE teachers of Muslims and others, such as parents and imams, involved in religious education to help prepare young Muslims for a rich spiritual life as Muslims in conversation with and respect for a multi-faith world. It will do this in a way that takes account of both the vertical, metaphysical and the horizontal, social axes of religious education and aims at a balance of knowledge *about*, knowledge *from* and knowledge *for* religion.

Muslim young people in the RE classroom

Taylor (2007) has discussed the process in the Christian West of 'disenchantment' whereby the belief in the external, ontological reality of spiritual forces, including God, His Angels, the Devil, and their power over the natural, physical world was first confined, with the Christian Reformation, to the private domain and then internalised as ethics and epistemology and finally displaced as the normal mindset of the Christian and Jewish populace by a natural-scientific world-view. This process of the privatisation and internalisation of faith in the Judaeo-Christian West has taken place to such an extent that in the contemporary political domain belief in the direct power of God over human affairs is regarded as symptomatic of a pathology on the understanding of what Wright (2007) calls 'comprehensive political liberalism'.

In contrast to this religiously 'disenchanted' prevailing political and psychological climate, Muslim pupils at primary and secondary level are likely to bring into the classroom an 'enchanted' (Taylor, 2007) world-view, as well as a relatively strong prior knowledge of aspects of their faith (Ipgrave, 2006). In the enchanted world-view of many young Muslims, the world of the unseen, including belief in the active daily intervention of God in the affairs of the world and the existence of angels and devils (*jinn*), as outlined in Chapter 5, is very much alive and makes a seminal contribution to their understanding and rationalisation of the world (Ipgrave, 2006).

In her ethnographic study into the 'distinctive features' – that is, in ICR terms, non-identity at the level of 1M (First Moment – being-as-such) – of 55 Muslim pupils in RE classes in four primary and four secondary schools in Leicester,

England, Ipgrave (2006) identifies five distinctive features of the type of religious beliefs and dispositions that Muslim young people bring into the RE classroom.

Belief in God
God is active in the world. Relationships with him involve fear but also love.

Spiritual perception of the world
The everyday world is inhabited by angels and *jinn*. Some objects (for example, pictures, the Qur'an) are in reality animate; their spiritual power means they can be used for protection or healing.

Absence of symbolic interpretation
Every phrase of the Qur'an is literally true. The significance of objects, rites and texts lies in their exoteric meaning, not in any exegesis or inward spiritualisation.

Eschatological preoccupation
Heaven and hell are ever-present realities. Individuals' destinies are determined by a judgement calculated on the merit (*thawab*) and demerit (*gunna*, Urdu from the Arabic *khati'ah*) of their actions.

Devotion
The Prophet Muhammad is a focus of devotion, possessing supernatural beauty and power.

(Ipgrave, 2006, p. 149)

These features, while possibly flavoured by the particular Islamic ethos of the Muslim community in Leicester, are highly characteristic of an 'enchanted' world-view in the externalisation of religious belief into the objective world, which has been observed elsewhere among Muslim young people in European schools (Rissanen, 2013). This world-view is likely to be at odds with, or at least in contrast to, the less enchanted mindsets of many adult RE teachers. While it is possible, even likely, that an scientific world-view in which natural and social causes and explanations 'trump' religious ones will inform the world-view of many, usually non-Muslim, RE teachers of young Muslims, a religious world-view in which religious causes and explanations 'trump' natural-scientific ones is likely to inform the meta-narrative of the universe for many young Muslims. This can either set up the conditions for a clash of fundamentalisms (Ali, 2003) in the RE classroom or create the potential for highly fertile cross-fertilisation of ideas and understandings, depending on the quality of the interaction between teacher and pupil and the levels of epistemic humility created by the teacher in the classroom (Conroy et al., 2013), to which we now turn (Ipgrave, 2006).

The experiences of teachers of Muslim young people

Ipgrave (2006) has pointed out, therefore, that the teaching of RE to Muslim young people is rich with opportunity for stimulating inter-faith exchange and fraught with potential dangers on the four-planar level (b) of inter-subjective (interpersonal) transactions: 'At the heart of [religious] education is the exchange between teacher and pupil. In a multi-faith class, this can be a living inter-faith encounter, of more immediacy than the politicised educational debate' (p. 148). RE teachers have noted the exciting opportunity for pupils of little or no religious faith that Muslim young people bring to the classroom for the exploration of what a lived faith means in four-planar social and transcendental reality. They also noted in Ipgrave's study a 'narrow-mindedness' and 'exclusivity' and propensity for the either–or Manichean mindsets that we noted in the Introduction were part of the defensive, post-colonial experience of the Muslim majority world and its diaspora. A further explanation of this 'arrogance' is that, perhaps because of their often religion-rich out-of-school cultures, Muslim children often bring a strong prior knowledge of Islam into the classroom which needs to be acknowledged and respected before humility can be encouraged.

However, as we shall explore more deeply in the next section, differences in interpretative world-view when thinking about Islam of the RE teacher and the Muslim pupil also represent a vital opportunity to break through 'either–or', Manichean world-views and to provide an esoteric/internal dimension to exoteric belief. In this regard, Ipgrave (2006, pp. 151–152) notes a tension that existed in the teaching of a 'Places of Worship' unit of work between a teacher's and a Muslim pupil's answer to the question, 'Why is it important for Muslim men to come to the mosque to pray?' The teacher expected replies in terms of the horizontal axis of 'community', 'sharing' and 'brotherhood'. The pupil's answer was, in the vertical axis, in line with sayings of the Prophet Muhammad: 'Because a prayer is worth more at the mosque than a prayer at home.' Here one can observe a creative tension in the differences of world-view and the potential for the teacher to ask, '*Why* did the Prophet Muhammad say that a prayer is worth more at the mosque than a prayer at home?' A response to this might, with entirely legitimate serious$_{(r+p)}$ Islamic reasoning, include both the 'vertical axis' consideration of what, metaphysically, the Muslim prayer is and why it might better be performed in company, and the horizontal axis, including themes of 'community', 'sharing' and 'brotherhood'. Thus, RE teachers have the opportunity to introduce an element of critical religious literacy to Muslim young people's understanding of their faith that is vital to their religious flourishing in a multi-faith world. For this to happen, however, it is critical that teachers themselves do not adopt an 'either–or' approach, and give credence to a pupil's initial exoteric position as part of an 'enchanted' world-view.

RE teachers in Ipgrave's study also noted the propensity of Muslim boys to 'flex their religious muscles' (Ipgrave, 2006, p. 150) by showing that they know more about Islam than the RE teacher and even the preparedness to enter into knowledge–power (Foucault, 1980) struggles with their teachers. This type of 'arrogance', which we might construe as an example of demi-real, 'hegemonic' 'laddishness' (L. Archer, 2003; B. Francis, 2000), was turned to good educational use by accomplished teachers in the study, who construed it as a willingness on the part of Muslim young people to enter wholeheartedly into debate. Thus, RE, like history, as we saw in Chapter 7, has been observed to represent a great opportunity to draw sometimes recalcitrant Muslim young people, prone to demi-real, hegemonic 'laddishness', into a life-meaningful engagement with the school curriculum. As we also saw in the previous chapter, such engagement in the spiritual dimension of success can have positive knock-on effects in the intellectual and affective-cultural dimensions of success.

Bearing in mind this identification of the nature of young Muslims in RE, it is the contention of this chapter:

- that effective religious education can help nurture Muslim embodied personalities and both nurture and nuance an 'enchanted' world-view in a way that acknowledges the human epistemic fallibility and the diversity of religious insight;
- that the undoubted importance of the spiritual dimension to the vast majority of Muslim young people and the importance of religion in the contemporary world means that this process is essential, and not an optional extra, for Muslim young people.

2E: absences of 'seriousness' $_{(e)}$, of governmental support, of pupil respect and of buy-in from the Muslim community

However, the delivery of these related aims for RE entails the necessary removal and transformation of significant and 'determinate absences' (Bhaskar, 1993/2008; see Chapter 4) in contemporary RE provision.

In Chapter 3, we saw that *'seriousness'* in the critical realist and philosophical sense means that your practices and behaviour are consistent with your knowledge and belief. It is built conceptually out of a critique of the philosophy of the Enlightenment philosophy of David Hume (1711–1776) as *'unserious'*. Bhaskar has effectively critiqued Humean actualist orthodoxy, and thus much modern and contemporary philosophy, as 'unserious' in its denial of deep ontological structure in favour of an actualism whereby natural (and social) phenomena are only explicable as constant conjunctions of events. This empiricist actualism, in its denial of deep structure, took Hume to a position where he could not philosophically sustain the rational belief that to leave a building by the ground-floor door was better than leaving it by the first-floor window because he believed that nature had no underlying causal laws or structures. This was an 'unserious' philosophical position because if he really believed it, he should have left buildings by the first-floor window on at least 50% of occasions!

We also in Chapter 2 saw how Islam is characterised by a commitment to religious 'seriousness' $_{(r)}$ and an a priori need for consistency between practice and belief.

This chapter introduces a more specific form of philosophical 'seriousness' – that is, seriousness-in-education, seriousness $_{(e)}$. Seriousness $_{(e)}$ refers to the consistency between the existence (ontology) of a phenomenon in the world and its epistemological representation as the subject of study on sites of education. This includes consistency between phenomena that are of value to pupils and their representation, or lack of it, on school curricula. It is the contention of this chapter that RE in Britain and the multi-faith West suffers from a lack of seriousness $_{(e)}$, especially, although not exclusively, for Muslim pupils. That is to say, there is a gap between the importance of religion as a generative mechanism in world affairs, as a central feature in the lives of young Muslims and many other young people of faith, and the status and quality of the provision of RE in schools. This lack of seriousness $_{(e)}$ is a product of contradictory dynamics in the national and international status of religion and the status of religion in educational policy, which I will now explain.

'God is back': religion is a prime motivating factor in contemporary national and global events

The secularisation thesis *predicted*, following the lead of Weber, Durkheim and Comte, and then *assumed*, the eventual collapse of faith and organised religion by the end of the twentieth century and its displacement by a liberal secular, empirical scientific world-view. However, religion appears to have made an extraordinary comeback in the twenty-first century, if, indeed, it ever went away. While it is fair to claim that in the industrial societies of the West, religious faith has become marginal in the public domain, in the private domain it still thrives; while in the developing world, religious faith and its public representations are on the increase in spite of increased and globalised industrialisation (Norris & Inglehart, 2004).

In the international arena, in the United States evangelical Christianity constitutes the world-view of millions of American citizens and forms a powerful political and educational lobby that underscored the interventionist neo-conservative foreign policy of the Republican administration from 2003 to 2009. In Turkey, the Justice and Development Party (*Adalet ve Kalkınma Partisi*, AK), a conservative democratic political party underpinned by Islamic ideals, has since 2002 had considerable success in turning around the country's failed economy, although in 2014 it fell foul of claims of human rights abuses. Despite recently tottering under the impact of repeated, highly damaging paedophilia scandals, Roman Catholicism is spreading in Africa and elsewhere. Even in Britain, which is by common consent in a more advanced stage of secularisation than most industrialised countries (White, 2004), the Anglican Church under both Archbishop Dr Rowan Williams and lately Archbishop Justin Welby has seen fit to add a moral and theological dimension to contentious public debates such as the place of Shari'a law in British life and the ethics of banking and welfare reform.

While it is easy to assume that much of the contemporary West is almost completely secularised, in Britain 46% of young people who self-identify as

Christian and 90% of young people who self-identify as Muslim regard 'religion' as their most important identifier (L. J. Francis & Robbins, 2005). While formal church attendance and other forms of institutional faith appear to be in steady and sharp decline, with an 11% drop in the numbers of confessing Christians in the United Kingdom between 2001 and 2011 (70% to 59% of the UK population; ONS, 2012), nevertheless *c.*70% of British people still believe in God (Economic and Social Research Council, 2008). Even in Britain, therefore, it would probably be more accurate to talk of a massive increase in religious individualism and the sharp decline of the institutions of religion, than a massive increase in secularisation.

Partly as a result of vocal Muslim public protest against Western foreign policy, their countering Islamophobia and real and imagined connections to terrorism, Islam and Muslims in the multi-faith West, and in particular Britain, for many have become the face of organised religion, in both its benign and its destructive manifestations. Despite there existing, in reality, a religiously diverse Asian population in Britain, whereas once to be Muslim meant to be Asian (Modood, 2003), for many, to be Asian now means to be Muslim. Consider the hostility faced in Britain by Sikhs, who are sometimes confused with, and even abused and attacked as, Muslims (DeJohn, Morales & Hutchinson, 2013). As I identified in the Introduction, the Islamist terrorist attacks of 9/11 and 7/7 have ramped up the connection in the minds of many people between organised religion and organised violence with a particularly Islamic hue.

Thus, it is fair to claim that the global socio-political climate is increasingly and overtly shaped by religious convictions and reactions, and that the personal lives of young people are inevitably increasingly shaped by the embrace or rejection of religious ideas, values and practices. At the same time, in the United Kingdom what Wright (2007) calls 'comprehensive liberalism' – a political world-view in which the maximising of individual autonomy becomes an end in itself – has meant that debate between religious and non-religious world-views has become increasingly fractious and incommensurable in the public sphere, with some religious positions on a range of issues – abortion and homosexuality, to name but two – driven to the extreme margins of political and educational discourse.

Decline in the status of religious education

The global political climate, characterised by the increasing visibility, importance and complexity of religion, would, therefore, appear to demand an increase in the sophistication of religious literacy developed for school pupils (Wright, 2007). However, the status of RE in English schools has been in steady and sharp decline since 1988 (Conroy et al., 2013; Ipgrave, forthcoming), and it is increasingly regarded by pupils and teachers as a 'Cinderella subject' (Kay, 1997). The marginalisation of RE from the systems of public exams and the concomitant lack of commitment to the subject from schools in term of staffing and resources mean that over a quarter of English secondary schools now opt to abandon RE before the statutory age of 16 (Paton, 2011).

It is appropriate to consider what has caused this unserious gap between the importance of private and public religion in the world and in the lives of young people and the status of the subject RE in English schools. There is a multiplicity of factors that have contributed to this lack of seriousness (e) in religious education.

First, RE inhabits a 'strange' (Conroy et al., 2013) obligatory/non-statutory, national/local status in the policy domain: RE provision is obligatory in English schools but its national framework is non-statutory. Thus,

> the deep localism manifest in England in the existence of SACREs [Standing Advisory Councils on Religious Education] can be replicated in no other subject … particular communities get directly to influence curriculum content and pedagogy in a way that would not be considered appropriate elsewhere.
>
> (Conroy *et al.*, 2013, p. 52)

This confusion between national and local aims and objectives for the subject is exacerbated in the political domain by the widespread belief that RE is not a 'proper' humanities discipline in the way that history and geography are. This belief has been led in the United Kingdom by leading Russell Group universities, including the Universities of London, Oxford and Cambridge, not including RE as a 'facilitating subject' for university entry. The Russell Group has been followed, or backed up, by government, as evidenced by the recent withdrawal by the Secretary of State for Education, Michael Gove, of financial aid for students undertaking teacher training (PGCE) for RE and its allocation for those training to teach Latin and Greek, neither of which is legally mandated. The claim is further reinforced by the fact that RE was excluded from the gold-standard English Baccalaureate while history and geography were included, despite vigorous campaigning and protest from the Religious Education Council (Conroy et al., 2013).

This lack of both academic and political backing, most recently from the United Kingdom's Coalition government, has interacted at the level (c) of irreducible institutions and forms with the inability of those in the RE community to define their subject clearly, which has played into the hands of educational policy-makers who do not have the best interests of RE at heart.[2] For a generation, as alluded to earlier, RE has been characterised by an absence of clarity of purpose and a lack of a clear rationale for the subject: is the purpose of religious education to contribute to the creation of the morally autonomous person, to provide a range of comparative facts about religion, and/or to help pupils lead the good life? What is the balance of knowledge about religion, knowledge from religion and knowledge for religion (Baumfield & Cush, 2013; Teece, 2010)? Should RE promote the quest for religious truth and/or an ethic of truthfulness, create community cohesion, celebrate diversity or all of the above? Wright (2007) cites David Day (1985) in identifying the 'permanent identity crisis' of religious education, and RE teachers have complained that a lack of subject

Table 8.1 The rank in popularity of different school subjects with 355 UK-based Muslim and non-Muslim boys

Position	Muslim	Non-Muslim
1st	PE	PE
2nd	Mathematics	Art
3rd	Science	English
4th	Art	Science
5th	English	History
6th	History	Mathematics
7th	Religious Studies	Geography
8th	Geography	Religious Studies

status in schools has been accompanied by an unrealistic burden of expectations about what RE in schools can achieve (Conroy et al., 2013).

As a result of the political downgrading of RE and the lack of clarity of purpose, RE suffers from a lack of resources in school and a lack of specialist subject knowledge and training (Conroy et al., 2013). RE provision in both primary and secondary schools is often assigned to history and citizenship teachers as a bolt-on additional duty. This contributes to a vicious cycle of loss of status and loss of quality of provision which impacts on the status of the subject with Muslim and other pupils. In my study of 295 Muslim young people in history education reported in the previous chapter, religious studies came seventh out of the eight core and foundation subjects in popularity across three of the four schools and eighth at the Faith School (!). Although this seventh position was one better than for the comparative non-Muslim sample, for whom RE came last, given the significance of religion in the boys' lives this fact evinces a high degree of lack of seriousness [e] in the lack of authentic impact of the subject on the Muslim young people's lives (see Table 8.1).

The absence of belief in RE for Muslim community educationalists

Furthermore, anecdotal discussion with the Muslim pupils' teachers at the Faith School suggested that the low status of the subject of RE at the Islamic Faith School was partly due to the fact the RE was undermined by the greater authority of Islamic madrasa-style religious education, which occurred in the mosque on the same school site (see Chapter 6). This fact is symptomatic of a more general lack of support for the subject from elements of the Muslim community and from prominent Muslim educationalists.

Precisely because both Islam and the spiritual dimension are significantly important for Muslim young people and for Muslim educators, RE has been a site of particular controversy for the Muslim community in England: both the relative absence of Islam in RE before the 1988 Education Reform Act and the presence of Islam on a more equal epistemic footing in RE with other religions and Christianity post-1988 has caused Muslim educationalists consternation

(Hull, 1998; Hunt, 1983; Zaki, 1982). This is because Islam for many Muslims in the post-colonial diaspora represents not only a religious world-view and way of life (*deen*), but also, as we have seen with the 'Gang Girls' in Chapter 6, an identity through which Muslims can resist racism and discrimination. Islam is the one aspect of life that had not, until its introduction into the RE curriculum, been 'colonised' by white Europeans.

Therefore, for some Muslim educationalists and community figures, the marginality of Islam in RE (compared to Christianity) has represented the marginality of Islam to British society and therefore something to be transformed; for others, the presence of Islam post-1988 in agreed RE syllabuses represents a threat to the monopoly within the Muslim faith community over the interpretation of Islamic values and the Islamic concept of education.

The former group (to which I belong) has recognised that, while multi-faith RE in schools is very much 'in process' (Conroy et al., 2013), and while it can never replace confessional Islamic education, such as the learning of the Qur'an through memorisation and exegesis, it is an essential complement to a traditional Islamic education that can develop religious literacy for a multi-faith world. RE can provide a critical bridgehead between Islamic education and the life of multi-faith society that, far from damaging Islamic identity and understanding, can enrich and deepen them, as is statutorily required by the National Curriculum.

The latter group, which includes a vocal constituency of Muslim parents, has at times advocated the complete removal of Islam from the RE classroom or the removal of Muslim pupils from RE. This attitude has on occasion resulted in mass Muslim community walkouts from RE (which are legal but undesirable; Hull, 1998) on the grounds that a non-Muslim RE teacher can never do justice to the immensity of Islamic praxis and that 'it were better for a religion not to be taught than to be taught badly' (Zaki, 1982). This position is indeed an intensified, particularised form of a more general fear among many Muslim educationalists and, indeed, parents that the aims of Western, secular education to create autonomous, morally liberal citizens are antithetical to the aims of Islamic education to create knowledgeable worshippers of God who understand their place within a divinely ordained cosmological order (Halstead, 2004).

Thus, for many Muslim educationalists and parents, non-confessional, multi-faith RE represents in microcosmic form everything that they fear is wrong with Western, liberal education: moral relativism, religious perennialism and political secularism (Wright, 2007). For this group, even the absence of Arabic-language labels and terminology can lead to the belief in the absence of Muslim-appropriate substance from the school RE curriculum.

The absence of seriousness $_{(e)}$ in RE in summary

At the level of 2E, absences of disciplinary clarity within the RE community, absences of university and political support for RE and absences of pupil respect and buy-in from Muslim parents and the Muslim community have generated an absence of 'seriousness'$_{(e)}$ for RE that presents a significant hurdle for the RE teacher to overcome in the task of addressing the ontology of the spirit effectively at the four-planar level (b) of personal interactions (including non-dual phases and states).

Nevertheless, while many of the absences that exist at the level of absence (2E) are structural and embedded at the four-planar level (c) of irreducible institutions and structures, there is much that RE teachers can do to apply their own transformative agency to the subject to revitalise and bring an element of seriousness$_{(e)}$ to RE provision, which, as we saw in Chapter 6, is not only essential for Muslim young people but also vital for young people of all faiths and none. The rest of this chapter is dedicated to outlining an ICR approach to help RE teachers bring about 'learning about' and 'learning from' and 'learning for' religion and to inject some welcome 'seriousness'$_{(e)}$ into the study of RE. It is my contention that this ICR approach to RE can help Muslim and other pupils in the pursuit, discovery and negotiation of absolute and contingent truths pertaining to the life of the spirit and help to create a more tolerant and religiously literate society.

3L: the fulcrum of ICR in the classroom, the embrace of difficult issues and the use of transcendence

Therefore, this section will suggest, at the level of 3L (Third Level – totality), tools for effecting a 'serious' and meaningful RE provision for young Muslims that, in line with obligatory, non-statutory requirements for English schools (Qualifications and Curriculum Authority, 2004) and locally agreed syllabuses, will help young Muslims learn about, from and for religion in a way that harnesses multi-faith RE perspectives and draws on the distinctive metaphysical nature of RE. This will be done by:

- using the fulcrum of ICR in the classroom in what I term the extra-faith, inter-faith and intra-faith modes, including embracing 'difficult issues';
- embracing 'difficult issues';
- exploring levels of transcendence.

The fulcrum of Islamic critical realism in religious education

The reader will remember from Chapter 3 that the core of the critical realist understanding of reality is grounded in three interrelated principles (see Figure 8.1):

1   ontological realism;
2   epistemological relativism;
3   judgemental rationality.

These were together described as the fulcrum of Islamic critical realism.

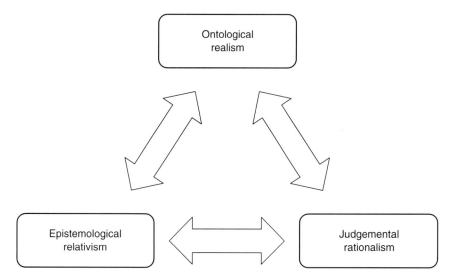

Figure 8.1 The fulcrum of ICR.

Ontological realism means that being exists independently of knowledge; for example, the sun exists in exactly the same way whether the universe is described in a geocentric or a heliocentric way. In the social-natural world, the objects of knowledge are existentially intransitive; that is to say, they exist independently of the agents of knowledge, otherwise there would be nothing to know in the first place. However, the social processes of knowing are causally interactive with the objects that they come to know.

When applied to the ontology of the spirit, ontological realism pertains to the essential being of spiritual phenomena: God can be said to exist (or not exist) independently of our knowledge of Him. Unseen spiritual realities, e.g. human/divine spirit, divine providence, intercession with God, can be allowed to exist (or not to exist) independently of our knowledge of or belief in them. Ontological realism about God claims not that God exists, but that the fact and realities of His existence are not dependent on our knowledge of Him or them.

Epistemological relativism asserts that are beliefs about and understandings and knowledge of being are socially produced, instantiated in historical and personal circumstances, fallible and transient. Epistemological relativism in the spiritual domain pertains to beliefs, knowledge and understandings of spiritual phenomena that usually take the form of religious traditions. To repeat a passage quoted in Chapter 3, to espouse the idea of epistemological relativism is to say that

> a belief about the reality or existence of god [*sic*] is quite consistent with ...
> the idea that god manifests himself or herself or itself in a variety of

different ways or is accessed by different people in different traditions in a plurality of different ways.

(Bhaskar, 2002/2012a, p. 31)

In other words, the fact that God has been known differently does not mean that the God that is known is different.

The compatibility of ontological realism and epistemological relativism necessitates *judgemental rationality*. That is to say, there exist or can be created rational criteria to adjudicate between different knowledges, understandings and values which are not all equally accurate, truthful, sustainable or useful. Judgemental rationality pertains to deliberation and deciding about the plausibility of spiritual phenomena and the traditions connected with them: the compatibility of ontological realism and epistemological relativism necessitates *judgemental rationality in that there must be coherent rational (doctrinal), emotional and experiential grounds for choosing one mode of spiritual access (religious tradition) as opposed to another if that decision is to be intellectually and spiritually sustainable.* Therefore, it is possible with these basic principles *both* to claim that God has been accessed and has revealed His Being through a variety of traditions *and* to choose one tradition as opposed to another, while still drawing on the insights of other faiths.

Chapter 3 made the case that this ICR fulcrum presents an intellectual framework that can offer young Muslims and other young people of faith:

* confidence in the rational possibility of the existence of essential phenomena as described by the Islamic faith at the level of ontological realism;
* humility with regard to their interpretation of these phenomena and their sectarian commitments, which includes openness to the spiritual insights of those of other faiths at the level of epistemology;
* intellectual rigour in the tools for making decisions and distinctions between competing truth-claims and the authenticity of different religious experiences at the level of judgemental rationality.

It outlines the possibility of a 'light' religious perennialism that is commensurate with Qur'anic teaching about the authenticity and inviolability of a variety of religions (e.g. Qur'an, 5:69); many spiritual roads lead potentially to the top of the ontological mountain, but they do not all necessarily do so with equal truth or efficacy.

From philosophy to pedagogy

SPIRITUAL BEING: THE EXTRA-FAITH MODE

The application of the fulcrum of ICR into the classroom involves condensing these complex philosophical ideas down to a pedagogical form. For these purposes, ontological realism becomes 'spiritual being' and is to be explored through what I call the 'extra-faith' mode. This is the mode at which the nature of spiritual and religious phenomena is examined ontologically in the classroom without reference to a religious tradition. It is the mode of looking at the field of absolute concerns of the life of the spirit generated by the universal quest for the meaning of life. The extra-faith mode is also the mode of identification by pupils in conversation with their teachers of universal religious phenomena that are fit for study and analysis. In teacher-training PGCE sessions that I have conducted at the University of Cambridge, the following spiritual phenomena have been identified (by no means exclusively and exhaustively) in the extra-faith mode as part of a universal patrimony of spiritual being: Justice, Destiny, Nature, God(s), Pilgrimage (see Figure 8.4), Prayer, the After-Life, Religious Books, Morality. Thus, it is the mode that in some ways combines the world religions' phenomenological approach with the current trends towards philosophy and ethics in the philosophical identification of universal religious phenomena.

The advantage of the extra-faith mode is that it can bring into the classroom examination at the very start of a unit of study those who have a commitment to faith and those who have no commitment to faith on an equal epistemic footing, which can help create a climate of consensual humility, something that is essential to the success of the shared quest for religious understanding (Conroy et al., 2013). Teachers can create a consensus in the extra-faith mode that these spiritual phenomena exist in the lives of religious people without any reference to the necessity of a truth-claim or lack of it. In other words, the class can agree to proceed according to the principle of ontological realism *as if* these spiritual phenomena exist (Berger, 1967 cited in Grimmitt, 1987). For even if they turn out to be false or even demi-real – that is, essentially and categorically false but effecting vicious causal changes in the world – they will be things that no class member can deny affect people's lives and minds.

Once this consensus is achieved and the pupils have identified a religious phenomenon, the teacher is free to explore the most basic nature of the phenomena, for example pilgrimage as a journey made with a spiritual purpose, so that all the children can get a clear idea of the nature of what they are studying – that is, what it is at the level of 1M, being-as-such, in a way that will also begin to suggest relativity and variety of religious understanding and the particular manifestations of that universal nature.

SPIRITUAL KNOWING AND UNDERSTANDING: THE INTER-FAITH MODE

Therefore, while spiritual being at the extra-faith mode refers to religious phenomena, metaphysical realities that are claimed by religions to exist in the ontology of the spirit, epistemological relativism becomes at the level of the classroom 'spiritual knowing and understanding' and is explored through the 'inter-faith' mode (see Figures 8.2 and 8.3).

The 'inter-faith' mode is the comparative mode of exploring different religious phenomenon as understood from the point of view of different faith traditions and different sectarian positions within traditions. It is the comparative

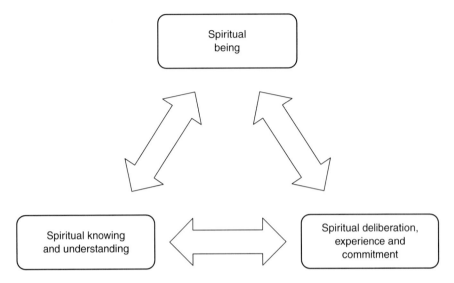

Figure 8.2 The fulcrum of ICR transposed into religious education (RE).

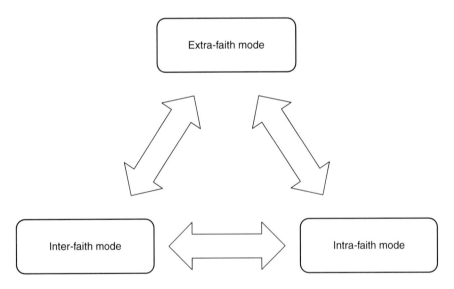

Figure 8.3 The pedagogical modes of the fulcrum of ICR in RE.

mode at which children can understand that similar phenomena of spiritual and religious being have been expressed similarly *and* differently in different faith traditions. It is the informative, 'learning about religion' mode in which the child can gather information about the faith of 'the other' compared with facets of his or her own faith. Thus, it is the mode of discovery that some religious phenomena and beliefs are universal, while others are not. It is the mode of visits to sacred sites and of exploration of the deep diversity of the human religious expression in artefacts, art and architecture. Such visits in the inter-faith mode may themselves challenge deeply held cultural prejudices of, and assumptions by, some children. For example, Conroy et al. (2013) describe the visit of Muslim girls to a Hindu temple, which, after resistance and reluctance, was deeply transformative of their opinion of the Hindu 'other'. In short, it is the mode of the comparative exposure to the most visible, audible elements of spiritual expression. It is the mode at which, for example, Muslim children can discover and explore how the Five Pillars of Islam are a particular manifestation of universal religious phenomena in a way that does not undermine their particularity but connects Islam to a universal human tendency to seek a systematic connection with truth-and-reality (*Haqq*; see Chapter 2).

The inter-faith is the mode of the comparative, multi-faith approach that has received a lot of RE policy and classroom attention since the 1988 Education Reform Act (Wright, 2007). Using the ICR fulcrum, it can be brought into a relationship with metaphysical and ontological reality in the extra-faith mode and deepened through further intellectual and spiritual analysis in the 'intra-faith' mode.

SPIRITUAL DELIBERATION, DECISION-MAKING AND COMMITMENT: THE INTRA-FAITH MODE

However, as we have seen earlier in the chapter, it is not enough for children to be exposed to the ontology of the spirit. Given that they are at the phase, especially in adolescence (Kroger, 1996), of negotiating and making their first independent decisions about their core, absolute values, they must be enabled to experience, decide, feel and, if and when appropriate, to commit. Therefore, in this classroom version of the ICR fulcrum, judgemental rationality becomes 'spiritual deliberation, experience and commitment' and is explored through the 'intra-faith' mode. The intra-faith mode is the mode for exploring, in depth, the spiritual experience of religious phenomena and being empowered through knowledge, analysis and discussion to make personal decisions and judgements about them and their claims to truth.

This is also the mode for the teasing out of the esoteric juice from exoteric faith positions that the children may already have (Ipgrave, 2006), for example the performance of ablution before prayer in Islam. It is the mode at which the skilled RE teacher can challenge Muslim children, at primary or secondary level, to explore the deeper meaning and spiritual rationality of beliefs and practices that they have learned at home or in the madrasa, in a similar or related way to that which I laid out in Part II of this book, in order that they can understand them properly and be enabled to articulate them to others. It is in this vital mode that contested sectarian positions can be explored: what they mean in life to those that believe them and for those who reject them.

For example, among PGCE trainees at Cambridge I have performed an exercise in distinguishing between Islamic primary sources, Islamist derivatives and violently extreme Islamist texts by identification of criteria of a lack of Islamic 'seriousness' in Manichean world-views and by furnishing elements of basic textual analysis for recognising an authentic Islamic text. That is to say, in the intra-faith mode Muslim and non-Muslim young people can be shown that there are simple ways to choose *for themselves* between healthy and unhealthy forms of spiritual doctrine and experience. Thus, the intra-faith mode can help them develop both spiritual literacy and other-regarding moral autonomy. The 'intra-faith' mode both challenges the intellectually lazy view that spiritual experience cannot be articulated or analysed, identified by Barnes (2001) as a weakness of the phenomenological approach to RE; and it also allows for the reality of the ineffable, unspeakable nature of direct experience of the holy, which is the experience of the mystic from a wide range of faith traditions (Bhaskar, 2000).

Thus, in the intra-faith mode children can also be introduced to the tools of religious plausibility, such as exegesis or textual analysis, and the notion of 'seriousness' (knowledge–practice consistency). It is the intra-faith mode that prevents the danger of children being left floundering defencelessly in a sea of moral relativity. By the principle of judgemental rationality, the fact that there exists an apparently universal (or near-universal) form of religious activity or phenomena, e.g. pilgrimage and prayer, and a diverse range of particular epistemically relative expressions of it, does not violate the possibility that one form of the phenomena may bring the adherent nearer God than others. Nor does it rule out the possibility that some forms of these universal phenomena may be demi-real or alethically false. The universalism inherent at the extra-faith mode, far from detracting from particular confessional commitments, can actually strengthen them if they are critically examined in the inter- and intra-faith

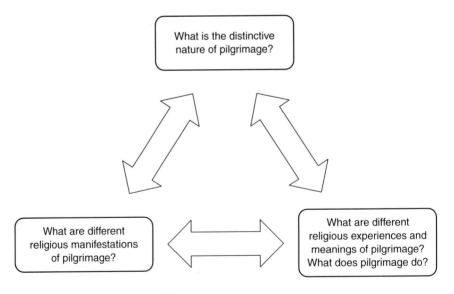

Figure 8.4 An example of the ICR fulcrum in use with the example of pilgrimage.

modes. The development of curricular material from this pedagogical framework will, I believe, help to enable pupils to justify and critique their own beliefs and to enter into a deep spiritual dialogue with the spiritual understandings of people of other faiths. The intra-faith mode can be a strong vehicle for philosophical seriousness by enabling the start of the safe negotiation of ultimate religious value and meaning in conversation with teachers and peers; thus, it can even, in the hands of a skilled and sensitive teacher, become the vehicle for the discovery of individual *dharma* (personal destiny) through the gradual controlled negotiation of core and secondary values.

Embracing the difficult issues

With regard to embracing and rejecting different sets of core and secondary values, the difficult issues of religion, such as violence and bigotry, are legitimate and necessary objects of study in the extra-faith, inter-faith and intra-faith modes. In the extra-faith mode, for example, the nature of violence can be explored: what is it that counts as religious violence? This might mean, for example, plotting a continuum from religious bullying and cultic behaviour to religiously inspired murders, past and present. It means showing in the inter-faith mode how religious violence has occurred within a vast range of religious positions, and examining in the intra-faith mode, using primary evidence, what motivates people in reality to be religiously violent, the impact on victims and what religious principles within particular faiths are flouted by religious violence undertaken in that faith's name.

As far as young Muslims are concerned, this approach to looking at religious violence by means of the ICR fulcrum would have the great advantage of avoiding the focus of religious violence being solely on Islam, as has become the norm in the discourses of securitisation (K. E. Brown, 2010), without being 'in denial' of the fact that skewed and violent interpretations of Islam will be part and parcel of the world-view to which some young Muslims will be exposed (Bunt, 2003). Young Muslims, in particular, need to be provided with the intellectual tools to approach the informal sites of religion on the internet and informal religious circles in a mature way, since they are such a prevalent feature of contemporary Islamic discourse (Bunt, 2003). The 'intra-faith' mode would enable an 'immanent critique' (Bhaskar, 1975) of these erroneous positions from within the principles of the Islamic faith, rather than an imposed liberal, moral secular agenda. It would enable pupils to see how and why such violent interpretations have got it wrong in terms of the true principles of Islam and what they do to the Muslim communities, societies and nations in which they take root.

Exploring transcendence: from denominational to transcendental religious education

We have seen how the fulcrum of ICR in the RE classroom in the extra-faith, inter-faith and intra-faith modes can help provide a more 'serious' experience of multi-faith religious education by bridging the gap between the importance of religion in the lives of young Muslim and other pupils and the RE classroom, and by injecting philosophical coherence into the study of the life of the spirit. Moreover, Conroy et al. (2013) point out that while other humanities subjects, e.g. literature, deal with the metaphysical conceits of their subjects as immanent expressions in the world, RE is unique in that it must, if it is to retain its distinctiveness as a subject, deal with transcendence (e.g. God, Paradise, Blissful enlightenment) qua transcendence. Conroy et al. (2013) also provide examples of RE teachers avoiding talk of the transcendent elements such as death and the afterlife for fear of offending both those among their pupils who were denominational believers and those who were not.

In this respect, the ICR notion of quotidian transcendence and the hierarchy of transcendence that we explored in Chapter 5 can, I believe, help RE teachers bridge the gap between predominantly empirical-scientific world-views and the predominantly metaphysical and transcendental world-views in RE. This is important, since not only is it essential for Muslim young people that the idea of religious transcendence is taken seriously and that transcendence is not reduced to circumstantial immanence, but also all children need to understand that every religion *sui generis* exists and needs to be studied in some respect on a transcendent plane if RE as a subject is to regain its particular identity.

We saw in Chapter 5 how Bhaskar (2002/2012a) has described three ways in which the world of duality and difference is ultimately underpinned by the world of non-duality and transcendental identity:

1   *The constitution of everyday life.* That is to say, transcendental identity is essential to the ordinary 'constitution, that is the reproduction and transformation, of everyday life' (Bhaskar, 2002/2012a, p. xi).
2   *As a basis of being and of the human self/soul*: the unified ultimatum or 'ground-state' (Bhaskar, 2002/2012a) out of which the stratified layers of all being, including human being, emerge.
3   *As the deep interior of the cosmos.* At this level, unity and transcendent identity are experiential rather than proven by argument, and akin to mystical intuitions as to the all-pervasive presence of the Absolute, i.e. God.

These three ideas of transcendence might be explored in the classroom to show pupils of faith and no faith that transcendence is part and parcel of everyday experiences of reality and that spiritual experience can therefore be quotidian and accessible, and not confined to churches, mosques, saints and beatific visions.

Thus, for example, the RE teacher might explore the most basic example of oral human communication, the conversation, as a phenomenon that necessarily involves acts of repeated transcendental identification because it involves the mutual transcendence of the separate consciousness in the creation of a shared context of meaning, as outlined in Chapter 5. This can be achieved through a practical classroom experiment to show that were a transcendental identification in consciousness not a possibility at the level (b) of personal relations, a conversation could not take place.

Similarly, the notion of the transcendentally real self/spirit/soul can be explored at the extra-faith and intra-faith levels without a commitment of religious faith through a classroom task of identification of whether pupils feel or can identify that there is anything essential or continuous to the sense of who they are. Once this non-confessional transcendental experiment has awakened pupils' minds to the possibility of soul, then the idea of the self/soul in different faith traditions can reasonably be explored in the inter-faith mode and a judgement of plausibility about the soul's existence made at the intra-faith mode.

Once the idea of transcendence as a quotidian part of life and then of faith has been introduced, the idea of the hierarchy of transcendence from the quotidian to the celestial might be explored as a critical extension exercise in understanding modes of religious experience for more religiously literate pupils.

1   At the bottom of the 'pyramid', pupils can explore a host of the everyday transactions that necessarily require a transcendental aspect for their effective operation – conversation, work and trade among them.
2   At a 'higher' level, pupils can explore the meanings of mutual transcendent enrichment through education and the sharing of ideas, and the experience of the sublime through aesthetic transcendence in art, music, sport and other

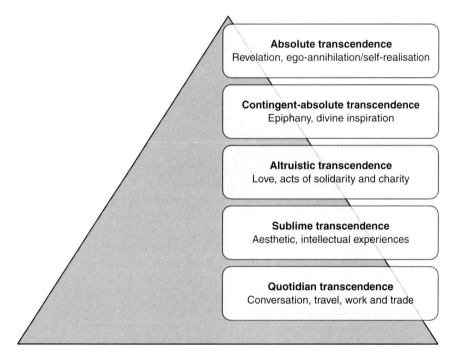

Figure 8.5 Stratified levels of transcendence.

forms of transcendental holistic activity and through scientific intellectual discoveries that involve the epistemological transcending of received knowledge.

3　At a yet 'higher' level, pupils can explore the meanings of transcendence of human love and of altruistic acts of solidarity, trust and devotion in which one human spirit or ground-state 'speaks' directly to another in service or sacrifice.

4　At an even 'higher' level still, pupils can explore the meanings of the experience of divine epiphany and inspiration.

5　At the pinnacle of transcendence, pupils can explore what is meant by the obliteration of the human ego and the assumption of the ground-state in the unity of God and similar acts of religious unveiling (Bhaskar, 2000), including the receipt of meaning directly from the presence of the Divine, Revelation.

Each one of these levels of transcendence can be examined in the extra-faith, inter-faith and intra-faith modes. Thus, the idea of transcendence as propounded by the philosophy of Islamic metaReality and ICR can be both a way into religious-style thinking for pupils from backgrounds in which religion does not feature and a way to extend religious literacy in gifted and interested pupils and those from religion-rich backgrounds, such as many Muslim young people.

4D: a transformative nexus of religious education: school, home, madrasa and peer group/internet

These tools can contribute to a serious experience of RE at the level of 3L in the classroom. We have seen from my dialectical Islamic critical realist analysis of the life of the Prophet Muhammad in Chapter 4 how the totality of the experience of Islam (at the level 3L) implemented in Madina became a transformative nexus of emancipated and enlightened behaviour on different sites in the Arabian Peninsula (before the power struggles and absences of authority on the death of Muhammad intervened in the dialectic once again).

It is the contention of this part of this chapter, analogously, that an implementation of a philosophically serious $_{(e)}$ education involves its necessary transformative connection to a variety of sites at which the spiritual dimension of Muslim young people is being affected by formal (school), semi-formal (madrasa) and informal (home and peer group) education. This is because the research presented in this chapter and the previous two chapters, and other research into young people (Muslim and other) in education (Alexander, 2000; L. Archer, 2003; Head, 1999; Shain, 2010), suggests that the non-school, semi-formal and informal sites of education are every bit as formative as the formal ones. It will be the task of dedicated RE teachers to create a sense of a joined-up religious world to nurture the development of an integrated spiritual dimension of young people in education.

Teacher–madrasa

We have seen already how the style of multi-faith religious education at school informed by the learning aims of the National Curriculum, namely to create other-regarding, respectful, truth-seeking, morally autonomous citizens (White, 2004; Wright, 2007), may be perceived by many Muslim young people and their parents to be at odds with the aims of a traditional Islamic education to create knowledgeable, morally obedient worshippers of God (Halstead, 2004).

I have already shown in Chapters 3 and 4 how critical spiritual rationality can be traditionally and authentically construed as part of an 'enchanted' Islamic world-view and as a necessary attitude of mind for study of the Qur'an. I suggested in Chapter 5 how the derivation of esoteric meaning of the basic practices of Islam can be made available to Muslim young people. It is therefore vital for the cultivation of an integrated Muslim spiritual dimension that the school and the madrasa, where traditional Islamic education is imparted to some 50% of Muslim schoolchildren in the United Kingdom (Coles, 2010), are in communication. RE teachers need to know about and even have some working knowledge of the religious texts and values that children are absorbing in madrasas to enable Muslim children to examine them critically and explore their meaning in the intra-faith mode at school. Qur'an teachers need to know what Muslim children are learning in RE so that critical, multi-faith perspectives can be more deeply embedded in their religious learning and exemplified by recourse to verses of the Qur'an (e.g. Qur'an 5:5). Where points of epistemic tension arise, these need to be discussed. If this communication does not happen, then the evidence presented in the previous chapter with history suggests that one or other of these authoritative centres of religious instruction will lose out in the minds of Muslim pupils, to the detriment of the development of their spiritual dimension and with the possible result that they occupy split, parallel religious universes. The history of RE in Britain also shows that a failure of communication between schools and madrasas can lead, at worst, to undesirable and unnecessary withdrawal of Muslim children from RE (Hull, 1998).

Teacher–parent

We noted in Chapters 6 and 7 the intellectual and emotional benefits for children of strong teacher–parent partnerships with regard to the study of history. It is inevitable that the religious/cosmic world-view of Muslim young people and their most basic religious instruction will have occurred at the hands of their parents or guardians and other close family members, such as siblings and aunts and uncles. Especially in the case of children of primary school age, teachers will do well to remember that they are interacting with the child and his or her parents, especially in matters of religious education, which Muslim parents usually take unusually seriously (Coles, 2010). Teacher–parent interaction is part and parcel of school life. Nevertheless, it is important that this interaction is meaningful with regard to RE and that neither teachers nor parents or guardians shy away from the discussion of difficult issues and differences between the religious educational culture of home and the religious educational culture of school if they arise.

Teacher–peer group–internet

We also saw in Chapters 6 and 7 how the peer group is a crucible for the identity formation of all young people and, in particular, the spiritual identity of Muslim young people. For almost all the Muslim young people in L. Archer's (2003) investigation, Shain's (2003; 2010) work and this study, the peer group was a crucial dimension for the formation of the spiritual dimension of Muslim youngsters. While it is uniquely difficult for teachers to get a detailed grasp of the ideas

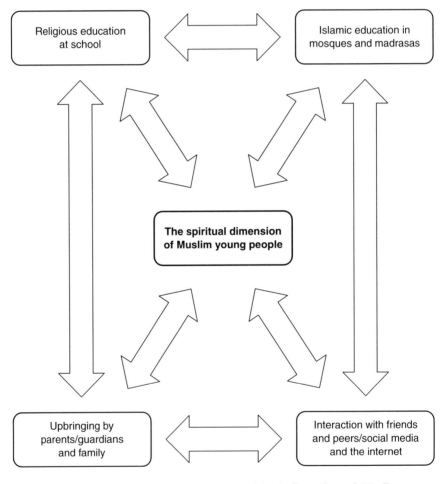

Figure 8.6 The transformative nexus for the spiritual dimension of Muslim young people.

that are circulating in young people's peer groups, it is quite practicable for teachers to tease out in class the religious dilemmas in the understanding of events and in the formation of young people's values that may be being debated and discussed within their peer groups. This is of particular importance for Muslim young people at secondary school level and in further education, given the prevalence and diversity of quality in religious understanding of Islam-related material that is available on the internet. Much of this material is interesting and worthy of discussion in class, but some of it is Manichean and divisive, and even violently extreme (Bunt, 2003; Wilkinson, 2011a). The critical interrogation of internet material and the frank recognition of the role of the internet in transmitting and reproducing religious power is a vital task for the thorough education of the spiritual dimension of Muslim young people. At the very least, young Muslims ought to be empowered through the development of judgemental rationality in the intra-faith mode that a judgement passed by an internet sheikh is not necessarily true, and they ought to have been equipped with necessary understandings to problematise apparently cast-iron and literalist religious interpretations as they are often simplistically presented online. This can only happen if the subject of internet religion is brought into the RE classroom in the extra-, inter- and intra-faith modes.

If this nexus of transformative religious education is established by RE teachers, madrasas and parents or guardians, then the spiritual dimension of Muslim young people stands a significant chance of being nurtured and informed in such a way as to enable their critical commitment to the core values and practices of the Muslim faith in a reflective way that is philosophically 'serious'. Such a nexus will, I believe, create a mature, critical openness in many Muslim young people to the insights and understanding of others, both within and outside the brotherhood (Umma) of Islam.

Summary: religious education – a return to 'seriousness'(e)

A return to seriousness(e) by closing the gap between the value of the ontology of the spirit in the world and lives of young Muslims and the status and quality of RE in schools will enable religious educators to connect with the faith of Muslim young people in a way that creates openness to the faiths and spiritual wisdom of others.

Grimmitt (1987), in line with other educationalists (Datta, 2002), has claimed that 'an educational process which isolates "academic knowledge" or "truth" from the social "life-world" of pupils does not assist them in valuing that world or re-appraising it' (p. 109). At present, the world of academic RE in schools and the informal (peer group/internet) and semi-formal (home–madrasa) religious worlds of Muslim young people often exist in relative isolation. Teachers have a crucial role, therefore, in creating a serious environment for the type of multi-faith RE which is a 'living multi-faith encounter' (Ipgrave, 2006) and in which the 'enchanted', religious world-view of young Muslims is regarded as a rational and valid response to the world, as well as open to critical rational debate and discussion.

The absence of 'serious' religious education in schools that provides for a rigorous engagement with transcendence and that provides the effective tools to understand, respect and draw from a diversity of religious traditions is likely highly detrimental for young Muslims. It leaves them unprepared to take their powerful faith identifications and practices with them effectively and fulfillingly into the world and may, occasionally, drive them into the arms of extreme and violent interpretations of their faith available on the internet and elsewhere.

A philosophically coherent provision of RE that takes religious transcendence seriously and that recognises the centrality of the spiritual dimension to the development of complete personhood in adolescence (Baker & Edwards, 2012) will help young Muslim children (and, indeed, all types of children) to embrace the increasingly complex world of the spirit with informed and sophisticated confidence.

Notes

1 The empirical demographic analyses suggested that Britain's minority communities were becoming more and more ethnically and culturally mixed (Casciani, 2005).
2 This blatant marginalisation and downgrading of RE as a school subject is in part at least the product of a political class that sees religious values and those that hold them as an obstacle to 'progressive', liberal politics (Morris, 2013).

9 Citizenship education

A pathway to full critical engagement

Introduction: the complexity of civic identification for young Muslims

From the very outset of this book, we have been aware that citizenship and civic belonging at the four-planar level (c) of social relations and irreducible structures, institutions and forms are key elements in the educational ontology of young Muslims. Muslim young people are facing complicated clusters of ethnic and national identifications that, as we have seen in Chapter 6, sometimes compete for 'hegemonic' dominance. Muslim young people are rarely indigenous, ethnic Britons and, although many were born and bred in the United Kingdom, they almost always have familial roots that lie elsewhere, and, to add to the complexity, the Islamic faith, which as we have seen is a crucial identifier for the vast majority of Muslim young people, is not a native British faith but one whose intellectual, cultural and spiritual roots emanate from outside the British Isles.

To further add to the complexity, young people, including young Muslims, inhabit a social world at the level (c) of irreducible institutions and forms which is in radical flux (Gearon, 2010). Both globalisation and intensified individualism (Ball, Maguire & Macrae, 2000), channelled through consumer outlets and habits and, lately, through social media, have challenged collective, national citizenship identifications, especially those in which citizenship is coterminous with a specific ethnicity. This has contributed to an increase of localism with globalisation (Easton, 2014) and even in some cases has threatened the existence of traditional nation-states. As I write, an upcoming referendum on Scottish separation from the United Kingdom challenges the 300-year-old constitutional structure of the United Kingdom – a political framework in which all Britons, young Muslims included, exist. The rise and/or decline of a composite national British, as opposed to more monolithic ethnic English, Welsh, Irish and Scottish identities, may be particularly meaningful for young Muslims who do not have an ethnically English, Welsh, Irish or Scottish identity to fall back on, with the weakening of 'Britishness'.

Nationhood and citizenship may be neither givens nor simple for young Muslims; rather, they are often highly contested, both within their peer groups and elsewhere. Nevertheless, research shows that it would be quite wrong to suppose that all or even most adult Muslims reject their British nationality and citizenship entitlements, and that their national citizenship is not important to them. Recent popular surveys have shown that, contrary to assumptions and stereotypes, adult Muslims tend to value their British citizenship as much as, if not more than, other groups, including white Britons (Binyon, 2007). As far as *young* Muslims are concerned, we saw in Chapter 7 how the civic dimension of success in the sense of institutional knowledge and knowledge for transformative belonging in Britain was the core *raison d'être* for the study of history at school for my sample for young Muslims: they wanted history to create a sense of informed critical attachment to their country. Therefore, in Chapter 6 I made the claim that at the level (c) of social relations and irreducible structures, institutions and forms, history in a past-oriented mode and citizenship education in a present-oriented mode (Barton, 2012) can complement each other to help to develop less alienated and more internally and externally integrated Muslim young people.

In this chapter, I am going to explore how citizenship education in this present-oriented mode can help young Muslims become informed and both transformed by and transformative of the civic and political worlds that they inhabit, especially those characterised as liberal democracies. I will indicate how citizenship education can help them successfully to negotiate a range of potentially dichotomised, Manichean socio-political positions and move successfully towards critically integrated, 'both/and' rather than 'either/or', approaches to their social and political lives in contemporary, multi-faith society. I will argue that these positions, which I characterize as positions of civic unity-in-diversity, will enable young Muslims both to participate in and transform shared public cultures and to be more authentically and seriously$_{(r+p)}$ Islamic. The structure of the chapter will follow the dialectical critical realist schema – MELD – with which I hope the reader will by now be familiar.

At the level of 1M (First Moment – identity-in-difference), I will explore who Muslim young citizens are, with recourse to the work of Archer and Shain, set in contrast to my own empirical evidence about the national and citizenship identifications of Muslim young people. This section will suggest that young Muslims are likely to value their citizenship entitlements and that they wish both to belong and to contribute civically and politically to the nations of which they are citizens, even if the achievement (Head, 1999) of authentic, hyphenated British-Islamic identities is not always simple. It argues that citizenship education in school ought to be in a position to help Muslim young people both to belong and to contribute to life in multi-faith societies.

However, this task is hampered because at the level of 2E (Second Edge – absence), citizenship education, even more than religious education, suffers from a significant absence of seriousness$_{(e)}$. That is to say, there is a dangerous gap between the importance of nurturing an informed, critical and committed citizenry, which is essential to the functioning of just, efficient democratic government and society, and the status and quality of citizenship education in schools. Since its introduction as a compulsory subject in schools in 2002, citizenship education has consistently been treated as a fringe subject in the school curriculum, if it is treated as an independent subject at all. I explain why this may be the case by recourse to a brief historical analysis of the 'slow and nebulous' development of the idea of the citizen in Britain and the more recent history of citizenship educational policy.

At the level of 3L (Third Level – totality), I explore how a 'serious'$_{(e)}$ strategy that is both informative and transformative for the young Muslim citizen can be developed by exploring issues in citizenship from the Islamic critical realist point of view of unity-in-difference. It will show how the ICR fulcrum of ontological realism, epistemological relativism and judgemental rationality can provide a route to serious$_{(e)}$ citizenship education that is non-doctrinaire and allows for the exploration of such themes as nationhood and national identity, democracy and governance, freedom of expression, the environment, the economy, culture and gender relations. This will provide a platform to revitalise the subject for young Muslims and other young people. At the level of 3L, I also suggest that creative links between citizenship, history and religious education can also lead to the generation of greater seriousness$_{(e)}$ for all three subjects.

Finally, at the level of 4D (Fourth Dimension – transformative praxis) I shall argue that citizenship education, above all the other humanities subjects, cannot be contained within the classroom but needs to be explored as a transformative praxis whereby young Muslims can be empowered outside school to engage with the local, national and international civic worlds.

1M: who is the young Muslim citizen?

Consistent with the ontological approach that has characterised my analysis of Muslim young people in education throughout this book, this section will examine at the level of 1M the nature of the young Muslim citizen, using both previous research and my own findings regarding the citizenship of Muslim young people in Britain (employing the sample of 307 Muslim young people reported in the previous three chapters). In so doing, it will challenge lazy assumptions in the media that young Muslims necessarily reject their British identities, as well as nuancing and adding an extra dimension to some serious academic findings to a similar, though more subtle, effect. I suggest that Muslim young people can and do feel that they belong and can contribute to Britain (and, indeed, elsewhere).

The displacement model of the nationhood of British Muslim boys: Muslim first; English last

Repeated media representations of Muslim young people have both set up and played into an 'either Muslim or British' dichotomy whereby Muslim young people are clearly expected to jettison their Islamic identities in favour of British ones (*Panorama*, 2009), or in other contexts, jettison their British-ness in favour of being a 'pure' Muslim. These representations have disseminated the idea that this rejectionistic dynamic is promoted, in particular, by Muslim faith schools (Siddique, 2010; Ware, 2010). Such reports and programmes have fed into, often sensationally, the construct of the Muslim as a 'feared/despised' (Goffman, 1986 cited in Sarra, 2011) 'other' leading a parallel life informed by values, such as extreme anti-Semitism, that are incompatible with enlightened, Western liberal ones.

Moreover, previous academic research into British Muslim adolescent identity, often conducted by researchers interested in the construction of gender-in-education (e.g. Alexander, 2000; L. Archer, 2003; Shain, 2010) has tended to identify Muslim young people, and especially boys, as rejecting their British nationality and resisting 'hegemonically' a sense of belonging in England as 'white', 'middle-class' and feminine.

For example, Alexander (2000), in her ethnographic study of 12 Bengali London-based teenage Muslims, characterises her sample as distinctly 'un-British' Muslims, preferring either their Bengali or Muslim identifiers at the expense of their British nationality. Likewise, L. Archer (2003) notes how her sample of 31 Muslim schoolboys from the north of England often distanced themselves from both their ethnic and their British national identifiers, preferring instead to identify themselves simply as Muslim. Similarly, Shain (2010) also observes Muslim boys in Britain as self-identifying as 'Muslim first', largely to the exclusion of national British and ethnic English identifiers. She (p. 56) suggests that Britishness among Muslim boys is often perceived as little more than a legal entitlement to a passport and the accidental rights of citizenship. In these findings, Muslim boys reject an attachment to Britishness as connected with an association with Englishness which they perceive as an ethnic category closely connected to 'being white'.

> 'First of all, I'm Muslim. After that I'm Pakistani. I wouldn't like to describe myself as English although I was born in this country. I always thought that after my education was complete, I would go back to Pakistan to live there.'
>
> (Zahid cited in Shain, 2010, p. 56)

Alexander (2000, p. 240) suggests that the growth of new hybrid British Islamic identity which actively rejects inclusion within wider British society has occurred.

The reasons for this distancing from national British/English national associations identified in previous research have been analysed as closely connected to the construction of masculinity and associated in particular with the 'hegemonic' construction of gender that we observed in Chapter 6 (Connell, 1995).

The reader will remember that Connell (1995) introduced the concept of 'hegemonic' gender as referring to the most powerful forms of gender operating within a culture at any one time. Gender models compete for dominance and, therefore, hegemonic masculinity, for example, describes 'those dominant and dominating modes of masculinity which claim the highest status and exercise the greatest influence and authority' (Skelton, 2001, p. 50 cited in L. Archer, 2003, p. 15). Hegemonic gender forms are not fixed, nor are they asserted consistently by all young people. They can endure over the course of a week, a year or even a generation in different contexts and times (L. Archer, 2003, p. 15). As Gramsci (1971 cited in L. Archer, 2003, p. 15) proposed, hegemony is never 'complete or absolute' but needs to be 'defended' and constantly reasserted against 'competing alternatives'.

Bearing this conception of hegemonic masculinity in mind, L. Archer (2003) notes that for her sample of 31 Muslim boys, the idea of identifying positively as a British national was construed hegemonically as 'feminine' and, instead, identification with the global brotherhood (the Umma) of Islam was often made as a corollary of rejection of the perception of individualised notions of white British masculinity. Shain (2010) expands upon this perspective by connecting the perception of white British masculinity in the minds of British Muslim boys with the perceived failures of white British men to embrace 'proper' family values, by, for example, looking after elderly relatives at home. This rejection of Britishness or Englishness as 'white' has also been observed to be accompanied by the embrace of 'black' hegemonic forms, namely the 'gangsta' and the 'lad'. These hegemonic forms, with which we became familiar in Chapter 6, enable Muslim boys to challenge 'white' stereotypes of Muslim boys as passive, studious Asians (Hopkins, 2004). Yet at the same time they are often uncomfortable and precarious positions, as Asian boys run the risk of not being perceived or perceiving themselves as 'black enough' compared with their African-Caribbean peers (L. Archer, 2003).

Conversely, although part of a relational male–female binary (L. Archer, 2003), Muslim girls have tended to associate more positively with the idea of being British than Muslim boys. Despite obvious differences in Muslim codes of dress and in the performance of gender to many 'hegemonic' Western liberal constructions of femininity, Muslim girls have often participated with greater success in the generation of hyphenated, Islamic-British identities, of which the business of Shazia Saleem, Ieat, mentioned in the Introduction, was one outward manifestation (Mondal, 2008; Shain, 2003).

My own empirical findings stand in contrast to and nuance those presented in some previous research. They suggest that second- and third-generation British Muslim young people, including boys, tend to value, rather than reject, their British citizenship and want to belong in England both in absolute terms and relative to the comparative non-Muslim sample, and to contribute to society in an informed way. These findings tally more closely with those of Mondal (2008) and some of those of Shain (2003), which suggest that for many young Muslims, Britishness provides a discursive space in which they can forge new Islamic identities and culturally hybrid responses to modernity. Britishness for many young Muslims is not set *against*, but rather can be as a platform *for*, Muslimness; and, conversely, Muslimness can be generative of 'new' forms of Britishness. The rest of the chapter will present the evidence for these assertions. It will conclude that Muslim young people are in the process of negotiating local, ethnic, national and international Islamic identities of great complexity that defy easy interpretation; and that citizenship education in school, under the right set of circumstances, can be well placed to help them in this complex task.[1]

The importance of national belonging for Muslim young people

To garner an understanding of the 'extensivity' of Muslim young people's citizenship and belonging, I gauged my sample of 307 Muslim young people's basic 'levels' of citizenship and belonging in the United Kingdom according to two survey variables:

4d Being British is important to me.

(Importance of being British)

5a I feel at home in England.

(Sense of Belonging in England)

According to these variables, my study showed that there was no significant difference between the Muslim and non-Muslim samples, either in their estimation of the 'importance of being British' or in their 'sense of belonging in England'. The proportion of the sample who 'agreed quite strongly' or 'agreed strongly' that 'Being British is important to me' was 72.5%, and 80.5% of the sample 'strongly' or 'quite strongly' agreed that 'I feel at home in England'.

While there existed no differences in citizenship and belonging between the Muslim and non-Muslim elements of the sample taken as a whole, there were significant differences in the basic 'levels' of 'Sense of Belonging in England' between Muslim pupils at the four sample schools taken individually. Boys at the Technology School agreed significantly less that 'I feel at home in England' (χ^2 (12)=22.703, p=0.030) than boys at the Community School or Specialist School. This was to be expected, perhaps, as Technology School boys represented the greatest proportion of recently migrant children, in particular Albanians, Afghans and Somalis, who might not expect to feel after a relatively short period in the United Kingdom that they belonged in England (Platt, 2001).

These high levels of citizenship and belonging recorded in my sample of Muslim young people were much more positive than might have been expected from earlier qualitative accounts of Muslim boys, which had suggested a marked absence of identification with British citizenship. Therefore, the 'blunt instrument' of the questionnaire survey suggested that some Muslim young people are at least as positive about their connection to Britain in both civic terms and emotional terms as their non-Muslim peers.

These positive 'extensive' quantitative findings about some Muslim young people's attitudes to their British citizenship were strongly corroborated at interview. In contrast to the experiences of Archer's and Alexander's cohorts, these positive associations with British citizenship were set in the broader context of the boys' finding Britain a largely welcoming place where opportunities to enjoy and improve their own and their families' lives were available, which, in some senses, are more typical of the migrant British experience (Koopmans & Statham, 1999).

Anas (Faith School, high-achieving, Indian-British), for example, was grateful for being British, as he felt that the Muslim community was more respected and more able to establish itself institutionally in Britain than in other European countries such as France.

ANAS: There's more respect in England. Like in France some women had [to remove] headscarves in schools […] they let us build a school here, they let us build *masjid*s (mosques) […] It's about the society you live in; no one really picks on you. Like in some other places around the world you normally get picked on or people degrade you.

Anas' identification of the relative religious freedom enjoyed in Britain echoes the findings of Mondal (2008) that the heightened Muslimness of third-generation British Muslims has precisely been enabled by their Britishness rather than blocked by it. The ability to enjoy a relatively full expression of Islamic praxis has created a sense of attachment to Britain compared with the rest of Europe, and even parts of the Muslim-majority world.

As well as this identification by one boy of the religious and cultural benefits of life in Britain, four boys highlighted the instrumental (for education and employment) benefits of being British and living in England. For example, Tariq (Faith School, middle-achieving, British-Pakistani), notwithstanding a certain naivety, compared the opportunities that were afforded him favourably with what he perceived to be on offer in Pakistan.

TARIQ: Because basically sometimes in Pakistan somewhere the people have to go miles just to go to a school or somewhere to learn and they don't have proper education. And over here in England you get the best education […] and you can get a job later on. Nice.

Similarly, Samir (Community School, middle-achieving, Bangladeshi-British) appreciated the relatively organised (compared with Bangladesh) British education system and the infrastructural benefits of clean streets and parks in Britain.

MATTHEW: [S]o you've obviously got memories of living in Bangladesh?
SAMIR: Yeah.
MATTHEW: How does it compare to living in Britain?
SAMIR: It's more organised here […] The education system is more easier, it helps, it helps you even more than … it does, the system is more faster so it benefits you because you're able to learn more quickly and able to take it in within the time that you're given.
MATTHEW: […] And how about life outside school: what's the difference between Bangladesh and Britain?

SAMIR: You're able to communicate, it's like there's more recreation so … and there isn't that much of like rubbish or anything, not so … because in Bangladesh it's more, it's polluted; there's … everything's just messed up. […] Yeah, just messed up and here it's more organised. The streets, they're cleaned every day and you're able to access parks and local leisure centres, which, you know, is kind of recreation, because after you've been in school for six hours it just gets you off in your mind.

Salman (Specialist School, middle-achieving, Bengali) responded positively to the idea of British citizenship on the basis of the positive immigrant experience enjoyed by him and his parents through which his family had achieved the economic goals of immigration and been well treated in the process.

SALMAN: I've ticked that box [Being British is important to me] because I thought my, my people, the people from my home country actually came here […] to get a job and to help their family, and I felt more at home 'cause people here, they actually took our people in and they treated them really good.

Indeed, Salman expressed a highly positive 'achieved' identity (Head, 1999) of hyphenated, British-Bangladeshi belonging, of being 'proud of being from both them places'.

SALMAN: I might have been brought up in Britain but the origin of my family was in Bangladesh and I think I should know more about, actually know about Britain and Bangladesh 'cause they're both like my home countries 'cause I was born in Britain but my parents were from, were born in Bangladesh and that, I'm actually proud of being from both of them places 'cause I would, like I would stand up and represent both countries.

These testimonies, in particular, present a picture of attachment and connection rather than the displacement suggested by the findings of Shain (2010) and Alexander (2000) alluded to earlier.

Complex negotiations of new ethno-national 'hybridity'

Such unequivocally positive attitudes were typical of 12 of my cohort of 24 interviewees; however, the views of four boys suggested that other Muslim young people are still very much in the process of working out how they 'fit in' to British life. The testimony of these boys suggested more complex and difficult dynamics involved of the process of internal and external integration in British life.

For example, Uthman's (Faith School, middle-achieving, Indian-British) account of the negotiation of national belonging was characterised by a poignant and very real sense of confusion.

UTHMAN: Sometimes I feel more part of India, sometimes England … because sometimes I don't like things down here [in England] then I like to do it there but sometimes when you don't … you can't do something there I think I'm happy to be here…. Like first I thought about India 'cause my dad's from India so I thought that Britain was India, and then it just that we're living in Britain so it's just like … I can't explain it but just tougher like … can't explain […]. It's a bit, it's a bit confusing like, yeah. I don't know anything.

Moreover, while Uthman's local associations with his home town, Leicester, were redolent with feelings of safety and hospitality, his associations with the rest of England and Britain were threatening; he viewed it as an unwelcoming place that was potentially the site of racism and of Islamophobia.

Another boy, Umar (Faith School, middle-achieving, Pakistani-British), described the unnerving experience of returning 'home' to Pakistan and being expected to support England at cricket when he wanted to support Pakistan, and the feeling 'of belonging nowhere and everywhere at the same time'. Benyamin (Technology School, high-achieving, Algerian-British) privileged his 'race' as an Algerian over his British nationality, and Pervez (Faith School, high-achieving, Pakistani-British) did not 'want to be referred to as "British" at all', despite Britain being the country of his birth, upbringing and education.

However, in my study these cases were exceptions to the more general rule suggested by the statistics and confirmed at interview that the young people in the sample were generally positive about 'being British' and felt that they 'belonged in England' more than they did not.

So who are British Muslim citizens?

Therefore, given that the findings of previous academic studies into the identities of Muslim boys alluded to here were undertaken by experienced and accomplished researchers using well-theorised research methodologies, it is worth asking: where does the truth of the citizenship, identity and belonging of British Muslim young people lie? The truth of citizenship, identity and belonging of Muslim young people in the civic dimension would appear to be a 'shifter', changing in response to different sites, people and places. This is especially the case with Muslim young people, who have to negotiate 'new' religious, 'non-native' British identities and may find some British environments welcoming and others threatening.

What my findings do, at the very least, indicate is that, given a sympathetic setting, Muslim young people in a multi-faith society such as Britain do wish to belong and to participate in the civic life of their nation as much as any group of young people. They tend to value – as much as, if not slightly more than, many young people – the opportunities for advancement and 'success' offered them by life in countries such as Britain, especially when it comes to gaining academic qualifications.

These findings also suggest a role for citizenship education in knitting together and informing these strands of Muslim young people's civic and national selves in the civic dimension of success and for the creation of safe intellectual and emotional environments in which a detailed, sensitive and informed exploration of Muslimness *and* Britishness can be negotiated. However, as we shall see from our analysis of the state of citizenship education in England at the level of 2E (Second Edge – absence), this is a role that citizenship education in English schools is not necessarily in a fit condition, at present, to assume.

2E: the absence of seriousness $_{(e)}$ in citizenship education

Why citizenship education is vital from a political and philosophical perspective

If citizenship is understood to be 'the system of values, efforts and institutionalised practices required for creating and maintaining conditions for living together in a complex society' (Dimitrov & Boyadjejieva, 2009, p. 156 cited in Reid, Gill & Sears, 2010), then clearly individuals need to be educated into a significant set of capabilities and develop an appropriate political awareness if they are to function as active and responsible citizens (Reid et al., 2010).

Moreover, from the philosophical point of view of critical realist theory the relationship of individual agency to civic and political structure also calls for robust critical education of the citizen. According to critical realists, social forms, groups and institutions have ontological reality that inevitably precedes the agency of individuals. For example, no one could say, 'I am a doctor' unless the medical profession existed. Likewise, no one could say, 'I am a politician' or 'I am a voter' without the pre-existent structure of something like a democratic state. 'The predicates designating properties special to persons presuppose a social context for their employment. A tribesman implies a tribe, the cashing of a cheque, a banking system' (Bhaskar, 1979, p. 209).

Similarly, Bhaskar (1979) reworks Saussure's conception of language as *langue*, the structure and forms of language, and *parole*, the individual's use of language, to exemplify this critical realist ontology of the social. Language as a social form – *langue* – clearly pre-exists the individual – he or she is born into it – but the individual acts on *langue* through *parole* to transformative effect. So, while the individual does not create language or any other social form, he or she may, under certain circumstances, transform it, or at least always has the potential to transform it. Thus, critical realists, e.g. Norrie (2010) and M. Archer (1998), conceive of society as relational: that is to say, the proper object of sociological knowledge is neither individuals nor groups but the identification and characterisation of the relational point of contact (Bhaskar, 1979, p. 40) between human agency and social structure. 'It is in the (explanation of) differentiation and stratification, production and reproduction, mutation and transformation … of the relatively enduring *relations* presupposed by particular social forms and structures that sociology's distinctive theoretical interest lies' (p. 41; emphasis added). Within this critical realist understanding of the primacy of social structure over individual agency *together with* the transformative understanding of the role of the individual within it, the necessity for a high-quality citizenship education to educate the individual in the essential and operational nature of the institutions of society, in order to endow him or her with the capability to transform them constructively, becomes immediately apparent.

However, this task of developing this informed and transformative civic dimension of Muslim and other young people in Britain and elsewhere is hampered by the state of the school subject, which at present, even more than religious education, evinces an absence of seriousness$_{(e)}$. That is to say, there is a gulf between the importance of citizenship, together with the actual quality of the engagement between the individual citizen and the structures of society, and the status and nature of the subject of citizenship in schools. Since its introduction as a statutory school subject in English schools in 2002, citizenship has had to fight for its status as an independent subject; it has received marginal status on school timetables (Davies, 2010b); it has seldom been taught by specialist citizenship teachers (Jerome, 2012) and thus is likely to be looked down upon by pupils (Chamberlin, 2003). The lack of seriousness$_{(e)}$ in relation to citizenship education entrenched in the English educational establishment was most clearly demonstrated by the recent decision of the Expert Panel of the recent National Curriculum Review in England to downgrade Citizenship from a Foundation (second-tier) Curriculum to a Basic (third-tier) Curriculum subject, i.e. as a non-subject 'to be added to other subjects', since 'we are not persuaded that study of the issues and topics included in citizenship education constitutes a distinct "subject" as such' (UK Gov., 2011a, p. 24).

I will now give a brief explanation as to why citizenship education in Britain has had such a chequered history and why, having not successfully established itself as a 'subject', it has such an insecure future, at least so long as it continues to be characterised by such an absence of seriousness$_{(e)}$.

The slow, somewhat nebulous development of the British citizen

Britain has a strong tradition of the political subject and a relatively (to other Western democracies) weak tradition of the citizen (Heater, 2010; Miller, 2000). In the Middle Ages, the rough division of male society into those who fought (the king and the nobility), those who prayed (the Church and the monastic orders) and those who worked the land (the peasantry) meant that to be a 'citizen' one was required to know one's place in an agrarian social order that had been ordained in an unchanging way by God. 'Citizens' in the original classical sense of those who had rights and responsibilities in urban societies were restricted to guilds and merchant classes of small boroughs, which were a relatively insignificant part of the overall political structure of English society.

The Christian Reformation in Europe, coupled with the massive expansion of ideas that followed the advent of printing, extended the possibility of rudimentary education to the 'lower orders' and thus loosened the bonds of strict hierarchical deference that had sustained the structure of medieval society.

In the European Enlightenment period of political restructuring that followed, the individual citizen as a legal and political entity gained increasing status and rights. However, while modern France, for example, was forged in the crucible of revolution at the beginning of the modern period (1789) that saw the over-throw of the *ancien régime*, the destruction of the monarchy and the formal establishment in republican law of the sovereign rights of the citizen, England/ Britain's period of Civil War, regicide, revolution and Restoration (1642–1689), by contrast, resulted in a substantial *devolution*, rather than revolution, of power from an absolute monarchic ruler advised by a Parliament of landowners to an empowered Parliament of landowners constrained by a constitutional monarchy. It did not go so far as establishing, or even nearly establishing, the democratic principle of 'one man, one vote'.

Thus, operationally the only 'citizens' of early modern England and then modern Britain, after the Union of the Parliaments of England and Scotland in 1707, were the landowning classes. During this phase in the development of British (for the first time) citizenship, the ideal for British citizens was perhaps best described by the sixteenth-century Scottish commentator George Buchanan: 'Those who obey the laws, who maintain human society, who would rather undergo every hardship and every peril for the well-being of their fellow coun-trymen' (Burns, 1951, p. 64 cited in Gearon, 2010, p. 11). It was a social belong-ing predicated on duties and sacrifice that largely downplayed citizenship entitlements of freedoms and rights.

Nevertheless, the eighteenth century saw great social and political changes in Britain, starting with the birth of the United Kingdom with the Union of the Parliaments of England and Scotland in 1707 after a century of amalgamated English/Welsh–Scottish monarchy. This brought about a national sense of belonging to a United Kingdom and of Britishness forged out of the commer-cial, political and military success of the Anglo-Scottish union, hostility to a deadly shared enemy – France – and a commitment, albeit to different types, of Protestant Christianity (Colley, 1992). Yet even in this emergence of a new fervent national consciousness, 'citizenship' in either the ancient sense or the modern democratic sense of a shared franchise was slow in forthcoming; the non-landed classes still had no vote and little voice, and society was still over-whelmingly and paternalistically agrarian, with its concomitant connection to a God-given social hierarchy and maintenance of this status quo. This was sym-bolised at such times and places as the weekly service in the parish church, which all tenants and workers were expected to attend and to sit in places in pews that were strictly symbolic of their places in a fixed social hierarchy (Copley, 2005).

Only the combination of industrialisation, which released workers from the land and landowners, and urbanisation, which exposed huge numbers of people to city life of unprecedented squalor, accelerated the United Kingdom towards universal suffrage and thus laid the conditions for mass political protest and eventually for relatively complete democratic citizenship. In the face of the political agitation of groups such as the Levellers and the Chartists, and terrified of full-scale Continental-style revolution, Parliament enacted the Reform Acts of 1832, 1867 and 1884, extending the male franchise until it was achieved fully, without property qualifications, in 1918. After the struggles of the suffragists and the suffragettes and the social upheavals caused by the First World War, women gained the vote finally in 1928 as the culmination of a 700-year devolution of power from the monarch to the subject that had begun in 1215 on the banks of the River Thames at Runnymede with the signing by King John of the Magna Carta.

Thus, despite recent Coalition governmental rhetoric about Britain's pre-eminent place in the 'birth' of modern parliamentary democracy, in reality the birth of democracy in the United Kingdom has had a painful, slow and hard-fought period of labour. Even today, Britons are still officially 'subjects' of a constitutional monarchy that operates with no official constitution, no declaration of rights and no citizen's charter (Heater, 2010). Thus, if we use the ideas of Thomas Hobbes, one of England's great political thinkers, the nature of the social contract between the ruler and the ruled in Britain was and is still far from clear. Britons, as citizens who determine the political destiny of the state which is under contract to protect them and uphold the law, have never entirely taken control of their own civic destiny from either landed or hereditary interests. The slow speed of political change over the past 700 years has generated and maintained the conditions of political stability, of which Britain is justly proud, but it has also generated an idea of the citizen that is patchy and incomplete. The deep irony of this is, of course, twofold: (1) that England *can* legitimately lay claim to being the cradle of parliamentary democracy; and (2) Britain has in John Locke, Thomas Hobbes, Adam Smith, T. H. Green and T. H. Marshall produced some of the seminal thinkers about citizenship of the modern age.

The emergence of citizenship education

This absence of constitutional clarity about the British citizen accounts, in part, for the history of citizenship education in Britain. Even in the twentieth century, when working-class, female and unpropertied Britons had gained the franchise, they were not educated as citizens because they were not expected to behave like 'active' citizens but rather more like (deferential) subjects in a fiercely classed social order. The landed classes, who until the latter part of the twentieth century predominated in Parliament, learned (and still learn) their political skills as 'citizens' with a real stake in the future of the state in the crucible of the major British public schools, through study of the classical rhetoricians and politicians such as Demosthenes and Cicero, and imitative exercises in formal argument and debate, such as practising speeches in formalised debates, recitations of literature and participation in sophisticated theatrical productions. It is no accident, for example, that contemporary Old Etonians distinguish themselves and are represented in disproportionate numbers in politics, acting, the law and the media. The gradual emergence of universal entitlements to education has not changed the fact that privately educated boys and girls are taught through exposure to a broad range of an active education in the liberal arts to be real, politically active citizens; whereas the working-classes pupils in state education have, with some notable exceptions, often been 'learning to labour' (Willis, 1977), with expectations that they will be relatively politically disengaged from the running of society at the level (c) of irreducible social institutions and forms reinforced by both hidden (Vallance, 1973) and absent (Wilkinson, 2014) school curricula.

Therefore, in the absence of formal citizenship education, throughout the twentieth century and through the furnace of two world wars it was school history rather than a specialist political subject that bore the brunt of the responsibility to teach citizenship (Phillips, 1998). At times, historians in school responded to a critical democratic and disciplinary duty to explore the country's political past through a balance of the heroic, antiquarian and critical styles of history that I explored in Chapter 6 (Aldrich, 2002; Aldrich & Dean, 1991; Macmillan, 2008); but often the political role of school history was reduced to the perpetuation of national myths and the uncritical celebration of national heroes in order to engender moral support and even material and physical sacrifice (Slater, 1989). So, until the end of the twentieth century what passed as citizenship education in England was rather more designed to assist the citizen/subject to respond to the demands of the state than it was to enable the citizen to get the state to respond to him or her. It was a citizenship of duties more than a citizenship of rights (Gearon, 2010). Thus, the 1949 pamphlet *Citizens Growing Up* (UK Gov., 1949/1961) suggested, for example, in a phrase little altered from Buchanan's sixteenth-century ideals, that 'a healthy democratic society can be encouraged if schools develop the old simple virtues of humility, service, restraint and respect for personality' (p. 41 cited in Davies, 2010b, p. 115). Moreover, rather than using political education to critique, challenge or clarify the nebulous British concept of the citizenship, educators were more likely to be wedded to it as a buffer against the fear of political indoctrination (Davies, 2010b). Indeed, the constitutional nebulousness of Britishness has itself come to be regarded as a hallmark of being British. This was suggested strongly by the winning suggestion for the *Times* (2007) competition for a motto to represent Britain, which was 'No motto please; we're British!'[2] (Hurst, 2007).

Thus, it was not until 1969, with the formation of the Politics Association, that the idea of a formal education for democratic citizenship took hold in England. The Programme for Political Education in the mid-1970s pushed the agenda, coinciding as it did with the lowering of the age of the franchise from 21 to 18 in 1971. This meant that it was now not only disingenuous but also downright irresponsible for government to keep citizenship education outside of the state education system (Davies, 2010a). However, despite some high-profile support and calls by Her Majesty's Inspectorate to provide pupils with political literacy, citizenship education was largely sidetracked in the 1970s by trendy thematic sub-disciplines such as peace and gender studies, followed by the Conservative backlash in the formation of the National Curriculum, which relegated citizenship education, as a non-traditional subject with little history in schools, to themes to be taught, patchily and often without teachers' understanding their rationale (Jerome, 2012), across other school subjects.[3]

However, the return to power of the so-called New Labour government in 1997 with its ideal of an active citizenry empowered through political devolution, related to the politics of the Third Way, led to the establishment of the Advisory Group for citizenship education in 1997. The influential Crick Report (1998) made a strong case for the implementation of an independent subject to be about and for political education, and articulated the three elements of citizenship education that were to become Key Concepts of Citizenship as an independent Foundation Subject on the National Curricula of 2002 and 2009. These were:

1   Democracy and Justice;
2   Rights and Responsibilities;
3   Identity and Diversity: Living together in the UK.

This new interest in citizenship as an independent subject was driven by the Labour government, and in particular the Rt Hon. David Blunkett MP, the then Secretary of State for Education and Employment, who realised that in a fast-globalising world the knowledge of and attachment of young people to Britain and its democratic processes could no longer be taken for granted (Heater, 2004). However, Crick himself was a political theorist and not an educator, and under-estimated how difficult it was, in practice, to establish a new school subject almost from scratch. The Programmes of Study for citizenship on the new National Curriculum (2002) were designed to give teachers plenty of autonomy to bring their own understandings of citizenship to bear on the creation of 'active citizens'. However, this failed to account for the fact that the majority of the new citizenship teachers themselves, from 2002 to 2009, were not subject specialists, and, owing to the nebulous nature of the tradition of British citizenship, as out-lined earlier, they often had no clear concept themselves of what a citizen was or should be (Jerome, 2012). The subject also suffered from having unclear disciplinary boundaries with other subjects, especially history, geography and religious education, whose teachers often resented the intrusion of citizenship into their disciplinary remit. As a result, citizenship education began to suffer from a crisis of subject identity, marginality on the secondary school timetable and a relative lack of respect from both school teachers and pupils (Jerome, 2012). Moreover, there is a certain irony in the fact that a new school subject was introduced to help pupils understanding the democratic processes of the nation-state at a time when, increasingly, globalisation was challenging the validity of the nation-state as humanity's pre-eminent organising principle.

These factors may partly explain why, despite a clear conceptual framework and Foundation status, citizenship struggled to embed itself in English schools throughout the 2000s. Nevertheless, the increasing civic and legal complexity faced by the citizen that results from globalisation does, in fact, intensify the need for 'a high-quality citizenship education [which] helps to provide pupils with knowledge, skills and understanding to prepare them to play a full and active part in society' (UK Gov., 2013d), and the need for that education to be sophisticated and effective to prepare pupils for civic life in a in a fast-changing and complex civic world.

The particular need for a serious $_{(e)}$ citizenship education for Muslim young people

Thus, if the case for the general necessity for seriousness $_{(e)}$ in citizenship education for all young people today is clear, the particular case for the necessity of seriousness $_{(e)}$ in citizenship education for Muslim young people is all the more so. We have seen how Muslim young people may face issues that need keenly to be addressed by citizenship education, primarily at the level (c) of social relations at the irreducible level of structures, institutions and forms, as well as at the level (d) of the internal stratification of the embodied personality.

For example, we have seen how young Muslims' emotional and political ties may straddle more than one nation and, increasingly, more than one ethnicity (Finney & Simpson, 2009); and how Muslim young people are likely to want to participate in national life, but also how they may feel alienated from active civic participation in the political life of the country, although local participation may be more appealing. To complicate matters, we saw in the Introduction how Islam, their faith, not only has a religious ethic of personal practice and piety, but also, traditionally, has a strong civic ethic and a civic-religious law (Shari'a). All these factors, coupled with the transnational civic and legal complexity faced by all young people today in their (often implicit) relations with local, national and European and global centres of law and political authority, make serious $_{(e)}$ education of the civic dimension of Muslim young people a non-negotiable necessity.

3L: a serious $_{(e)}$ citizenship education

At the level of 3L (Third level – totality), I shall now explore how a 'serious' $_{(e)}$ strategy for citizenship education that is both informative and transformative for the young Muslim citizen can be developed for exploring issues in citizenship from an Islamic critical realist point of view. It will show how

- the idea of unity-in-difference;
- the notion of the primacy of structure over individual agency; and
- the ICR fulcrum of ontological realism, epistemological relativism and judgemental rationality

can provide a route to serious citizenship education that is non-doctrinaire and allows for the exploration of such themes as nationhood and national identity, governance, law, freedom of expression, the environment, the economy, culture and gender relations, which will provide a platform to revitalise the subject for young Muslims and other young people.

The basis: civic unity-in-difference

Banks (2004) writes:

> One of the challenges to diverse democratic nation-states is to provide opportunities for different groups to maintain aspects of their community cultures while building a nation in which these groups are structurally included and to which they feel allegiance. *A delicate balance of diversity and unity should be an essential goal of democratic nation-states and of teaching and learning in democratic societies.*
>
> (p. 298; emphasis added)

In respect of civic unity-in-diversity, we have seen in Chapters 3–5 that while original and dialectical critical realism thematises difference, non-identity, real change and duality as being real and necessary features of the natural and social worlds, the philosophy of metaReality (PMR) thematises unity as the necessarily prior substratum to duality. This is because, while unity can exist without duality, duality cannot exist without unity. 'Thus concepts of identity, unity, etc. are ontologically, epistemologically and logically *prior* to concepts of non-identity, etc.' (Bhaskar, 2002/2012c, p. xlv).

In civic ICR terms, the essential unity of humankind has primacy over its difference and diversity, and both unity and diversity are in the gift of God (Qur'an, 3:10–19).

Non-duality and transcendental identification

We also saw in Chapter 5 that Bhaskar (2002/2012a) has described three ways in which the world of duality and difference is ultimately underpinned by the world of non-duality and transcendental identity:

1   *The constitution of everyday life*. That is to say, unity and transcendental identity is essential to the ordinary 'constitution, that is the reproduction and transformation, of everyday life' (Bhaskar, 2002/2012a, p. xi).
2   *As a basis of being and of the human self/soul*: the unified ultimatum or 'ground-state' (Bhaskar, 2002/2012a) out of which the stratified layers of all being, including human being, emerge.
3   *As the deep interior of the cosmos*. At this level, unity and transcendent identity are experiential rather than proven by argument and akin to mystical intuitions as to the all-pervasive presence of the Absolute, i.e. God.

Transcendence as constitutive of everyday civic life

Crucially, for a civic understanding of transcendence, transcendence is not limited to or even primarily experienced as an other-worldly notion of divinity but is posited by natural necessity in our daily actions of normal life. That is to

say, transcendental unity is quotidian and essential to the operation and reproduction of daily life. '[T]he transcendence of duality is a pervasive reality in
human action and social life and ... "the process of enlightenment is a natural
extension" of this always-already quotidian transcendence' (Hartwig, 2012).

Thus, for example, we have seen how the most basic example of oral human
communication, the conversation, necessarily involves acts of repeated transcendental identification because it involves the mutual transcendence of the
separate consciousness of two embodied personalities in the creation of a shared
context of meaning. Were a transcendental identification in consciousness not a
possibility at the level of personal relations, a conversation could not occur. To
repeat here another effective quotidian example of transcendental unity, without
the existence of transcendental holism one could not

> possibly steer one's way around the pavements of a busy London street
> unless some kind of almost miraculous holistic, synchronicitous perform-
> ance was taking place. Otherwise one would be bumping into people all the
> time. One could easily show this by simulating on a computer the chances
> of crashes or accidents, which are in actual life extremely rare.
>
> (Bhaskar, 2002/2012c, p. 5)

This idea of the quotidian nature of unity-in-diversity, as well as the ICR of the
primacy of structure over agency that we looked at earlier in the chapter, can be an
effective starting point for a serious civic education, since it is necessary for
Muslim young people, and young people in general, to understand that they cannot
'opt out' of political and civic participation in society, because they are necessarily
born into it; that meaningful civic relationships are unavoidably 'intrinsic' and not
'extrinsic' to everyday life (Bhaskar, 1993/2008); and that this transcendence in
the civic dimension is something that all human beings share. Thus, civic and
political education can be shown a priori not to be an optional extra to other high-
status school subjects, but an intrinsic part of preparing to become a fully realised
human being. Citizenship is a natural and unavoidable part of the human condition,
even though, of course, its contingent, historical particularities are social products.

This initial idea of the necessity of unity-in-diversity might be explained by a
teacher through inquiries to show the interdependence of the different institutions of society and how 'the good of each is dependent on the good of all', or
similar. If a strong existential case is made to pupils for the necessity of citizenship education by individual teachers, this may go some way towards compen-
sating for its lack of status and identity in schools and provide the context for a
more particular establishment of its relevant and important themes.

The fulcrum of Islamic critical realism in citizenship education

Once the teacher has made a strong, serious case for the necessity of citizenship
education, using this idea of the essential nature of quotidian transcendence and
the primacy of structure over agency, he or she can use the fulcrum of ICR –

ontological realism, epistemological relativism and judgemental rationality – to explore the themes and sub-themes that were identified by the Crick Report to introduce a deep civic criticality that will actively encourage the philosophical interrogation of, as well as the civic participation in, the values and processes of democracy.

The reader will remember from Chapters 3, 7 and 8 that the core of the critical realist understanding of reality is grounded in three interrelated principles:

1   ontological realism;
2   epistemological relativism;
3   judgemental rationality.

These were together described as the fulcrum of Islamic critical realism (see Figure 9.1).

As we have seen, *ontological realism* means that being exists independently of knowledge. For example, the sun exists in exactly the same way whether the universe is described in a geocentric or a heliocentric way. In the social-natural world, being exists relatively independently of knowing in that the agents of knowledge are always implicated in the objects of knowledge that they come to know. But objects of knowledge also exist independently of knowledge, otherwise there would be nothing to know in the first place. When applied to political understanding, we might say that political structures and relationships exist independently of whether or not we participate in them, or believe that we participate in them.

Epistemological relativism asserts that beliefs about and understandings and knowledge of being are socially produced, instantiated in historical and personal circumstances, fallible and transient. Epistemological relativism in the civic

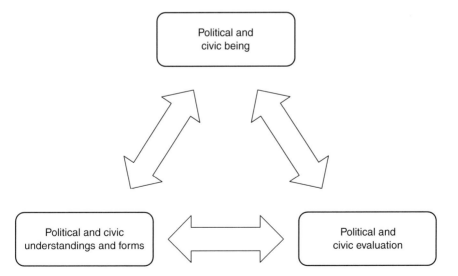

Figure 9.1 The fulcrum of ICR transposed into citizenship education.

domain pertains to beliefs, knowledge and understandings of political power that usually take the form of traditions and methods or models of governance: democracy, oligarchy, monarchy, dictatorship, theocracy, to name but five (not to mention myriad hybrid variants of these).

The compatibility of ontological realism and epistemological relativism necessitates *judgemental rationality*. That is to say, there exist rational criteria to adjudicate between different political understandings and values which are not all equally accurate, just, truthful, sustainable or useful. Judgemental rationality pertains to deliberation and deciding about the efficacy and equity of political phenomena and the traditions connected with them: the compatibility of ontological realism and epistemological relativism *necessitates judgmental rationality; there must be coherent rational (philosophical), emotional and experiential grounds for choosing one mode of political organisation as opposed to another.*

Therefore, it is possible with these basic principles to admit that there are a variety of valid systems of governance that have existed and still do exist in the political world both potentially and actually and yet that they are not all equally just or sustainable and that there exist or can be devised criteria to decide between them. They also form the basis for pupils to make a critical commitment to democracy without its being imposed on them as an a priori.

From philosophy to pedagogy

Political and civic being: the extra-systemic mode

The application of the fulcrum of ICR into the classroom involves condensing these complex philosophical ideas down to a pedagogical form. For these purposes, ontological realism becomes 'civic being' and is to be explored through what I call the 'extra-systemic' mode. This is the mode at which the nature of political phenomena is examined philosophically in the classroom without a priori commitment to a particular mode of governance, e.g. liberal democracy. This is also the mode of identification by pupils in conversation with their teachers of universal civic and political phenomena that are fit for study and analysis. Following the guidance of the Crick Report and other teaching training guides (Gearon, 2010), the extra-systemic mode might, *inter alia*, include the ontological exploration of the nature of:

- government and governance;
- justice and law;
- nationality and national belonging;
- culture and the arts;
- gender relations;
- relating to the environment.

The advantage of the extra-systemic mode is that teachers can show pupils that these political and social-civic phenomena are universals, in that they have

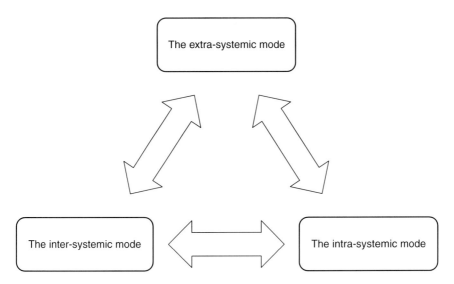

Figure 9.2 The modes of the fulcrum of ICR transposed into citizenship education.

been a feature, in some way, of the life of every human civilisation, and, at the same time, begin to suggest that they are not fixed – that the nature of these phenomena and how they are manifested at particular historical moments is contested and both changeable and open to re-evaluation. The extra-systemic mode ought neither to drive pupils into an a priori decision about the best systems of governance, justice and so forth, nor be felt to drive pupils into an a priori decision about the best systems of governance, justice and so forth. Ironically, by not artificially championing liberal democracy as the best option a priori, the extra-systemic mode can set up the conditions for a citizenship education that is genuinely democratic.

Political and civic understanding and forms: the inter-systemic mode

Therefore, while the extra-systemic mode refers to civic phenomena and political realities that have universal existence independent of a particular manifestation of them, epistemological relativism becomes at the level of the classroom the exploration of particular institutional expressions of political systems, and is explored through the 'inter-systemic' mode. The 'inter-systemic' mode is the comparative mode of exploring different civic phenomena as understood from the point of view of different political and civic traditions and different sectarian positions within traditions. It is the comparative mode in which children can understand that political phenomena have been expressed similarly and differently in different political traditions. It is the informative mode, learning about citizenship, politics and law, in which the child can gather information about political systems and their origins, including different types of democracy. As far as Muslims are concerned, it would be important that in the extra-systemic mode the nature and particular features of both democracy and theocracy are explored, since both have in limited and more comprehensive guises formed part of the civic history of the Muslim community (Feldman, 2003).

The inter-systemic mode is the mode of the comparison of the features of different types and models of legislature, of different types of justice and law, and different types of justice and punishment, both contemporaneous ones and those of the recent and distant past. This exploration would necessarily for young Muslims need to include the defining features of English common law, French public and private law and the Islamic Shari'a, to give but three out of a range of possible examples. The inter-systemic mode is the mode of gathering knowledge necessary both for the effective identification and understanding of the types of political institutions that will govern children's lives, and for the deep critical reflection of the intra-systemic mode. It is also the mode of visiting and enacting dramatically different institutional phenomena, such as cases heard in courts of law. In the inter-systemic mode, it will be important for teachers to explore the

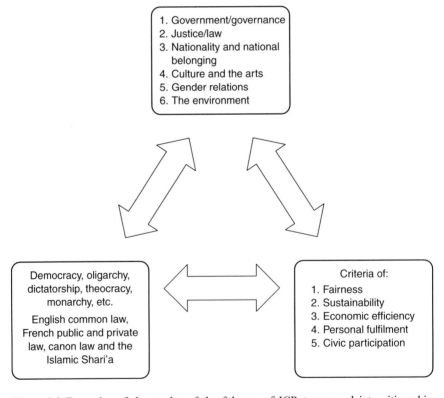

Figure 9.3 Examples of the modes of the fulcrum of ICR transposed into citizenship education.

relationship between Islamic civic ideas and British democratic ones. For example, a legitimate comparison might be made between the Magna Carta of 1215, which was a written agreement between the sovereign and representatives of his people, and the Constitution of Madina drawn up by the Prophet Muhammad as a binding civic charter, which we looked at in Chapter 4. The point here will be to show how the principle of civic justice and responsibility is both shared and similarly and differently expressed across different cultures and periods of time, and to show how principles such as equality before the law, as we saw in Chapter 4, have both a liberal democratic and an Islamic heritage.

Political and civic evaluation: the intra-systemic mode

The intra-systemic mode is the mode for experiencing and evaluating political and civic forms. It is the mode, for example, for evaluating the strengths and weaknesses of democracy and understanding why and how people have fought and died for the establishment and preservation of democratic values. In this respect, citizenship education needs to work collaboratively with history departments so that the civic meaning of episodes such as the English Civil War and the French Revolution is teased out both in the history and in the citizenship classroom, preferably in parallel.

ARTS AND CULTURE

Vitally, the intra-systemic is the mode of understanding how cultural forms and the arts can both reflect and transform society. For example, an in-depth study of the role of theatre through the ages in partnership with history might encourage young Muslims to probe beyond the superficial issues of the current complexion of artistic forms to look at their function in society, as well as their intrinsic contribution to the sum of beauty and knowledge. This would help young Muslims make up their own minds about whether cultural forms such as music and theatre, whose status is disputed in Islamic law, are permitted (*halāl*) or forbidden (*harām*) not on the basis of a disputed and antiquated interpretation of an antiquated religious source, but on the basis of understanding the social, spiritual and civic function that the arts have performed in life in society. The especially well-informed teacher might, for example, be able to relate this process of cultural reflection to the living Islamic jurisprudential criterion of custom (*'Urf*) (Hallaq, 2001). This material for essential cultural reflection needs to be coupled with spiritual considerations undertaken with and in RE about whether cultural forms promote or hinder the development of the type of transcendental spirituality outlined in Chapter 5.

This combination of serious$_{(e)}$ religious and citizenship education in the intra-faith/systemic mode would provide young Muslims with the mindsets to distinguish between healthy and unhealthy cultural forms that respectively generate or block the possibility of consistency between the ground-state/spirit/soul and the embodied personality. It will give them the necessary mechanisms of internal distinction to decide how best to participate in and, where necessary, transform the cultural life of societies of which they now form an intrinsic part. The combination of serious $_{(e)}$ religious and citizenship education that was both informative and transformative might go a long way to reduce the instances of dichotomised, either–or mindsets by showing young Muslims that full civic participation is not only existentially unavoidable and democratically necessary, but also, Islamically speaking, highly desirable.

EXAMINING ISLAMIC FORMS OF GOVERNANCE

The ICR fulcrum can also provide a useful tool to help teachers of Muslims explore highly charged political idea(l)s of the Umma (global brotherhood), *Khilafa* (the Islamic state or governance by a caliph) and Shari'a law (Islamic law) that many Muslim young people are likely to be exposed at home and that non-Muslim children may be aware of through the media. These can be brought into the classroom and critically interrogated. It is important that citizenship teachers are aware that these discourses exist in the mainstream Muslim community so that they can, at least, tease out some of the historical complexity of these civic phenomena and show, where appropriate, that many of the principles underlying Islamic law, e.g. public good (*maslaha*), also exist in British and other non-Islamic legislatures. This will diffuse the idea of Muslim 'good' and non-Muslim 'bad' in some Muslim youngsters, as well as the converse – Muslim 'bad' and non-Muslim 'good' – in non-Muslim youngsters, and show how the pursuit of justice is a universal phenomenon. By recognising the existence of Islamic civic phenomena in the present and the past, such as the *awqaf* (charitable endowments), guilds and the class of lawyer-scholars (*'ulamā*), whose historical role we explored in Chapter 1, teachers can create the type of civic awareness from within Muslim youngsters' understandings of their faith that will lead to fuller participation in society by young Muslims, by disabusing them of the idea that full participation in the life of society is in any way un-Islamic.

NATIONALITY AND NATIONAL BELONGING

Similarly, teachers can explore the extra-systemic idea of nationality and, in partnership with history, reflect at the inter-systemic level upon the distinctive hybridity of British nationality that is reflected, among other things, in the English language (Datta, 2002). Armed with this knowledge, young Muslims can be enabled in the intra-systemic mode to embrace their status as 'new' Britons as part of a long-standing tradition of migration to Britain, and to 'imagine' (Anderson, 1983) the language of Islam potentially as one component part of our rich national cultural and linguistic heritage. In short, rather than being exposed to myths of static, monolithic Britishness, young Muslims can be encouraged by serious $_{(e)}$ citizenship education to become a part of a dynamic and fluid tradition of negotiating and renegotiating national participation and belonging through engagement with civic unity-in-diversity.

Vitally, serious$_{(e)}$ citizenship education will also need to explore the changing nature of gender relations in society both by recourse to current liberal democratic ideas about the changing and 'shifting' roles of men and women in society and what it means to be either a man or a woman, and by recourse to Islamic idea(l)s of masculinity and femininity. Citizenship education can help debunk the myth of the anti-intellectual hegemonic 'gangsta' or 'Gang Girl' who featured as an archetype in previous chapters by recourse to the Islamic ideals of male and female scholarship and intellectual achievement. Islamic positions and ideals can also serve the critical function of putting current Western gender assumptions into critical relief. For example, the loss of status of the traditional female home-maker in the West can be explored from the Islamic position of the deep traditional respect accorded to wives and mothers, and issues such as the impact of working mothers on parenting can be explored from a variety of points of view in the intra-systemic mode. It will be vital that Muslim boys and girls are afforded space for critical reflections such as these as they start to consider their places and status in the adult world of work.

RELATIONS WITH THE ENVIRONMENT

A critical realist citizenship would also explore the nature of material and ethical relations with the environment in the extra-systemic, the inter-systemic and the intra-systemic modes. It could consider different models of relating to the environment from capitalist models that privilege the free market over environmental considerations, to deep ecological positions based, for example, on James Lovelock's idea of a self-regulating Gaia (1979). Within this consideration of the environment in the inter-systemic modes, citizenship teachers might explore the Qur'anic idea of stewardship (*khalifa*) over the creation (Qur'an, 2:30), and in the intra-systemic mode invite Muslim pupils to explore reflectively what that ideal might entail in practical civic terms for the Muslim believer in his or her treatment of the world around us. This can lead to a consideration of the role and the ethics of environmental activism and, perhaps, to exposing students to the ideas and concrete realities of Greenpeace and Friends of the Earth. Thus, the skilled citizenship teacher can, using the fulcrum of ICR, expand the knowledge base of the young Muslim and create a closer existential connection between the worlds of British majority and Islamic minority society through the intra-faith mode. The skilled teacher can present young Muslims with civic scenarios redolent with ethical overlap and creative tension, rather than Manichean opposition and incommensurability.

4D: transformative praxis: taking citizenship education out of the classroom

In summary, the fulcrum of ICR can become a pedagogic tool that joins up strong theoretical and conceptual political and civic knowledge to a reflective ethic of personal and practical commitment to participate in civic life. It is based philosophically upon the premise that unity-in-diversity is the ontological bedrock of society, in which institutional structure *both* predominates over individual agency *and* can be transformed by it. This task of linking agency with structure means that, more than any other subject at the level of 4D (Fourth Dimension – transformative praxis), citizenship education needs to be carried outside of the classroom into the community.

Successive studies, e.g. Torney-Purta, Lehmann, Oswald & Wolfram (2001), Campbell (2008) and Saha (2001), have shown the value of extra-classroom activities in the development of effective citizenship awareness (Keser, Akar & Yildirim, 2011) in terms of the development of greater civic participation of pupils in after-school life and 'active citizenship' that has been one of the distinctive contributions of recent developments in English citizenship education (Jerome, 2012). Since citizenship is above all else a praxis, the integrated practical implementation of theory and knowledge, children need to be exposed to and absorb institutional circumstances in which citizenship at the level (c) of social relations and irreducible structures, institutions and forms is forged in society in a concrete practical way.

We saw in Chapter 6 how for Rami (Community School, middle-achieving, British-Pakistani), a historical visit to the Houses of Parliament brought the concrete day-to-day operation of democracy vividly alive. Likewise, visits to and tastes of working experience with courts of law, local councils, charities and NGOs can introduce young Muslims to a universe of civic experience and deliberation, about which they need to know for the effective operation of their own lives and in which they are entitled to become involved. This job of bridging the gap between the home and the civic institutions of society is a vital function that schools can perform for young Muslims. This will at once both demystify and 'enchant' their civic world-view with the possibility of participation and social change, in a parallel to the way in which the study of the suffragettes in history had done for pupils at the Faith School. Again, this task of interacting educationally at the level (c) of social relations and irreducible structures, institutions and forms will encourage the development of the 'critical Muslim patriot', who, as we saw in Chapter 6, is connected to and informed about civic life in Britain and able, when necessary, to work to transform it on a micro, meso or even macro level to address injustices when they occur.

Conclusion: a pathway to full civic engagement

We have seen how, in a situation analogous to that of the RE classroom, the presence of substantial numbers of Muslim young people in the citizenship classroom represents an opportunity for teachers to add an extra dimension of deep criticality to the exploration of citizenship for all young people. Using the philosophical tools of unity-in-difference, the primacy of the structure over transformative agency and the fulcrum of ICR, citizenship teachers can explore the themes and concepts introduced by the Crick Report in a deeply critical way by mobilising the extra-systemic, inter-systemic and intra-systemic modes. They need to include some consideration and incorporation of the Islamic perspectives on civic life that are part and parcel of the Muslim world-view which informs the outlook of many young Muslims. If teachers can create such a challenging provision, then, in partnership with history and RE, serious $_{(e)}$ citizenship education can help nurture the critical Muslim patriot who feels connected to and knowledgeable about the civic life of Britain and the wider world, and enabled to actively transform society, as and when necessary, locally, nationally or even on the international stage.

Notes

1 For a full account of the methodology and the sample used for this empirical research, please refer to pp. 124–127.
2 This was also a popularist 'raspberry' against the 'Britishness' agenda of the unpopular then British prime minister, Gordon Brown.
3 It is worth bearing in mind that the NC school subject disciplines were almost exact replicas of the Board School Curriculum of the 1870s.

10 Conclusion

A call for existential seriousness $_{(r+p+e)}$ to regenerate the Happy Muslim Consciousness

Feldman (2003) asks the question 'Can democracy be made to flourish in the lands where Islam prevails?' and he answers that since both democracy and Islam are packages of flexible, 'mobile' universal ideas, under the right conditions Islamic democracy is perfectly plausible. This book has addressed an inverse question: 'Can Islam and young Muslims flourish in lands where liberal democracy (or at least a sincere aspiration for it) prevails?' I have answered this question with a clear and resounding 'Yes'. It is eminently possible and desirable for Islam and Muslims to flourish in a multi-faith, democratic world, but it does require some favourable philosophical and political preconditions.

The philosophical and political preconditions of seriousness $_{(r+p+e)}$

The philosophical precondition for young Muslim success that has been a theme throughout this book is the establishment by empowered adults in the lives of young Muslims, such as parents and guardians, humanities teachers and Qur'an teachers, of three key types of necessarily interrelated existential 'seriousness'. These three key types, which constitute a large but not exhaustive part of possible types of existential seriousness, are seriousness $_{(p)}$ – that is, philosophical seriousness; seriousness $_{(r)}$ – that is, religious seriousness; and seriousness $_{(e)}$ – that is, educational seriousness.

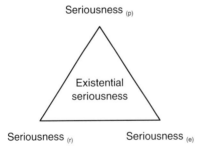

Figure 10.1 The components of existential seriousness.

I explained in Chapter 2 that seriousness$_{(r)}$ is the intelligible, realistic and sincere marriage of practice and belief by those who practise Islam, and indeed other faiths not specifically discussed in this book. Seriousness$_{(r)}$ will permit the sloughing off of false, demi-real (Bhaskar, 1993/2008), unrealistic and immoderate forms of Islamic praxis and enable young Muslim to begin to create a coherent relationship between the eternal principles of their faith and the lived contexts of the contemporary multi-faith world.

Seriousness$_{(r)}$ is mirrored philosophically by seriousness$_{(p)}$, which is philosophical consistency between thought/knowledge and action/the world. Seriousness$_{(p)}$ set up the necessary philosophical conditions for an Islamic critical realism to tease out the deep spiritual rationality that is already inherent in Islamic praxis. The seriousness$_{(p)}$ of the philosophy of critical realism lays the conditions for the work of underlabouring of Islamic critical realism to rediscover an ethos of the Muslim faith that is highly suitable for the promotion of human flourishing in a multi-faith world. Unserious$_{(r)}$ faith positions, in which knowledge and belief are not consistent with each other, are embedded in contemporary intellectual cultures dominated 'hegemonically' (Gramsci, 1971) by an absence of seriousness$_{(p)}$. This situation has led to 'either–or' world-views by which either worldly success in secular liberal democracies is achieved by Muslims at the price of jettisoning the practice of their faith, or an Islamic praxis is preserved in intellectual and spiritual isolation from the society that provides its social and cultural context. Both these are unserious default positions and have generated the Unhappy Muslim Consciousness.

The third component part of existential seriousness, educational seriousness – seriousness$_{(e)}$ – meant a consistency between the ontological status and importance of a phenomenon in the world and the epistemological representation of it as a subject in school. I made the case in Chapters 8 and 9 that both religious and citizenship education in Britain and other multi-faith Western democracies manifest a deep absence of seriousness$_{(e)}$. I argued that the mobilisation of RE and citizenship to engage Muslim young people with their faith in relation to the faiths of others, as well as with their citizenship rights and duties entails removing (or at least closing) the gap between the essential, unavoidable importance of religion and citizenship in the multi-faith, globalising world and the at present incoherent and low-status situation of the corresponding subjects in school.

I have explored these three component types of existential 'seriousness' which together, I have suggested, would help regenerate the Happy Muslim Consciousness, by which the life of the Muslim spirit would be aligned purposively, authentically and transformatively with the conditions of life in a liberal democracy.

Removing absence to transform educational praxis

I have also suggested that the process of accomplishing seriousness$_{(r+p+e)}$ would entail the removal (or absenting) of different types of intellectual 'absence'. Therefore, the dialectical critical realist idea of the removal or 'absenting' of absence as a route to greater seriousness and greater epistemic consistency and ontological wholeness also reoccurred throughout the book. This idea of trans-formative absence has been related to the notion that while to some extent the embodied personality of the individual is always the product of and constrained by the civic and educational structures into which he or she is 'thrown' (Norrie, 2010), the individual can be educated through effective history, RE and citizen-ship education to be informed about and transformative of the structural world around him or her.

I have argued that this transformative role of humanities education is of par-ticular importance for young Muslims who are negotiating, with varying degrees of success, complex and challenging 'new' globalising, Western national, local and faith-based identities. Young Muslims may well also face the need to trans-form the structures of society in order to find a place for themselves in a social world in which people may be fearful of the 'new' Muslim presence, as a feared or despised 'other', or not know quite how Islam and its adherents can 'fit into' contemporary multi-faith and secular life. I have shown how the fulcrum of Islamic critical realism – ontological realism, epistemological relativism and judgemental rationality – can provide the basis of a pedagogical framework for history, RE and citizenship that enables teachers to fulfil their National Curric-ulum brief in an information and transformation-rich way which engages pupils existentially and thus will help in turn to generate returns to seriousness$_{(e)}$ in these crucial subjects.

As far as the political preconditions of educating Muslim young people for success are concerned, it has been a contention of this book that serious$_{(r+p)}$, reflective Islam is highly commensurate with democratic political liberalism because the aim of both sets of praxes is to 'underlabour' for the good life (Wright, 2007) and for human flourishing. This is because both Islam and polit-ical liberalism recognise the sanctity of the life of the self and the necessity for self-fulfilment to occur in relation to respectful regard for the self-fulfilment of others. Neither Islam nor political liberalism is an end in itself; they create polit-ical and intellectual environments in which the flourishing of the individual in relation to the other (and the Transcendental Other) can be pursued.

By contrast, I have suggested that literalist, Manichean Islam, based on demi-real dichotomies, and 'comprehensive' liberalism do, perhaps, represent incom-mensurable world-views because they set themselves up as ends in themselves with their own entrenched culture and immobile ideas, rather than promoting human flourishing and the good life. Many of the knotty issues faced by Muslim young people result from the fact that literalist, Manichean Islam, which is the residue of vicious aspects of the Islamic reformist movement explored in Chapter 1, and which is often cut off from the exegetical moorings and the flexible legal traditions of Islam, predominates in semi-formal Islamic educational settings, such as university Islamic societies and some mosques. The inflexible puritan-ism of literalist Islam is itself fuelled by the increasingly inflexible, comprehen-sively liberal political culture of Europe. Adherents to comprehensive liberalism are prepared to tolerate no political or moral principle other than the moral autonomy of the individual, and thus will not tolerate some mainstream traditional religious opinions as part of the political and cultural lives of democratic nations. Literalist Islam and comprehensive liberalism, as ideologies, share very little common ground.

In this regard, Britain and Europe and, indeed, much of the world appear to be poised on a knife-edge. Political forces that favour cultural and national isolation are in the ascendency in Britain and elsewhere in Europe, and some of these forces, in particular in continental Europe, are predicated upon sharp rejection of the Islamic 'other' as incompatible with the values of liberal democracy. The framing of Muslims as 'the enemy within' has become increasingly acceptable in some political quarters (Ansari, 2004), and this idea has been unwittingly exacerbated by the tendency of mainstream media outlets such as the BBC to give extreme Islamist voices undue attention in an effort to present both sides of complicated arguments in simplistic and publicly digestible ways.

The opportunity for and of Islam

Against this dichotomising and demonising cultural and political backdrop, one important aim of this book has been to suggest that, while Muslims with their Islamic faith face real problems which need urgent solutions, they are not in themselves 'a problem'. To the contrary, the book has suggested that Islam as a *deen* can recover its traditional role as a platform for educational and other types of success by using the ideas and opportunities created by a philosophy such as Islamic critical realism. It has made a strong case for the fact that Islam can be a means and a medium by which young Muslims can interact productively with a multi-faith world.

This means that, with the underlabouring help of an appropriate theological philosophy, Islam can find a new role for itself as one of a family of faiths, the one that is believed by Muslims, naturally enough, to be the most truthful and complete way to engage in a relationship with God and fellow humankind, but not as containing an exclusive monopoly of wisdom, insight, spirituality or truth. Thus, multi-faith democratic contexts represent an enormous opportunity for Islam and Muslims to move away creatively from the intellectual and spiritual traumas of colonialism and post-colonialism that we looked at in Chapter 1 to become, once again, one of the responsible, reflective voices that shape, rather than merely being shaped by, the world.

It is not only the case, however, that liberal democracy represents an opportunity for Muslims and Islam; Muslims and Islam represent an opportunity for other citizens of liberal democracies to expand their horizons intellectually, culturally and spiritually and to be empowered to embrace the challenges and opportunities presented by globalisation (Ajegbo, 2007).

We have seen in Chapters 7–9 how the presence of substantial numbers of Muslim young people in history, RE and citizenship classrooms represents an opportunity for an extra dimension to be added to the exploration of the spiritual and civic dimensions for all young people. We have seen how the Muslim

presence in the history classroom can inspire a broader, richer historical narrative in which our shared national history and events of great national moment,
such as the Anglo-Saxon and Viking civilisations, the Crusades, the Spanish
Armada and the British Empire, can be set in a richer, more interesting international context in a way that will generate a better history for all pupils. It
should, for example, be a matter of course that, in the same way that no teacher
would consider omitting to teach the history of slavery or the Holocaust, the
history of the contribution of Islamic civilisations to the intellectual and technological progress of humanity is taught, because without it a narrative of human
progress in schools makes no historical sense for anyone.

This broadening of curricular historiography means that seismic international
and national events such as the First World War need to be studied in a 'totalising' way that avoids damaging curricular 'sub-totalities' that can lead to alienation and cultural prejudice. We have seen that such a provision would aim at
the ideal of the 'critical patriot' whose duty to country includes shedding frank,
critical light on episodes of national disgrace, such as Britain's participation in
slavery, as well as looking for inspiration in figures and events in which Britain
has led the technological, political and moral way in the world.

In religious education, we saw in Chapter 8 how the presence of Muslim children from strong, traditional faith backgrounds with 'enchanted' religious world-
views presents an opportunity for children from other backgrounds to explore
with their teachers what it means to live according to a faith tradition. They
provide the occasion for teachers to examine critically the possible meanings of
a spiritual ontology that includes God, Angels, Revealed Books, divinely
inspired Prophets and the Day of Judgement, a topic which I developed in
Chapter 5. We have seen how the fulcrum of Islamic critical realism and the idea
of transcendence can be tools that allow for the detailed exploration of spiritual
phenomena in a way that allows for, but does not demand, a commitment of faith
and can nurture the types of mindsets that are open the spiritual insights of
others.

Similarly, the presence of Muslim young people in the citizenship classroom
presents the opportunity for an informed and more deeply critical examination of
civic and political phenomena that many of us may take for granted. Muslims
and Islam, with their own traditions of governance and civic organisation, can
provide the necessary critical perspective to allow all of us to ask the difficult
civic questions: what is the nature of governance and justice? Is liberal democracy unquestionably the best form of political governance, and, if so, why?
What is the role of the arts in the life of a democracy and are there any necessary
limits to freedom of expression? On what ethical grounds should human beings
be custodians of the environment? How should men and women relate to each
other fairly and what are equitable gender roles in a modern liberal democracy?
Thus, the presence of Muslims and their Islamic heritage can challenge our civic
and intellectual complacency in a mirror image of the necessity for Muslims to
reflect coherently and seriously about the institutions of the democratic world in
which we all live.

In short, far from being an ever-present threat and danger, the Muslim presence in the classrooms of Britain and other Western nations can be the yeast in the dough of a more general intellectual and spiritual revival that challenges all of us to examine deeply what and why we think, behave and believe as we do and, if we find that our thought, behaviour and beliefs are 'unserious', to change or transform them accordingly.

From the terrors of performativity to serious$_{(r+p+e)}$ transformativity

The final message and recurring theme of this book has been an even more general one. The type of informative and transformative education of the human person, be he or she Muslim or otherwise, that can potentially be accessed through the humanities subjects using an 'underlabouring' philosophy such as Islamic critical realism is increasingly taking place in a reductionist, 'bobby-basics', performative (Ball, 2003) educational policy culture. This culture stretches schools, teachers and pupils on the rack of myriad league tables, the minutiae of detailed and unrelenting targets and other apparatus of the 'terrors of performativity' (Ball, 2003). The performative educational culture has shoved the idea both of the human person and of the humanising role of the humanities subjects to the margins of the curriculum and has focused more and more time and money on boosting 'literacy' and 'numeracy' without a serious$_{(r+p+e)}$ consideration of why, ultimately, we are trying to make young people literate and numerate in the first place. For this reason, this book has consistently given priority to ontology by asking *who* is being educated and *why*, and by setting out a richly theorised and evidenced ontology of the young Muslim learner in the humanities classroom. In a constricted educational policy culture, the agency of teachers in knowing *who* their pupils are and *how* to cater informatively and transformatively to their educational needs to become even more than usually central to the full flourishing of pupils.

Taking a fresh look at Islam and the education of young Muslims in a multi-faith world is, I believe, one of the most important educational tasks of our time; but it can only be accomplished effectively if educational policy-makers, thinkers, school managers, parents, guardians and teachers remember, and are constantly reminded, that it is in the balanced development of the whole human being, in all his or her related, articulated dimensions, that the true meaning of education lies.

Appendix

Possible reasons for differences in empirical findings about Muslim boys' identities

Given that the findings of previous studies into the identities of Muslim boys alluded to here were undertaken by experienced and accomplished researchers using well-theorised research methodologies, it is worth reflecting on the possible reasons for the differences between my findings and theirs.

There are possible issues of ethnicity. Archer has alluded to the fact that Asian researchers, such as Shain, may share an 'insiderness' with Asian pupils that allows pupils to express certain points of view about racism that otherwise would be silenced (L. Archer, 2002). I am not Asian British, I am English British, and therefore there is a possibility that my 'whiteness' may have silenced some of the boys' more controversial and negative opinions about being British in an attempt to please a relatively empowered British 'native'. However, the converse is also true: that as a male Muslim I shared a high degree of 'insiderness' with my research subjects, which would permit them to speak up, and I was also careful to build up rapport at the beginning of each interview. Moreover, the boys were under no apparent pressure to represent their views positively in the questionnaire surveys, as these were completed anonymously in class.

Furthermore, the different gender of the researchers may account for some of the difference in the findings. The fact that the majority of previous research has been performed by female researchers may have contributed to precisely the 'gendered' posturing of resistance by the boys that the researchers themselves have identified as part of the 'masculine' adolescent performance of identity. The boys had no 'need' to 'perform' their masculinity to me, another Muslim male.

The different contexts and geographical settings of the research undoubtedly played a part. The fact that the questionnaires and surveys were undertaken in a school setting rather than in a setting outside school may have had a positive impact on the findings. It was possible that Muslim boys at least wish to appear to 'resist' school when interviewed in a setting outside it, while they were happier to appear to 'conform' within it. This picks up on L. Archer's (2003) idea of localised hegemonic masculinities that are highly particular to context.

More important, perhaps, is the fact that my study was undertaken in Muslim-dense schools in cosmopolitan Muslim-dense areas in London and the Midlands, where British and Muslim identities may be more readily available, than for Muslim boys in much more marginal communities in white British areas of, for example, the North. In the north of England, where Archer's research was carried out, competition for jobs and employment is also more intense and has contributed to higher levels of inter-cultural tension and the need for Muslim young men, in particular, to distance themselves from white 'Englishness'.

Moreover, times have changed. Nearly half a generation (15 years) has elapsed since the fieldwork of Archer and Alexander, and more recent research, e.g. that of Hussain (2008), shows that the identifications of the Muslim community are very much 'in motion'. It may be that since 2000, despite the impact of 9/11 and 7/7, and the Prevent agenda, young Muslims are finding it more 'normal' to identify both as British and Muslim (cf. Mondal, 2008). It is possible that the attention, although almost always negative, given to Muslims since 9/11 and 7/7 means that Muslim boys at least feel a part of the normal, national landscape rather than simply an ignored absence (Bhaskar, 1993/2008).

References

Abdalati, H. (1975). *Islam in focus*. Oak Brook, IL: American Trust Publications.

Adey, K., & Biddulph, M. (2001). The influence of pupil perceptions on subject choice at 14+ in geography and history. *Educational Studies, 27*(4), 439–450.

Ahmad, T. (Writer). (2011, 14 February). Lessons in hate and violence, *Dispatches* [Television programme]. Channel 4.

Ahonen, S. (2001). Politics of identity through history curriculum: Narratives of the past for social exclusion – or inclusion? *Journal of Curriculum Studies, 33*(2), 179–194.

Ajegbo, K. (2007). *Curriculum review: Diversity and citizenship* (the Ajegbo Report). Nottingham: Department for Education and Skills.

Alderson, P. (2013). *Childhoods real and imagined*. London: Routledge.

Aldrich, R. (2002). *A century of education*. London: RoutledgeFalmer.

Aldrich, R., & Dean, D. (1991). The historical dimension. In R. Aldrich (ed.), *History in the National Curriculum*. London: Kogan Page.

Alexander, C. E. (2000). *The Asian gang: Ethinicity, Identity, Masculinity*. Oxford: Berg.

Ali, T. (2003). *The clash of fundamentalisms*. London: Verso.

Allawi, A. A. (2009). *The crisis of Islamic civilization*. New Haven, CT: Yale University Press.

Anderson, B. (1983). *Imagined communities*. London: Verso.

Ansari, H. (2004). *'The infidel within': Muslims in Britain since 1800*. London: C. Hurst.

Apple, M., & King, N. (1983). What do schools teach? In H. Giroux & G. Purpel (eds), *The hidden curriculum and moral education: Deception or discovery?* (pp. 82–99). Berkeley, CA: McCutchan.

Apple, M. W. (1990). *Ideology and curriculum* (2nd edn). New York: Routledge.

Apple, M. W. (1993). The politics of official knowledge: Does a national curriculum make sense? *Teachers College Record, 95*(2), 222–241.

Archer, L. (2002). 'It's easier that you're a girl and that you're Asian': Interactions of 'race' and gender between researchers and participants. *Feminist Review, 72*, 108–132.

Archer, L. (2003). *Race, masculinity and schooling: Muslim boys and education*. Maidenhead: Open University Press.

Archer, M. (1998). Realism in the social sciences. In M. Archer, R. Bhaskar, A. Collier, T. Lawson & A. Norrie (eds), *Critical realism: essential readings*. London: Routledge.

Archer, M. A., Collier, A., and Porpora, D. V. (2004). *Trancendence: Critical realism and God*. London: Routledge.

Armstrong, K. (2000). *Islam: A short history*. London: Phoenix.

Austin, J. L. (1962). *How to do things with words*. London: Oxford University Press.

Averroes. (1179/2001). *Faith and reason in Islam: Averroes' exposition of religious arguments* (I. Najjar, Trans.). Oxford: Oneworld Publications.

Axelrod, T. (2010, 22 March). Anti-Semitic attacks rising in Scandinavia. JTA. Retrieved 3 January 2011 from http://jta.org/news/article/2010/03/22/1011279/report-anti-semitic-attacks-in-rise-in-scandanavia

al-Azem, T. (2012). Legal rule-making in the Madhab-law tradition. Paper presented at the Cambridge Muslim College.

Azzām, Abd al-Rahman (1938/1993). *The eternal message of Muhammad* (C. E. Farah, Trans.). Cambridge: Islamic Texts Society.

Baker, D., & Edwards, N. (2012). What would Catherine of Sienna do? Spiritual formation and the brains of adolescent girls. *Religious Education, 107*(4), 371–387.

Ball, S. J. (2003). The teacher's soul and the terrors of performativity. *Journal of Education Policy, 18*(2), 215–228.

Ball, S. J., Maguire, M., & Macrae, S. (2000). *Choice, pathways and transitions post-16*. London: RoutledgeFalmer.

Banks, J. A. (2004). Teaching for social justice, diversity, and citizenship in a global world. *Educational Forum, 68*(4), 296–305.

Banks, J. A. (2006). Teaching Black history with a focus on decision-making. In J. A. Banks, *Race, culture, and education: The selected works of James A. Banks* (pp. 19–28). London: Routledge.

Barnes, L. P. (2001). What is wrong with the phenomenological approach to religious education? *Religious Education, 96*(4), 445–461.

Barton, K. C. (2012). Agency, choice and historical action: How history teaching can help students think about democratic decision making. *Citizenship Teaching and Learning, 7*(2), 131–142.

Barton, K. C., & James, J. H. (2010). Religion in history and social studies. *Perspectives: Newsmagazine of the American Historical Association, 48*(5).

Barton, K. C., & Levstik, L. S. (2004). *Teaching history for the common good*. Mahwah, NJ: Lawrence Erlbaum.

Barton, K. C. and McCully, A. W. (2007) Teaching controversial issues where controversial issues really matter. *Teaching History, 127*, 13–19.

Baumfield, V., & Cush, D. (2013). Religious education at the crossroads (again): The search for a subject identity? *British Journal of Religious Education, 35*(3), 231–235.

BBC. (2007, 30 April). Profile: Mohammad Sidique Khan. *BBC News*. Retrieved 21 March 2014 from BBC http://news.bbc.co.uk/1/hi/uk/4762209.stm

Becher, R. (1984). Parent involvement: A review of research and principles of successful practice. National Institute of Education, Washington, DC.

Bentley, H., & Ziegler, J. (2006) *Traditions and encounters: A global perspective on the past*. New York: McGraw-Hill.

Bhaskar, R. (1975). *A realist theory of science*. Leeds: Leeds Books.

Bhaskar, R. (1979). *The possibility of naturalism*. Brighton: Harvester Press.

Bhaskar, R. (1991). *Philosophy and the idea of freedom*. Oxford: Blackwell.

Bhaskar, R. (1993/2008). *Dialectic: The pulse of freedom*. London: Routledge.

Bhaskar, R. (1997). Philosophy and scientific realism. In M. Archer, R. Bhaskar, A. Collier, T. Lawson & A. Norrie (eds), *Critical realism: Essential readings* (pp. 16–47). London: Routledge.

Bhaskar, R. (2000). *From East to West*. London: Routledge.

Bhaskar, R. (2002/2012a). *From science to emancipation*. London: Routledge.

Bhaskar, R. (2002/2012b). *Reflections on MetaReality*. London: Routledge.

Bhaskar, R. (2002/2012c). *The philosophy of MetaReality*. London: Routledge.

Bhaskar, R. (2009). *Contexts of interdisciplinarity: Interdisciplinarity and climate change*. London: Institute of Education, University of London.

Bhaskar, R. (2013). Prolegomenon: The consequences of the revindication of philosophical ontology for philosophy and social theory. In M. S. Archer & A. M. Maccarini (eds), *Engaging with the world: Agency, institutions, historical formations* (pp. 11–21). London: Routledge.

Bhaskar, R., & Danermark, B. (2006). Metatheory, interdisciplinarity and disability research: A critical realist perspective. *Scandanavian Journal of Disability Research, 8*(4), 278–297.

Binyon, M. (2007, 17 April). Poll of Muslims in London shows hidden face of a model citizenry. *The Times*.

Birt, J. (2010). The challenge facing Muslims in the West. Paper presented at the the Muslim Council of Britain Annual General Meeting, the East London Mosque.

Blackhirst, R. (2003). *Authochthony and the symbolism of Islamic prayer*. Religioperennis.

Bloch, M. N., & Tabachnick, B. R. (1994). Improving parental involvement as school reform: Rhetoric or reality? In K. N. Borman & N. P. Greenman (eds), *Changing American education: Recapturing the past or inventing the future* (pp. 261–293). Albany: State University of New York Press.

Booth, M. (1993). History. In A. S. King & M. J. Reiss (eds), *The multicultural dimension of the National Curriculum* (pp. 78–90). London: Falmer Press.

Bourdieu, P., & Passeron, J.-C. (1977). *Reproduction in education, society and culture*. London: Sage.

Brighouse, T., & Woods, D. (1999). *How to improve your school*. London: Routledge.

Brown, G. (2006). A speech to the Fabian Society: The future of Britishness. Retrieved 1 June 2009 from www.fabians.org.uk/events/speeches/the-future-of-britishness

Brown, G. L. (2009). The ontological turn in education. *Journal of Critical Realism, 8*(1), 5–34.

Brown, K. E. (2010). Contesting the securitization of British Muslims. *Interventions, 12*(2), 171–182.

Bruner, J. (1997). A narrative model of self-construction. *Annals of the New York Academy of Sciences, 818*(1), 145–161.

Bullock, A. [Sir] (Chair). (1975). *A language for life: Report of the Committee of Enquiry* (the Bullock Report). London: HMSO.

Bunt, G. R. (2003). *Islam in the Digital Age*. London: Pluto Press.

Bunting, M. (2011, 6 February). Blame consumer capitalism, not multiculturalism. *Guardian*.

Cameron, D. (2011). Muslims must embrace our British values. Paper presented at the Munich Security Conference 2011, Munich. Retrieved 15 September 2012 from www.telegraph.co.uk/news/newstopics/politics/david-cameron/8305346/Muslims-must-embrace-our-British-values-David-Cameron-says.html

Campbell, D. (2008). Voice in the classroom: How an open classroom climate fosters political engagement among adolescents. *Political Behavior, 30*(4), 437–454.

Cannadine, D. (2013a, 13 March). The future of history. *The Times Literary Supplement*.

Cannadine, D. (2013b). *The undivided past*. London: Allen Lane.

Casciani, D. (2005). Analysis: Segregated Britain? *BBC News*. Retrieved 29 March 2014 from http://news.bbc.co.uk/1/hi/uk/4270010.stm

Chamberlin, R. (2003). Citizenship? Only if you haven't got a life: secondary school pupils' views of Citizenship Education. *Westminster Studies in Education, 26*(2), 87–97.

Chapman, A. (2011). Historical interpretations. In I. Davies (ed.), *Debates in history teaching* (pp. 96–108). London: Routledge.

Coffey, A. (1999). Locating the self. In A. Coffey, *The ethnographic self: Fieldwork and the representation of identity* (pp. 17–38). Thousand Oaks, CA: Sage.

Cohen, S. (1973). *Folk devils and moral panics*. London: Paladin.

Coles, M. I. (2010). *Every Muslim child matters: Practical guidance for schools and children's services*. Stoke-on-Trent: Trentham Books.

Colley, L. (1992). *Britons: Forging the nation 1707–1837*. New Haven, CT: Yale University Press.

Collier, A. (2004). The Masters of Suspicion and secularisation. In M. A. Archer, A. Collier & D. V. Porpora, *Transcendence: Critical realism and God* (pp. 82–91). London: Routledge.

Connell, R. W. (1995). *Masculinities*. Cambridge: Polity Press.

Conroy, J. C., Lundie, D., Davis, R. A., Baumfield, V., Barnes, L. P., Gallagher, T., … Wenell, K. (2013). *Does religious education work?* London: Bloomsbury.

Copley, T. (2005). *Indoctrination, education and God*. London: Society for Promoting Christian Knowledge.

Cowling, R. (Writer). (2009). *The Muslim Tommies* [Television programme]. R. Cowling (Producer). BBC.

Crick, B. (Chair). (1998). *Education for citizenship and the teaching of democracy in schools: Final report of the Advisory Group on Citizenship* (the Crick Report). London: Qualifications and Curriculum Authority.

Cronon, W. (2000). Why the past matters. *Wisconsin Magazine of History, 84*(1), 2–13.

Crozier, G. (2005). Beyond the call of duty: The impact of racism on black parents' involvement in their children's education. In G. Crozier & D. Reay (eds), *Activating participation: Parents and teachers working towards partnership* (pp. 39–56). Stoke-on-Trent: Trentham Books.

Datta, M. (2002). *Bilinguality and literacy: Principles and pratice*. London: Continuum.

Davies, I. (2010a). Defining citizenship education. In L. Gearon (ed.), *Learning to Teach citizenship in the secondary school* (2nd edn, pp. 22–33). London: Routledge.

Davies, I. (2010b). England: Searching for citizenship. In A. Reid, J. Gill & A. Sears (eds), *Globalization, the nation-state and the citizen: Dilemmas and directions for civics and citizenship education* (pp. 114–127). New York: Routledge.

Davison, G. (2000). *The use and abuse of Australian history*. Crows Nest, NSW: Allen & Unwin.

DeJohn, I., Morales, M., & Hutchinson, B. (2013, 22 September). Hateful mob attacks Sikh who says he was mistaken for a radical Muslim. *Daily News* (New York). Retrieved 10 March 2014 from www.nydailynews.com/new-york/mob-attacks-sikh-mistaken-radical-muslim-article-1.1464357

Dewey, J. (1916). *Democracy and education*. New York: Macmillan.

DeWitt, J., & Storksdieck, M. (2008). A short review of school field trips: Key findings from the past and implications for the future. *Visitor Studies, 11*(2), 181–197.

Dutton, Y. (1999). *The origins of Islamic law: The Qur'an, the Muwatta' and Madinan Amal*. Richmond, Surrey: Curzon Press.

Easton, M. (Producer). (2014, 9 April). UK becoming 'more local and global'. *BBC News*. Retrieved 1 May 2014 from www.bbc.co.uk/news/uk-26885743

Eccles, J. S., Early, D., Fraser, K., Belansky, E. & McCarthy, K. (1997). The relation of connection, regulation, and support for autonomy to adolescents' functioning. *Journal of Adolescent Research, 12*(2), 263–286.

Eccles, J. S., & Harold, R. D. (1996). Family involvement in children's and adolescents' schooling. In A. Booth & J. F. Dunn (eds), *Family–school links: How do they affect educational outcomes?* (pp. 3–34). Mahwah, NJ: Lawrence Erlbaum.

Ellis, R. (1997). Revelation, wisdom, and learning from religion: A response to D. G. Attfield. *British Journal of Religious Education, 19*(2), 95–103.

Epstein, D., Elwood, J., Hey, V., & Maw, J. (eds). (1998). *Failing boys? Issues in gender and achievement*. Buckingham: Open University Press.

Epstein, J. L., & Becker, H. J. (1982). Teachers' reported practices of parent involvement: Problems and possibilities. *Elementary School Journal, 83*(2), 103–113.

Equality and Human Rights Commission. (2010). *How fair is Britain?* London: Equality and Human Rights Commission.

Economc and Social Research Council. (2008). *Britain in 2008: The state of the nation*. London: ESRC.

Fadel, M. (2013). 'No salvation outside Islam': Muslim modernists, democratic politics, and Islamic theological exclusivism. In M. H. Khalil (ed.), *Between heaven and hell: Islam, salvation, and the fate of others* (pp. 35–62). New York: Oxford University Press.

Feinstein, S. G. (2009). *Secrets of the teenage brain: Research-based strategies for teaching and reaching today's adolescents* (2nd edn). Thousand Oaks, CA: Corwyn.

Feldman, N. (2003). *After jihad: America and the struggle for Islamic democracy*. New York: Farrar, Straus & Giroux.

Feldman, N. (2008). *The fall and rise of the Islamic state*. Princeton, NJ: Princeton University Press.

Ferguson, N. (2011). *Civilization: The West and the rest*. London: Allen Lane.

Fielding, M. (2000). Community, philosophy and education policy: Against effectiveness ideology and the immiseration of contemporary schooling. *Journal of Education Policy, 15*(4), 397–415.

Finney, N., & Simpson, L. (2009). *'Sleepwalking to segregation'? Challenging myths about race and migration*. Bristol: Policy Press.

Fiss, O. M. (1996). *The irony of free speech*. Cambridge, MA: Harvard University Press.

Foucault, M. (1980). Two lectures. In C. Gordon (ed.), *Power/knowledge: Selected interviews and other writings 1972–1977* (pp. 78–108). New York: Pantheon Books.

Francis, B. (2000). *Boys, girls and achievement: Addressing the classroom issues*. London: RoutledgeFalmer.

Francis, B., Skelton, C., & Read, B. (2009). The simultaneous production of educational achievement and popularity: How do some pupils accomplish it? *British Educational Research Journal, 36*(2), 317–340.

Francis, L. J., and Robbins, M. (2005). *Urban hope and spiritual health: The adolescent voice*. Peterborough: Epworth Press.

Freedland, J. (2005, August 3). The identity vacuum. *Guardian*. Retrieved 12 October 2010 from www.theguardian.com/world/2005/aug/03/race.july7

Friedmann, Y. (2003). *Tolerance and coercion in Islam: Interfaith relations in the Muslim tradition*. Cambridge: Cambridge University Press.

Friedmann, Y. (2012). Is there no compulsion in religion? In L. Ridgeon (ed.), *Islam and religious diversity* (Vol. 1, pp. 87–120). London: Routledge.

Frosh, S., Phoenix, A., & Pattman, R. (eds). (2002). *Young masculinities*. Basingstoke: Palgrave.

Garton Ash, T. (2006, August 10). What young British Muslims say can be shocking –some of it is also true. *Guardian*. Retrieved 12 October 2010 from www.theguardian.com/commentisfree/2006/aug/10/comment.race

Gearon, L. (ed.). (2010). *Learning to teach citizenship in the secondary school*. London: Routledge.

Gellner, E. (1983). *Muslim society*. Cambridge: Cambridge University Press.

al-Ghazāli. (*c*.1090/1983). *Inner dimensions of Islamic worship* (M. Holland, Trans.): Markfield, Leicestershire: The Islamic Foundation.

Gilliat-Ray, S. (2010). *Muslims in Britain: An introduction*. Cambridge: Cambridge University Press.

Glaser, B. G. (1992). *Emergence vs forcing: Basics of grounded theory analysis*. Mill Valley, CA: Sociology Press.

Gledhill, R., & Webster, P. (2008, 8 February). Archbishop of Canterbury argues for Islamic law in Britain. *The Times*.

Gonzalez-DeHass, A. R., Willems, P. P., & Holbein, M. F. D. (2005). Examining the relationship between parental involvement and student motivation. *Educational Psychology Review, 17*(2), 99–123.

Goodson, I. F. (1990). 'Nations at risk' and 'national curriculum': Ideology and identity. *Journal of Education Policy, 5*(5), 219–232.

Gramsci, A. (1971). *Selections from the prison notebooks*. London: Lawrence & Wishart.

Green, E. H. (2009). Speaking in parables: The responses of students to a Bible-based ethos in a Christian city technology college. *Cambridge Journal of Education, 39*(4), 443–456.

Gregg, M., & Leinhardt, G. (1994). Mapping out geography: An example of epistemology and education. *Review of Educational Research, 64*(2), 311–361.

Grever, M., Haydn, T., & Ribbens, K. (2008). Identity and school history: The perspective of young people from the Netherlands and England. *British Journal of Educational Studies, 56*(1), 76–94.

Grimmitt, M. (1987). *Religious education and human development*. Great Wakering, Essex: McCrimmon.

Gubrium, J. F., & Holstein, J. A. (eds). (2003). *Postmodern interviewing*. Thousand Oaks, CA: Sage.

Haddad, Y. Y. (ed.). (2002). *Muslims in the West: From sojourners to citizens*. New York: Oxford University Press.

Hakim, C. (2011). *Honey money: The power of erotic capital*. London: Penguin Books.

Hallaq, W. (2001). *Authority, continuity and change in Islamic law*. Cambridge: Cambridge University Press.

Halstead, M. (2004). An Islamic concept of education. *Comparative Education, 40*(4), 517–529.

Haraway, D. (1988). Situated knowledges: The science question in feminism and the privilege of partial perspective. *Feminist Studies, 14*(3), 575–599.

Hart, G. H., & Maraldo, J. C. (eds). (1976). *The piety of thinking: Essays by Martin Heidegger*. Bloomington: Indiana University Press.

Hartwig, M. (ed.). (2007). *Dictionary of critical realism*. London: Routledge.

Hartwig, M. (2012). Introduction. In R. Bhaskar, *The Philosophy of MetaReality*. London: Routledge

al-Hassani, S. T. S. (ed.). (2012). *1001 inventions: The enduring legacy of Muslim civilization*. Washington, DC: National Geographic.

Haw, K., & Shah, S. (1998). The Nazrah story. In K. Haw (ed.), *Educating Muslim girls: Shifting discourses* (pp. 139–160). Buckingham: Open University Press.

Haydn, T. (2003). Computers and history: Rhetoric, reality and the lessons of the past. In T. Haydn & C. Counsell (eds), *History, ICT and learning in the secondary school* (pp. 11–37). London: RoutledgeFalmer.

Head, J. (1999). *Understanding the boys: Issues of behaviour and achievement*. London: Falmer Press.

Heater, D. (2004). *A history of education for citizenship*. London: RoutledgeFalmer.

Heater, D. (2010). A history of citizenship in Britain. In L. Gearon (ed.), *Learning to teach citizenship in the secondary school* (pp. 7–21). London: Routledge.

Hegel, G. W. F. (1807 trans. 1977). *Phenomenology of spirit* (A. V. Miller, Trans.). Oxford: Clarendon Press.

Hewer, C. (2001). Schools for Muslims. *Oxford Review of Education, 27*(4), 515–527.

Hirst, P. (1974). *Knowledge and the curriculum*. London: Routledge & Kegan Paul.

Hoch, P. (1979). *White hero, black beast: Racism, sexism and the mask of masculinity*. London: Pluto Press.

Hoover-Dempsey, K. V., Bassler, O. C., & Brissie, J. S. (1987). Parent involvement: Contributions of teacher efficacy, school socioeconomic status, and other school characteristics. *American Educational Research Journal, 24*(3), 417–435.

Hopkins, P. (2004). Young Muslim men in Scotland: Inclusions and exclusions. *Children's Geographies, 2*(2), 257–272.

Hopkins, P. (2009). Critical social identities and reflexive positionalities: Researching Muslims in Britain. Paper presented at the Researching Muslims in Britain Conference, Cardiff University, 15 April.

Hostettler, N. (2012). *Eurocentrism: a Marxian critical realist critique*. Abingdon: Routledge.

Hull, J. M. (1998). Religious education and Muslims in England: Developments and principles. *Muslim Education Quarterly, 15*(4), 10–23.

Hunt, D. (1983). The teaching of Islam in schools: A reply. *British Journal of Religious Education, 5*(2), 96–99.

Huntington, S. P. (1996). *The clash of civilizations*. New York: Simon & Schuster.

Hurst, G. (2007, 22 November). Maverick streak makes mockery of hunt for a British motto. *The Times Online*. Retrieved 1 May 2014 from www.thetimes.co.uk/tto/news/politics/article2024244.ece

Husband, C. (1994). The political context of Muslim communities' participation in British society. In B. Lewis & D. Schnapper (eds), *Muslims in Europe* (pp. 79–97). London: Pinter.

Hussain, S. (2008). *Muslims on the map: A national survey of social trends in Britain*. London: Tauris Academic Studies.

Hussein, I. (2003). Time in the Qur'an. Retrieved 6 October 2010 from www.islam-frominside.com/Pages/Articles/The%20concept%20of%20time%20in%20the%20Quran.html

Imtiaz, S. M. A. (2011). *Wandering lonely in a crowd: The Muslim condition in the West*. Leicester: Kube.

Ipgrave, J. (2006). Issues in the delivery of religious education to Muslim pupils: Perspectives from the classroom. *British Journal of Religious Education, 21*(3), 146–157.

Ipgrave, J. (forthcoming). Multiculturalism, communitarianism, cohesion, and security: The impact of changing responses to British Islam on the nature of English religious education. In R. Heffner & A. Seligman (eds), *Civic enculturation and citizenship in North America and Western Europe*.

'Iyad, Qadi (*c*.1100/1982). *Foundations of Islam*. Norwich: Diwan Press.

'Iyad, Qadi (*c*.1100/1991). *Recognition of the rights of the Chosen One* (A. Bewley, Trans.). Granada: Madinah Press.

Jackson, P. (2006). Thinking geographically. *Geography, 91*(3), 199–204.

Jalalayn. (1505/2013). Tafsir al-Jalalayn (The commentary of the two Jalals). Retrieved 3 May 2014 from Royal Aal al-Bayt Institute for Islamic Thought, www.altafsir.com/ Tafasir.

Jerome, L. (2012). *England's citizenship education experiment*. London: Bloomsbury.

Kamali, M. H. (1997). *Freedom of expression in Islam*. Cambridge: Islamic Texts Society.

Katyal, K. R., & Evers, C. W. (2007). Parents – partners or clients? A reconceptualization of home–school interactions. *Teaching Education, 18*(1), 61–76.

Kay, W. (1997, 21 November). Cinderella of the education system. *Times Educational Supplement*.

Kersten, C. (2011). *Cosmopolitans and heretics: New Muslim intellectuals and the study of Islam*. London: Hurst.

Keser, F., Akar, H., & Yildirim, A. (2011). The role of extracurricular activities in active citizenship education. *Journal of Curriculum Studies, 43*(6), 809–837.

Kessler, E. (2013). *Jews, Christians and Muslims in encounter*. Norwich: SCM Press.

Kisby Littleton, F. (2009). *Representations of the Islamic world in history textbooks for English schools, 1799–2002: A case study of the Crusades*. London: Institute of Education, University of London.

Koopmans, R., & Statham, P. (1999). Challenging the liberal nation-state? Postnationalism, multiculturalism, and the collective claims making of migrants and ethnic minorities in Britain and Germany. *American Journal of Sociology, 105*(3), 652–696.

Kroger, J. (1996). *Identity in adolescence: The balance between self and other*. London: Routledge.

Leaman, O., & Rizvi, S. (2008). The developed *kalām* tradition. In T. Winter (ed.), *The Cambridge companion to classical Islamic theology* (pp. 77–96). Cambridge: Cambridge University Press.

Lee, P. (1992). History in schools: Aims, purposes and approaches: A reply to John White. In P. Lee, J. White, P. Walsh & J. Slater (eds), *The aims of school history: The National Curriculum and beyond* (pp. 20–34). London: Tufnell Press.

Lee, R. D. (1997). *Overcoming tradition and modernity*. Boulder, CO: Westview Press.

LeSieur, M., Russo, A., & Russo, J. (Writers). (2006). *You, me and Dupree* [Film]. M. Parent, S. Stuber & O. Wilson (Producers). Universal Pictures.

Levstik, L. S., & Barton, K. C. (2011). *Doing history: Investigating with children in elementary and middle schools* (4th edn). New York: Routledge.

Lewis, B. (1994). Legal and historical reflections on the position of Muslim populations under non-Muslim rule. In B. Lewis & D. Schnapper (eds), *Muslims in Europe* (pp. 1–18). London: Pinter.

Lewis, P. (2002). *Islamic Britain: Religion, politics and identity among British Muslims*. London: I. B. Tauris.

Little, D. (1993). Evidence and objectivity in the social sciences. *Social Research, 60*(2), 363–396.

Loewen, J. W., & Deininger, W. T. (1997). Lies my teacher told me: Everything your American history textbook got wrong. *History: Reviews of New Books, 25*(3), 100–101.

Lovelock, J. (1979). *Gaia: A new look at life on Earth*. Oxford: Oxford University Press.

Mac an Ghaill, M. (1994). *The making of men: Masculinities, sexualities and schooling*. Buckingham: Open University Press.

Macmillan, M. (2008). *The uses and abuses of history*. London: Profile Books.

Mahmutćehajić, R. (2011). *On the other: A Muslim view*. Bronx, NY: Fordham University Press.

Malcolm, N. (2013). Positive views of Islam and of Ottoman rule in the sixteenth century: The case of Jean Bodin. In A. Contadini & C. Norton (eds), *The Renaissance and the Ottoman World* (pp. 197–217). Farnham: Ashgate.

Masood, E. (2009). *Science and Islam: A history*. London: Icon Books.

Matar, N. (1998). *Islam in Britain, 1558–1685*. Cambridge: Cambridge University Press.

Matthews, J. A., & Herbert, D. T. (2008). *Geography: A very short introduction*. Oxford: Oxford University Press.

McConaghy, C. (2000). *Rethinking indigenous education: Culturalism, colonialism and the politics of knowing*. Brisbane: Post Pressed.

Mernissi, F. (1975). *Beyong the veil: Male–female dynamics in modern Muslim society*. Cambridge, MA: Schenkman.

Michot, Y. (2006). *Ibn Taymiyya: Muslims under non-Muslim rule*. Oxford: Interface Publications.

Miller, D. (2000). Citizenship: What does it mean and why is it important? In N. Pearce & J. Hallgarten (eds), *Tomorrow's citizens: Critical debates in citizenship and education* (pp. 26–35). London: Institute for Public Policy Research.

Mirza, M., Senthilkumaran, A., & Ja'far, Z. (2007). *Living apart together: British Muslims and the paradox of multiculturalism*. London: Policy Exchange.

Modood, T. (1994). The end of a hegemony: The concept of 'Black' and British Asians. In J. Rex & B. Drury (eds), *Ethnic mobilisation in a multi-cultural Europe* (pp. 87–96). Aldershot: Avebury Press.

Modood, T. (2003). Muslims and the politics of difference. *Political Quarterly, 74*(1), 100–115.

Modood, T. (2007). British Muslim perspectives on multiculturalism. *Theory, Culture and Society, 24*(2), 187–213.

Mondal, A. A. (2008). *Young British Muslim voices*. Oxford: Greenwood World.

Moosavi, L. (2014). The racialization of Muslim converts in Britain and their experiences of Islamophobia. *Critical Sociology*. doi:10.1177/0896920513504601

Morey, P., & Yaqin, A. (2011). *Framing Muslims*. Cambridge, MA: Harvard University Press.

Morris, R. (2013, 9 September). Why Sarah Teather has let the Liberal Democrats down. *Guardian*. Retrieved 17 February 2014 from www.theguardian.com/commentis-free/2013/sep/09/sarah-teather-let-liberal-democrats-down

Nast, H. J. (1994). Women in the field: Critical feminist methodologies and theoretical perspectives – opening remarks on 'Women in the Field'. *Professional Geographer, 46*(1), 54–66.

Nawawi. 40 Hadith Nawawi. Retrieved 1 April 2014 from http://sunnah.com/nawawi40

Nieto, S. (2006, December). Creating multicultural learning communities: Strategies for reaching all students. Presentation to Sturbridge (MA) Communities and Schools for Success.

Norrie, A. (2010). *Dialectic and difference: Dialectical critical realism and the grounds of justice*. London: Routledge.

Norris, P., & Inglehart, R. (2004). *Sacred and secular: Religion and politics worldwide*. Cambridge: Cambridge University Press.

Norton, C. (2013). Blurring the boundaries: Intellectual and cultural interactions between the Eastern and Western; Christian and Muslim worlds. In A. Contadini & C. Norton (eds), *The Renaissance and the Ottoman world* (pp. 1–22). Farnham: Ashgate.

al-Oadah, S. (2014). Obeying the law in non-Muslim countries. Retrieved 23 April 2014 from http://en.islamtoday.net/node/604

Oliver, N. (2012). *Vikings: A history*. London: Weidenfeld & Nicolson.

Omissi, D. (1999). *Indian voices of the Great War: Soldiers' letters, 1914–18*. London: Palgrave.

Ormsby, E. (1984). *Theodicy in Islamic thought*. Princeton, NJ: Princeton University Press.

Ormsby, E. (2008). *Ghazali: The revival of Islam*. Oxford: Oneworld Publications.

Otto, R. (1923/1950). *The idea of the holy* (2nd edn). Oxford: Oxford University Press.

Oyserman, D., Brickman, D., & Rhodes, M. (2007). School success, possible selves, and parental involvement. *Family Relations, 56*, 479–489.

Palloff, R. M., & Pratt, K. (2007). *Building online learning communities*. San Francisco: Jossey-Bass.

Panorama (2009, 22 February). Muslim first, British second [Television programme]. BBC.

Parekh, B. (Chair). (2000). *The future of multi-ethnic Britain* (the Parekh Report). London: Runnymede Trust.

Paton, G. (2011, 9 July). Religious education in schools 'under threat'. *Telegraph*. Retrieved 17 February 2014, from www.telegraph.co.uk/education/education-news/8625861/Religious-education-in-schools-under-threat.html

Pew Research. (2011). *The future of the global Muslim population* (Report). Retrieved 26 March 2014 from www.pewforum.org/2011/01/27/the-future-of-the-global-muslim-population/

Phillips, R. (1998). *History teaching, nationhood and the state*. London: Cassell.

Phillips, R., Goalen, P., McCully, A., & Wood, S. (1999). Four histories, one nation? History teaching, nationhood and a British identity. *Compare, 29*(2), 153–169.

Platt, L. (2001). *Migration and social mobility: The life chances of Britain's minority ethnic communities*. York: Joseph Rowntree Foundation.

Postman, N., & Weingartner, C. (1969). *Teaching as a subversive activity*. New York: Delacorte Press.

Pring, R. (2010, 12 January). Reclaiming education. Paper presented at the Critical Realism Group Seminar, Institute of Education, University of London.

Pring, R. (2013). *The life and death of secondary education for all*. London: Routledge.

Qualifications and Curriculum Authority. (2004). *The non-statutory national framework for religious education*. London: Qualifications and Curriculum Authority.

Qualifications and Curriculum Development Agency. (2009). National Curriculum. London: Qualifications and Curriculum Development Authority.

Qualifications and Curriculum Development Agency. (2010). *History Key Stage 3 – Programme of Study*. London: Retrieved 4 April 2011 from http://curriculum.qcda.gov.uk/key-stages-3-and-4/subjects/key-stage-3/history/programme-of-study/index.aspx

Qutb, S. (1964/1981). *Milestones*. Karachi: International Islamic.

Ramadan, T. (1999). *To be a European Muslim*. Leicester: Islamic Foundation.

Ramadan, T. (2006). The Way (*al-Sharia*) of Islam. In M. Kamrava (ed.), *The New Voices of Islam* (pp. 65–98). London: I. B. Tauris.

Ramadan, T. (2007a). Foreword. In M. L. N. Wilkinson, *The Demise of Imam Faustus*. Chesham: Othello Press.

Ramadan, T. (2007b). *The Messenger: The meanings of the life of Muhammad*. London: Penguin.

Ramadan, T. (2009). Determining the sources of Islamic law and jurisprudence. In T. Ramadan, *Radical reform: Islamic ethics and liberation* (pp. 85–100). New York: Oxford University Press.

Ramadan, T. (2010). *The quest for meaning: Developing a philosophy of pluralism.* London: Penguin Books.

Ramadan, T. (2012). *Islam and the Arab awakening.* New York: Oxford University Press.

Rampton, A. (Chair). (1981). *West Indian children in our schools: Interim report of the Committee of Inquiry into the Education of Children from Ethnic Minority Groups* (the Rampton Report). London: HMSO.

Rapoport, Y., & Ahmed, S. (2010). *Ibn Taymiyya and his times.* New York: Oxford University Press.

Reid, A., Gill, J., & Sears, A. (2010). The forming of citizens in a globalising world. In A. Reid, J. Gill & A. Sears (eds), *Globalization, the Nation-State and the Citizen* (pp. 3–16). New York: Routledge.

Religion of Peace, The. (2014). Muslim loyalty to non-Muslim governments. Retrieved 15 April 2014 from www.thereligionofpeace.com/quran/014-loyalty-to-non-muslim-government.htm

Richardson, H. (2011, 25 August). Why boys trail further behind girls at GCSE top grades. *BBC News.* Retrieved 23 April 2013 from www.bbc.co.uk/news/education-14664916

Rissanen, I. (2013). Developing religious identities of Muslim students in the classroom: A case study from Finland. *British Journal of Religious Education, 36*(2), 123–138.

Ritchie, D. (Chair). (2001). *Oldham independent review: One Oldham, one future* (the Ritchie Report). Oldham: Oldham Independent Review.

Rogers, M. A., Theule, J., Ryan, B. A., Adams, G. R., & Keating, L. (2009). Parental involvement and children's school achievement. *Canadian Journal of School Psychology, 24*(1), 34–57.

Sachedina, A. (2013). Islamic theology of Christian–Muslim relations. In L. Ridgeon (ed.), *Islam and religious diversity* (Vol. 4, pp. 113–128). London: Routledge.

Saeed, A. (2006). *Islamic thought: An introduction.* London: Routledge.

Saha, L. (2000) Political activism and civic education among Australian secondary school students. *Australian Journal of Education, 44*(2), 155–174.

Said, E. (1978). *Orientalism.* New York: Vintage.

Sarra, C. (2011). *Strong and smart – Towards a pedagogy for emancipation: Education for first peoples.* Abingdon: Routledge.

Sayer, A. (1984). *Method in social science* (2nd edn). London: Routledge.

Sayyid, S., & Vakil, A. (eds). (2010). *Thinking through Islamophobia: Global perspectives.* London: C. Hurst.

Schiffauer, W. (1988). Migration and religiousness. In T. Gerhol & Y. G. Lithman (eds), *The new Islamic presence in Western Europe* (pp. 146–158). London: Mansell.

Scott, D. (2010). *Education, epistemology and critical realism.* London: Routledge.

Scott, D. (2011). PISA, international comparisons, epistemic paradoxes. In M. Pereyra, H.-G. Kottoff & R. Cowen (eds), *PISA under examination: Changing knowledge, changing tests and changing schools* (pp. 97–107). Rotterdam: Sense Publishers.

Şentürk, R. (2002). Adamiyyah and 'Ismah: The contested relationship between humanity and human rights in classical Islamic law. *İslâm Araştırmaları Dergisi, 8,* 39–69.

Sewell, W. H. Jr (2005). Refiguring the 'social' in social science: An interpretivist manifesto. In W. H. Sewell Jr, *Logics of history: Social theory and social transformation* (pp. 318–372). Chicago: University of Chicago Press.

Shah-Kazemi, R. (2013). The metaphysics of interfaith dialogue: Sufi perspectives on the universality of the Quaranic message. In L. Ridgeon (ed.), *Islam and Religious Diversity* (Vol. 4, pp. 69–112). London: Routledge.

Shain, F. (2003). *The schooling and identity of Asian girls.* Stoke-on-Trent: Trentham Books.

Shain, F. (2010). *The new folk devils: Muslim boys and education in England.* Stoke-on-Trent: Trentham Books.

Sheldon, S. B., & Epstein, J. L. (2002). Improving student behavior and school discipline with family and community involvement. *Education and Urban Society, 35*(1), 4–26.

Shepard, W. (2004). The diversity of Islamic thought: Towards a typology. In S. Taji-Faouki & B. M. Nafi (eds), *Islamic thought in the twentieth century* (pp. 61–103). London: I. B. Tauris.

Sherif, F. (1995). *A guide to the contents of the Qur'an.* Reading: Garnet.

Siddique, H. (2010). BBC's Panorama claims Islamic schools teach antisemitism and homophobia. *Guardian*, 22 November.

Singh Ghuman, P. A. (1997). Assimilation or integration? A study of Asian adolescents. *Educational Research, 39*(1), 23–35.

Skelton, C. (2001). *Schooling the boys: Masculinities and primary education.* Buckingham: Open University Press.

Slater, J. (1989). *The politics of history teaching: A humanity dehumanized?* Special Professorial Lecture, Institute of Education, London.

Slater, J. (1992). Where there is dogma, let us sow doubt. In P. Lee, J. Slater, P. Walsh & J. White (eds), *The aims of school history: The National Curriculum and beyond* (pp. 45–53). London: Tufnell Press.

Smith, C. (2010). *What is a person?* Chicago: University of Chicago Press.

Smith, R. (1995). What makes a good teacher? In B. Moon & A. Shelton Mayes (eds), *Teaching and learning in the secondary school* (pp. 103–106). London: Routledge.

Swann, M. [Lord Swann] (Chair). (1985). *Education for all: Report of the Committee of Enquiry into the Education of Children from Ethnic Minority Groups* (the Swann Report). London: HMSO.

Taji-Farouki, S., & Nafi, B. M. (eds). (2004). *Islamic thought in the twentieth century.* London: I. B. Tauris.

Tawney, R. H. (1926/2013). *Religion and the rise of capitalism* (A. Seligman ed.). London.

Taylor, C. (2007). *A secular age.* Cambridge, MA: The Belknap Press of Harvard University Press.

Teece, G. (2010). Is it learning about and from religions, religion or religious education? And is it any wonder some teachers don't get it? *British Journal of Religious Education, 32*(2), 93–103.

Thompson, M. (2004). *The pressured child: Helping your child find success in school and life.* New York: Ballantine Books.

Tillich, P. (1952/2000). *The courage to be.* New Haven, CT: Yale University Press.

Torney-Purta, J., Lehmann, R., Oswald, H., & Wolfram, S. (2001). *Citizenship and education in twenty-eight countries.* Amsterdam: International Association for the Evaluation of Educational Achievement.

Treiger, A. (2012). *Inspired knowledge in Islamic thought: Al-Ghazālī's theory of mystical cognition and its Avicennian foundation.* London: Routledge.

Tryer, D., & Ahmad, F. (2006). *Muslim women and higher education: Identities, experiences and prospects.* Liverpool: Liverpool John Moores University.

UK Gov. (1949/1961). *Citizens growing up*. London: HMSO.

UK Gov. (2008). *Ethnicity and education: The evidence on minority ethnic pupils aged 5–16*. London: Department for Children, Families and Schools.

UK Gov. (2011a). *The Framework for the National Curriculum: A report by the Expert Panel for the National Curriculum review*. London: Department for Education.

UK Gov. (2011b). *GCSE and equivalent attainment by pupil characteristics in England, 2009/10*. London: Department for Business Innovation and Skills. Retrieved 3 October 2012 from www.education.gov.uk/rsgateway/DB/SFR/s000977/index.shtml

UK Gov. (2012). *Census 2011*. London: Office for National Statistics. Retrieved 19 February 2014 from www.ons.gov.uk/ons/guide-method/census/2011/index.html?utm_source=LCRN+News+Service&utm_campaign=2da3bf9763-LCRN_Resource_eNews_Volume_2_Issue_42_10_2011&utm_medium=email

UK Gov. (2013a). *GCSE and equivalent attainment by pupil characteristics in England, 2011/12*. London: Department for Education.

UK Gov. (2013b). *National Curriculum consultation framework document for history*. London: Department for Education.

UK Gov. (2013c). *Statutory guidance: National Curriculum in England: History programmes of study*. London: Department for Education.

UK Gov. (2013d). *Statutory guidance: National Curriculum in England: Citizenship programmes of study for Key Stages 3 and 4*. London: Department for Education. Retrieved 11 January 2014 from www.gov.uk/government/publications/national-curriculum-in-england-citizenship-programmes-of-study/national-curriculum-in-england-citizenship-programmes-of-study-for-key-stages-3-and-4

UK Gov. (2013e). *Summary of DFID's work in Pakistan 2011–2015*. London: Department for International Development.

Vallance, E. (1973). Hiding the hidden curriculum: An interpretation of the language of justification in nineteenth-century educational reform. *Curriculum Theory Network, 4*, 5–21.

van Driel, B. (ed.). (2004). *Confronting Islamophobia in educational practice*. Stoke-on-Trent: Trentham Books.

Vasagar, J., & Sparrow, A. (2010, 5 October). Simon Schama to advise ministers on overhaul of history curriculum: Education secretary Michael Gove tells Tory conference move will ensure no pupil leaves school without learning 'narrative British history'. *Guardian*.

Vidal Rodeiro, C. L. (2009). *Uptake of GCSE and A-level subjects in England by ethnic group 2007*. Cambridge: Cambridge Assessment.

Walsh, P. (1992). History and love of the past. In P. Lee, J. Slater, P. Walsh & J. White (eds), *The aims of school history: The National Curriculum and beyond*. London: Tufnell Press.

Ware, J. (Writer). (2010, 27 November). *Panorama*: British schools, Islamic rules [Television programme]. L. Telling (Producer). BBC.

Weber, M. (1958/2003). *The Protestant ethic and the spirit of capitalism* (T. Parsons, Trans.). New York: Dover Publications.

Wegner, G. P. (1990). Germany's past contested: The Soviet–American conflict in Berlin over history curriculum reform, 1945–48. *History of Education Quarterly, 30*(1), 1–6.

Wemyss, G. (2009). *The Invisible Empire: White discourse, tolerance and belonging*. Farnham: Ashgate.

Whitburn, R., Hussain, M., & Mohamud, A. (2012) 'Doing justice to history': The learning of African history in a North London secondary school and teacher development in the spirit of *ubuntu*. *Teaching History, 146*, 18–27.

White, J. (2004). Should religious education be a compulsory school subject? *British Journal of Religious Education, 26*(2), 151–164.

Wilkinson, M. L. N. (2007). The National Curriculum for History: Is it failing Muslim boys? Master of Research (MRes) dissertation, King's College London, London.

Wilkinson, M. L. N. (2011). History Curriculum, Citizenship & Muslim Boys: Learning to Succeed? PhD dissertation, King's College London, London.

Wilkinson, M. L. N. (2011). *Regina* v. *Faraz*. London: Crown Prosecution Service (unpublished).

Wilkinson, M. L. N. (2013). Response to the draft National Curriculum for History. Cambridge: Curriculum for Cohesion.

Wilkinson, M. L. N. (2014). The concept of the absent curriculum: the case of Muslim contribution and the English National Curriculum for History. *Journal of Curriculum Studies, 46*(4), 419–440.

Willis, P. (1977). *Learning to labour*. Aldershot: Gower.

Wilson, B. L., & Corcoran, T. B. (1988). *Successful secondary schools*. Lewes: Falmer Press.

Winter, T. (2007). Ishmael and the Enlightenment's *crise de coeur*. In B. B. Koshul & S. Kepnes (eds), *Scripture, Reason, and the Contemporary Islam–West Encounter* (pp. 149–176). New York: Palgrave Macmillan.

Winter, T. (2008). Introduction. In T. Winter (ed.), *The Cambridge companion to classical Islamic theology*. Cambridge Cambridge University Press.

Winter, T. (2010). Terrorism and Islamic theologies of religiously-sanctioned war. In D. Fisher & B. Wicker (eds), *Just War on Terror? A Christian and Muslim Response* (pp. 9–24). Farnham: Ashgate.

Wittgenstein, L. (1922). *Tractatus logico-philosophicus* (F. P. Ramsey & C. K. Ogden, Trans.). New York: Kegan Paul.

Wright, A. (2007). *Critical religious education, multiculturalism and the pursuit of truth*. Cardiff: University of Wales Press.

Xu, J., & Corno, L. (2003). Family help and homework management reported by middle school students. *Elementary School Journal, 103*(5), 503–517.

Xu, J., & Yuan, R. (2003). Doing homework: Listening to students', parents', and teachers' voices in one urban middle school community. *School Community Journal, 13*(2), 25–44.

Zaki, Y. (1982). The teaching of Islam in schools: A Muslim viewpoint. *British Journal of Religious Education, 5*(1), 33–38.

Zaman, M. Q. (2002). *The Ulama in contemporary Islam: Custodians of change*. Princeton, NJ: Princeton University Press.

Ziai, H. (2008). Islamic philosophy (*falsafa*). In T. Winter (ed.), *The Cambridge companion to classical Islamic theology* (pp. 55–76). Cambridge: Cambridge University Press.

Ziegler, S. (1987). *The effects of parent involvement on children's achievement: The significance of home/school links*. Toronto: Toronto Board of Education.

Index

Page numbers in *italics* denote tables, those in **bold** denote figures.

7/7 118, 196, 202, 255; bombers 32, 195; post 7/7 118, 196
9/11 8, 118, 202, 255; post 9/11 118, 196
1944 Education Act 192
1988 Education Reform Act 192, 194, 204, 211

absence 67–71; absenting of 66–7, 85, 89, 154; determinate 33, 66, 120, 139, 143, 148n2, 151, 154, 159, 169, 174, 200; of Islam 16, 119, 204; of law 79, 81; noxious 77, 88; philosophical 33, 39, 65–6; of pupil respect and buy-in from Muslim community 200, 205; relative 85, 122, 151, 168, 170, 172, 204; removal of 66–7, 154
absence of seriousness 222; in education 231, 249; in citizenship education 230; in RE 205
absent curriculum 152–67, **153**, 175
absent parent 169, 177, 185
absent pedagogy 167–9, 177, 185
Adey, K. 132, 142
affective-cultural 171, 177, 182; dimension of being 147, 151; dimension of success (ADS) 13, 132, 140–1, 143, 145, 149n7, 150n12, 166, 169–70, 172, 178, 184, 200
Ahonen, S. 126, 166
Ajegbo, K. 251; Ajegbo Report 140, 166
Alderson, P. 40, 57, 154
Alexander, C.E. 30, 118–19, 122–3, 127, 216, 224, 226, 228, 255
Alexander the Great 176
al-Ghazali, A.H.M.M. 9–10, 70, 112
Allawi, A.A. 18, 136, 181
Anderson, B. 5, 244

Angels 12, 45, **54**, 61, 72, 78, 103, 105, 112, 197–8, 252; *'Azrael* (Azrael) 106; *Israfil* (Raphael) 106; *Jibra'il* (Gabriel) 11, 74, 76–7, 105–7; *Mikail* (Michael) 106; archangel 106
anti-Western 34, 136–7
Apple, M.W. 10, 152, 154–5, 159
Archer, L. 5–6, 10, 118–23, 125, 127, 135, 142, 148n5, 148n6, 174, 190, 200, 216, 218, 222, 224–6, 254–5
Archer, M. 10, 57, 230
Articles of the Islamic Faith 12, 88; Angels 12, 45, 54, 61, 103, 105–6, 112, 197, 252; Day of Reckoning 12, 79, 103, 106, 108, 112; Divine Decree 12, 44, 58, 103, 107–8; Prophets 12, 15n2, 45, 106–7, 176, 252
Averroes 9–10, 40–1, 48, 71, 106, 112

Baker, D. 15n5, 190, 220
balance of power 192; sacred–civic 18
Ball, S.J. 118–19, 221, 253
Bangladesh 227–8; history 160, 172, 178
Bangladeshi 31, 120; boys 125; British 160, 170, 227–8; girls 121; history 161; youth 122, 149n6
Banks, J.A. 144, 237
Barnes, L.P. 193–4, 212
Barton, K.C. 126, 134, 139, 143, 146, 161–2, 164–5, 222
Battle of Badr 83
Battle of Uhud 83–4
BBC 3–4, 251; Panorama 223
Becher, R. 185–6
Bhaskar, R. 7, 10, 13, 19, 32–3, 39–40, 42–4, 46–7, 51–3, 56–8, 60, 64–70, 86–7, 89–92, 94–6, 98, 101, 104–5,

110–11, 120, 129–31, 135, 139, 141, 143, 154, 177, 200, 207–8, 212–14, 216, 230, 237–8, 249, 255
Birt, J. 31, 188
Blackhirst, R. 110–11
Bourdieu, P. 159, 171
boycott 76; political 161
British Muslim 229; Asian 118; boys 148n4, 188, 223, 225; children 195; communities 149n6; girls 148n4; identity 3, 126, 224; males 8, 32, 125; third-generation 225, 227; young 5–6, 8, 117, 119, 121, 127, 133, 148n4, 165, 181, 190
Brown, G. 127, 184; former Prime Minister 133, 247n2
Brown, G.L. 130, 152
Brown, K. E. 8, 118, 213
Bullock Report 193
Bunt, G.R. 32, 213, 219

Cannadine, D. 20, 126, 148n2
capitalism 20; free-market 19
Casciani, D. 195, 220n1
Catholic 19–20, **54**, 201; monarchs 16
Christendom 12, 188; Christianity 29, **54**, 57, 68, 194, 201, 204–5, 232
Christian 7, 33, 35n6, 74, 188, 194, 202; Britain 29; community 80; congregations 68; Constantinople 16; Europe 12, 81, 102; Europeans 28; faith-school 176; families 193; Gospels 29, 76; individuals 20; majority 9; medieval conceptions 28; members of staff 182; monk 73; non-Christian 28, 193; non-realist 57; populace 197; prejudice 136; Reformation 197, 231; religious backgrounds 193; religious freedom 81; thinkers 105; Victorian Evangelicals 192; religion 58; West 19, 21–22, 28, 197
civic engagement 246
Cohen, S. 28, 31, 146
colleges 13; technology 139
Collier, A. 57, 60
commitment 43, 219, 232, 246; confessional 212; to democracy 240; to educational achievement 120, 174; to faith 64, 80, 209, 252; lack of 202; metaphysical 47; mutual 99, 137; philosophical 40; sectarian 208; to secular education 118; to seriousness 47–8, 64, 109, 200; shared 39, 42; spiritual **210**, 211, 215
Community School 127, 134, 136–8, 140,

144, 160–1, 165, 167, 169–72, 175, 226–7, 246
Companions of Muhammad 11, 14n1, 41, 45, 59, 76, 78–9, 81–2, 85–7
Connell, R.W. 6, 122, 224
Conroy, J.C. 167, 192, 196, 198, 202–5, 209, 211, 214
Crick, B. 235; Crick Report 235, 239–40, 246
critical engagement 183, 221
critical realism 10, 35, 39–40, 57, 71, 88–9, 94, 104, 113, 129, 145–6, 152, 154, 156; dialectical 65, 67, 69, 85, 237; Islamic 12, 14, 15n5, 41–2, 48, **50**, 61, 64n1, 65, 70, 117, 127, 129, 206, 238–9, 249–53; original 51–2, 66
Cronon, W. 126, 136, 155, 182, 185
curriculum 166; absent 119, 151, **153**, 156–9, 165–7, 169, 175, 177, 185; null 152, 158; unenacted 153, 162, 164–5; unselected 159, 162

Dar al-Islam (the place of Islam) 12, 16, 61; *see also* Islam
Datta, M. 219, 244
Davies, I. 231, 234
Day of Reckoning 12, 79, 103, 106, 108, 112
demi-reality (*kufr*) 95–8, 106, 108, 110
democracy 5, 17, 34, 150n14, 161, 223, 235, 239–40, **242**, 243, 246, 249; liberal 14, 19, 24, 240–1, 248, 251–2; parliamentary 233; representational 27
Dewey, J. 134, 164
DeWitt, J. 168–9
dialectical 70; absenting of absence 67, 85, 154; change 65–6, 71, 89–90, 98, 100, 102, 154; critical realism 65, 67, 69, 85, 89, 237; critical realist 66, 69, 87–8, 177, 191, 222, 249; disenchantment 34; Islamic critical realism 70, 90, 216, 222, 237, 249; level 139, 185; moment 10, 14, 50, 117, 151–2, 187; movement 44, 98; process 88; pulse of freedom 70–1; tendency 99, 108
divine 62, 87, 113n1, 205; attuned behaviour 82; command 79, 106–7; communication 105; Decree (*Qadr*) 44, 58, 95–6, 98; epiphany 94, 216; guidance 71; immanence 104; inspiration **93**, **215**, 252; intervention 70, 79; justice 14n2; knowledge 64; mercy 79, 102, 105; plan 55, 83, 99, 112–13; prerogative 48; Presence 105,

divine *continued*
108; Providence 54, 207; Purpose 84;
Qur'anic injunction 84; revelation 12,
15n4, 61, 71, 94, 107, 216; source 110;
spirit (*ruh*) 54, 92, 207; teaching 59;
transcendence 90; unity 74, 78–9, 107;
Will 83; worship 103

Eccles, J.S. 171, 174
education 4, 11, 53, 91, 93, 121, 130, 136,
138, 142, 191–2, 216, 227, 229, 232;
citizenship 222– 3, 226, 230–1, 233–6,
238, **239**, **241–2**, 243–7, 249–50; ethical
67; formal 5, 23, 224, 234; higher 31,
121, 124–5; history 117, 128, 130–1,
133, 142–3, 145, 147, 148n2, 169, 177,
179, 183, 187–8, 204; humanities
15n4–5, 117, 119, 129–31, 145, 147,
151, 250; informal 33; Islamic 32–3,
205, 217, **218**; mosque-based 141;
multicultural 193; ontological
monovalence 151; political 234–5, 238;
Reform Act 192, 194, 204, 211;
religious 6, 8–9, 13–14, 32–3, 117–19,
126, 128, 146–7, 148n3, 191–2, 195–7,
199, 200, 202–4, 206, **210**, 213–14,
216–17, **218**, 219–20, 222–3, 231, 235,
252; secular 118, 205; sites 201; system
40, 227, 234; transformative 253;
Western 42
educational 8–9; achievement 5, 17,
120–2, 190; architecture 11;
environments 6, 32, 118, 175;
philosophy 14, 15n4, 35, 42; policy
118–19, 201, 203, 223, 253; praxis 249;
processes 10, 35, 119, 144, 219; success
118, 127–9, 131, 147, 190;
underachievement 31, 121
embodied personality 55, 86, 92, 94, 96–9,
101, 105–6, 108–12, 120, 122, 145–6,
170, 196, 243, 250; emergent 132–3;
internal stratification 13, 53, 95, 135,
147, 236
embracing difficult issues 206, 213, 218
empirical 52, 55, 62–3, 106–7; actualism
48, 51; considerations 155; depth 151;
empirical-material forms 78; empirical-
practical realities 118; ethnographic
work 191; findings 131, 225;
grounding 145; level 55, 63, 66, 83, 92,
96, 108; research 117, 127; science 19,
23, 158–9; scientific world-view 201,
214
engagement 246; critical 183, 221;

obstacles to 166, 190; transformative
117
epistemological relativism **50**, **54**, 56–60,
63–4, 64n1, 128, **179**, 180–1, 206, **207**,
208–9, 223, 236, 239–41, 250
Epstein, D. 121, 174
Epstein, J.L. 185–6
Equality and Human Rights Commission
188, 195
existential 7, 9; absence 71, 89; case 238;
change 66, 76; connection 62, 245;
dichotomies 42; engagement 250;
intransitivity 207; necessity 244;
recognition of being 102; seriousness
248, 249; truth 104; unity 108
extremism 137, 195; Islamic 192;
Preventing Violent Extremism
policy agenda 118, 255; violent 32, 118,
126

faith 4, 6, 9, 11, 17–18, 23, 27–8, 31–2, 39,
41–5, 48, 56, 60, 63, 84–5, 128, 133,
146, 190–3, 196–7, 199, 201, 206, 208,
214, 221, 236, 244, 251; Abrahamic 75,
80; based 5, 7, 187; based identity 119,
190, 260; commitment 252; declaration
of 86, 109; default positions 33–4, 249;
Faith Girls 120, 123–4; identifications
220; institutional 202; Muslim 7–8, 10,
12, 28, 32, 35, 39, 83, 92, 119, 195, 205,
219, 223, 249; new 75, 77, 79; other 4,
7, 35, 51, 64–5, 68, 119, 190, 208, 210,
213, 249; religious 5, 199, 201, 215;
shared 88; traditions 56, 190, 209–10,
212, 215, 252; UK 194; values 176
Faith school 127, 138, 140, 142, 150n16,
165, 167–71, 173–6, 184, 186, 196,
227–9, 246; Islamic 8, 128, 159, 164,
204; Muslim 32, 195, 223; system 195
Feldman, N. 16–22, 27–8, 42, 82, 242,
248
femininity 132; Muslim 30, 141, 245;
hegemonic 123; Western 225
First Moment (1M) 98; being-as-such 50,
62, 65–6, 70–1, 75, 89, 117–18, 151,
191–2, 197, 209, 223; identity-in-
difference 95, 112, 222
First World War 23, 27, 155, 158, 162–5,
178, 181, 233, 252
Five Pillars of Islam 12, 15n2, 44, 81, 88,
108–9, 113, 211; Fast (*Sawm*) 12, 43,
81, 103, 111–12; Hajj 8, 12, 43, 103,
112–13; Obligatory Prayer 12, 44, 47,
81, 109–11; Social Welfare Tax (*Zakat*)

12, 43, 46, 68, 81, 103, 109, 111;
  Witnessing 12, 103, 109
Foucault, M. 53, 131, 199
Fourth Dimension (4D): transformative
  praxis 65–6, 69–70, 85–7, 98–9, 117,
  152, 177, 185, 187, 192, 216, 223, 226,
  245–6
Francis, B. 118, 121, 123, 174, 200
Francis, L.J. 119, 190, 202
Friedmann, Y. 75, 81

al-Ghazali 9–10, 70, 112
Gearon, L. 221, 232, 234, 240
gender 5, 55, 187; gendered selfhood 125,
  128, 147; gender-in-education 10, 122,
  224; hegemonic forms 122, 125, 147,
  190, 224–5; non-gendered 113n1;
  performance 6, 120, 225, 254; relations
  30, 42, 124, 223, 236, 240, 242, 245;
  roles 252; separation 176
globalising world 148n2, 188, 235, 249
Goodson, I.F. 10, 187
Gramsci, A. 20, 122, 225, 249
Green, E.H. 176, 233
Grimmitt, M. 209, 219
Ground of All Being 96, 104, 106–10
ground-state 89, 91–2, 94–8, 100–5,
  108–12, 145–7, 197, 214, 216, 237, 243;
  Divine 94; human 96, 106–7; in
  pregnancy 99

al-Hassani, S.T.S. 18, 180
Halstead, M. 205, 217
Hartwig, M. 52, 64n1, 90, 238
Haw, K. 122, 124
Haydn, T. 126, 183–4
Head, J. 12, 15n5, 121, 174, 191, 216, 222,
  228
Heater, D. 231, 233, 235
Hegel, G.W.F. 10, 44, 65, 193
Hegelian 34, 67; dialectics 70
hegemonic masculinities 122, 148n5, 254;
  and femininities 123
hiatuses 42, 66–8, 80–1, 84, 87, 99, 154–5
Hopkins, P. 31, 127, 190, 225
Hostettler, N. 66, 154
Hull, J.M. 194–5, 205, 217
human relationships 87; quality 45
Husband, C. 28–9
Hussain, S. 31n2, 118, 121–2, 255

identity 34, 65, 71, 82, 92, 94, 98–101, 132,
  141, 205, 214, 221, 228–9, 235, 237;
  British Muslim 3, 126, 224; building

166, 218; crisis 203; faith-based 119,
  190; gangsta 123; historical 28; Islamic
  5, 35, 121, 205, 224; lack of 238; learner
  188; Muslim 6, 120, 190; national 122,
  126, 187–8, 196, 223, 236; performance
  of 254; religious 120, 190, 196; spiritual
  218; transcendent 83, 90, 98, 214, 237;
  transcendental 89–90, 214, 237
identity-in-difference 95, 97–8, 112, 222;
  difference-in-identity 72
inclusion 113n1, 165, 182–3, 194, 224;
  ontology of inclusion 177
intellectual 17, 19, 25–6; absences 67, 249;
  analysis 211; anti-intellectual 245;
  agenda 22, 27; being 11; benefits 22,
  217; challenges 24; contexts 61; crisis
  22; cultures 249; dimension 13, 170–2,
  177–8, 182, 184; discoveries 93, 216;
  environments 230, 250; establishment
  188; experiences **93**, 98, **215**;
  framework 208; fringe 35n6; levels 126;
  misjudgement 72; options 34;
  participation 159; and political 18, 21–2;
  progress 179, 252; revival 23, 253; roots
  11, 221; significance 119; and spiritual
  15n5, 21–2, 24–5, 58, 80, 208, 211, 249,
  251, 253; stagnation 17; tension 28;
  tools 64, 213; traditions 9–10, 53;
  trauma 251; voices 26
intellectual success 134, *140*, 149n10, 166;
  dimensions of (IDS) 132–5, 139–40,
  143, 145–7, 151, 160, 178, 191, 200
interaction 95, 97, **218**; human 54, 74, 131;
  parent 141–2; personal 95–7, 100, 206;
  teacher-parent 217; teacher-pupil 198
inter-faith 33, 199, 206; mode 191, 209,
  210, 211, 213, 215–16
internet 9, 12–13, 32–3, 181, 183, 191–2,
  213, 216, **218**, 219–20
inter-subjective (interpersonal) transactions
  13, 53, 95, 143, 199
intra-faith mode 191, 206, **210**, 211–13,
  215–17, 219, 243, 245
Ipgrave, J. 191–9, 202, 211, 219
Iran 26–7
Iranian 23
Islamic 88; belief 89, 105–6; civilisation
  17–19, 119, 137, 139, 148n2, 157, 178,
  252; doctrine 10, 41–2, 109; education
  32–3, 175, 205, 217, **218**, 250; ethics 88,
  100–2; *Hijra* 76, 79; practice 12, 15n2,
  35, 44, 88; law 7, 11–12, 15n4, 16, 18,
  21, 25, 29, 41, 88, 100–1, 243–4;
  scholarship 11, 18, 33, 245; traditional 35

Islamic critical realism (ICR) 210; critical
realist transcendence 93; fulcrum of ICR
50, **54**, 61–4, 127, **179**, **207**, **210**, 238; in
citizenship education **239**, **241–2**,
245–6; in the classroom 206, 208, 213,
240; pedagogical modes **210**
Islamic *deen* (life-transaction) 11–12, 100,
103, 107, 112–13, 117, 196, 205, 251;
religion 12, 25, 59, 191, 196;
scholarship 11, 18, 33
Islamic faith 3–5, 14, 29, 31, 33, 40, 58,
82, 117, 124, 126, 147, 208, 213, 221,
251; Articles of 12, 14n2, 88; Five
Pillars 12, 15n2, 44, 81, 88, 108–9, 113,
211; school 8, 127–8, 159, 164, 204
'Iyad, Q. 44, 82, 104

Jackson, P. 146, 148n1
Jalalayn 45, 61–2, 93
Jerome, L. 231, 235, 246
Jews 28, 68, 80–1, 138, 168; anti-Jewish
feeling 137; community 80, 102; Jewish
81, 84; members of staff 182; migration
192; people 137, 197; scholar 189n4;
State of Israel 26; theology 33
Jihad 94, 97, 147; violent jihadist groups
24–5
judgemental rationality **50**, **54**, 59–60, 62,
128, **179**, 180, 182–3, 206, 208, 211–12,
219, 223, 236, 239–40, 250; exegetical
107; historical 181; sensitive 87;
spiritual 63; tools of 61, 64

Kamali, M.H. 31, 62
Kessler, E. 102, 189n4
Kroger, J. 191, 211

Lee, P. 143, 184
Lee, R.D. 19–20, 29
Levstik, L.S. 134, 139
Lewis, B. 29, 188
Lewis, P. 122, 171
liberal democracy 14, 19, 24, 240–1,
248–9, 251–2

Madina 8, 14n1, 17, 41, 75, 79, 82, 85, 88,
216; Christian tribes 81; community 20,
25, 80; Constitution of Madina 80, 243;
Madinan Helpers (*Ansar*) 83–4
madrasas 20, 150n16, 176, 191–2, 211,
216–17, **218**, 219; Islamic 204;
Pakistani 32
Mahmutcehajic, R. 33–4, 44, 46, 56, 66,
78, 84, 105, 112

Malcolm, N. 18, 21, 81
marriage 21, 75–6, 79, 84, 98–100, 102; of
belief and action 48, 249; homosexual
29; of Muhammad 73, 77; outside 101;
partners 46; social institution 55
masculinity 120, 148n5, 254; hegemonic
122–3, 148n5, 224–5, 254; Islamic 245;
negotiations of 132
Matar, N. 20–1
material transactions with nature 13, 53,
95–7, 131, 146
media 4, 6, 13, 30, 223, 233, 244; British
31; multi-media 167; outlets 29, 251;
political 126; social 9, **218**, 221
metaReal 92, 103; understanding 90, 95,
101
metaReality 46–7, 71, 87–91, 94, 98–100,
108, 216, 237
modernity 20–1, 26–7, 94, 225; challenges
of 22, 24; conditions of 19, 94; early 16,
19; postmodernity 16, 25, 27
Modood, T. 30, 123, 202
Mondal, A.A. 6, 49, 119, 178, 225, 227,
255
mosques 8, 13, 18, 20, 27, 53, 80–1, 147,
174–6, 192, 194, 199, 204, 214, **218**,
227, 250; mosque-based 141, 151, 178,
186
Muhammad Messenger of God 12, 86,
109; *see also* Prophet Muhammad
multi-faith 4, 12, 17, 61, 68, 219;
Abrahamic believers 80–1; Britain 3,
15n3; contexts 3, 6, 8, 14, 28, 30, 33–5,
39, 117; democracies 6, 35, 249; Islamic
philosophy 33; religious education 191,
199, 205–6, 214, 217; settings 32, 35,
117; societies 9, 49, 82, 146, 188, 205,
222, 229; West 28, 201–2
multi-faith world 4, 10–12, 14, 15n3, 28,
33–5, 50, 61, 87, 197, 199, 205, 251,
253; contemporary 6, 117, 249;
democratic 248
Muslim 205; diaspora 27–8, 137, 199,
205; families 12, 124; learners 132,
147, 151, 192, 253; Reformers 22; *see
also* British Muslim; Muslim boys;
Muslim community; Muslim
Consciousness; Muslim girls; Muslim
young people
Muslim boys 8, 118, 121–2, 132, 135, 137,
141, 148n5, 149n7, 172–4, 176–8,
184–5, 190, 199, *204*, 226, 229, 245,
254–5; British 148n4, 188, 223–5;
working-class 123, 125

Muslim community 6, 8, 29–30, 34, 59–60, 77–9, 83–5, 87, 89, 148n4, 152, 186–7, 191–2; global 32; groups 194–5, 198, 200, 204, 227, 242, 244, 255; Madinan 20, 81, 83; scholarly 15n4; walkouts 205

Muslim Consciousness 249; Happy 42, 49, 248–9; Unhappy 33, 44, 249

Muslim girls 120; Faith Girls 120, 123–4; Gang Girls 120, 123–4, 205

Muslim young people 3, 5–10, 31–3, 35, 87, 117–20, 126, 129, 132–4, 136, 138, 140–3, 145, 149n6, 151, 153, 157, 159, 162, 168, 172, 173, 180, 182–4, 188, 199, 200, 204, 206, 212, 214, 216–17, 221, 223–4, 244, 249; Asian 122–3; British 121, 125, 127, 131, 165, 190, 225, 229; citizenship education 236, 238, 246, 252; contemporary 87; development 127, 148n1; education 248, 250–1; experiences of NCH 128, 166–7; external integration 144, 146, 222; in humanities education 131, 147; national belonging 226, 228–30; spiritual dimension 190–2, 196–8, **218**, 219; success 148, 169, 177–8

National Curriculum for History (NCH) 126–9, 132, 134–5, 137–41, 143–5, 149n7–8, 150n16, 157–9, 161–2, 166–7, 169–72, 175, 177–8, 183–7

non-identity 66, 70–2, 77, 89–90, 92, 99–101, 108, 237; being-as-non-identity 50, 62, 75, 191, 197; epistemological 65; ethical 74; existential 76; of Muhammad 82, 87

non-Muslim (*kafir*) 3, 5, 14, 25, 27–8, 30–1, 33, 109, 134–6, 141–2, 144–5, 147, 149n6, 149n8, 162, 166–8, 198, 225; agency 164; authorities 19, 76; children 14, 244; counter-othering 28–33; forms 27; friends 3–4; habits 6; lands 32, 102; law 9; Muslim–non-Muslim 31, 137, 146, 180–1; parents 169; peers 42, 226; perceptions 146; powers 22; scholars 40; students 178; teacher 205; young people 121, 127, *204*, 141, 212, 244

Norrie, A. 10, 57, 65–9, 87, 100, 154–5, 230, 250

nurseries 13

obedience 4, 9, 44, 74, 107; civil disobedience 69; to the law 103

Obligatory Prayer 12, 44, 47, 81, 109–11

obstacles 24, 49, 97, 186, 220; cultural 121, 124; to engagement 166, 190; to ontological wholeness 67, 154; political 80; social 122; to understanding 154, 164

ontological realism **50**, 51, **54**, 56–9, 62–4, 106, 128, **179**, 180–1, 206, **207**, 208–9, 223, 236, 239–40, 250

opportunity 15n5, 103, 163–4, 167, 182, 188, 199, 200, 246, 252; for and of Islam 251; lack of 32

Ormsby, E. 10, 48, 67, 70

othering/counter-othering 28–33; *see also* non-Muslims

Ottoman 16; caliphate 17; Canon law 35n5; Empire 20–1, 23, 162–3, 181–2; Istanbul 81; period 18, 22; Turkey 18, 181

out-of-school 11; culture 137, 147, 199; history *140*, 141, 145, 169, 185–6; peer group 13

Oyserman, D. 172, 174

Pakistan 16, 24, 165, 224, 227, 229; creation of 164, 181; history 160, 173, 175, 178; Islamic Republic of 26

Pakistani 224; boys 122; British 134, 136, 138, 149n6, 150n16, 164–5, 168, 171, 173–5, 227, 229, 246; component of Partition 164–5; girls 121; heritage 125; madrasas 32; pride 120; youth 31–2

Parekh Report 161

Partition of India 27, 165, 181; Pakistani component 164

peer group 54, 122, 130–2, 147, 191–2, 216, 218–19, 221; out-of-school 13

Pew Research 27

Phillips, R. 126, 187, 234

philosophical seriousness 42–3, 47, 213, 248

philosophical theology (*kalam*) 9; Islamic 10, 33, 40–1, 44, 47

Pilgrimage (*Hajj*) 43, 103, 109, 209, **212**; Lesser Pilgrimage (*Umra*) 85; *see also* Five Pillars of Islam

Platt, L. 149n6, 226

plurality 58, 208; ethical and religious 12, 193

Preventing Violent Extremism policy agenda 118, 255

primary school 4, 13, 119, 169, 204; children 217

Pring, R. 118–19, 148n2

Prophet Muhammad 7–8, 11, 14n1, 41, 59, 64, 74–5, 77–80, 84, 100, 108–9, 113, 198–9, 243; absence 41; lessons of 87; life of 65, 70–1, 87–90, 97–8, 154, 216; migration 17; seriousness 46; Sunna 7, 21, 44
Protestant 19, **54**; Christianity 232; liberal 194

Qualifications and Curriculum Authority 192, 206
Qualifications and Curriculum Development Agency 126, 134–5, 140
Qur'an 7, 10–11, 21–2, 24, 40–2, 44, 46, 48, 51, 58–9, 61–5, 68, 71, 78, 82–7, 92–3, 96–8, 103–12, 113n1, 124, 171, 176, 198, 205, 208, 217, 237, 245, 248; Revelation 90
Qur'anic 100; message 74–5, 79; principle 9, 47, 80; tetrapolity 100–2; verse 45, 76; world-view 64, 100
Qutb, S. 24–5, 61

Ramadan 72–4, 85–6, 109, 121; Fast of Ramadan (*Sawm*) 43, 81, 103, 111–12
Ramadan, T. 15n4, 17, 21, 30, 34, 59–60, 63, 72, 74, 77, 81–4, 86, 107, 121, 143, 188
Rapoport, Y. 24–5
re-enchantment 63, 98–9; dialectics of 87; rational 64–5, 88
reimagining the nation 177, 187
relationship 19, 249; harmonious 161; human 45, 87; Islamic 24, 46, 185, 243
Religion of Peace 32
religiosity 132; personal 19, 21; excess of 56; high levels 190; religious aberrations 42, 56
religious education 6, 8–9, 13–14, 32–3, 117–19, 126, 128, 146–7, 148n3, 191–2, 195–7, 199, 200, 202–4, 206, **210**, 213–14, 216–17, **218**, 219–20, 222–3, 231, 235, 252
removing absence 66–7, 154, 249
Rogers, M.A. 170, 188n2

Sachedina, A. 20, 33, 45, 84
Sahaba 20, 81
Said, E. 28, 30
Sarra, C. 28, 30, 224
Sayer, A. 13, 44, 127
Schiffauer, W. 27, 31
school 10–12, 31, 119, 123, 125, 128, 136–7, 139, 142, 149n9, 152; British 5,

118; buildings 53, 131; curricula 31–2, 147, 166, 185, 187, 200–1, 223, 234; English 117, 148n2–3, 149n6, 153; faith 8, 32, 127–8, 138, 140, 142, 150n16, 159, 164–5, 167–71, 173–6, 184, 186, 195–6, 204, 223, 227–9, 246; of law 14n1, 18–20, 24–5, 41, 59; mainstream 32–3, 122; management 53, 119, 131, 152, 156–7, 159, 166, 169; out-of-school culture 137, 147, 199; peer group 13, 147; research 139, 158–9, 163; state 32, 127, 149n6, 187, 195; subjects 53, 126, 131, 133, 142, 165, 174, 191, *204*, 202n2, 231, 235, 238, 247n3; timetable 235; *see also* secondary school
Scott, D. 119, 127, 129, 134
secondary school 13, 175, 204; English 119, 202; Muslim girls 120, 123; Muslim young people 151, 191, 197, 219; timetable 235
Second Edge (2E): absence 65, 70, 75, 98, 117, 139, 151–2, 167, 169, 191, 200, 205–6, 222, 230
Second World War 27, 97; post-Second World War 192
secular 21, 31, 34, 92, 250; academic discourse 33; education 118, 196, 205, 213; legal framework 28; liberal 29–30, 201, 249; nationalist governments 26; nationalist monarchy 27; nation-states 21; social attitudes 68; spheres 176; values 61, 118
secularisation 201–2
secularism 29; nationalist 23, 28; political 205
secularist 22–3, 33
self-realisation 13, 65, 69, **93, 215**
Sentürk, R. 80, 101
serious education (e) 216; citizenship 223, 236, 243–5, 247; religious 243–4; strategy 223, 236
seriousness 7, 45, 47–8, 200, 250; existential **248**, 249; Islamic 111–12, 212; lack of 43–4, 191, 201, 203–4, 231; philosophical (p) 42–3, 47–8, 201, 213, **248**, 249; religious (r) 43–7, 200, **248**, 249; return to 219; (r+p) 44–5, 48–50, 56, 61, 63–4, 87, 103, 109, 111–12; (r + p + e) 248–9; spiritual (s) 39, 42
seriousness-in-education 191, 200–1, 203–4, 223, **248**, 250; citizenship education 230, 236; absence of 204–6, 222, 231, 249; religious education 203, 219

Shain, F. 5, 10, 118–20, 122–5, 127, 135, 141, 148n6, 190, 216, 218, 222, 224–5, 228, 254
shared commitment 39, 42
Shari'a 14n1, 21, 23, 28, 102; courts 29; Five Pillars of Islamic practice 12, 88; Islamic 84, **242**; law 11, 16–18, 27, 100–1, 29, 201, 236, 244; level of proof 82; tradition 18–19, 25
Shepard, W. 22–3
Shi'a 35n4, **54**; Islam 10, 26; Muslims 15n2, 18, 26–7
Siddique, H. 137, 195, 223
Skelton, C. 118, 122, 225
Slater, J. 139, 234
Smith, C. 52, 130
social media 9, **218**, 221
social relations at the irreducible level 13, 53, 95, 135, 143–4, 151, 236
Specialist School 127, 136–7, 159–60, 163, 169, 171, 183–4, 226, 228
spiritual dimension 13, 56, 178, 220; of being 55; of Muslim young people 178, 190–2, 204, 216–17, **218**, 219; of success (SDS) 132, 135–40, 147, 149n11, 177, 200
Standing Advisory Councils on Religious Education (SACREs) 203
status 138, 165, 169, 232, 243–4, 249; of citizenship education 222, 231, 235; high 238; highest 122, 224; of human beings before God 69; loss of status 76, 78, 110, 204, 245; of RE 201–4, 219; of Revelation 59; special 82; spiritual 80, 83; of women 30, 245
stewardship 101, 245
submission 44, 47, 103
success 11, 30, 133, 135, 139; academic 120, 124, 171; affective-cultural dimension 132, 140–1, 149n7, 150n12; civic 133, *140*, 143–5, 150n14; civic dimension 132, 143, 222, 230; educational 31, 118, 127–9, 131, 147, 190; holistic *140*, 141, 143–5, 177, 184, 188n2; instrumental dimension 132, 142–3, 150n13; intellectual 134, *140*, 143, 149n10, 166; intellectual dimension of (IDS) 132–5, 140, 143, 146, 178; spiritual 4, 132, 139, *140*, 145, 191; spiritual dimension 132, 135, 139, 147, 149n11, 200; worldly 19, 249
Sunni 10, 15n2, 18, 25–7, 35n4, **54**
Swann, M. 193; Swann Report 152, 193

Taylor, C. 64, 105, 197
teachers 4, 6, 9, 11, 13–14, 15n5, 23, 53, 69–70, 91, 100, 118, 120, 124–5, 129, 131–2, 134, 136–7, 139, 142, 151, 153, 156–7, 159, 161, 164, 168, 182–4, 191, 200, 202, 204, 213, 218, 230, 238, 240, 242–3, 247, 250, 252–3; citizenship 14, 204, 231, 235, 244–6; expectations 122, 199; good 167; history 8, 126, 128, 140, 160, 163–4, 167, 182–3; humanities 248; laziness 160; less-recognised 7; parent–teacher partnerships 185–7, 217; religious (RE) 8, 186, 191, 195, 197–9, 203, 205–6, 211, 214, 216, 219; training 70, 161–2, 203, 209; views 172, 178
Technology School 127, 135–9, 143, 160, 167–9, 171, 226, 229
terrorist 8, 192; attacks 118, 202; counter-terrorism trials 8; suicide bomber 4
terrors of performativity 119, 253
the Devil 29, 96, 197
theological crisis 22, 26
theological philosophy (*falsafa*) 9–10; Islamic 40–1, 48, 60, 251
The Religious Education Council (REC) 196, 203
The Revelation of God 11, 21, 40–1, 44, 59, 74, 79, 82–3, 89–90, **93**, 94, 106–7, **215**, 216
the Sunna 7, 11, 14n1, 21, 24, 41, 44, 47–8, 84, 103–4, 107–9, 111
Third Level (3L): totality 65–8, 70, 79–80, 92, 99, 117, 151, 177, 185, 191, 206, 216, 223, 236; curricular 69, 152; First World War 155, 163; inclusive 67, 154; Indian Independence 164–5; of the Islamic faith 82, 84–6, 216; Madinan 81, 84, 88; partial 67–8, 9, 88, 154–5, 163, 165; of personhood 143–5; sub-totality 67–9, 72, 152, 154–5, 163–4; of the world 43
transcendence 67, 71, 88, 94, 99, 105, 154, 191, 206, 213, 237, 252; absolute **93**, 106–7, **215**; aesthetic 93, 215; altruistic **93**, 98, **215**; contingent-absolute **93**, 106–7, 112, **215**; critical realist 93; dialectics of 98; of duality 90, 238; in education 91; of God 104; of human love 94, 216; principles of 108; quotidian 90, **93**, 103, 113, 214, **215**, 238; religious 214, 220
transformation 42, 99, 146, 214, 230, 237, 250; of absences 200; epistemological 87; of Islam 80, 85; social 17, 27, 64–5, 67, 69–71, 85, 89, 143, 154; spiritual 71

transformative 77, 111, 182, 191, 211,
    222–3, 236, 244, 249; ability 146;
    absence 66–7, 154, 250; act 109; agency
    206; attitude 50; education 253; effect
    230; engagement 117; giving 112;
    impact 144; lawfulness 102; nexus 192,
    216, **218**; package 148n1; praxis 65–6,
    69–70, 85–8, 99, 152, 177, 185, 187,
    245–6; religious education 219;
    understanding 231
transforming communities of learners
    184–5, 187
Treiger, A. 48
Tusi school of Twelver Shi'ism 10

UK Government 5, 27, 31, 121–2, 148n2,
    148n4, 165, 177, 231, 234, 236
Umma of Islam 6, 16, 18, 26, 80, 120, 219,
    225, 244
unbelief (*kufr*) 12, 94, 96–8, 105–6, 108,
    110; Dar al-Kufr (the Place of Unbelief)
    61; pagan 89
underlabour 39–40, 42, 48, 61, 64–5, 108,
    117, 127, 250; underlaboured 40, 87;
    underlabouring 39–42, 49–50, 88, 249,
    251, 253
Unhappy Muslim Consciousness 33, 44,
    249
unity-in-difference 92, 99, 223, 236–7,
    246
unity-in-diversity 95, 222, 237–8, 244,
    246
unity-in-duality 98, 100, 112

Universities 3, 12–13, 23, 35n6, 121, 205;
    Islamic societies 250; Russell Group
    203; University of Cambridge 7, 196,
    209
unserious 33, 42–3, 46–8, 58, 147, 176,
    200, 203, 249, 253

Vallance, E. 152, 154, 157, 234

War on Terror 8, 118, 131
Weber, M. 19, 201
White, J. 201, 217
Wilkinson, M.L.N. 32, 118–19, 122, 125,
    129, 148n2, 181–2, 219, 234
Willis, P. 123, 137, 234
Wilson, B.L. 141, 170
Winter, T. 10, 16, 17, 25, 61
Wittgenstein, L. 57, 194
Wright, A. 192, 194, 196–7, 202–3, 205,
    211, 217, 250

Xu, J. 171, 174

young Muslims 3–6, 9, 11–12, 14, 26,
    30–2, 34–5, 39, 42, 49, 50, 64, 70, 88,
    100, 117–18, 121, 126, 151, 181–2,
    190–2, 196–8, 200–1, 206, 208, 213,
    219–23, 225, 236, 242–8, 250–1, 253,
    255

Zaki, Y. 205
Zaman, M.Q. 19, 26
Ziai, H. 10, 40–1